Microprocessors
and Microcomputer Technology

T. Hanley
M Sc, PGCE (LOND), Grad. Dip. Computing

Senior Lecturer in Computing, City of Westminster College. City and Guilds of London Institute Visiting Assessor for Information Technology

DP Publications Ltd
Aldine Place
London W12 8AW
1993

Acknowledgements

I wish to thank Paul Frisby for the production of all the diagrams from my freehand sketches and his invaluable assistance with the checking of the final manuscript. I would also like to thank Mariagrazia Lardani for producing the diagrams for the sample chapter and Rae Green who helped with the technical editing. I am grateful to Carl Miller for his support and encouragement during the writing.

A CIP catalogue record for this book is available from the British Library

ISBN 1 85805 030 8
Copyright T. Hanley © 1993

All rights reserved
No part of this publication may be reproduced, stored in a retrieval system, or transmitted in any form or by any means, electronic, mechanical, photocopying, recording, or otherwise, without the prior permission of the copyright owner.

Printed by
Loader Jackson Printers
Arlesey, Bedfordshire

Preface

Aims of the book

1. The primary aim of this book is to provide a straightforward and simplified approach to the understanding of microprocessors and microcomputer technology. It is intended for those with little or no understanding of the subject.
2. This text covers the syllabus requirements of the following public examination bodies.

City & Guilds of London Institute

- 223 Microcomputer Technology
  Paper 1 (233-1-01) and Hardware assignments (223-1-03)
- 224 Electronics Servicing Part II
  Paper 224-2-13 (Digital Electronics)
- 7261 Information Technology
  Module 303 (Microprocessors)
- 2344/5 Electronics Office Systems Maintenance
  Module 303 (Microprocessors)

It is also suitable for BTEC National microelectronics and digital systems and other courses at a comparable level.

Need

Since the first microprocessor appeared in the early seventies an explosive growth in microprocessor applications has been taking place. Typically, these range from the now commonplace personal computer, to business and commercial usage, to complex control systems for industrial processes. The microelectronics revolution is increasingly gaining momentum and large numbers of people will need to be trained in microcomputer systems and information technology to keep pace with this rapid expansion. New courses are evolving to meet the demand for more skilled personnel in computing.

Due to the widespread use of personal microcomputers and associated peripheral equipment, subjects such as microprocessors and microcomputer technology are now appearing in many courses. These courses provide training in a diverse range of disciplines, ranging from data processing and information technology, to maintaining personal computer systems.

Approach

The book can be used in conjunction with a course of lectures or on courses with little lecturer contact time. Extensive use of diagrams, practical illustrative examples throughout, in-text questions and answers and concise, coherent presentation of information facilitate student interest and understanding of complex concepts. Convoluted descriptions have been deliberately avoided.

Questions

To ensure that readers have absorbed and understood the topic under discussion, short answer questions (SAQs) with answers are used throughout each chapter.

End of chapter

Each chapter finishes with a summary. Typical multiple choice examination questions and short answer questions appear at the end of each chapter. The answers to all multiple choice questions are given in Appendix A.

Lecturers' supplement

A lecturers' supplement, containing the answers to the end of chapter 'short answer questions', is available free of charge to lecturers who are using the book as a main course text. Applications, on departmental headed paper, should be made to the publishers.

Tom Hanley
August 1993

Contents

Preface *iii*

1 **Microcomputers & Microprocessors**
  1.1 Introduction to digital systems *1*
  1.2 The stored-program concept *2*
  1.3 Microprocessor integrated circuits *3*
  1.4 Personal computers *5*
  1.5 A typical single board microcomputer *8*
  1.6 The architecture of a basic microcomputer *9*
  1.7 A summary of key terms for microcomputing *14*
  1.8 Overview of a microcomputer system *18*
  Summary *20*
  Chapter review questions *20*

2. **Number Systems & Computer Arithmetic**
  2.1 An introduction to number systems *23*
  2.2 Basics of the decimal, binary, hexadecimal and octal number systems *23*
  2.3 Converting numbers from one base to another *30*
  2.4 Binary arithmetic *37*
  2.5 Representation of positive and negative numbers in binary *41*
  2.6 Twos complement addition & subtraction *42*
  2.7 Addition and subtraction of hexadecimal numbers *45*
  2.8 Fixed-point and floating-point numbers *46*
  2.9 Binary codes: BCD, ASCII and EBCDIC *48*
  Summary *52*
  Chapter review questions *53*

3 **Logic Gates**
  3.1 Introduction *56*
  3.2 The basic combinational logic gates:
  AND, OR, NOT, NAND, NOR, EX-OR and EX-NOR *57*
  3.3 Boolean algebra *66*
  3.4 Universal logic *72*
  3.5 Analysis of combinational logic circuits *76*
  3.6 Practical applications of logic gates *78*
  3.7 Tri-state gates *84*
  Summary *85*
  Chapter review questions *85*

4 **Sequential Logic Elements Counters & Shift Registers**
  4.1 Introduction to memory elements *90*
  4.2 The S-R flip-flop *90*
  4.3 The clocked S-R flip-flop *93*
  4.4 The D-type flip-flop *97*
  4.5 Master-slave and edge triggered flip-flops *99*
  4.6 Practical applications of flip-flops:
  Mechanical switch debouncing, frequency division *102*
  4.7 Digital counters *105*
  4.8 An asynchronous 4-bit binary up-counter *107*
  4.9 A BCD up-counter *109*
  4.10 An asynchronous 4-bit binary down counter *112*
  4.11 Synchronous counters *114*

Contents

    4.12 A 4-bit synchronous binary up-counter *114*
    4.13 Shift registers *115*
    4.14 Serial-in serial-out shift registers *116*
    4.15 Serial-in parallel-out shift registers *118*
    4.16 Parallel-in serial-out shift registers *119*
    Summary *120*
    Chapter review questions *120*

5 Logic Families

    5.1 Introduction *126*
    5.2 Levels of integration *126*
    5.3 IC packages *127*
    5.4 Criteria for selecting a logic family *129*
    5.5 The TTL logic family *134*
    5.6 MOS logic families *138*
    5.7 Handling MOS devices *140*
    Summary *141*
    Chapter review questions *142*

6. Inside the Microprocessor – a First Look

    6.1 Microprocessor architecture *146*
    6.2 Microprocessor word lengths *147*
    6.3 Directly addressable memory *148*
    6.4 An example of memory addressing *150*
    6.5 Speed of operation of the microprocessor *151*
    6.6 Inside the microprocessor *152*
    6.7 The internal microprocessor buses *154*
    6.8 The microprocessor block diagram *154*
    6.9 The microprocessor's registers *155*
    6.10 The ALU *156*
    6.11 The microprocessor's control circuitry *158*
    6.12 The general purpose registers *160*
    Summary *161*
    Chapter review questions *162*

7. Other Microprocessor Registers

    7.1 The accumulator *165*
    7.2 Status register *166*
    7.3 Program counter *168*
    7.4 Instruction register *170*
    7.5 Stack pointer *172*
    Summary *175*
    Chapter review questions *176*

8. Other Features Of Real Microprocessors The Fetch-Decode-Execute Cycle

    8.1 Data bus control logic *180*
    8.2 Address control logic *181*
    8.3 Data/address/control bus buffers *182*
    8.4 The microprocessor fetch-decode-execute cycle *182*
    8.5 How the microprocessor executes an instruction *184*
    8.6 Another example of the fetch-decode-execute cycle *187*
    8.7 Using the ALU to perform arithmetic operations *190*
    8.8 The Zilog Z80 microprocessor *194*
    8.9 Programming model of the Z80 MPU *195*

Summary *195*
Chapter review questions *196*

9. Microcomputer Memories

9.1 Introduction *199*
9.2 Read only memories *203*
9.3 ROM signals and architecture *205*
9.4 Popular EPROMS *207*
9.5 RAM signals and architecture *209*
9.6 An example of a popular SRAM chip *211*
9.7 Memory maps *213*
9.8 Memory decoding *214*
9.9 Practical decoding systems *216*
9.10 SIMMs and SIPs *219*
Summary *220*
Chapter review questions *221*

10. Microprocessor Input/Output ICs Interfacing & Peripherals

10.1 Parallel I/O *223*
10.2 Block diagram of a parallel port *227*
10.3 A programmer's model of the Z80 PIO *229*
10.4 Z80 PIO programming modes *231*
10.5 Serial input/output *234*
10.6 Overview of serial programmable ICs *236*
10.7 Memory-mapped and I/O mapped ports *238*
10.8 Methods used to transfer data between a microcomputer and its peripherals *240*
10.9 Interfacing external devices to a microcomputer *241*
10.10 Interfacing buses and standards *246*
10.11 Peripheral equipment *248*
Summary *251*
Chapter review questions *252*

11. Microcomputer Programming

11.1 Software development *255*
11.2 Program design *258*
11.3 The microprocessor's instruction set *262*
11.4 Addressing modes *267*
11.5 Programming examples *269*
11.6 Interfacing examples *278*
11.7 Debugging programs *293*
11.8 The monitor *293*
Summary *294*
Chapter review questions *295*

12. Mass Storage

12.1 An introduction to mass storage *297*
12.2 How binary data is stored in magnetic media *298*
12.3 Floppy disks *300*
12.4 Interfacing a floppy disk drive to a microcomputer *302*
12.5 Hard disks *307*
12.6 Hard and floppy disks compared *308*
12.7 Floppy disk care and handling *309*
12.8 Other magnetic storage media *309*
Summary *310*
Chapter review questions *311*

13. Troubleshooting On Digital/Microprocessor-Based Systems

13.1 Logic probe *314*
13.2 Logic pulser *315*
13.3 Current tracer *319*
13.4 Logic clip *322*
13.5 Logic comparator *323*
13.6 Logic analyser *324*
13.7 Signature analyser *326*
13.8 Self-test programs *328*
13.9 Memory testing *329*
Summary *330*
Chapter review questions *331*

Appendices

A: Answers to end of chapter multiple choice questions *334*
B: A microcomputer clock circuit *334*
C: Centronics signals *335*
D: RS-232 signals *336*
E: Program flowchart symbols *337*
F: Z80 instruction set *338*
G: Z80 flag register *345*

Index *346*

1: Microcomputers and Microprocessors

The profound effect of digital computers on society is now quite evident. Microprocessors and microcomputers are widely used in industry, science, mathematics and business. It is therefore essential to have an understanding of how microprocessor-based systems and microcomputers may be used and how they operate.

This chapter introduces the essential hardware components of a basic microcomputer system and provides an overview of the different types of software.

1.1 INTRODUCTION TO DIGITAL SYSTEMS

A number of important discoveries and inventions led to the development of the digital microcomputer, known today as the personal computer (PC). Personal computers have changed the world we live in, by transforming the way we handle information. Some of the landmarks which led to the development of the microcomputer include:

a. The invention of the transistor in 1948 at Bell Laboratories by John Bardeen, Walter Brattain and William Shockley. For this and for all the development work on semiconducting devices they were awarded the Nobel prize for physics in 1956.

   The **transistor**, is essentially, a solid-state **electronic switch.**

b. The first integrated circuit (IC) which was invented in 1959 by Texas instruments. An integrated circuit is a semiconductor circuit that contains a number of transistors on a tiny piece or chip of silicon and connects the transistors and other electronic components without wires. The first IC. contained only six transistors; the latest microprocessor the Intel 486 used in many of today's systems and personal computers has 1.2 million transistors. Today ICs can be built with several million transistors.

c. The first microprocessor, the Intel 4004, which was developed for use in the hand held calculator was introduced in 1971 and subsequently adopted for a number of industrial uses, such as traffic light systems. The 4004 microprocessor had 2,300 transistors.

A **digital computer** is a very flexible **general-purpose machine** that can be applied to a wide and ever-increasing range of applications. Basically, its function is to **process data**. As far as the computer is concerned, this data has to be numerical. If we, the users, have some non-numerical data, such as, a letter to a company, which has to be word processed, it is necessary that the non-numerical data be translated into numbers before the computer receives it. The data is represented by combinations of 0s and 1s. Here we are dealing with two unique digits; 0 and 1. Such a numbering system is known as the **binary** (two state) system.

Instructions and data for the computer are coded in binary **digit** form. For this reason they are referred to as **digital** computers.

1: Microcomputers and microprocessors

In the binary system, the term **BI**nary digi**T** is often abbreviated to the term **BIT**. A bit can have the value 0 or 1. Sometimes the value of the bit is called the logic level.

The first microprocessor, the Intel 4004, processed data in groups of four bits.

Within the computer the binary digits or bits are represented as follows:

+5 Volts = Logic 1 or Logic level 1

0 Volts = Logic 0 or Logic level 0

Fig 1.1 illustrates a typical four bit data word.

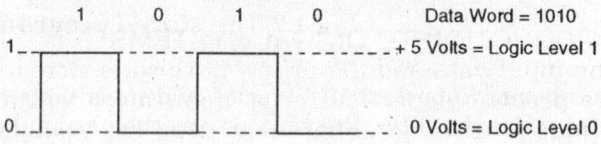

Fig 1.1 A four bit data word

Q Short answer question 1.1

State the basic function of a digital computer.

A Answer to SAQ 1.1

To process data

1.2 THE STORED-PROGRAM CONCEPT

To perform even the simplest task, a computer needs to be told exactly how to do it. A computer operates under **program control,** meaning that the computer's actions are controlled by a series of instructions that make up **a computer program** and since this program is stored within the computer, all digital computers are said to operate using the stored-program concept which is illustrated in Fig 1.2

When a computer **executes** a program, **it carries out the instructions**, one by one, that make up the program, which is stored in its memory.

1: Microcomputers and microprocessors

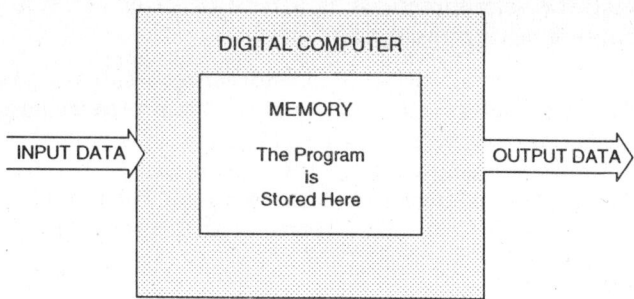

Fig 1.2 The stored program concept

The input data and the program which is stored in the memory of the computer are problem dependent; each application will need its own input data and a unique program to process that data. For example, in order to print salary slips for a group of employees, a wages program must first of all be written and then entered into the memory of the computer. Individual employee details (the input data) can then be entered into the computer, in turn, and their pay slips (the output data) produced.

Advantages of digital computers

a. Because digital computers are programmable they can be applied to a diverse range of applications. Each application requires a unique program, which can be entered into the computer and then executed.

b. Once the program has been entered into the computer, it can execute the program, to process the data, at very high speed.

c. Different sets of input data can be input, in turn, to the computer and the same program can produce different sets of output data or results.

 Short answer question 1.2

What is meant by the stored-program concept?

 Answer to SAQ 1.2

In order to solve a problem, using a computer, a set of instructions, called the program has to be written and entered into the memory of the machine. The processor then executes the instructions, one-by-one, until the program is completed.

1.3 MICROPROCESSOR INTEGRATED CIRCUITS

The microprocessor is a special kind of Integrated Circuit (IC). It is a general purpose device which may be programmed and applied to a wide range of applications. The microprocessor is at the heart of every microprocessor-based product, including microcomputers.

The two chief functions of the microprocessor are **processing** and **control.** The role of the microprocessor is to process data (carry out arithmetic calculations etc.) in accordance with a program of instructions which is stored in the memory of the system. Processing takes place within the Arithmetic Logic Unit (**ALU**). During the execution of a program the Control Unit (**CU**) of the microprocessor keeps itself and all of the other parts of the system (memory and I/O ports) working together and in the right time sequence.

The **Microprocesssor** is also known as the MicroProcessorUnit (**MPU**). Although it is frequently also referred to as the Central Processing Unit (**CPU**) care must be taken when using the latter term. Sometimes the CPU is taken to mean the arithmetic logic unit (ALU), control unit (CU) and the main store; the main store consists of those locations that may be addressed by the central processor. Throughout this text the use of the phrase CPU will be avoided and microprocessor or MPU or simply the processor will be used.

A typical 8-bit microprocessor is about 50mm long and 12mm wide. Careful examination of Fig 1.3 (a) reveals two sets of leglike protrusions, called **pins**. These pins are either soldered directly onto the printed circuit board or fitted into integrated circuit holders which are soldered to the printed circuit board. This type of **packaging** is called a Dual In-line (**DIL**) Package. The device in the figure has 40 pins. A 16-bit microprocessor, the Intel 80186, is shown in Figure 1.3(b).

For further details of IC packaging refer to Chapter 5, Section 5.3

Short answer question 1.3

What are the two chief functions of a microprocessor?

Answer to SAQ 1.3

To process data and control the other units (memory and input/output ports) of the system.

(a) an 8-bit microprocessor   (b) a 16-bit microprocessor

Fig 1.3 Microprocessor integrated circuits

1.4 PERSONAL COMPUTERS

A personal computer (PC) is a small, relatively inexpensive microcomputer marketed for individual use. All PCs use some kind of **microprocessor** chip as the **processing element**.

Personal computers began to appear during the mid to late 1970s. One of the first and most popular personal computers was the Apple II, introduced in 1977 by Apple Computer.

IBM soon realised that the world market for personal computers was about to grow rapidly and they entered the microcomputer industry in 1981 with the introduction of a new personal computer; what we now commonly refer to as the IBM PC.

Their original PC had only two floppy disk drives for storage, whereas modern systems can have a hard disk that is capable of providing GigaBytes of storage (Giga = 1000 million; Byte = 8 Bits).

The IBM PC gained popularity very quickly with the result that a number of computer manufacturers fell by the wayside.

Other companies adopted to IBM's dominance by building IBM clones; computers that were almost the same internally as the IBM PC but they cost much less.

All IBM and compatible P.C. systems divide into two distinct groups, XT and AT designs. Fig 1.4 summarises these two basic system types.

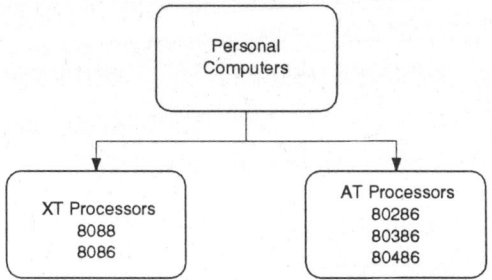

Fig 1.4 General classes of machines; XT and AT

The **XT** (eXtended Technology) corresponds closely to the original IBM PC (1981) design. By today's standards it **lacks power and expandability** (limited expansion). For this class of machine there is now a growing body of software and applications which it cannot run.

The **AT** (Advanced Technology) design was introduced in 1984 and has been developed over the years so that it offers the best performance available. The 80286, usually referred to as the 286 is now diminishing in popularity as the more powerful 386s and 486s are available at very competitive prices.

The other main distinction between Personal Computers is the type of processor that they use. The processor is the chip that runs the program to perform a task and so it determines the power of the machine. Basically, processor power depends on the type of device being used and the speed of the clock (See Chapter 6 – Section 6.5).

The leading manufacturers of microprocessors for personal computers are Intel and Motorola. IBM PCs and IBM clones or compatibles use Intel microprocessors, whereas Apple Macintosh computers use Motorola microprocessors.

Table 1.1 shows some popular microprocessors and their corresponding external data bus width, measured in bits. The size of the data bus is an important factor when comparing processors because, in general, the system with the widest system (external) data bus, can potentially, work faster.

Microprocessor	External data bus width (bits)
Intel 8085	8
Zilog Z80	8
MOS Technology 6502	8
Intel 8088	8
Intel 8086	16
Intel 80286	16
Intel 80386SX	16
Intel 80386DX	32
Intel 80486	32
Motorola 68000	16
Motorola 68010	16
Motorola 68020	32

Table 1.1 External bus widths for microprocessors

Multiple choice question 1.1

Comparing XT and AT personal computers. The AT:
a) is slower
b) works at about the same speed
c) is faster
d) always works twice as fast

Answer to MCQ 1.1

c

The microcomputer or personal computer is a complete computing system built around a microprocessor. Fig 1.5 illustrates such as product.

1: Microcomputers and microprocessors

Fig 1.5 A modern microprocessor-based microcomputer.
This product is built around the Intel 80386 microprocessor.
Courtesy of Research Machines (RM) Oxford

The most important part of any machine is the motherboard. Fig 1.6 indicates some of the main components in a Research Machines motherboard. These include:
- the microprocessor
- Random Access Memory (RAM)
- Read Only Memories (ROM)
- Input-Output (I/O) Ports for peripheral devices, such as, the keyboard, mouse and monitor

Fig 1.6 The mainboard or motherboard for
a Research Machines microcomputer.

1: Microcomputers and microprocessors

1.5 A TYPICAL SINGLE BOARD MICROCOMPUTER

Microprocessors (MPUs) are powerful computing devices, but they are not much good by themselves; they have to be supported by other components and integrated circuits. It is, however, the most important unit in the system and can be thought of as acting like its 'brains'.

Just as a human brain needs feet, hands, eyes, ears, nose, and a mouth to be able to direct physical actions, such as, those required for drinking a cup of tea, a microprocessor needs to be connected to other devices before it becomes a useful system.

Fig 1.7 shows a single board microcomputer system. Examination of the diagram reveals many other components besides the microprocessor. These include:

Random Access Memory (RAM)
Read Only Memory (ROM)
An Input/Output Port
A keyboard
An in-built seven segment display
Resistors
Capacitors
Transistors

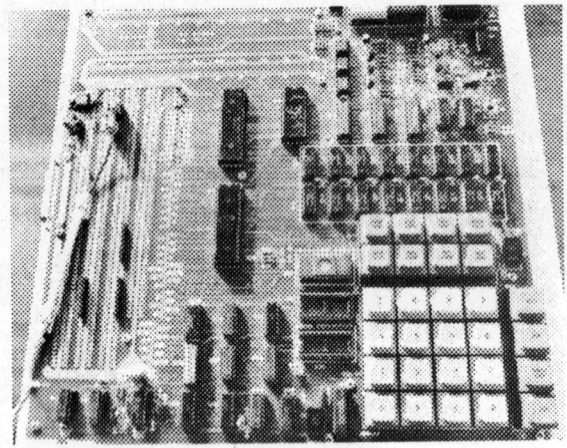

Fig 1.7 A single board microcomputer based on the 8-bit Z80 microprocessor

Short answer question 1.4

Name THREE different types of components found within a microcomputer system.

1: Microcomputers and microprocessors

> **Answer to SAQ 1.4**
>
> i) Integrated circuits such as the MPU, ROM, RAM and the Input/Output port.
> ii) Resistors
> iii) Capacitors

1.6 THE ARCHITECTURE OF A BASIC MICROCOMPUTER

By **architecture** we mean a description of its hardware (physical) parts, how they are connected, and how they communicate with each other. Block diagrams are used extensively to describe all kinds of systems. A **block diagram** is a graphic description of individual parts of a system and how they interact. Fig 1.8 is a block diagram showing the combination of microprocessor, memory and input and output ports which forms what is known as a **microcomputer**. The function of each unit of the system is as follows:

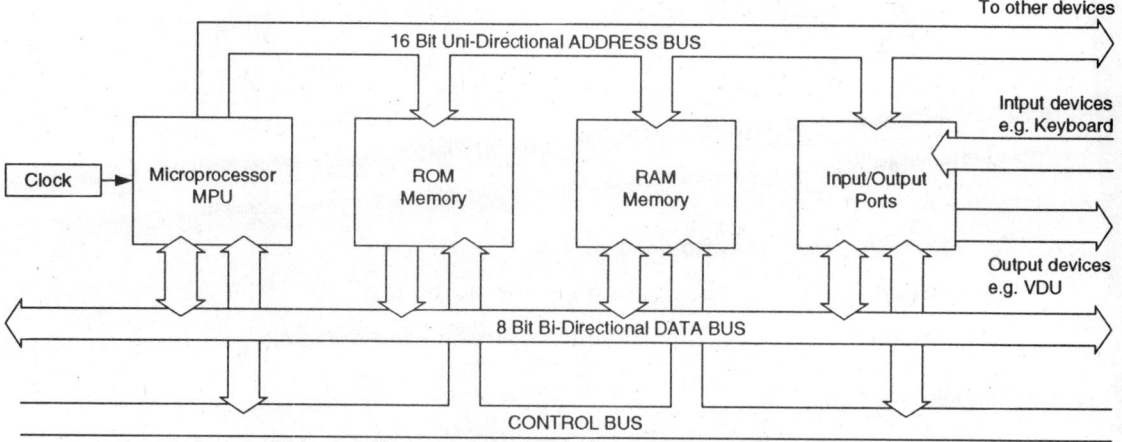

Fig 1.8 A basic microcomputer system

THE MICROPROCESSOR

The microprocessor is a single chip which is capable of **processing** data and **controlling** all of the components which make up the microcomputer system. It is often called the microprocessor unit (MPU) or simply the processor. It contains all the circuits needed to create the 'brain' of a microcomputer.

The internal architecture of the microprocessor is, as might be expected, complex and will be examined in detail in Chapters 6, 7, and 8. However, as far as the user is concerned, a typical MPU chip contains:

    a. **Temporary storage** in the form of a number of **registers** which can each hold a number of bits of binary information, representing program instructions or data.

b. The **Arithmetic Logic Unit (ALU)**. This part of the microprocessor performs both arithmetic (such as addition and subtraction) and logical operations (we'll find out about these in Chapter 3).

c. **Timing and control circuits** that keep all of the other parts of the system (memory and I/O ports) working together and in the right time sequence.

Multiple choice question 1.2

When a microcomputer carries out calculations they are performed within the:

a) RAM
b) ROM
c) Input/Output port
d) Microprocessor

Answer to MCQ 1.2

D

THE MEMORY

The duties of the memory are:

a. to store programs and data.
b. to provide data to the microprocessor on request
c. to accept new data from the microprocessor for storage

ROM

ROM stands for Read Only Memory. The software in the ROM is fixed during manufacture and cannot be changed; no information can be written into ROM. All types of ROM (see Chapter 9) are **non-volatile** which means that when the microcomputer power supplies are switched off, the information stored in ROM is not lost. When the microcomputer is turned on, the ROM locations contain the same values that they did before it was turned off.

Those programs which are permanently stored in ROM are often called **firmware.**

ROM is used to store operational programs called **monitors.** A monitor is a program that lets the user communicate with the microprocessor, using the keyboard and display. For example, the monitor provides a facility that permits the running of the user's program. The main facilities available with a monitor for a single board microcomputer are stated in Chapter 11.

RAM

RAM stands for **R**andom **A**ccess **M**emory. RAM has both read and write capability, meaning that it is designed to have information written into it and also read out from it. Unlike ROM, RAM is **volatile,** meaning that the memory keeps the information stored in it only as long as the power supply to the microcomputer is left switched on. If we turn off the power to the system, or if the power fails, the data stored in RAM is lost. When we turn off the microcomputer, all the information stored in RAM is destroyed. When we turn the computer on, random values are found in the RAM memory locations. These random values are called **garbage** because they have no meaning to us. RAM can, however, be made non-volatile by providing back-up power supplies to maintain power when the mains supplies are turned off or fail. RAM is used to store the program which we want to run currently.

Multiple choice question 1.3

Which one of the following is TRUE?

a) RAM is non-volatile

b) ROM is non-volatile

c) Both RAM and ROM are volatile

d) The ROM contains garbage at switch on

Answer to MCQ 1.3

B

THE INPUT OUTPUT (I/O) DEVICE

I/O means input/output and is the link between the microprocessor and the outside world. Also known as input/output ports. An input port is a circuit through which an external device can send signals to the processor. An output port is a circuit that allows the microprocessor to output signals to external devices. Both input and output ports may be implemented in a single IC package. Both input to and output from the processor via the I/O ports is done under program control. This topic is covered in Chapters 10 and 11.

BUSES

Fig 1.8 illustrates that the system components – RAM, ROM and I/O ports are interconnected by a bus system. The term **bus** refers to a group of wires or conduction tracks on a printed circuit board (also ribbon cable etc.) through which binary information is transferred from one part of a microcomputer to another. The MPU has three buses which it uses to communicate with the other parts of the system. These are, the **address bus**, the **data bus** and the **control bus**.

The data bus

The **data bus** carries the data which is being transferred throughout the system. Examples of data transfers are:

i   program instructions being read from RAM into the processor
ii data being read from RAM into the processor
iii results being sent from the processor to RAM
iv data being sent from the processor to the output port
v   data being read in from the port to the processor

There are 8 data pins on an 8-bit microprocessor, labelled D_0 to D_7 and the data bus has eight lines, one for each pin. So the data bus can carry simultaneously 8-bit data words. The data bus is **bi-directional**, which means that data can travel in both directions.

The size of a bus, known as its width, is important because it determines how much data can be transferred at one time.

The address bus

An address is a binary number that identifies a specific memory storage location or I/O port involved in a data transfer. The address bus is used to transmit the address of the location to the memory or the port. An 8-bit microprocessor has 16 address pins, labelled A_0 to A_{15} and the system address bus has 16 lines, one for each address pin on the processor. The address bus is **unidirectional** (one way): addresses are always issued by the microprocessor.

Every piece of information (instructions and data) stored in the memory, has its location identified by an **address**.

The control bus

The **control bus** is another group of pins on the MPU. READ is an example of a control bus signal. This signal is generated by the timing-control circuits of the microprocessor whenever it needs to read information from the memory or an input/output port via the data bus. From the data bus the data is taken into the microprocessor. Each line of the control bus goes only one way. Some lines, such as, READ and WRITE, are output lines, while others which we will discuss later, act as inputs to the MPU (interrupts).

1: Microcomputers and microprocessors

 Short answer question 1.5

The microprocessor has just performed an arithmetic operation and the 8-bit result 0101 1111 is left in one of its internal registers. The result is to be stored in RAM at address 0010 0000 0000 0000. Draw the basic microcomputer system block diagram highlighting which components of the system are involved in the data transfer. The binary numbers appearing on the address and data bus must be clearly indicated on the diagram.

Are any signals within the control bus active during the transfer of the data from the MPU to RAM?

Which part of the system issues the RAM address 0010 0000 0000 0000 where the data is to be stored?

 Answer to SAQ 1.5

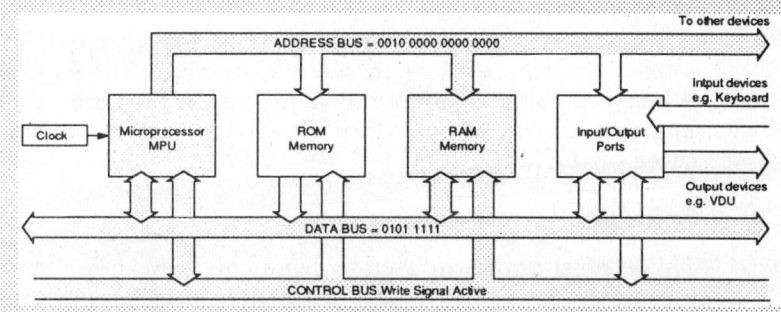

Fig 1.9

The memory WRITE signal within the control bus will be active.

The address where the data is to be stored is issued by the microprocessor.

 Short answer question 1.6

What is meant by the term bus?

 Answer to SAQ 1.6

A bus is a common communications pathway used to carry information between the various elements of a computer system.

13

1.7 A SUMMARY OF KEY TERMS FOR MICROCOMPUTING

- ☐ Hardware
- ☐ Program
- ☐ Software
  - ■ Systems software
  - ■ Applications software
- ☐ Machine code
- ☐ High-level Languages
- ☐ Assembly language

Hardware

Hardware is the name for the **physical components** of a digital computer system. Examples of hardware are: microprocessor chips, memory chips, input/output port chips, printed circuit boards, peripherals-keyboards, printers, screens.

Program

A program is a complete **set of instructions**, written in computer language, that tells the computer how to solve a problem. The program is stored in memory. When you ask the computer to execute a program it reads in and executes the instructions one by one, until all the instructions in the program have been executed by the MPU.

Software

This is a general term used to denote all forms of **programs** which can be used on a computer system together with their associated documentation. The two main classes of software are: **applications software** and **systems software**.

Applications software

This is software which is often produced by a **software house**, which is a commercial organisation specialising in the development of software which is designed to be put to specific practical use. Applications software falls into two categories: **Applications packages** and **Specialist applications software.**

a. An **applications package** is a set of programs with associated documentation which enables a computer to be used for a specific application. A vast selection of applications packages, which are available from many sources, have been written for use with personal computers. The most popular ones are: **Word processing, Databases** and **Spreadsheets.**

   Word Processing (WP) is one of the most common applications of computer systems. A word processing package is a program which enables you to create a document, store it on a disk, display it on a screen, modify it by entering commands from the keyboard or mouse and output the document to a printer to obtain **hard copy**. A system dedicated to this application is often referred to as a word processor.

Databases. A database is a collection of useful information organised in a specific manner. For instance, you can view a personal telephone directory as a database with a list of names in one column and their telephone numbers in another. A **database package** is a program which is actually a set of tools with which you can organise and manipulate data in a simple yet effective manner. For example, the names in the telephone directory could be arranged alphabetically by surname.

Spreadsheets. A spreadsheet is a table of values arranged in rows and columns where each value sits in a cell. A spreadsheet package is a program which allows you to create and manipulate spreadsheets. A simple example of a useful spreadsheet application is one that calculates mortgage payments for a house. For this application you would define five cells:

1. the total cost of buying the house
2. the deposit
3. mortgage rate
4. mortgage term
5. monthly payment

Once you have defined how these cells depend on each other, you could enter numbers and play with various possibilities. For example, you could use the spreadsheet package to find out how the repayments would vary for mortgage terms from five to twenty five years, whilst keeping all the other values constant.

b. **Specialist applications software** is also available (or may be written by the user) which is designed to carry out particular tasks. Examples are:

i) a program for solving equations for electronic circuitry design
ii) a payroll program
iii) stock control programs

Short answer question 1.7

Name two common software applications packages

Answer to SAQ 1.7

Word Processing and Database packages

System software

In practice most people have little difficulty understanding the meaning of hardware and applications software. The hardware is self evident in a typical computer room; items, such as, the computer unit, printers, display units, document scanners etc. Most people gain an idea of what is meant by applications software

1: Microcomputers and microprocessors

in terms of instructing the computer to carry out tasks for their specific applications. But system software is often much more of a mystery.

The simplest definition of systems software is that it is the software which bridges the gap between the applications software and the hardware as illustrated in Fig 1.10.

Fig 1.10 Systems software as a link between hardware and applications programs

The term **systems software** refers to programs which are related to the control and management of the computer system as a whole, rather than to a particular application. One of the main items of systems software is the **operating system** which has many functions in managing machine resources such as memory and disk space and starting the system at switch on. Other items of systems software include **language processors** and **utilities** (see section 1.8).

Machine code

Machine code is the **language** that the **MPU can interpret directly** because each instruction and every piece of data is represented by a unique pattern of binary digits (bits). For instance, the following piece of machine code would load a particular register (the accumulator – see Chapters 6,7 and 8), within the Z80 MPU, with the 8 bits of data stored in RAM at address 0010 0001 0000 0000 and then halt the processor:

Instruction 1	0011	1010
	0000	0000
	0010	0001
Instruction 2	0111	0110

Fig 1.11 Machine code program

Clearly, machine instructions, written in **machine code**, which consist entirely of binary numbers (often expressed in hexadecimal for convenience) are almost impossible for humans to understand. Frequently, machine code is either referred to as **object code** or the **object program**. Each microprocessor has its own unique set of machine instructions, called the instruction set, which it understands. Because object code is so difficult to write and understand, programmers use either a high-level programming language or an assembly language.

High-level Languages

These are programming languages which are easier to write and understand. Unlike machine code which is processor specific, high-level languages enable a programmer to write programs that are more or less independent of a particular type of computer. Such languages are considered high-level because their instructions frequently contain words from the English language.

Pascal, Cobol and **Fortran** are examples of some commonly used high-level programming languages. Programs written in a high-level language are known as **source programs.** The instructions which make up a source program are not directly understood by the MPU because they are not written in binary. The source code has therefore to be translated into object code using a program known as a **compiler**.

Assembly language

Assembly language is a means of programming where every instruction is specified by the programmer, but with various aids in the language to make it more convenient than machine code written using just binary numbers. For example, the two machine code instructions in Fig 1.11 would be written as:

        Instruction 1   LD   A, (2100)
        Instruction 2   HALT

This is now our **source code** in the assembly language.

From the foregoing example it is clear that assembly language is preferable to machine language. However, because it is not written in binary, the microprocessor will not understand it and like the high-level language the assembly source code must be translated into object code. This is done using a program called an **assembler**. Each type of MPU has its own machine language and assembly language. Assembly language is used in applications where speed is essential; an assembly language program runs faster than a high-level language program.

Short answer question 1.8

State the name of the program for translating

i)   assembly language source code to object code

ii)   Pacal source code to object code

Answer to SAQ 1.8

i)   Assembler

ii)   Compiler

1.8 OVERVIEW OF A MICROCOMPUTER SYSTEM

A general overview of a typical computer system is given in Fig 1.12 The diagram illustrates that any system may be sub-divided into hardware and software components. The **hardware** is the **physical parts** of the system. **Software** refers to **programs** and is divided into two categories – **systems software** and **applications software**. Typical examples of applications software are word processing, database and spreadsheet packages. Specialist applications software is also available or it may be produced by the user. An example of this type of software would be a program which could aid a design engineer to model and analyse electrical or electronic circuits.

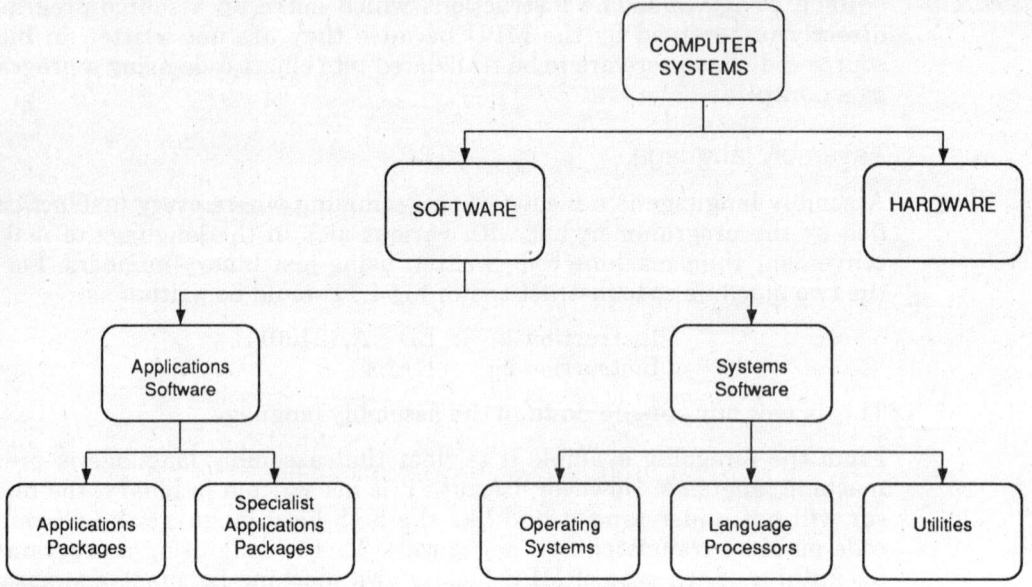

Fig 1.12 Overview of a microcomputer system

Systems software includes:

The operating system. The most popular operating system for microcomputers is **MS-DOS** (MicroSoft-Disk Operating System). As soon as your personal computer is switched on the operating system is loaded into RAM memory, and it remains in control of the system at all times. The operating system performs many tasks, such as, handling peripheral devices used for input, output and storage. For instance, if you wish to print your wordprocess document a request is made from the applications package to the operating system which then issues the appropriate hardware instructions to the device concerned; the printer. One of the chief responsibilities of an operating system is the management of computer files. Your source program for an assembly language or a high level language which is saved on disk is an example of a computer file. Files are loaded into the computer's memory when the information they contain is to be used and the operating system controls both the storing and the loading of computer files.

Language processors or translators. Examples are **compilers** (for Pascal, Cobol etc.) **interpreters** (for some versions of Basic) and **assemblers** for assembly language programming.

Utilities which are usually provided free with the operating system. Common examples are **FORMAT** which prepares a disk so that the computer can read or write to it and **DISKCOPY** for copying disks.

Short answer question 1.9

Name any TWO items of systems software.

 Answer to SAQ 1.9

i) the operating system

ii) language translators (assemblers, compilers, interpreters)

SUMMARY

- A digital computer is general-purpose system which may be programmed to perform a variety of tasks.
- The element within a microcomputer which has the dual functions of processing data and controlling the various elements of the system is the microprocessor.
- Personal computers or microcomputers fall into two general classes XT and AT.
- XTs are based on the 8088 processor, or the slightly faster 8086
- ATs can be based on a number of processors. 286, 386 or 486 processors may be used. ATs cost more than XTs.
- In order to be able to run modern applications and software packages an AT system is required.
- A typical microprocessor contains temporary storage (registers), an Arithmetic Logic Unit (ALU) and timing and control circuits.
- A basic microcomputer system consists of the microprocessor, RAM, ROM and input/output ports.
- A microcomputer has three buses. The address, data and control buses.
- Hardware refers to the physical parts of the system
- A program is a list of instructions
- Software is a term used to denote all types of programs
- The two main classes of software are Systems software and applications software.
- Items of systems software are the Operating System, Language Processors (or Translators) and Utilities.
- A system may be programmed in machine code, assembly language or a high-level language.

CHAPTER REVIEW QUESTIONS

Section A: Multiple choice questions (Answers in Appendix A)

1. The transistor is:
    a) a semiconductor circuit that contains a number of components
    b) a solid-state electronic switch
    c) the component which processes data within an MPU
    d) the main component within a microcomputer

2. Which one of the following voltage levels is used to represent binary 1 within a microcomputer?
    a) 0 V
    b) +15 V
    c) +25 V
    d) +5 V

3. The two chief functions of a microprocessor are
    a) performing arithmetic and logic operations
    b) controlling the memory and port
    c) processing data and controlling the system components
    d) running systems and applications programs

4. A compiler is a program for converting
    a) assembly language source code to object code
    b) object code to assembly language source code
    c) object code to high-level language source code
    d) high-level language source code to object code

5. Which one of the following can an MPU interpret directly?
    a) machine code
    b) assembly language
    c) high-level language
    d) an applications program

6. The user's high-level language program is stored in
    a) the input/output port
    b) ROM
    c) MPU
    d) RAM

7. Refer to Fig 1.13

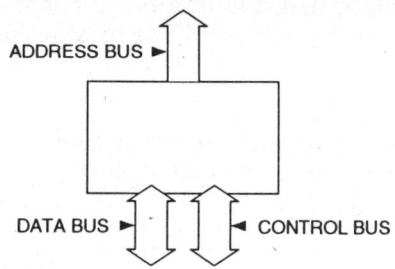

Fig 1.13

Which one of the following parts of a basic microcomputer is shown in Fig 1.13?

a) RAM
b) ROM
c) Input/Output port
d) Microprocessor

8 The main components of a microcomputer are

a) address bus, data bus, control bus and MPU
b) temporary storage, RAM, ROM and input/output ports
c) MPU, ROM, RAM and input/output ports
d) busses, ROM, RAM and input/output ports

9 Which one of the following buses is UNIDIRECTIONAL?

a) address bus
b) data bus
c) control bus
d) input/output bus

10 One reason for writing a program in assembly language rather than using a high-level language is that it

a) executes faster
b) executes slower
c) is quicker to write
d) doesn't need a translation program

Section B: Short answer questions

1 A digital computer is said to be a general-purpose machine. Briefly explain what this means.

2 What is meant by the stored-program concept?

3 There are two general classes of personal computers XT and AT. Which processors may be used in AT designs?

1: Microcomputers and microprocessors

4. Draw a block diagram of a basic microcomputer and explain the function of each unit of the system. Your answer should include the MPU, ROM, RAM, Input/Output port and the mechanism by which these components communicate.

5. Draw a diagram which gives a general overview of a typical microcomputer system. Your answer must include hardware and software (system software and applications software)

    With the aid of the diagram describe the main items of systems software.

6. State one main difference between ROM and RAM.

7. What is firmware?

Chapter 2

Number Systems and Computer Arithmetic

The first part of this chapter is a review of the decimal number system which we work with in our everyday lives. You should also be familiar with other number systems, such as, binary, hexadecimal and octal and conversions between these different number systems. Binary (two-state) is particularly important because microprocessor-based systems and microcomputers are implemented using hardware components which have two stable states. The hexadecimal number system which is used extensively in microcomputer systems to represent large binary numbers will be examined in some detail. Representation of positive and negative numbers within the microcomputer plus commonly used binary codes are also introduced in this chapter.

2.1 AN INTRODUCTION TO NUMBER SYSTEMS

For everyday use people are trained to work with the **denary** or **decimal** number system which employs ten different symbols, namely **0,1,2,3,4,5,6,7,8,9**.

Digital computers, however, employ a different and much simpler system of numbers. They work with binary numbers and instructions coded in binary number form. Therefore, it is important that we develop a good working knowledge of binary numbers, computer arithmetic using binary numbers, and microprocessor instructions coded in binary patterns, so we can begin to understand how microprocessors and microcomputer systems operate. The binary system uses only two separate symbols, 0 and 1, to represent numbers and instructions (machine instructions) for a digital computer.

Other number systems which may be used in digital computing are the base-8, octal and the base-16, hexadecimal, systems.

2.2 BASICS OF THE DECIMAL, BINARY, HEXADECIMAL AND OCTAL NUMBER SYSTEMS

Decimal Numbers

The decimal system is the most commonly used number system in the world. For example, when you examine your bank balance or telephone a friend you are dealing with decimal numbers. The **decimal system**, also called the **base-10** system, because it **has 10 digits**, has evolved naturally as a result of the fact that a person has ten fingers. Examination of the characteristics of the decimal system will help us to develop an understanding of other number systems which are used in digital computers.

2: Number systems and computer arithmetic

Using the 10 symbols 0,1,2,3,4,5,6,7,8,9 as digits of a number, we can express any quantity. The decimal system uses a **positional-value** or **place value** system in which the value of a digit depends on its position within the number. For instance, consider the decimal number 753.

We know that:

$$7 \text{ represents } 7 \text{ hundreds ; seven hundreds} = 7 \times 100 = 7 \times 10^2$$
$$5 \text{ represents } 5 \text{ tens } \quad ; \text{ five tens} \quad = 5 \times 10 = 5 \times 10^1$$
$$3 \text{ represents } 3 \text{ units } \quad ; \quad\quad\quad\quad\quad = 3 \times 1 = 3 \times 10^0$$

So $753 = 7 \times 10^2 + 5 \times 10^1 + 3 \times 10^0$
$\quad\quad\quad = 7 \times 100 + 5 \times 10 + 3 \times 1$
$\quad\quad\quad = 700 + 50 + 3$
$\quad\quad\quad = 753$

The 7 carries the most weight of the three digits and is referred to as the most significant digit (MSD). The three carries the least weight and is called the least significant digit (LSD).

The decimal positional values (weights) are illustrated in Fig. 2.1

Positional values or column weights $\rightarrow$	10^4	10^3	10^2	10^1	10^0
	10000	1000	100	10	1

Fig. 2.1 Decimal position values as powers of ten

Example: The decimal number 4507 is made up thus:

10^4	10^3	10^2	10^1	10^0
(10000)	(1000)	(100)	(10)	(1)
0	4	5	0	7

$= 0 \times 10000 + 4 \times 1000 + 5 \times 100 + 0 \times 10 + 7 \times 1$
$= \quad\quad\quad 0 + 4000 \quad + 500 \quad + 0 \quad + 7$
$= 4507$

To distinguish between different number systems, the base is shown as a subscript. For instance, the decimal number 4507 in the previous example would be written as 4507_{10}.

Short answer question 2.1

What base does the decimal number system use?

2: Number systems and computer arithmetic

Answer to SAQ 2.1

10

Binary Numbers

Unfortunately, the decimal number system is not particularly suitable for direct use in digital electronic circuits. It is very difficult to design digital circuitry so that it can work with ten different voltage levels; each one representing one of the decimal numbers 0 to 9. On the other hand, it is very easy to design circuits that operate with only two voltage levels. For this reason, digital systems use the binary (two-state) system as the basic number system of its operations, although other systems are often used in conjunction with binary. Because binary numbers contain only two different digits, 0 and 1, the binary number system is said to have a base of two.

Like the decimal system, the binary number system assigns a weight to each column. In the decimal number system, each column has a weight that is a power of ten. This is done because the decimal number system has a base of ten. The binary number system has a base of two and so its column weights are powers of two. Fig. 2.2 illustrates the first eight column weights for binary numbers.

Positional values or column weights	→	2^7	2^6	2^5	2^4	2^3	2^2	2^1	2^0
Decimal equivalents	→	128	64	32	16	8	4	2	1

Fig. 2.2 Binary position values as powers of two and their decimal equivalents.

Multiple choice question 2.1

The binary number system has a base of

a) 10

b) 8

c) 16

d) 2

Answer to MCQ 2.1

D

Example: The eight bit binary number 0110 1111 has the following meaning.

Bit No.	Bit 7	Bit 6	Bit 5	Bit 4	Bit 3	Bit 2	Bit 1	Bit 0
Column Weights	2^7	2^6	2^5	2^4	2^3	2^2	2^1	2^0
Decimal equivalent	128	64	32	16	8	4	2	1
Binary Number	0	1	1	0	1	1	1	1

$$\begin{aligned}
0110\ 1111 &= 0 \times 2^7 + 1 \times 2^6 + 1 \times 2^5 + 0 \times 2^4 + 1 \times 2^3 + 1 \times 2^2 + 1 \times 2^1 + 1 \times 2^0 \\
&= 0 \times 128 + 1 \times 64 + 1 \times 32 + 0 \times 16 + 1 \times 8 + 1 \times 4 + 1 \times 2 + 1 \times 1 \\
&= 0\ \ \ \ \ + 64\ \ \ \ + 32\ \ \ \ + 0\ \ \ \ + 8\ \ \ \ + 4\ \ \ \ + 2\ \ \ \ + 1 \\
&= 111_{10}
\end{aligned}$$

From the foregoing example we have seen that conversion from a binary to its equivalent decimal number is very straightforward. All we need to remember is the column weights as we move from right to left;

Left ⟵───────────────────────────────⟶ Right

⟵─── 128 64 32 16 8 4 2 1

A binary 1 in a given position must be multiplied by the relevant column weight, a binary 0 in any position indicates a zero. Stated in another way, it means that we simply add the decimal weights of all bits that are 1.

Table 2.1 lists the decimal numbers 0 to 25 and shows their binary equivalents

Decimal Number	Binary Number	Decimal Number	Binary Number
0	00000	13	01101
1	00001	14	01110
2	00010	15	01111
3	00011	16	10000
4	00100	17	10001
5	00101	18	10010
6	00110	19	10011
7	00111	20	10100
8	01000	21	10101
9	01001	22	10110
10	01010	23	10111
11	01011	24	11000
12	01100	25	11001

Table 2.1 Decimal and corresponding binary numbers

2: Number systems and computer arithmetic

Short answer question 2.2

Convert 10101_2 to its decimal equivalent

Answer to SAQ 2.2

$10101_2 = 1 \times 2^4 + 0 \times 2^3 + 1 \times 2^2 + 0 \times 2^1 + 1 \times 2^0$

$ 16 +0 +4 +0 +1$

$ 21_{10}$

Octal numbers

Although digital computers work with binary numbers and instructions coded in binary number form, most humans find binary difficulty to handle, especially when dealing with long binary patterns consisting of maybe 8, 16, 32 or even 64 bits. For example, the address bus of an 8 - bit microcomputer system is 16 bits long. Because binary numbers are tedious and error-prone when used by human operators alternative shorthand methods for representing long binary numbers are available. External to a computer, binary numbers may be represented by any other convenient number system. You might therefore suggest working in decimal. However, decimal is not the most convenient method since it is not easy to relate each digit in a decimal number to a specific number of bits in its binary equivalent because ten is not an exact power of two.

Octal and **hexadecimal** number systems are used as **shorthand representations of long binary numbers.**

The octal number system, as the name suggests, has a **base of 8** and uses the eight symbols **0,1,2,3,4,5,6,7**. In order to represent these 8 octal digits in binary we need to use three bits. See Table 2.2

Octal	Binary
0	000
1	001
2	010
3	011
4	100
5	101
6	110
7	111

Table 2.2 The eight octal digits and corresponding binary representation

In the octal system positional or place values increase in powers of 8. Fig 2.3 gives the first five column weights for the octal number system and corresponding decimal values.

2: Number systems and computer arithmetic

Positional values as powers of eight →	8^4	8^3	8^2	8^1	8^0
Decimal equivalents →	4096	512	64	8	1

Fig 2.3 Octal position values as powers of 8 and their decimal equivalents

Example: Convert 216_8 to decimal.

An octal number can be easily converted to its decimal equivalent by multiplying each octal digit by its positional weight.

$$\begin{aligned} 216_8 &= 2 \times 8^2 + 1 \times 8^1 + 6 \times 8^0 \\ &= 2 \times 64 + 1 \times 8 + 6 \times 1 \\ &= 128 + 8 + 6 \\ &= 142_{10} \end{aligned}$$

Q Short answer question 2.3

Convert 90_8 to decimal

A Answer to SAQ 2.3

$$\begin{aligned} 90_8 &= 9 \times 8^1 + 0 \times 8^0 \\ & 72 + 0 \\ & 72_{10} \end{aligned}$$

Hexadecimal numbers

Many computers utilise the hexadecimal system, rather than octal, to represent large binary numbers. We use hexadecimal representation in place of binary for programming microcomputers. **Hexadecimal** numbers, usually abbreviated to **'Hex'**, are **base 16** numbers. Thus, it has 16 distinct symbols. It uses the digits **0 through 9** plus the letters **A, B, C, D, E and F** as the 16 symbols. We need to remember that the first six letters of the alphabet A, B, C, D, E and F correspond to 10, 11, 12, 13, 14, and 15 in decimal. In order to represent the sixteen distinct hex symbols we need four bits. Table 2.3 gives the hexadecimal numbers form 0 to 20, together with their decimal and binary equivalents.

2: Number systems and computer arithmetic

Decimal	Hexadecimal	Binary
0	0	0000
1	1	0001
2	2	0010
3	3	0011
4	4	0100
5	5	0101
6	6	0110
7	7	0111
8	8	1000
9	9	1001
10	A	1010
11	B	1011
12	C	1100
13	D	1101
14	E	1110
15	F	1111
16	10	0001 0000
17	11	0001 0001
18	12	0001 0010
19	13	0001 0011
20	14	0001 0100

Table 2.3 Hexadecimal (Hex) numbers and their binary and decimal equivalents

From table 2.3 we see that each hex character can serve as a shorthand notation for a 4-bit binary number. Note that numbers above 15_{10} require more than one hex character. Positional or place values follow the same pattern as decimal, binary and octal; hex uses base 16 so the place values for the first five columns are as shown in Fig 2.4

Positional value $\longrightarrow$	16^4	16^3	16^2	16^1	16^0
Decimal equivalents $\longrightarrow$	65536	4096	256	16	1

Fig. 2.4 Hexadecimal place values as powers of 16 and their decimal equivalents.

Hexadecimal numbers may be denoted either by using the subscript 16 or the letter 'H' after the last character/s. For instance, the hexadecimal characters 12AF may be written as $12AF_{16}$ or 12AFH.

Example: Calculate the decimal number corresponding to 123H

2: Number systems and computer arithmetic

$$123\text{H} = 1 \times 16^2 + 2 \times 16^1 + 3 \times 16^0$$
$$= 1 \times 256 + 2 \times 16 + 3 \times 1$$
$$= 256 \quad + \quad 32 + 3$$
$$= 291_{10}$$

2.3 CONVERTING NUMBERS FROM ONE BASE TO ANOTHER

When you work with microprocessors it is important that you are able to handle number conversions involving decimal, binary, octal and hexadecimal. We have already seen how to convert from binary, octal and hexadecimal to decimal.

Multiple choice question 2.2

The binary number 0011 1111 corresponds to the decimal number,

a) 31
b) 36
c) 63
d) 18

Answer to MCQ 2.2

c

Multiple choice question 2.3

The octal number 23 is equivalent to which of the following decimal numbers ?

a) 5
b) 17
c) 19
d) 29

Answer to MCQ 2.3

c

2: Number systems and computer arithmetic

Multiple choice question 2.4

15H is equal to which of the following decimal numbers?

a) 6

b) 4

c) 12

d) 21

Answer to MCQ 2.4

D

Conversion of decimal numbers to binary numbers

This conversion may be carried out by two different methods:

a. By a combination of intuition and trial and error.

    Example: 57_{10} may be converted to binary by writing down the binary column weights and then trying to work out which columns should have a one, so that when the columns with the 1s are added together the sum is equal to 57_{10}

Decimal Number	Binary Columns								Binary Number
	2^7	2^6	2^5	2^4	2^3	2^2	2^1	2^0	
	128	64	32	16	8	4	2	1	
57	0	0	1	1	1	0	0	1	0011 1001

Explanation: The number 57 is less than both 128 and 64 therefore a 0 is placed in these columns. However it is greater than 32 so a 1 is placed in the 32s column. This leaves 57 − 32 = 25, which is greater than 16, so a 1 is placed in the 16s column. This then leaves 25 − 16 = 9. This is greater than 8, so a 1 is placed in the 8s column. The remainder of 9 − 8 (1) is less than 4 or 2 so a 0 is placed in these columns. Finally a 1 is placed in the 1s column giving the binary number 0011 1001.

b. An alternative and more systematic method consists of dividing the decimal number successively by 2, until the result of the last division is zero. The remainder is noted after each division. The equivalent binary number is then found by writing the remainders so that the last remainder is the most significant bit (MSB) of the binary number.

Example: Convert 49_{10} to binary.

2: Number systems and computer arithmetic

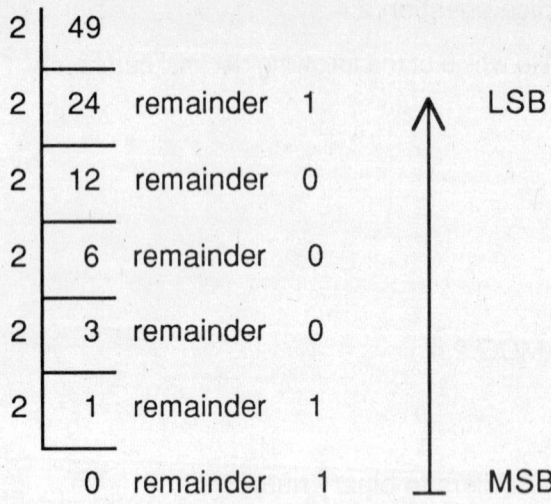

Therefore $49_{10} = 1\ 1\ 0\ 0\ 0\ 1_2$

Q Short answer question 2.4

Using the successive division by two method convert 34_{10} to binary.

A Answer to SAQ 2.4

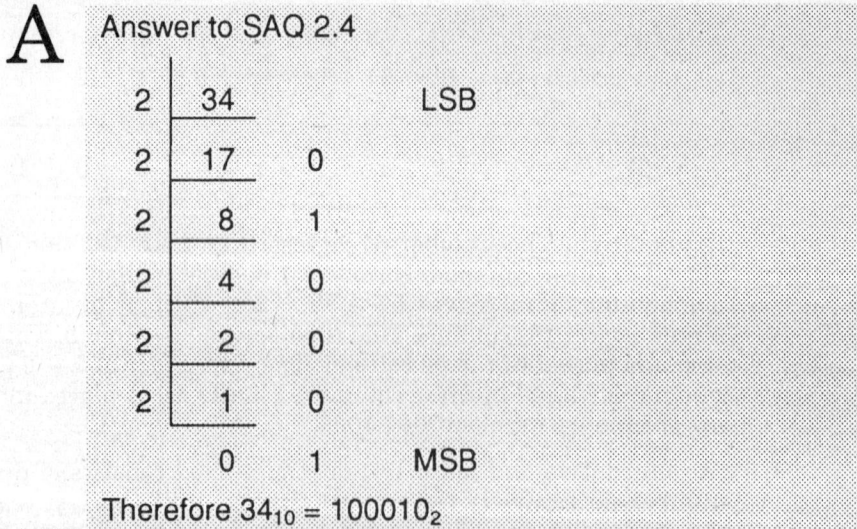

Therefore $34_{10} = 100010_2$

Conversion from decimal to octal

Previously we saw that decimal numbers could be converted to binary by two different methods:

2: Number systems and computer arithmetic

a. By writing down the binary column weights and then by a mix of intuition and trial and error attempting to place 1s in the appropriate binary column/s.

b. By using the more elegant technique known as the successive division method.

The successive division method may be used to convert from decimal to any other number base by applying the following simple rule.

'The decimal number to be converted is successively divided by the base of the number system it is to be converted into, until the result of the division is 0'

Example: Convert 139_{10} to octal

```
8 | 139
8 |  17    remainder of 3      LSB
8 |   2    remainder of 1       ↑
      0    remainder of 2      MSB
```

Hence $139_{10} = 213_8$

Q Short answer question 2.5

Using the successive division method convert 156_{10} to octal

A Answer to SAQ 2.5

```
8 | 156
8 |  19    4      LSB
8 |   2    3
      0    2      MSB
```

Therefore $156_{10} = 234_8$

2: Number systems and computer arithmetic

Conversion from decimal to hexadecimal

The procedure for converting from decimal to hexadecimal is similar to binary and octal except that successive division by 16 (because hex is base 16) is carried out. For example, to convert 135_{10} to hexadecimal (hex):

```
16 | 135
16 |   8   remainder of 7    ↑  LSD
   |   0   remainder of 8       MSD
```

Therefore $135_{10} = 87H$

Q **Short answer question 2.6**
Check that the answer obtained in the last example is correct.

A **Answer to SAQ 2.6**

$87H = 8 \times 16 + 7 \times 1$
$ 128 + 7$
$ 135_{10}$

Conversion between binary and octal

To convert from **binary to octal** the binary number must be split into groups of three bits (because each octal digit is represented by three bits), starting at the right and working towards the left. Each group is then separately converted into octal. When dealing with binary words which cannot be divided up into groups of three bits it is necessary to add leading insignificant 0s. For example, to convert 01100011_2 to octal the steps are:

a) Finish ←———————————————————————— Start
 0 1   1 0 0   0 1 1

b) Add a leading insignificant zero so that the left hand group has three bits

 0 0 1   1 0 0   0 1 1
 _/   _/   _/
 1   4   3

Therefore, $001\ 100\ 011_2 = 143_8$

To convert **octal to binary** simply write down the 3-bit binary number for each octal digit. For example,

$$5037_8 = 101\ 000\ 011\ 111_2$$

2: Number systems and computer arithmetic

Conversion between binary and hexadecimal

The conversions between hexadecimal and binary are done in exactly the same manner as octal and binary except that groups of four bits are used.

Binary to hex conversion is performed by arranging the binary number in groups of four bits working from right to left. As an example, imagine that the data bus of an 8-bit microcomputer has the binary information 01101010 on it.

The conversion technique is to split the binary number into two groups of four bits, and then assign the appropriate hex character to each group:

$$01101010 = \underbrace{0110}_{6} \quad \underbrace{1010}_{A}$$

We now see that the information on the data bus can be conveniently represented by 6AH.

Short answer question 2.7

The address bus of a microcomputer has the binary address 0100111100110000 on it. Express the address in hex.

Answer to SAQ 2.7

4F30H

To convert **from hex to binary** each of the hex characters is converted separately to its corresponding 4-bit binary number thus:

$$7BD9H = 0111\ 1011\ 1101\ 1001_2$$

Binary fractions

In any number system a point (.) may be used to separate the whole and fractional parts of the number. For instance, in decimal 12.15, 12 is the whole part and 0.15 the fractional part of the number.

The column weights to the right of the decimal point, and moving from left to right, are:

$$
\begin{array}{cccc}
10^{-1} & 10^{-2} & 10^{-3} & 10^{-4} \\
= \quad 1/10 & 1/100 & 1/1000 & 1/10000 \\
= \quad 0.1 & 0.01 & 0.001 & 0.0001
\end{array}
$$

Therefore $12.15_{10} = 1 \times 10^1 + 2 \times 10^0 + 1 \times 0.1 + 5 \times 0.01$
$$= 10 + 2 + 0.1 + 0.05$$
$$= 12.15_{10}$$

Similarly, the binary column weights for the fractional part of a binary number are:

$$2^{-1} \quad 2^{-2} \quad 2^{-3} \quad 2^{-4}$$
$$1/2 \quad 1/4 \quad 1/8 \quad 1/16$$

Examples: Convert 12.125_{10} to binary.

First of all convert the whole part of the decimal number into binary (either by column weights or successive division by 2 - see previous examples):

$$\text{Whole part} = 12_{10} = 1100_2$$

To convert the decimal fraction 0.125 to a binary fraction repeatedly multiply by 2 and record any carries in the integer position. Note that the repeated multiplications continue until a product of exactly 1.00 is reached (most of the time 1.00 will not occur so you should terminate the process after the required accuracy is reached)

$0.125 \times 2 = 0.25$; whole part = 0 = MSB; remainder = 0.25
$0.250 \times 2 = 0.500$; whole part = 0 ; remainder = 0.5
$0.5 \times 2 = 1.00$; whole part = 1 ; no remainder

Therefore $12.125_{10} = 1100.001_2$

Convert 110.101_2 to decimal

The whole part of the binary number, namely 110 is converted to decimal first:

$$110_2 = 6_{10} \text{ (see previous examples)}$$

The fractional part 0.101 is converted to binary using the column weights for the fractional part of a binary number.

$$2^{-1} \quad 2^{-2} \quad 2^{-3}$$
$$1/2 \quad 1/4 \quad 1/8$$

$0.101 = 1 \times 1/2 + 0 \times 1/4 + 1 \times 1/8$
$ = 0.5 \quad + 0 \quad + 0.125$
$ = 0.625$

Hence $110.101_2 = 6.625_{10}$

Short answer question 2.8

Convert 111.1_2 to decimal

2: Number systems and computer arithmetic

Answer to SAQ 2.8

Whole part of number = $111_2 = 7_{10}$
Fractional part   = $0.1_2 = 1 \times 2^{-1} = 1 \times 1/2 = 1 \times 0.5 = 0.5$
Therefore $111.1_2 = 7.5_{10}$

Short answer question 2.9

Convert 56.15_{10} to binary

Answer to SAQ 2.9

Whole part of number = $56_{10} = 111000_2$
Fractional part = 0.15_{10}

0.15 × 2 = 0.30; Whole part = 0 = MSB ; remainder = 0.3
0.3 × 2 = 0.6 ; Whole part = 0   ; remainder = 0.6
0.6 × 2 = 1.2 ; Whole part = 1   ; remainder = 0.2
0.2 × 2 = 0.4 ; Whole part = 0   ; remainder = 0.4
0.4 × 2 = 0.8 ; Whole part = 0   ; remainder = 0.8
0.8 × 2 = 1.6 ; Whole part = 1   ; remainder = 0.6
and so on....

In this case the fractional part does not work out evenly, so we have to make an approximation of 001 001

Therefore $56.15_{10} = 111000.001001_2$

2.4 BINARY ARITHMETIC

When the microprocessor is performing arithmetic operations, it is working with numbers coded in binary patterns of 1s and 0s.

Although the processor is only capable of performing a limited number of operations, it can do so at very high speeds. Addition is one of the most important operations in digital computers. As we shall see in this chapter, the operations of subtraction, multiplication and division actually use only addition as their basic operation.

Binary addition

Binary addition and decimal addition are done in the same general way. So let us first review decimal addition:

2: Number systems and computer arithmetic

```
MSD        LSD
 3    5     7
+5    2     4
_____
 8    8     1
```

The least significant digit(LSD) is operated on first to produce a sum of 11, which produces a carry of 1 into the second column and a sum equal to one in the first column. The carry into the second column then produces a sum of 8 in that column. Finally the MSDs are added giving a sum of 8 in the third column.

The same general steps are followed in binary addition. However, there are only four possible results from adding two binary digits. **The binary addition rules are:**

$$0 + 0 = 0$$
$$0 + 1 = 1$$
$$1 + 0 = 1$$
$$1 + 1 = 0 \text{ and carry } 1$$

To add two binary numbers we simply arrange the binary numbers in vertical columns, taking care to align columns of equal weight under one another.

Example: Add $0\ 1\ 0\ 1_2$ to $1\ 0\ 0\ 1_2$

```
MSD       LSD
 0   1  0  1
+1   0  0  1
_____
 1   1  1  0
```

Explanation. Adding the two 1s in the first column produces a sum of 0 and a carry of 1 into the next column. Adding the 1 which was carried over from the first column to the 0s in the second column gives a sum of 1 in that column. In column three $0 + 1 = 1$ and in the fourth column $1 + 0 = 1$.

Binary subtraction

Binary subtraction is similar to decimal subtraction. The rules for binary subtraction are:

$$0 - 0 = 0$$
$$1 - 0 = 1$$
$$1 - 1 = 0$$
$$0 - 1 = 1 \text{ and borrow } 1$$

Only the result $0 - 1$ requires an explanation.

```
2s         1s
column     column
_____
            0
          - 1
_____
         1 borrow 1
```

2: Number systems and computer arithmetic

This means that in order to subtract the 1 from the 0 in the first column it will only be possible if we borrow a one from the next higher-order column, whose value is 2 times the preceeding column (the first column). We can then subtract the 1 in the first column from the two which has been borrowed from the second column, but we must indicate that in order to subtract 1 from 0 a borrow from the next column is necessary ; borrow 1.

Example: Subtract 0110_2 from 0111_2

```
   0 1 1 1
 - 0 1 1 0
 ---------
   0 0 0 1
```

A subtraction which yields a negative binary result poses the problem how can we represent negative numbers in binary. This topic is covered in the next section.

Multiple choice question 2.5

Adding the binary numbers 10000 and 00111 gives:

a) 10000111_2

b) 1000000111_2

c) 11101_2

d) 10111_2

Answer to MCQ 2.5

D

Binary multiplication

To multiply two binary numbers use the following rules:

$$0 \times 0 = 0$$
$$0 \times 1 = 0$$
$$1 \times 0 = 0$$
$$1 \times 1 = 1$$

Decimal and binary multiplication use the same method; shift left and add. It is best illustrated by an example which finds the product of 110_2 and 101_2.

2: Number systems and computer arithmetic

```
            1 1 0
            1 0 1
          -------
            1 1 0     Multiply the top number by the LSB of the bottom number
          0 0 0       Shift left one place and × the top no. by next significant bit
        1 1 0         Shift left one place and × the top no. by the MSB
        ---------
        1 1 1 1 0     add the 3 partial results to obtain the final answer
```

Hence $110_2 \times 101_2 = 11110_2$

Q Short answer question 2.10

By converting all numbers to decimal check that the answer obtained in the multiplication example is correct.

A Answer to SAQ 2.10

$110_2 = 6_{10}$
$101_2 = 5_{10}$
$6_{10} \times 5_{10} = 30_{10}$

$11110_2 = 1 \times 16 + 1 \times 8 + 1 \times 4 + 1 \times 2 + 0 \times 1$
$ = 16 + 8 + 4 + 2 + 0$
$ = 30_{10}$

The add-shift principle is used by the ALU of the computer to perform multiplication.

Binary division

Division is the reverse of multiplication. That is, we subtract one number from another until we cannot subtract it anymore. The number of times that we are able to subtract the first number tells us how many times it can be divided into the second number. Binary division can therefore be performed by a process of **subtracting and shifting**.

Example: Divide 1100_2 by 110_2

```
                        1 0
                     -------
          1 1 0 )    1 1 0 0
                    1 1 0 ↓
                    -------
                    0 0 0 0
```

The process of division is a little more difficult than multiplication because we have to guess the partial results and then test our guess.

Q Short answer question 2.11

Check the answer obtained in the division example.

A Answer to SAQ 2.11

$1100_2 = 12_{10}$ and $0110_2 = 6_{10}$

Dividing 12_{10} by 6_{10} gives 2_{10} which is equal to 10_2

2.5 REPRESENTATION OF POSITIVE AND NEGATIVE NUMBERS IN BINARY

When representing negative decimal numbers we merely precede the number with a minus sign. For instance, minus 40 is written as –40.

However, we cannot use this system within the computer because all of our numbers are written as binary patterns of 1s and 0s; there is no negative sign.

So far in our discussion we have only considered positive or unsigned binary numbers. An 8-bit unsigned binary number may therefore have values between $0000\ 0000_2$ and $1111\ 1111_2$; 0 to 255 in decimal.

Clearly, there is a need to be able to store and process both positive and **negative** numbers within the computer, and produce the correct signed result after ALU operations have taken place. The standard method used is the **two's complement notation**, which automatically produces the correct signed result for arithmetic operations.

Using the twos complement notation, the most significant bit (MSB) of each number is used to indicate the sign of the number. Thus with an 8-bit microcomputer each number is represented as follows:

Bit 7							Bit 0
MSB							LSB
S							

Bit 7, the MSB is the Sign bit 'S'

S = 0 for pOsitive numbers and zero

S = 1 for negative numbers

Examples:

i) 0011 1111 ; Is a positive number because bit 7 = 0

ii) 1001 1110 ; Is a negative number because bit 7 = 1

For positive numbers, the remaining seven bits, bit 0 to bit 6, indicate the magnitude of the number, which is calculated in the usual manner from the binary column weights. Thus: $0000\ 1111_2 = +15_{10}$

For negative numbers, the two's complement is obtained by applying the following rules:

i) Write down the binary representation of the number as if it is a positive number; ignore the minus sign.

ii) Invert or complement all bits of the number by changing all 0s to 1s and all 1s to 0s. This then gives what is called the **one's complement**

iii) Finally, add 1 to the result obtained at ii). This gives the two's complement of the number.

Example: Obtain the two's complement representation of -74_{10}

i) $+74_{10} = 0100\ 1010_2$

ii) $1011\ 0101$

iii) $1011\ 0101 + 1 = 1011\ 0110$

Hence, $-74_{10} = 1011\ 0110_2$

Examination of the result shows that Bit 7, the sign bit = 1, which indicates that the result is negative. Whilst this is encouraging it does little to convince us that the magnitude is in fact 74_{10}.

To determine the magnitude of the number, we must now find the two's complement of $1011\ 0110$.

i) Obtain the one's complement (change all 0s to 1s and all 1s to 0s). This gives:

    $0100\ 1001$

ii) add 1 to the LSB of the result.

    $0100\ 1001 + 1$

    $= 0100\ 1010$

    $= +74_{10}$

Because bit 7 is a 1(1011 0110) we know that the number is negative.

Therefore $1011\ 0110 = -74_{10}$

2.6 TWO'S COMPLEMENT ADDITION & SUBTRACTION

Binary addition using 2s complement notation

Example: Using 8-bit numbers, express 40_{10} and -28_{10} in 2s complement notation and then add the two numbers.

2: Number systems and computer arithmetic

a) $+40_{10} = 0010\ 1000_2 =$ 2s complement of 40_{10}

b) Now obtain the 2s complement representation of -28_{10}

    i) $+28_{10}$ = $0001\ 1100_2$

    ii) $1110\ 0011$; 1s complement

    iii) $1110\ 0011 + 1 = 1110\ 0100$

    So $-28_{10} =$ $1110\ 0100_2$; 2s complement form

Combining the results from a) and b) and adding gives:

$$
\begin{array}{rcl}
+40_{10} & = & 0010\ 1000_2 \\
-28_{10} & = & 1110\ 0100_2 \\
\hline
+12_{10} & = & [1]\ 0000\ 1100_2
\end{array}
$$

Note that the final carry [the 1 in bit 8 position] produced in the addition MUST be ignored. Bits 0 to 7 do of course represent $+12_{10}$

Binary subtraction

Example: Using 8-bit 2s complement notation perform the calculation $15_{10} - 22_{10}$

a) $+15_{10}$ = $0000\ 1111_2$; in 2s complement form

b) $+22_{10}$ = $0001\ 0110_2$

    i) $1110\ 1001$; 1s complement

    ii) $1110\ 1001 + 1 = 1110\ 1010$

Hence, $-22_{10} =$ $1110\ 1010_2$; 2s complement

Combining the results of a) and b) and adding we get:

$$
\begin{array}{rcl}
+15_{10} & = & 0000\ 1111_2 \\
-22_{10} & = & 1110\ 1010_2 \\
\hline
 & = & 1111\ 1001_2
\end{array}
$$

Therefore the result is: $1111\ 1001_2$

Bit 7 of the result is a 1, hence the number is negative.

Short answer question 2.12

Show that the result obtained in the last example $= -7_{10}$

Answer to SAQ 2.12

Proving that $1111\ 1001_2 = -7_{10}$

Bit 7 is a 1, therefore the number is negative. Obtain the magnitude of the number by finding its 2s complement.

i)   0000 0110   = Ones complement of number

ii) 0000 0110 + 1

     0000 0111   = Two's complement of number

From ii) the magnitude is 7

Hence, $1111\ 1001_2 = -7_{10}$

The foregoing examples of addition and subtraction have clearly shown that when 2s complement notation is used to represent both positive and negative numbers a result with the correct sign is automatically produced.

Finally, to avoid errors, when using 2s complement notation, we should be aware of the range of numbers which can be accommodated if an 8-bit system is being used. The range of possible numbers is given in Table 2.4. Note that the maximum positive number is +127 and the maximum negative number is -128. If this range is ignored and we try to do an arithmetic operation such as, adding two numbers whose sum exceeds +127 then an error will occur.

Decimal number	Twos complement
+127	0 1111111
+126	0 1111110
.	.
.	.
.	.
+2	0 0000010
+1	0 0000001
0	0 0000000
−1	1 1111111
−2	1 1111110
.	.
.	.
−127	1 0000001
−128	1 0000000

Table 2.4 Representation of signed binary numbers in twos complement form

2.7 ADDITION AND SUBTRACTION OF HEXADECIMAL NUMBERS

Addition of hex numbers

The procedure for adding hex numbers is similar to that used for binary, except that a carry is generated when a sum equals or exceeds 16.

Example: Add 29H and 58H

      29H   Explanation:
+ 58H   Addition of the LSDs gives 17; sum =1, carry=1
               Adding the 5 and the 2 in the next column, plus the
+ 81H   1 which was carried over gives, 5 + 2 + 1 = 8

Subtracting hex numbers

When we deal with computer memories in chapter 9 you will see that the memory map for an 8-bit microcomputer has addresses which are quoted in hex. For instance, the RAM might be shown thus:

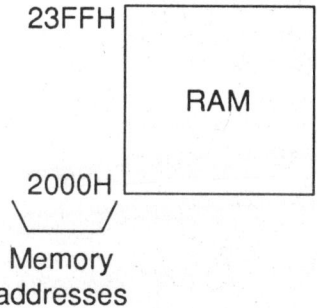

Memory addresses

A common problem is to be able to determine the number of bytes (in decimal) which the RAM can store. This may be solved using hex subtraction.

No. of bytes which the RAM can store = 23FFH − 2000H

$$\begin{array}{r} 23\text{FFH} \\ -\,2000\text{H} \\ \hline 03\text{FFH} \end{array}$$

$$\begin{aligned} 03\text{FFH} &= 3 \times 16^2 + F \times 16^1 + F \times 16^0 \\ &= 3 \times 256 + 15 \times 16 + 15 \times 1 \\ &= 768 \quad\;\, + 240 \quad\;\, + 15 \\ &= 1023_{10} \end{aligned}$$

Including the first location zero, the total number of storage locations is 1024_{10}

2: Number systems and computer arithmetic

Multiple choice question 2.6

Adding 89H and 74H gives:
a) DFH
b) 163H
c) FDH
d) DFH

Answer to MCQ 2.6

C

Multiple choice question 2.7

The result of subtracting 9AH from DBH is:
a) 14H
b) 41H
c) 175H
d) 141H

Answer to MCQ 2.7

B

2.8 FIXED-POINT AND FLOATING-POINT NUMBERS

a. **Fixed-point numbers**

All of the numbers we have been dealing with so far are fixed-point numbers. In fixed-point number format, the **decimal (or binary) point** is assumed to be at a **fixed position in the computer word.** Including the possibility of a fractional decimal number the column weights are:

$$10^2 \quad 10^1 \quad 10^0 \quad . \quad 10^{-1} \quad 10^{-2} \quad 10^{-3}$$
$$100 \quad 10 \quad 1 \quad . \quad 0.1 \quad 0.01 \quad 0.001$$

_____↑_____/
fixed decimal point

and the fixed point is shown where the power of the base changes from positive to negative.

Some fixed point numbers are: 12.56, 156.123 and −0.003412

Fixed-point notation has certain disadvantages. When using 8-bits and 2's complement numbers the range of numbers is only from -128_{10} to $+127_{10}$. Even if we use two bytes (double precision) to represent a twos complement number the range is still only -32768_{10} to $+32767_{10}$. We are still limited to a precision of about 1 part in 60,000. Also if fractional calculations are to be carried out the number of bits used to represent a fixed-point number will become large and processing time will slow down.

To overcome these disadvantages we use floating point arithmetic.

b. **Floating-point numbers**

We use floating-point notation because it has the advantage of being able to accommodate a much wider range of numbers for a given number of bits than fixed-point.

Floating-point numbers in decimal are widely used in engineering and science and are often referred to as scientific notation. Most likely your pocket calculator will be capable of performing these kinds of calculations. Some examples will help clarify the meaning of floating-point numbers.

	Fixed-point Representation	Floating-point Representation Eng/Science	Computing
1	6 40.15	6.4015×10^2	0.64015×10^3
2	0.000 123	1.23×10^{-4}	0.123×10^{-3}
3	120.567	1.20567×10^2	0.120567×10^3

Fig 2.5 Fixed-point and Floating-point numbers

If you compare fixed-point with floating-point notation for engineering and science for each of the three examples you will notice that in order to arrive at the scientific notation the decimal points have been moved or **floated** along the digits to position it between the first and second non zero MSDs. Computer science uses a slightly different notation which is shown in the right hand column.

In general the floating-point representation of a number (N) to any base may be written as:

$$N = \pm M B^{\pm e}$$

Where M is the Mantissa

B is the base of the number system

e is the exponent

In the first example above where we have

2: Number systems and computer arithmetic

$$6.4015 \times 10^2$$

6.4015 is the mantissa

10 is the base

2 is the exponent

Sometimes the result **6.4015 × 10²** may be printed as **6.4015E+02**. Here base 10 is assumed and the 'E' stands for **Exponent** and is used to separate the mantissa from the exponent.

Short answer question 2.13

What is the main advantage of floating-point over fixed-point number representation for computer systems ?

Answer to SAQ 2.13

Floating-point notation has the advantage of being able to accommodate a much wider range of numbers for a given number of bits than fixed-point.

2.9 BINARY CODES: BCD, ASCII and EBCDIC

Binary Coded Decimal (BCD) numbers

Because the computer works with binary numbers, conversions between decimal and binary are being performed frequently. Conversions for large numbers can become long and tedious. For this reason, another code for representing decimal numbers, which offers a compromise between the decimal system, which people feel comfortable with, and the binary system which is used by digital computers, is sometimes used. The code used is known as **Binary Coded Decimal** or **BCD** for short. **BCD** is a **numeric code** in which each decimal number is represented by a group of **4 bits**. Table 2.5 gives examples of two BCD codes. The 8421 is the most popular. Here each BCD number is given the same weighting as pure binary. In the 2421 system, the MSB has a weighting of 2, the next digit has a weighting of 4, the next digit 2 and finally the LSB has a weighting of 1.

2: Number systems and computer arithmetic

Decimal number	8421 BCD	2421 BCD
0	0000	0000
1	0001	0001
2	0010	0010
3	0011	0011
4	0100	0100
5	0101	0101
6	0110	0110
7	0111	0111
8	1000	1110
9	1001	1111

Table 2.5 Examples of two BCD codes

Examples: Convert each of the decimal numbers to 8421 BCD code

i) 146_{10} =   (0001   0100   0110)$_{8421\ BCD}$

ii) 987_{10} =   (1001   1000   0111)$_{8421\ BCD}$

iii) 7325_{10} =   (0111   0011   0010   0101)$_{8421\ BCD}$

Short answer question 2.14

Convert 8365_{10} to 8421 BCD

Answer to SAQ 2.14

8365_{10} = 1000 0011 0110 0101$_{8421\ BCD}$

Alphanumeric codes

So far we have only considered how the computer handles numbers coded in binary form. However everyday applications such as, word processing or entering your program into the computer through a keyboard involves **alphanumeric characters** such as **numbers**, **letters** of the alphabet and **special characters like + – / * ?**.

In the same way as different codes (such as BCD) exist to represent numbers, several standard codes have been defined which are used to represent alphanumeric characters. The most widely used codes are ASCII and EBCDIC.

The **American Standard Code for Information Interchange – ASCII** is used almost universally for information interchange between microcomputers, computer peripheral equipment and data communications links.

Table 2.6 lists the ASCII code for numbers, letters of the alphabet (upper case and lower case) and other common symbols such as + – / % ? @.

CHAR	ASCII CODE in HEX	CHAR	ASCII CODE in HEX
Decimal Numbers		OTHER COMMON SYMBOLS	
		:	3A
0	30	;	3B
1	31	<	3C
2	32	=	3D
3	33	>	3E
4	34	?	3F
5	35		
6	36	Space	20
7	37	!	21
8	38	"	22
9	39	#	23
		$	24
LETTERS: Lower case in brackets		%	25
		&	26
A (a)	41 (61)	'	27
B (b)	42 (62)	(	28
C (c)	43 (63)	)	29
D (d)	44 (64)	*	2A
E (e)	45 (65)	+	2B
F (f)	46 (66)	'	2C
G (g)	47 (67)	-	2D
H (h)	48 (68)	.	2E
I (i)	49 (69)	/	2F
J (j)	4A (6A)	[	5B
K (k)	4B (6B)	\	5C
L (l)	4C (6C)	]	5D
M (m)	4D (6D)		
N (n)	4E (6E)		
O (o)	4F (6F)		
P (p)	50 (70)		
Q (q)	51 (71)		
R (r)	52 (72)		
S (s)	53 (73)		
T (t)	54 (74)		
U (u)	55 (75)		
V (v)	56 (76)		
W (w)	57 (77)		
X (x)	58 (78)		
Y (y)	59 (79)		
Z (z)	5A (7A)		

Table 2.6 The ASCII codes for numbers, alphabet letters and other common symbols

2: Number systems and computer arithmetic

In ASCII each character is represented by 7 bits. Therefore 128 different characters may be defined. Errors could occur as data is being transmitted from one unit of a system to another. For instance a corruption (loss of a single bit/s) might take place in the cables between a computer and a terminal. In order to provide a form of **error checking** within the **ASCII** code an eighth bit is added and this is known as the **parity bit**.

The parity bit is added to give an indication as to whether or not an error has occurred in transmission. The **parity bit** may be **odd** or **even**. The transmit / receive equipment agrees which one to use; even or odd.

Example: Even Parity

The parity bit is made so that the data word being transmitted will have an even (2,4,6,8) number of 1s. For instance:

i) Data word = 0111 1111 then Parity bit = 1 and 1111 1111 is transmitted as the ASCII character. The receive equipment therefore receives an even number of bits and is happy.

ii) Data word = 0100 1000 then Parity bit = 0 and 0100 1000 is transmitted as the ASCII character. Again the receive equipment counts the number of 1s in the data word and finds an even number of 1s (two) and therefore assumes that the correct data word has been received.

Odd Parity

The parity bit is made so that the data word being transmitted will have an odd (1,3,5,7) number of 1s. For example:

i) Data word = 0111 1111 then the Parity bit = 0 because the data word already has an odd number of bits (7) and so the eighth bit, the parity bit is left at zero. The ASCII character 0111 1111 is then transmitted.

ii) Data word = 0101 1111. In this case the word to be transmitted has an even number of 1s (6) but as odd parity is required the parity bit (8th bit) is set to 1 and the ASCII character 1101 1111 is transmitted.

Parity checking can only indicate that the data word is incorrect - it cannot detect the faulty bit. It should also be remembered that it is not a fool-proof method. For example: If 0111 1111 is being transmitted and odd parity is being used and two of the 1s are dropped during transmission the receiving equipment will still receive an odd (5) number of 1s and the error will not be detected. For more exhaustive error checking other techniques such as, cyclic redundancy checking (CRC) are employed.

Chapter 10 introduces devices having a number of programmable features which include the parity bit for error checking.

Another alphanumeric code is the Extended Binary Coded Decimal Interchange Code – **EBCDIC** – which was developed by IBM for use on their computers.

2: Number systems and computer arithmetic

SUMMARY

Number system	Base	Symbols used
Decimal	10	0,1,2,3,4,5,6,7,8,9
Binary	2	0 and 1
Octal	8	0,1,2,3,4,5,6,7
Hexadecimal	16	0,1,2,3,4,5,6,7,8,9 and A,B,C,D,E,F

- A decimal number can be converted to any other number base by successively dividing by the base of the number system it is to be converted into. Carry on dividing until the result of the division becomes zero.

- The octal and hexadecimal number systems are used as shorthand representations of long binary numbers. For microcomputer work the hexadecimal (hex for short) is vitally important.

- To convert a binary number to hexadecimal start at the right hand side of the number and split it up into groups of four bits. Should the last group not contain four bits then add insignificant leading zeros. Convert each group of four bits, separately, to hex.

- To convert from hex to binary, replace each hex symbol by its corresponding four bit value. See Table 2.3.

- The rules for binary addition are:

    | 0 | + | 0 | = | 0 |
    | 0 | + | 1 | = | 1 |
    | 1 | + | 0 | = | 1 |
    | 1 | + | 1 | = | 0 and carry 1 |

- The rules for binary subtraction are:

    | 0 | − | 0 | = | 0 |
    | 1 | − | 0 | = | 1 |
    | 1 | − | 1 | = | 0 |
    | 0 | − | 1 | = | 1 borrow 1 |

- The standard method for representing signed numbers within a micrcomputer is the TWOS COMPLEMENT notation.

- Using 8-bit twos complement the range of numbers is from -128 to +127 (decimal).

- Floating-point numbers are used in preference to fixed-point because they have the advantage of being able to accommodate a much wider range of numbers for a given number of bits.

2: Number systems and computer arithmetic

☐ Common binary codes are:
B.C.D. Binary Coded Decimal
A.S.C.I.I.   American Standard Code for Information Interchange
E.B.C.D.I.C. Extended Binary Coded Decimal Interchange Code
BCD is a numeric code, whereas ASCII and EBCDIC are alphanumeric codes.

CHAPTER REVIEW QUESTIONS

Section A: Multiple choice questions (Answers in Appendix A)

1   An ASCII code is a
   a) sixteen bit code
   b) four bit code
   c) seven bit code
   d) twelve bit code

2   The random access memory for a microcomputer is located in the memory space 2000H to 27FFH. The total amount of RAM available is:
   a) 8kB
   b) 4kB
   c) 2kB
   d) 1kB

3   The number of bytes of memory occupied by an assembler which is located on the memory map of a microcomputer between addresses F000H and FFFFH is:
   a) 4096_{10}
   b) 2048_{10}
   c) 1024_{10}
   d) 8192_{10}

4   The twos complement representation of -56_{10} is
   a) 1100 1000_2
   b) 0011 1000_2
   c) 1100 0111_2
   d) 0111 1100_2

2: Number systems and computer arithmetic

5   Which one of the following is the result of dividing $0011\ 1000_2$ by 1000_2?
    a) 1100_2
    b) 1110_2
    c) 0011_2
    d) 0111_2

6   The ASCII code is
    a)   seldom used
    b)   the same as BCD code
    c)   a numeric code
    d)   an alphanumeric code

7   Even parity is being used for error checking of computer data. If the data word to be transmitted is 0101 0111, the value of the parity bit will be
    a)   0
    b)   1
    c)   1 or 0
    d)   01

8   You would use floating-point numbers to represent
    a)   very large or small numbers
    b)   only large positive numbers
    c)   only large negative numbers
    d)   negative numbers within a computer

9   The hexadecimal number A23F is represented in binary by
    a)   1010   0010   0011   1110
    b)   1010   0100   0011   1111
    c)   1010   0010   0011   1111
    d)   1111   0011   0010   1010

10 The range for 8-bit twos complement numbers, expressed in decimal, is from
    a)   -127 to +128
    b)   -127 to +127
    c)   -128 to +128
    d)   -128 to +127

Section B: Short answer questions

1   Convert the following decimal numbers to 8-bit binary numbers
    i)   40
    ii) 112

2   Convert the following 8-bit binary numbers to decimal
    i) 0011   1111
    ii) 0111   1111

3   Convert the binary number 0101 1011 to octal

4   Convert the following binary numbers into hexadecimal representations:
    i)   1111   0011
    ii) 0101   1110
    iii) 0010   0000   1100   1010

5   Convert the following hexadecimal numbers to binary numbers:
    i)   23FF
    ii) ABCD
    iii) 7E56

6   Represent the decimal number 749 in 8421 BCD.

7   Use twos complements to evaluate $36_{10} - 24_{10}$

    Check your answer by converting the final binary number into decimal.

8   Add the following binary numbers
    i) 0001   0000 and 0000   1111
    ii) 0011   1100 and 0001   0111

9   Subtract 0101_2 from 1110_2

10 Express the decimal number 1257.15 in floating-point representation

12 Convert 39.75_{10} to binary

13 Convert 101.011_2 to decimal

Chapter 3

Logic gates

A range of electronic logic devices for use in digital systems and computers have been developed. The most basic of these is the **logic gate**. Logic gates, are manufactured as integrated circuit (IC) units employing transistors, diodes, resistors and interconnecting conductors etc. In this chapter the operation of **AND, OR, NOT, NAND, NOR** and **EX-OR** gates is described as well as **combinational logic** systems. **Boolean algebra** is introduced and some common applications of logic gates presented.

3.1 INTRODUCTION

Digital computers store, process and transmit information between the various elements of the system in binary form. In a digital system, the binary information is represented by two voltage levels, generally +5 and 0 volts. So **5 volts** is used to represent **binary 1** or **logic 1** or **logic level 1** and **0 volts** is used to represent **binary 0** or **logic 0** or **logic level 0**. Sometimes binary 1 and binary 0 are known respectively as the **HIGH** and **LOW** levels.

To illustrate the idea of a digital signal consider two examples.

Example 1

A single line (for instance, a single copper track on a printed circuit board) within a system can only be at one of two levels as shown in Fig 3.1. From time 0 to t_1 the line is at binary 0 and between t_1 and t_2 it is at binary 1. It is important to understand that at any given time only one logic level (1 or 0) can exist on that line. The line could be part of one of the microcomputer buses.

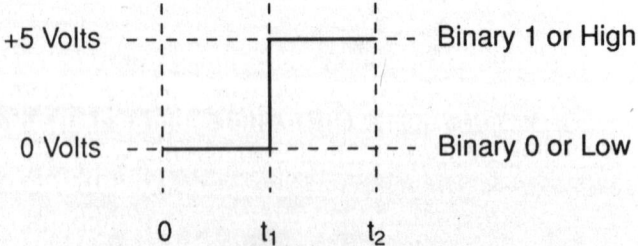

Fig 3.1 A simple binary signal

Example 2

The data bus of an 8-bit microcomputer system has eight lines and conveys 8-bit binary numbers between the MPU, ROM, RAM and PORT of the system. Assume that the data on this bus is 1010 1011. Fig 3.2 illustrates the 8-bit digital signal in which the 8-bit number is represented as a series of 8 pulses. The 1s (High levels) are denoted by 5 volt signals and the 0s (Low levels) by 0 volts.

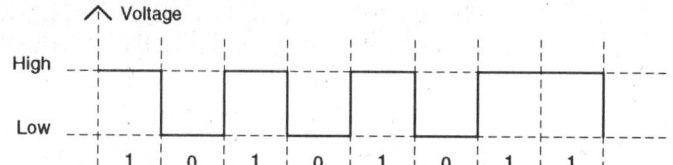

Fig 3.2 Digital signal representation of the binary data
1010 1011 on the data bus of a microcomputer.

Q Multiple choice question 3.1

The signals within the data bus of a microcomputer are

a) analogue
b) a mix of digital and analogue
c) binary digital
d) multi-level digital signals

A Answer to MCQ 3.1

c

3.2 THE BASIC COMBINATIONAL LOGIC GATES: AND, OR, NOT, NAND, NOR, EX-OR and EX-NOR gates.

Systems constructed so that the inputs and outputs can only take either one of two allowed states are termed logic systems or circuits. If each **output** of such a system **depends only on the present states of the inputs** to the circuit it is called a **combinational logic circuit**. In other words, this type of circuit does not possess any memory capability. Devices which are capable of remembering binary data are knows as sequential logic elements. Sequential elements and systems are discussed in Chapter 4.

A '**Gate**' can be regarded as a **barrier**, which when closed prevents the passage of information, but if open allows the signal/s to pass through freely.

Logic gates are **two-state electronic components** used in logic networks to **control** the **flow of digital signals** or information throughout the system. The output of a gate will depend on the input signal(s) and the type of gate. The operation of a gate may be described either by **Boolean Algebra** or a **Truth Table**.

The characteristics of digital devices make it possible to use Boolean algebra as a mathematical tool for the analysis and design of digital circuits and systems.

In Boolean algebra **binary 1** is called the **true** value and **binary 0** the **false** value. In digital electronics the values are **HIGH** and **LOW**;

3: Logic gates

Binary 1 = 5 volts = HIGH = TRUE
Binary 0 = 0 volts = LOW = FALSE

We will use the simple electrical circuit of Fig 3.3 as the vehicle for introducing truth tables. It consists of a 5 volt supply and a relay.

The relay consists of a copper winding and two contacts X,Y. If a voltage is applied to the relay input, contacts X,Y will close.

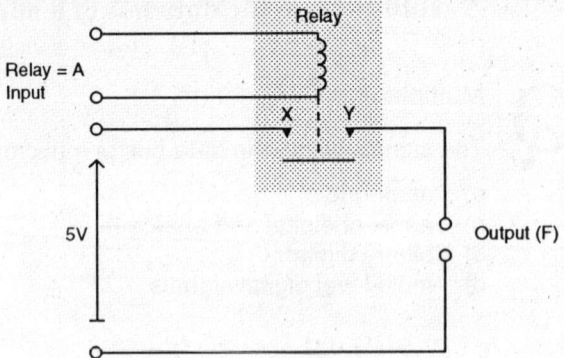

Fig 3.3 A simple relay circuit

With no input to the relay, (A = 0) contacts X,Y are open and there is no output at F. The input is 0 or LOW or FALSE and the output is 0 or LOW or FALSE.

If an input is applied to the relay (A = 1) contacts X,Y will close and 5 volts will appear at the output. The input is now 1 or HIGH or TRUE and the output is 1 or HIGH or TRUE.

The complete operation of the circuit is summarised in Table 3.1. This kind of table is called a **truth table**.

Input A	Output F
0	0
1	1

Table 3.1 Truth table for a simple electrical circuit

A truth table defines the output of a logic gate or system for all possible combinations of inputs.

Truth tables will be used to describe the operation of all of our logic gates. They can also be used to describe other types of logic elements as well as complete logic systems.

All combinational logic gates have at least one input line and a single output. Any input(s) to, or output from, a logic gate can only be at one of two logic levels; HIGH or LOW. The output from any logic gate is determined by its present inputs.

AND GATE

The simple electrical relay circuit of Fig 3.4 illustrates the principle of operation of a logic AND gate. Each logic gate has its own unique identification symbol.

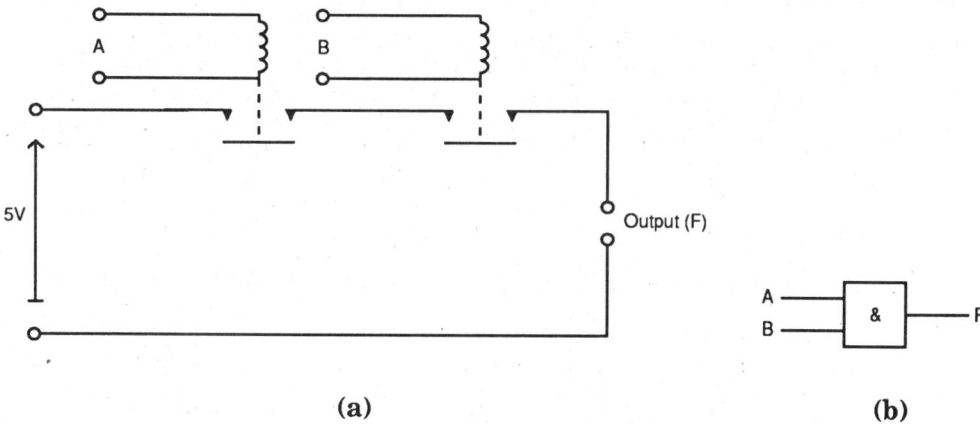

Fig. 3.4 AND gate (a) relay circuit and (b) Logic symbol

The AND gate can have two or more inputs. The two inputs to the relays are A and B. When the input to either or both relays is binary 0 (no input voltage applied) then one or both of the relays will not be energised and its associated contacts will be open and therefore the output (F) will also be binary 0 (no output voltage at F). If, and only if, both inputs A and B, to the relays, are at binary 1 (an input voltage applied) will both sets of relay contacts be closed giving an output of 5 volts or binary 1. This is summarised in Table 3.2

Inputs A	B	Output F
0	0	0
0	1	0
1	0	0
1	1	1

Note. In practice the AND gate may have more than two inputs. For any number (n) of inputs the total number of possible input combinations is 2^n.

Check. For a two input gate the number of possible combinations is $2^2 = 4$.

Table 3.2 Truth table for a two-input AND gate

From the truth table for the **AND** gate we see that in order to obtain a HIGH output, both of the inputs, **A and B**, must be at a **HIGH** level.

In **Boolean algebra** we can describe the operation of the AND gate thus:

$$\text{Output (F)} = A \text{ AND } B$$

The AND operator is denoted by a dot (.) so we can write:

$$\textbf{Output (F)} = \textbf{A} \cdot \textbf{B}$$

3: Logic gates

Short answer question 3.1

With the aid of a TRUTH TABLE describe the operation of a three input AND logic gate. Write down the Boolean equation for the output (F).

Answer to SAQ 3.1

Let the inputs to the gate be A,B,C
The total number of possible combinations of inputs is $2^3 = 8$

| Inputs | | | Output |
A	B	C	F
0	0	0	0
0	0	1	0
0	1	0	0
0	1	1	0
1	0	0	0
1	0	1	0
1	1	0	0
1	1	1	1

An output of 1 only occurs when all of the inputs (A, B and C) are HIGH.

The Boolean equation for the output (F) is:

$F = A$ AND B AND C
$= A \cdot B \cdot C$

OR GATE

When describing the AND gate a relay switching circuit was used to illustrate the AND function. The main reason for this was to show that the AND gate is merely an electronic switching device whose output depends on its present inputs. Whilst all of the other gates to be described could be considered in terms of relay logic or switches, this is felt to be generally unnecessary. For design, analysis or troubleshooting the truth table or the Boolean equation representing the output provides a full description of each gate.

The OR gate can also have two or more inputs. It **gives an output of 1, if any one of its inputs are at binary 1**. No matter how many inputs, only the case where all inputs are 0 will give an output of 0. The truth table and logic symbol for a three input OR gate are given in Fig 3.5

3: Logic gates

Inputs			Output
C	B	A	F
0	0	0	0
0	0	1	1
0	1	0	1
0	1	1	1
1	0	0	1
1	0	1	1
1	1	0	1
1	1	1	1

(a)

(b)

Fig 3.5 OR gate (a) truth table and (b) logic symbol

In this case the total number of possible input combinations is 2^3 or 8. Carefully note the pattern for writing down the input combinations. The information contained in the truth table may be summarised as:

'The output is equal to 1 if one or more of the inputs are at binary 1.'

This translates to Boolean algebra thus:

Output = A OR B OR C
Output = A + B + C
Read the Boolean operator '+' as 'OR'

Multiple choice question 3.2

Which one of the following is the correct truth table for a two input OR gate?

B	A	(A) Output 1	(B) Output 2	(C) Output 3	(D) Output 4
0	0	0	0	1	1
0	1	1	1	1	1
1	0	1	1	1	1
1	1	0	1	0	1

A Answer to MCQ 3.2

B

NOT GATE

The **NOT** gate, also known as an **INVERTER**, has only one input and one output, and its output is always the opposite of its input. That is, if its input is 1 (**TRUE**),

3: Logic gates

the output is 0 (FALSE) and vice versa. Figure 3.6 shows the symbol for the inverter, or NOT function, and its truth table.

The output from a NOT gate is:

'F equals not A (or A bar)'. In Boolean algebra this is written as:

Output (F) = $\overline{A}$

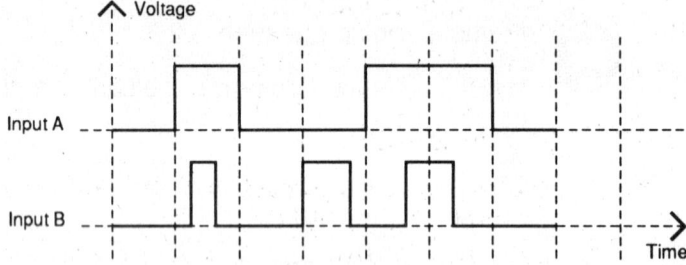

Input A	Output F
0	1
1	0

(a)   (b)

Fig 3.6 NOT Gate (a) Symbol and (b) Truth Table

The three gates just described – AND, OR, NOT – form the basic design elements or building blocks for all digital logic systems. Any logic operation may be implemented using combinations of these three gates.

Q Short answer question 3.2

A two-input AND gate has the following signals applied to its inputs:

Sketch the output timing waveform (voltage against time)

A Answer to SAQ 3.2

Both inputs, A and B, must be at a HIGH level in order to produce a HIGH level signal at the output.

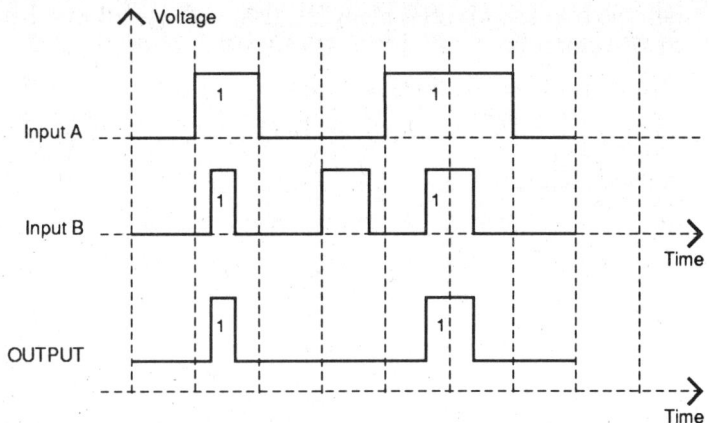

Multiple choice question 3.3

Which three input logic gate has an output (F) = A . B . C?

a) NAND
b) EX-OR
c) NOT
d) AND

Answer to MCQ 3.3

D

NAND and NOR GATES

Two other gates have been developed from the three basic AND, OR, NOT gates. These are the NAND and NOR gates.

The names NAND and NOR are contractions of the following logic functions

$$\text{NAND} = \text{NOT AND} = \overline{\text{AND}}$$
$$\text{NOR} = \text{NOT OR} = \overline{\text{OR}}$$

These functions are described in detail in the following sections.

NAND GATE

The **NAND** gate is a combination of an **AND** gate followed by a **NOT** gate. This is illustrated in Fig 3.7, together with the NAND gate symbol and truth table. The **output** from a NAND gate is opposite to that of an AND gate and is always 1, except when all of the inputs are 1. It may help if you regard the NAND gate as being 'zero sensitive', meaning that **a 0 on any of its inputs will produce a 1 at the output.**

The little circle, or 'bubble', is used here, as it is in the inverter, to mean 'not' or 'invert'. To perform the NAND operation, we AND the input values, then invert that result.

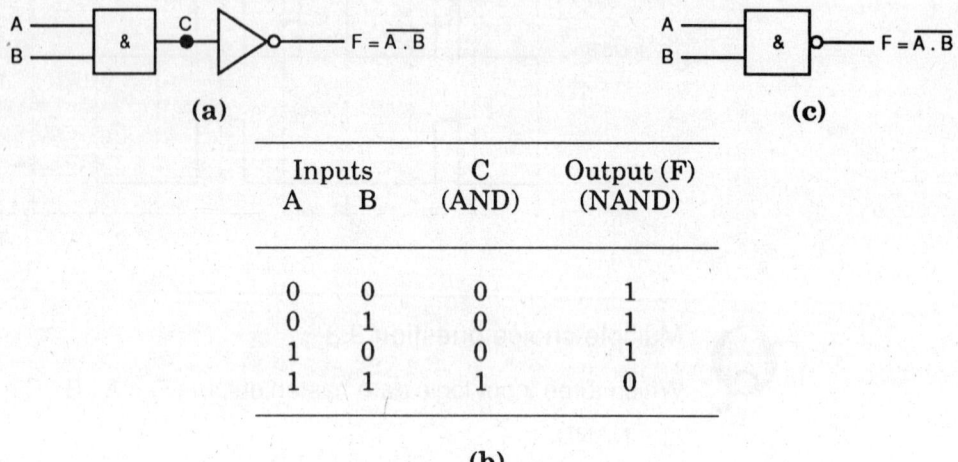

(a)   (c)

Inputs A B	C (AND)	Output (F) (NAND)
0 0	0	1
0 1	0	1
1 0	0	1
1 1	1	0

(b)

Fig 3.7 NAND Gate (a) Equivalent circuit
(b) Truth Table (c) Logic symbol

The output from the **NAND** gate is '**NOT an AND**'. For the two input gate:

Output (F) = NOT (A AND B)

F = $\overline{A \cdot B}$ in Boolean algebra

NOR GATE

The NOR gate is a combination of an OR gate followed by a NOT gate; **NOT OR** which is abbreviated to **NOR**. Inverting the result of an OR operation gives us the equivalent of a NOR function, where **all inputs must be low to obtain a high output**. If any of the inputs are HIGH, the output will be low. Fig 3.8 shows a two-input NOR gate equivalent logic circuit, logic symbol and truth table.

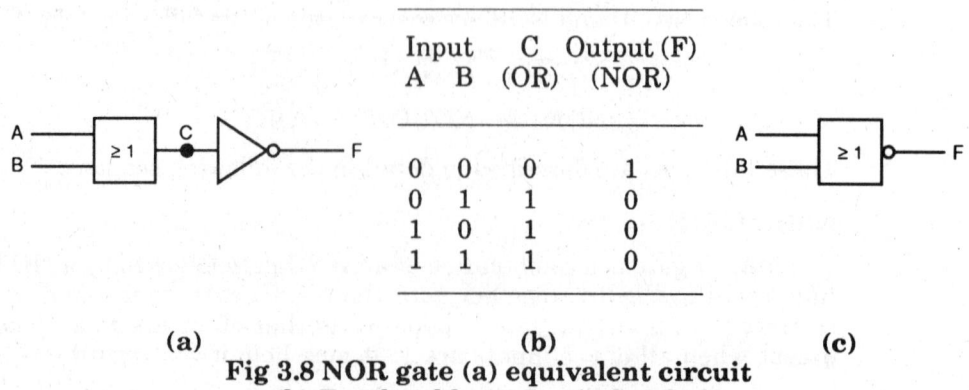

Input A B	C (OR)	Output (F) (NOR)
0 0	0	1
0 1	1	0
1 0	1	0
1 1	1	0

(a)   (b)   (c)

Fig 3.8 NOR gate (a) equivalent circuit
(b) Truth table (c) Logic Symbol

The output (F) from the NOR gate is: $F = \text{NOT}(A + B)$
$$F = \overline{A + B}$$

EXCLUSIVE-OR GATE

An EXCLUSIVE-OR (EX-OR) gate has two-inputs and gives an **output of 1 if either but not both of its inputs are at 1.** The symbol and truth table for an EX-OR gate are shown in Fig 3.9

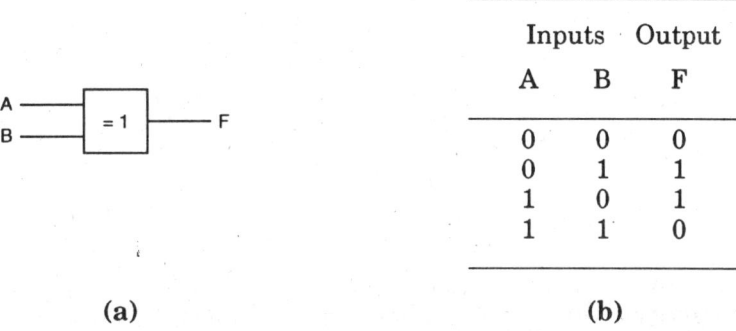

(a)   (b)

Fig 3.9 EX-OR gate (a) Logic Symbol (b) Truth Table

Examination of the EX-OR truth table shows that an output occurs for two different input conditions:

a. When B = 1 (B) AND A = 0 ($\overline{A}$) OR
b. When B = 0 ($\overline{B}$) AND A = 1 (A)

Combining a. and b. we get, Output (F) = B . $\overline{A}$ + $\overline{B}$. A which may be rewritten as:

Output (F) = A . $\overline{B}$ + $\overline{A}$. B

This is the Boolean equation representing the output from an EX-OR logic gate, which may be written in shorthand as:

$$\text{Output (F)} = A \oplus B$$

EX-OR gates and circuits built from them have many important practical applications. These include, logic circuits for performing binary addition, parity checkers and generators. Signature analysers (Chapter 13 section 13.7) which are used for troubleshooting microprocessor-based products also use exclusive-or gates.

 Short answer question 3.3

An EXCLUSIVE NOR or EQUALITY gate has two inputs, A and B, and produces a high whenever the two inputs are equal. This means that it is equivalent to an EX-OR followed by a NOT gate. Draw the truth table for this gate and suggest an appropriate logic symbol. Write down the Boolean equation for its output.

3: Logic gates

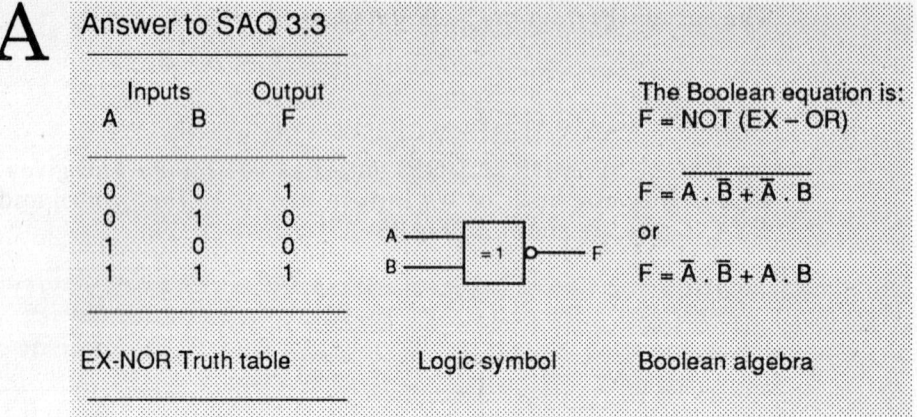

A Answer to SAQ 3.3

| Inputs | | Output |
A	B	F
0	0	1
0	1	0
1	0	0
1	1	1

EX-NOR Truth table · Logic symbol · Boolean algebra

The Boolean equation is:
F = NOT (EX − OR)

$F = \overline{A.\overline{B} + \overline{A}.B}$

or

$F = \overline{A}.\overline{B} + A.B$

3.3 BOOLEAN ALGEBRA

Boolean algebra was developed by the British mathematician and logician **George Boole** (1815-1864) who was born in Lincoln UK. He learned his early mathematics from his father, an amateur mathematician and optical instrument maker. He became a school teacher at the age of 16, and was later appointed Professor of mathematics at Queen's College, Cork, Ireland (Now UCC).

Boolean algebra is the mathematical technique used when considering problems of a logical nature.

Until 1938 Boole's algebra was restricted to the field of mathematics. However, at that time, an American scientist Claude Shannon who was researching communication systems realised that Boolean algebra could usefully be applied to telephone switching networks.

With the development of computers, the use of Boolean algebra in the electronics industry increased to where it is now mainly used by scientists, engineers and mathematicians to aid them in the design of logic systems.

Conventional algebra uses continuous variables (for example, the variable 'x' in ordinary algebra can take any value) and is based on standard arithmetic with the four operators of add, subtract, multiply and divide. When Boolean algebra is used these operations no longer apply; the operations of **Boolean** algebra must be used and these are the logical **operators AND** (.), **OR** (+), **NOT** (−) which have already been introduced in the section dealing with logic gates. Unlike variables in ordinary algebra which can take any value, **Boolean variables** are only allowed to take either one of two states, called **TRUE** and **FALSE** (or 1 and 0) and the rules for the manipulation of these variables is not the same as the rules used in conventional algebra.

Boolean logic is especially important for computer science, because it fits nicely with the binary numbering system, in which each bit has a value of either 1 or 0.

Some important relationships (theorems or rules) in Boolean algebra are given in Table 3.3

RELATIONSHIPS IN BOOLEAN ALGEBRA

T1	(a)	$A + B$	$= B + A$
	(b)	$A \cdot B$	$= B \cdot A$
T2.	(a)	$(A + B) + C$	$= A + (B+C)$
	(b)	$(A \cdot B) \cdot C$	$= A \cdot (B \cdot C)$
T3.	(a)	$A \cdot (B + C)$	$= A \cdot B + A \cdot C$
	(b)	$(A + B) \cdot (A + C)$	$= A + B \cdot C$
T4.	(a)	$A + A = A$	
	(b)	$A \cdot A$	$= A$
T5.	(a)	$\overline{(\overline{A})}$	$= \overline{A}$
	(b)	$\overline{(\overline{A})}$	$= A$
T6.	(a)	$A + A \cdot B$	$= A$
	(b)	$A \cdot (A + B)$	$= A$
T7.	(a)	$0 + A$	$= A$
	(b)	$1 \cdot A$	$= A$
	(c)	$1 + A$	$= 1$
	(d)	$0 \cdot A$	$= 0$
T8.	(a)	$\overline{A} + A$	$= 1$
	(b)	$\overline{A} \cdot A$	$= 0$
T9.	(a)	$A + \overline{A} \cdot B$	$= A + B$
	(b)	$A \cdot (\overline{A} + B)$	$= A \cdot B$
T10.	De Morgans Theorem		
	(a)	$\overline{A + B + C + \ldots}$	$= \overline{A} \cdot \overline{B} \cdot \overline{C} \ldots$
	(b)	$\overline{A \cdot B \cdot C \cdot \ldots}$	$= \overline{A} + \overline{B} + \overline{C} \ldots$

Table 3.3 Boolean relationships

Although, at first glance, the above rules may appear quite daunting, they are in fact very simple. One means of proving that the relationships stated in Table 3.3 are correct, or in indeed, that any logical expression is identical to another, is the use of a **truth table**.

Consider T3 (b): $(A + B) \cdot (A + C) = A + B \cdot C$

This equation involves three variables – A, B and C, hence there are eight possible input combinations. We will use a truth table to verify that the left hand side of the equation [$(A + B) \cdot (A + C)$] is identical to the right hand side $(A + B \cdot C)$. Let the left hand side and right hand side of the equation, be known respectively as LHS and RHS.

3: Logic gates

| Inputs | | | | | LHS | | | RHS |
A	B	C	(A+B)	(A+C)	(A+B).(A+C)	A	B.C	A+B.C
0	0	0	0	0	0	0	0	0
0	0	1	0	1	0	0	0	0
0	1	0	1	0	0	0	0	0
0	1	1	1	1	1	0	1	1
1	0	0	1	1	1	1	0	1
1	0	1	1	1	1	1	0	1
1	1	0	1	1	1	1	0	1
1	1	1	1	1	1	1	1	1
					*			*

Table 3.4 Truth table for T3(b)

Truth table 3.4 shows that the columns representing (A+B).(A+C) and A + B . C, marked with an asterisk, are identical. Therefore (A+B).(A+C) = A + B . C

Q Short answer question 3.4

With the aid of a TRUTH TABLE prove that A + $\overline{A}$. B = A + B

(Table 3.3 T9 (a))

A Answer to SAQ 3.4

| Inputs | | | | LHS | RHS |
A	B	$\overline{A}$	$\overline{A}$.B	A + $\overline{A}$.B	A + B
0	0	1	0	0	0
0	1	1	1	1	1
1	0	0	0	1	1
1	1	0	0	1	1
				*	*

The left hand side (LHS) and the right hand side (RHS) of the equation are identical.

Q Short answer question 3.5

Using a TRUTH TABLE show that B + $\overline{B}$. $\overline{A}$ = $\overline{A}$ + B

3: Logic gates

A Answer to SAQ 3.5

| Inputs | | | | | LHS | RHS |
A	B	$\bar{A}$	$\bar{B}$	$\bar{B}.\bar{A}$	$B+\bar{B}.\bar{A}$	$\bar{A}+B$
0	0	1	1	1	1	1
0	1	1	0	0	1	1
1	0	0	1	0	0	0
1	1	0	0	0	1	1

The left hand side (LHS) and the right hand side (RHS) of the equation are identical.

Q Short answer question 3.6

Show that   (i) $A = \bar{\bar{A}}$

              (ii) $A + \bar{A} = 1$

              (iii) $A.\bar{A} = 0$

A Answer to SAQ 3.6

| Input | | (i) | (ii) | (iii) |
A	$\bar{A}$	$\bar{\bar{A}}$	$A+\bar{A}$	$\bar{A}.A$
0	1	0	1	0
1	0	1	1	0

Column A is identical to column $\bar{\bar{A}}$

Column $A + \bar{A} = 1$

Column $\bar{A}.A = 0$

Q Short answer question 3.7

Prove that

(i) $\overline{A+B} = \bar{A}.\bar{B}$ { De Morgans theorems }

(ii) $\overline{A.B} = \bar{A}+\bar{B}$

3: Logic gates

> **A** Answer to SAQ 3.7
>
> | Inputs | | LHS of (i) | LHS of (ii) | | | RHS | RHS |
> |---|---|---|---|---|---|---|---|
> | A | B | NOR | NAND | $\bar{A}$ | $\bar{B}$ | (i) | (ii) |
> | 0 | 0 | 1 | 1 | 1 | 1 | 1 | 1 |
> | 0 | 1 | 0 | 1 | 1 | 0 | 0 | 1 |
> | 1 | 0 | 0 | 1 | 0 | 1 | 0 | 1 |
> | 1 | 1 | 0 | 0 | 0 | 0 | 0 | 0 |
>
> ∴ LHS of (i) = RHS of (i)
>
> ∴ LHS of (ii) = RHS of (ii)

WHY BOOLEAN ALGEBRA?

We will now illustrate the practical significance of Boolean algebra, using the logic circuit of Fig 3.10

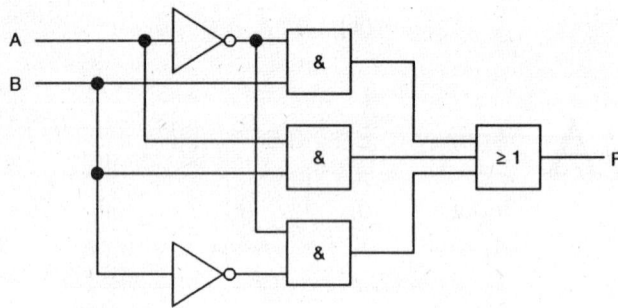

Fig 3.10 A combinational logic circuit

To obtain the Boolean function, which represents the output, from a logic diagram, proceed as follows:

1. Clearly identify each gate and write the name next to it
2. Working from the input towards the output, label the outputs of all gates with some convenient letter (The output from the last gate is usually denoted by the letter F, which stands for Function)
3. On the logic diagram write the Boolean expression for the output of each gate.
4. Write down the Boolean expression for the overall output (F)
5. Use Boolean algebra (or any other method) to check whether or not the system can be minimised; implemented using fewer gates
6. Draw the logic diagram

7. Check your solution by drawing truth tables for both the original circuit and the simplified one

Redrawing the logic diagram of Fig 3.10 and applying steps 1 to 4 gives:

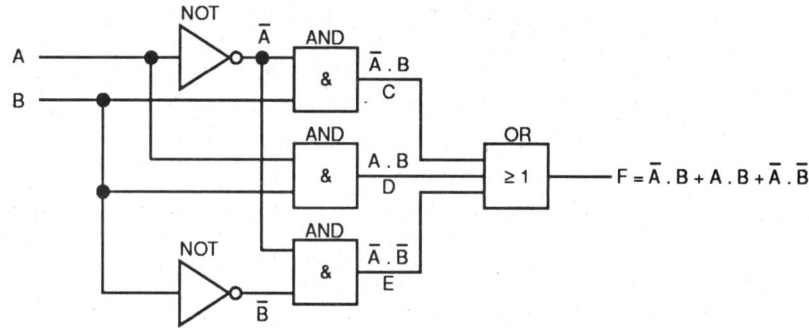

Fig 3.11 Analysing a combinational logic circuit

$$\begin{aligned}\text{The output (F)} &= \overline{A}.B + A.B + \overline{A}.\overline{B} \\ &= B.(\overline{A}+A) + \overline{A}.\overline{B} \\ &= B + \overline{A}.\overline{B} \\ &= B + \overline{A}\end{aligned}$$

Hence $\overline{A}.B + A.B + \overline{A}.\overline{B} = B + \overline{A}$ \qquad (1)

Having now simplified the Boolean algebra we can draw the logic circuit corresponding to the right hand side of the equation. Thus:

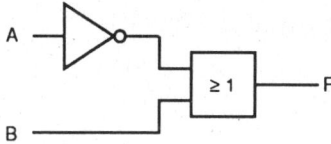

Fig 3.12 Logic diagram for RHS of equation (1)

In order to verify that the solution is correct draw the truth table for the left hand side (LHS) of equation (1) which relates to the original logic circuit of Figs 3.10/11 and compare that with the truth table for the right hand side (RHS) of the equation, which corresponds to the simplified logic circuit – Fig 3.12

Inputs A	B	$\overline{A}$	$\overline{B}$	C $\overline{A}.B$	D $A.B$	E $\overline{A}.\overline{B}$	LHS of equation $\overline{A}.B + A.B + \overline{A}.\overline{B}$
0	0	1	1	0	0	1	1
0	1	1	0	1	0	0	1
1	0	0	1	0	0	0	0
1	1	0	0	0	1	0	1

Table 3.5 Truth table for LHS of equation (1)

3: Logic gates

INPUTS			RHS of equation
A	B	$\bar{A}$	$\bar{A} + B$
0	0	1	1
0	1	1	1
1	0	0	0
1	1	0	1

Table 3.6 Truth table for RHS of equation (1)

The truth tables show that the RHS of the Equation is identical to the LHS of the equation.

To build the original circuit (corresponding to the LHS of equation 1) would require:

$2 \times$ NOT gates
$3 \times$ AND gates
$1 \times$ OR gate

The total number of ICs required is THREE.

The gates needed for the simplified circuit (the RHS of equation 1) are:

$1 \times$ NOT
$1 \times$ OR

In this case we only need TWO ICs

If it is possible to simplify a given logic circuit, using Boolean algebra, then a number of advantages are evident.

1. Less ICs needed, therefore it will be cheaper to build the system
2. The system will be more reliable (less parts to go wrong)
3. It will consume less power and therefore generate less heat within the system.
4. Printed circuit board size reduced
5. If the IC count is reduced, it will result in a simpler circuit, which may make troubleshooting easier.

3.4 UNIVERSAL LOGIC

Digital circuits are more frequently constructed with NAND or NOR gates than with AND, OR, NOT gates. NAND and NOR gates are easier to fabricate and are the basic gates used in all IC digital logic families.

Both **NAND** and **NOR** gates are described as **universal logic gates** because either gate can be used to generate the three basic logic functions, AND, OR,

NOT, from which all logic circuits can be built. In practice this means that the digital logic system may be built using just one type of gate. This would require the stocking of only one type of spare part (NAND or NOR) and is more convenient and economical.

USING NAND GATES TO GENERATE THE NOT, AND, OR FUNCTIONS

The methods of generating the three basic functions using NAND gates only are illustrated in Fig 3.13. In each case a truth table is used to verify the result.

(a) **NOT** Function

Truth Table

Input A	Output F
0	1
1	0

The two inputs to the NAND gate are connected together electrically.

When A = 0 both of the NAND gate inputs are at 0, giving an output of 1.

When the input A = 1, both of the NAND gate inputs are at 1 giving an output of 0. Therefore this arrangement behaves just like a NOT gate.

(b) **AND** Function

Truth Table

Inputs A	B	C (NAND)	Output (F) (NOT C)
0	0	1	0
0	1	1	0
1	0	1	0
1	1	0	1

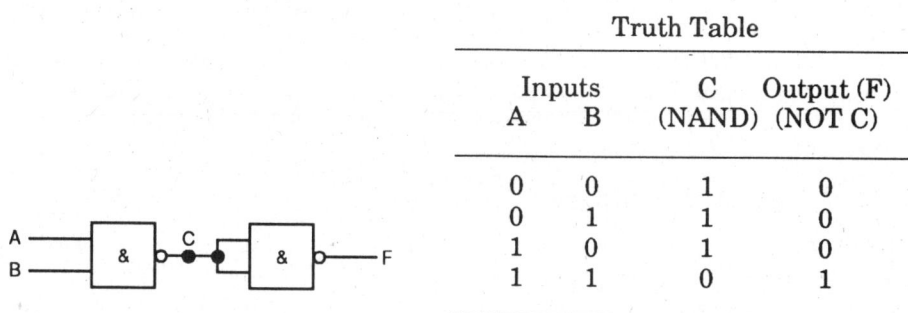

The output from the first NAND gate is C and this provides the input to the second NAND gate which is acting as a NOT gate. Examination of the output column shows that the only time the output is at 1 is when both of the inputs A and B are at 1. Therefore this combination of NAND gates is generating the AND function.

(c) OR Function

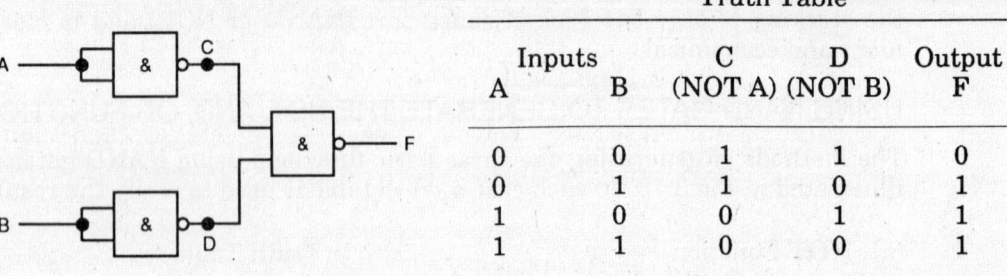

Truth Table

| Inputs | | C | D | Output |
A	B	(NOT A)	(NOT B)	F
0	0	1	1	0
0	1	1	0	1
1	0	0	1	1
1	1	0	0	1

Fig 3.13 Using NAND gates to generate the NOT, AND, OR functions

Examination of the output column shows that a 1 on any input gives a high output. It is therefore acting like an OR gate.

USING NOR GATES TO GENERATE the NOT, AND, OR functions.

(a) **NOT** Function

Truth Table

Input A	Output F
0	1
1	0

Both inputs of the NOR are now connected together electrically.

When the input A = 0 then both inputs to the NOR gate are 0 giving an output of 1. Conversely when A = 1, both of the NOR gate inputs are at 1 and its output is 0. Therefore it functions as a NOT gate.

(b) **AND** Function

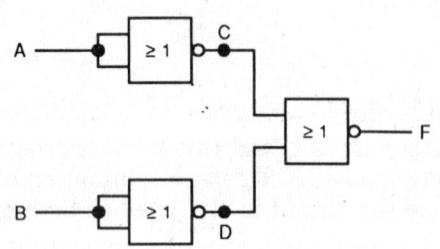

Truth Table

| Inputs | | C | D | Output |
A	B	(NOT A)	(NOT B)	F
0	0	1	1	0
0	1	1	0	0
1	0	0	1	0
1	1	0	0	1

3: Logic gates

The truth table shows that the output is 1 only when both of the inputs A AND B are at 1. This satisfies our definition of the basic AND gate.

Short answer question 3.8

Explain how the 'C' column is derived for the AND function when using NOR gates only.

Answer to SAQ 3.8

Column C = NOT A ; C is the inverse of the A input

(c) **OR** Function

Truth Table

Inputs A	B	C (NOR)	Output (F = NOT C)
0	0	1	0
0	1	0	1
1	0	0	1
1	1	0	1

From the truth table we see that the output is HIGH whenever one or more of the inputs, A or B, is high. This is, of course, equivalent to a basic OR gate.

Fig 3.14 Using NOR gates only to generate the NOT, AND, OR functions

Short answer question 3.9

Refer to the OR function using NOR gates.

Explain how the logic levels for the C output are derived.

Answer to SAQ 3.9

A and B are inputs to a NOR gate. Therefore C = NOT (A + B)

75

SUMMARY of LOGIC GATES: TRUTH TABLES & SYMBOLS

BS	MS	GATE	TRUTH TABLES
A,B → [&] → F	A,B → AND-shape → F = A . B	AND	Inputs A B / Output F 0 0 / 0 0 1 / 0 1 0 / 0 1 1 / 1
A,B → [≥1] → F	A,B → OR-shape → F = A + B	OR	Inputs A B / Output F 0 0 / 0 0 1 / 1 1 0 / 1 1 1 / 1
A → [1]o → F	A → ▷o → F = $\bar{A}$	NOT	Inputs A / Output F 0 / 1 1 / 0
A,B → [&]o → F	A,B → NAND-shape → F = $\overline{A.B}$	NAND	Inputs A B / Output F 0 0 / 1 0 1 / 1 1 0 / 1 1 1 / 0
A,B → [≥1]o → F	A,B → NOR-shape → F = $\overline{A+B}$	NOR	Inputs A B / Output F 0 0 / 1 0 1 / 0 1 0 / 0 1 1 / 0
A,B → [=1] → F	A,B → XOR-shape → F = A ⊕ B	EX-OR	Inputs A B / Output F 0 0 / 0 0 1 / 1 1 0 / 1 1 1 / 0

Fig 3.15 BS and American (MS) Logic gate symbols and truth tables

3.5 ANALYSIS OF COMBINATIONAL LOGIC CIRCUITS

Those readers who are familiar with analogue circuits, such as, Radio and TV, will be aware that the analysis process is difficult. In the case of combinational logic circuits, analysis is a simple task. The aim of any circuit analysis is to start from a circuit diagram which shows how the various electronic components are interconnected and to obtain an exact description of the behaviour of the system. When the circuit is a combinational logic one, the result of an analysis will be either a **Boolean expression** or a **truth table.** By combinational logic circuits we mean any circuit which is constructed from any mix of logic gates and which does not have any memory capability. We have already seen examples of how to analyse logic circuits by using TRUTH TABLES in the section 3.3 'Why Boolean algebra'.

The analysis process for digital logic circuits is best illustrated by example. Draw the truth table for the logic circuit of Fig 3.16

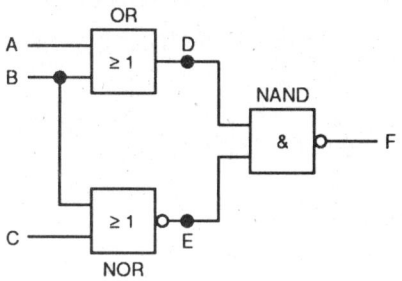

Fig 3.16 A combinational logic circuit

The circuit has three inputs, A, B and C, therefore there are eight possible input combinations. The truth table shows all possible input combinations, plus the output D from the OR gate, the output E from the NOR gate. The final output from the system is F. Remember that the D output is found by ORing together the A, B inputs. (C plays no part). NORing the B and C inputs produces the E output (this time A plays no part). Finally, the overall output (F) is found by NANDing together the D and E signals. Now carefully work your way through the circuit and compare your answer with table 3.7

| Inputs | | | D = A + B | E = NOT (B + C) | Output F = NAND |
A	B	C	(OR Gate)	(NOR Gate)	F = NOT (D AND E)
0	0	0	0	1	1
0	0	1	0	0	1
0	1	0	1	0	1
0	1	1	1	0	1
1	0	0	1	1	0
1	0	1	1	0	1
1	1	0	1	0	1
1	1	1	1	0	1

Table 3.7 Truth table for the combinational logic circuit of Fig 3.16

Points to note:

i) The output from the OR gate is determined by A,B

ii) The output from the NOR gate depends on B,C

iii) $D = A + B$

iv) $E = \text{NOT}(B + C) = \overline{B + C}$

v) $F = \text{NOT}(D + E) = \overline{D + E}$

3: Logic gates

Short answer question 3.10

Use a truth table to show that $A + A \cdot B = A$

Verify your answer by using Boolean algebra.

Answer to SAQ 3.10

TRUTH TABLE

| Inputs | | (A . B) | Output |
A	B		F = A + A . B
0	0	0	0
0	1	0	0
1	0	0	1
1	1	1	1

If we now examine the output column (the left hand side of the equation) and compare it with the 'A' column (the right hand side of the equation) the two are identical: Hence, $A + A \cdot B = A$

This in effect means that we can dispense with both the AND and OR gate and connect 'A' directly to the output 'F'.

Using basic Boolean relationships we can also prove that $A + A \cdot B = A$

From the left hand side of the equation we can simplify thus:

$A = 1 \cdot A$ (From T7 (b), therefore $A + A \cdot B = 1 \cdot A + A \cdot B$

Now take out the common factor 'A' and we get:

$1 \cdot A + A \cdot B = A \cdot (1 + B)$

But from T7 (c) we know that $(1 + B) = 1$

Hence it simplifies to $A \cdot (1) = A \cdot 1 = A$ (which is the right hand side of the equation)

So we have now proved by truth table and Boolean algebra that:

$A + A \cdot B = A$

3.6 PRACTICAL APPLICATIONS OF LOGIC GATES:

Addition circuits and a coin-operated cold drinks dispenser

By connecting together the correct combinations of logic gates it is possible to solve a wide range of problems.

3: Logic gates

A few practical examples will serve to tie some of the basic logic concepts together. A procedure which is helpful to follow in developing a desired logic circuit can be outlined as follows:

1. Clearly state the problem
2. Prepare a truth table from the problem description
3. Obtain a Boolean expression for the output (F)
4. If possible, simplify the Boolean expression
5. Draw the logic circuit diagram
6. Verify that your solution is correct.

Example 1

Design a logic circuit which is capable of adding two single-order bits. This type of circuit is known as a HALF-ADDER.

If you are unsure of binary addition, refer to Chapter 2, Section 2.4, before progressing.

The truth table for the circuit is:

Inputs		Outputs	
A	B	SUM	CARRY
0	0	0	0
0	1	1	0
1	0	1	0
1	1	0	1

Table 3.8 Truth table for a half-adder

Three alternative methods will now be presented.

Method 1

From the truth table, the logic expressions for the outputs are:

A SUM occurs for two sets of input conditions:

i) When B = 1 (B) AND A = 0 ($\bar{A}$) ; $\bar{A} \cdot B$

   OR

ii) When B = 0 ($\bar{B}$) AND A = 1 (A) ; $A \cdot \bar{B}$

Combining i) and ii) the SUM = $A \cdot \bar{B} + \bar{A} \cdot B$ (1)

The CARRY occurs when A = B = 1, therefore CARRY = $A \cdot B$

3: Logic gates

In order to implement the logic expressions for the SUM and CARRY we need:

2 × NOT gates
2 × AND gates } For the SUM
1 × OR gate

and 1 × AND gate for CARRY.

Hence, the desired logic circuit is:

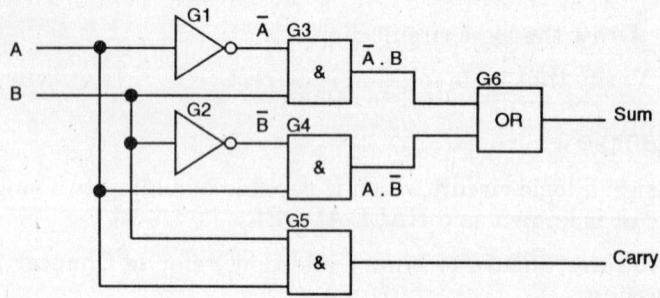

Fig 3.17 Half-adder using AND, OR, NOT gates

Q Short answer question 3.11

Verify that the logic circuit of Fig 3.17 performs binary addition

A Answer to SAQ 3.11

Inputs					Outputs from		
A	B	G1	G2	G3	G4	G5 (CARRY)	G6 (SUM)
0	0	1	1	0	0	0	0
0	1	1	0	1	0	0	1
1	0	0	1	0	1	0	1
1	1	0	0	0	0	1	0

The CARRY and SUM outputs are correct for a half-adder

Method 2

By inspection of the truth table, the SUM output corresponds to an EX-OR gate and the carry to an AND gate. Therefore the logic circuit of Fig 3.18 also acts as a half-adder.

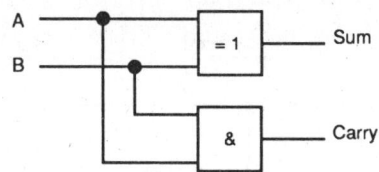

Fig 3.18 Half-adder using an EX-OR and AND gates

Method 3

Universal logic was covered in Section 3.4, where either NAND or NOR gates can be used to generate other functions, such as, AND, OR, NOT. The solution from method 1, using AND, OR, NOT gates is reproduced here for convenience. See Fig 3.19

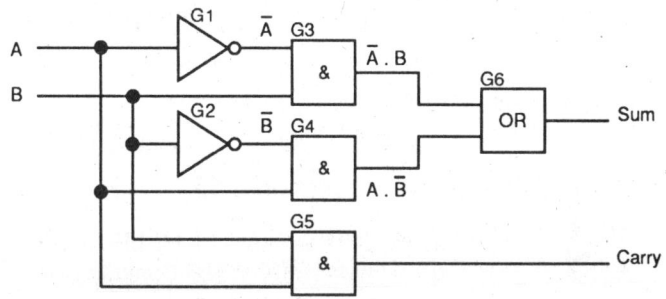

Fig 3.19 A Half-adder logic circuit

We now replace each AND, OR, NOT with its equivalent NAND gate/s. The resultant circuit is given in Fig 3.20.

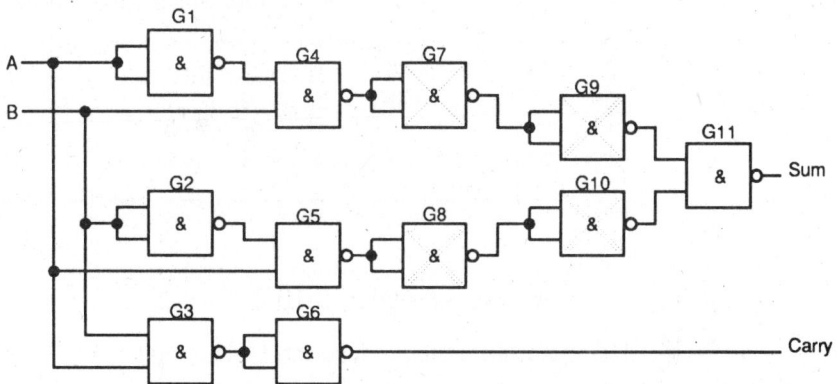

Fig 3.20 Half-adder using NAND gates only

In Fig 3.20 logic gates G7 and G9 are two NOT gates connected in cascade. Using the Boolean identity $\bar{\bar{A}} = A$, G7 and G9 are redundant. Similar reasoning applies to G8 and G10, so they may also be eliminated from the circuit. The final version of our universal logic circuit is shown in Fig 3.21

3: Logic gates

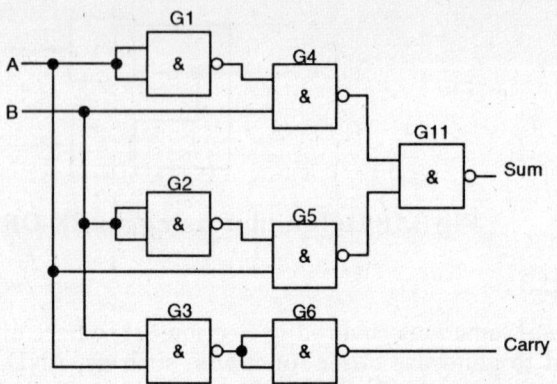

Fig 3.21 Half-adder using fewer NAND gates

The original version (Fig 3.17) of the half-adder using AND, OR, NOT gates required THREE different types of IC. Using universal logic NAND gates the circuit can be constructed from just TWO ICs of the same type. (Each IC contains four independent NAND gates)

Q Short answer question 3.12

Verify that Fig 3.21 works as a HALF-ADDER.

A Answer to SAQ 3.12

Inputs					Outputs from			
A	B	G1	G2	G3	G4	G5	G6 (CARRY)	G11(SUM)
0	0	1	1	1	1	1	0	0
0	1	1	0	1	0	1	0	1
1	0	0	1	1	1	0	0	1
1	1	0	0	0	1	1	1	0

Q Short Answer question 3.13

Using a truth table analyse the logic circuit of Fig 3.22

What function does the circuit perform?

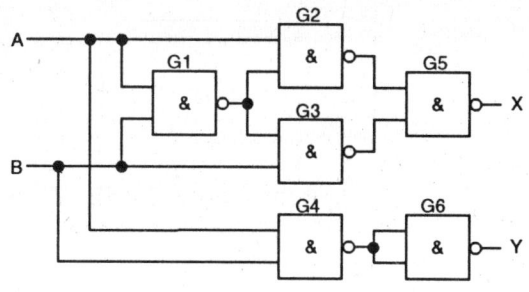

Fig 3.22

> **A** Answer to SAQ 3.13
>
> | Inputs | | Outputs from | | | | | |
> |---|---|---|---|---|---|---|---|
> | A | B | G1 | G2 | G3 | G4 | G5 (X) | G6 (Y) |
> | 0 | 0 | 1 | 1 | 1 | 1 | 0 | 0 |
> | 0 | 1 | 1 | 1 | 0 | 1 | 1 | 0 |
> | 1 | 0 | 1 | 0 | 1 | 1 | 1 | 0 |
> | 1 | 1 | 0 | 1 | 1 | 0 | 0 | 1 |
>
> The circuit is a half-adder. The X output is the SUM and Y the CARRY

Example 2

A coin-operated cold-drink dispenser will provide a cold drink (D) under the following conditions:

The correct coin (C) is inserted   AND

A paper cup is in position (P)   AND

The selector is set at Orange (O) OR Sprite (S) OR Lemonade (L)

One means of solving this kind of problem is to write down the Boolean equation for the output, where the output in this case is a drink (D) being made available.

D = C AND P AND (O OR S OR L)

    = C . P . (O + S + L)

Examination of the Boolean equation indicates that the circuit can be implemented by using one three input OR gate and one three input AND gate. The logic circuit is shown in Fig 3.23

3: Logic gates

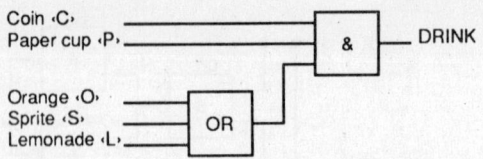

Fig 3.23 A cold drinks dispenser

3.7 TRI-STATE GATES

Tri-state gates, also known as 3-state drivers or 3-state buffers, have many applications in circuits where several signals are connected to common lines (buses). You will recall from Chapter 1 that the MPU, ROM, RAM and the Input/Output port of a microcomputer are interconnected via bus lines. Consequently, tri-state buffers are in-built to all of these devices.

Fig 3.24 (a) shows a tri-state gate. If the Enable (E) input is HIGH then the data at input 'A' is transferred to the output (F). However, if the enable input line is LOW the gate is disabled or inhibited and data cannot be transmitted from the input to the output. The output is effectively disconnected and is said to 'float'. Hence, a tri-state gate output may be HIGH, LOW or FLOATING (sometimes called the high impedance HIGH-Z state; effectively disconnected)

(a)   (b)

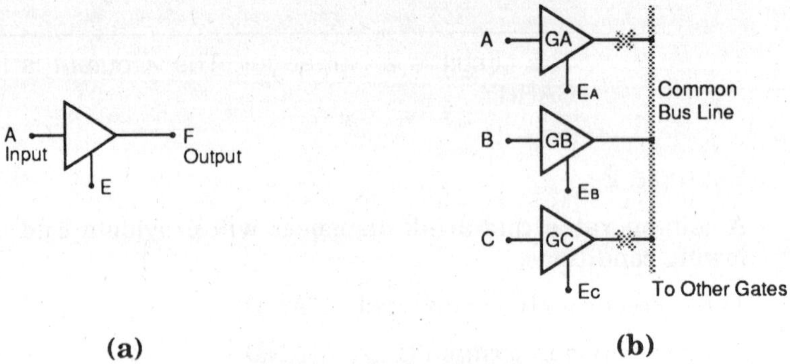

Fig 3.24 Tri-state gates

The tri-state gate discussed is an ACTIVE HIGH device, however, it should be noted that ACTIVE LOW gates are also available.

We will examine the application of tri-state buffers in ROM and RAM memory integrated circuits in Chapter 9 – Microcomputer memories, but we can understand the basic idea from Fig 3.24 (b).

Here we have three logic signals A, B, and C connected to a common bus line through tri-state buffers. This arrangement permits us to transmit any one of these signals over the bus line to other circuits by enabling the appropriate buffer. For instance, consider the case where $E_A = 0$; $E_B = 1$ and $E_C = 0$. Gate GB is enabled, while gates GA and GC are inhibited. Therefore the data at B can be safely transferred onto the bus. The 'X's on the diagram denote a HI-Z state, which means that the outputs of those gates are essentially disconnected from the bus.

Where common bus lines are shared by devices it is imperative that only one device is allowed to communicate with the bus at any given time, otherwise **bus contension** would ensue.

SUMMARY

- A logic gate is a switching device which is used to control the flow of signals in a system.
- Logic gates, such as AND, OR, NOT, NAND, NOR, EX-OR are all combinational logic elements.
- Logic gates are widely used in digital systems and computers.
- The operation of any logic gate or combinational logic system may be described by means of a TRUTH TABLE.
- A truth table defines the output of a logic gate or system for all possible input combinations.
- The output from a tri-state gate may be HIGH, LOW or high impedance (disconnected).
- Boolean algebra can be used to simplify logic circuits.
- NAND and NOR gates are known as universal logic elements because either of them can be used to generate other functions such as AND, OR, NOT.
- A half-adder is a logic circuit which is capable of adding two single order bits.
- A full-adder is a logic circuit which can add three 1-bit numbers, two of which are the bits to be added and the third any carry from a previous stage

CHAPTER REVIEW QUESTIONS

Section A: Multiple choice questions (Answers in Appendix A)

1. Refer to Fig 3.25

    Which logic function does this circuit generate?
    a) EX-OR
    b) NOR
    c) NAND
    d) AND

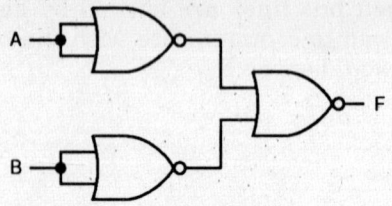

Fig 3.25

2. Which one of the following Boolean expressions represents the SUM output from a HALF-ADDER?
   a) A . B
   b) A + B
   c) $\bar{A}.\bar{B} + A.B$
   d) $A.\bar{B} + \bar{A}.B$

3. Refer to Fig 3.26

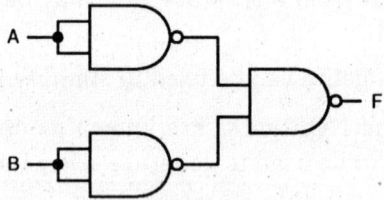

Fig 3.26

The Boolean expression for the output (F) is:
   a) A + B
   b) A . B
   c) $\overline{A + B}$
   d) $\overline{A . B}$

4 Refer to Fig 3.27

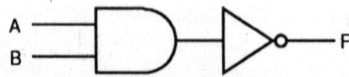

Fig 3.27

The logic function generated by this circuit is:
   a) EX-OR
   b) NOR
   c) NAND
   d) AND

5   Refer to Fig 3.28

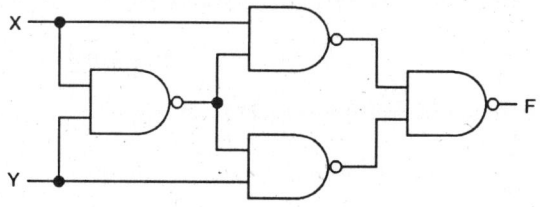

Fig 3.28

Which of the following logic gates is equivalent to this circuit?

a) AND
b) OR
c) NOT
d) EX-OR

6   The two inputs to a NAND gate are X and Y. Which one of the following is the Boolean representation of the output?

a) X . Y
b) X + Y
c) $\overline{X . Y}$
d) $\overline{X + Y}$

7. Which one of the following is the correct truth table for a two input NAND gate?

(a)

A	B	Output
0	0	0
0	1	1
1	0	1
1	1	1

(b)

A	B	Output
0	0	1
0	1	0
1	0	0
1	1	1

(c)

A	B	Output
0	0	1
0	1	1
1	0	1
1	1	0

(d)

A	B	Output
0	0	0
0	1	0
1	0	0
1	1	1

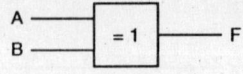

Fig 3.29

8. The logic gate shown in Fig 3.29 is
   a) OR
   b) EX-OR
   c) EX-NOR
   d) NOR

9. A logic gate has four inputs. The total number of possible input combinations is
   a) 4
   b) 8
   c) 16
   d) 32

10. A full-adder is a logic circuit which can add two single order bits plus a carry-in from a previous adder. Its incomplete truth table is given in Table 3.10. The missing entry in the outputs for SUM and CARRY$_{out}$ are:

    a) 0 0
    b) 0 1
    c) 1 0
    d) 1 1

Inputs			Outputs	
A	B	C_{in}	Sum	Carry$_{out}$
0	0	0	0	0
0	0	1	1	0
0	1	0	1	0
0	1	1	0	1
1	0	0	1	0
1	0	1	0	1
1	1	0	0	1
1	1	1	?	?

Table 3.10

Section B: Short answer questions

1. What is a logic gate?
2. LIST the three basic logic gates
3. What is meant by ' universal logic '?
4. Draw the logic circuit corresponding to the Boolean equation

$$F = A . \overline{B} . \overline{C} + A . B . C$$

5. Refer to Table 3.11 and write down the Boolean equation for the output (F)

A	B	C	F
0	0	0	0
0	0	1	0
0	1	0	0
0	1	1	1
1	0	0	0
1	0	1	0
1	1	0	0
1	1	1	1

Table 3.11

6. State one practical application of Boolean algebra.

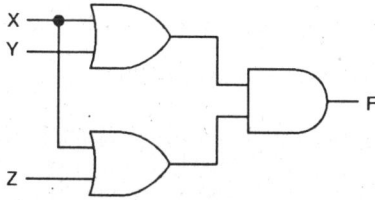

Fig 3.30

7. Draw the TRUTH TABLE for the logic circuit of Fig 3.30
8. Use Boolean algebra to minimise the logic circuit of Fig 3.30
   Draw the simplified logic circuit. Check your answer using a truth table.
9. Implement your solution for Question 8, using only:
   i) NAND gates
   ii) NOR gates
10. Check your answers for Question 9 parts (i) and (ii)
11. What is 'bus contention' and how can it be eliminated?

Chapter 4
Sequential Logic Elements: Counters and Shift Registers

The elements used in sequential logic systems are introduced in this chapter. The operation of S-R, D-Type and J-K flip-flops is examined. A number of practical applications of these devices are presented. These include: frequency division, mechanical switch debouncing, counters and shift registers.

4.1 INTRODUCTION TO MEMORY ELEMENTS

The combinational logic circuits described in Chapter 3, have outputs that depend solely on the inputs. An important feature of combinational logic circuits is that output states previously held by such circuits have no effect on their present behaviour. Without modification they are not capable of 'remembering' or 'storing' any past information. However, most digital systems, microprocessor-based products and computers require memory elements.

When the **output** of a circuit **depends on past inputs** (and hence on existing or previous outputs) **as well as the order in which the present inputs are applied**, the circuit is termed a **sequential circuit**. If the circuit is to retain information about past inputs it must of course contain some form of memory.

Sequential logic systems are usually divided into two groups: **synchronous** and **asynchronous** systems. A synchronous system only responds to its inputs if a clock (an electronic circuit which generates a continuous wavetrain of pulses of very stable frequency) signal is present at some common control input to all sections. In an asynchronous system there is no common control; a change in one section of the system causes further changes in other sections and so on. Practical examples of synchronous and asynchronous systems are given later in this chapter.

The basic memory element used in sequential logic systems is the **bistable,** which is also known by the names **flip-flop** or **latch**, but we will generally use flip-flop because it is the most common designation for digital systems.

A **bistable** is an electronic circuit which has **two stable states** and can be switched from one to the other by applying appropriate inputs. The basic flip-flop is a memory cell which can store one bit (0 or 1).

4.2 THE S-R (SET-RESET) FLIP-FLOP

The simple S-R (Set-Reset) flip-flop may be constructed in many ways using either NAND or NOR gates. Fig 4.1 shows two different implementations.

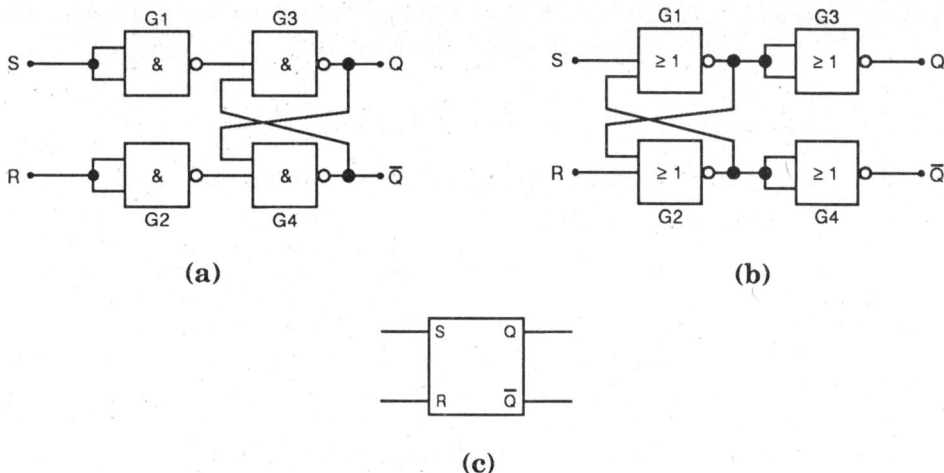

Fig 4.1 The S-R flip-flop using (a) NAND and (b) NOR gates (c) Logic symbol.

Consider the NAND gate version. Before attempting to explain its operation it is worth remembering that a NAND gate is 'zero sensitive'; meaning that as soon as a zero is applied to any of its inputs the output will become 1. As the flip-flop has two inputs we must analyse the circuit for all four possible input combinations.

Referring to Fig 4.1 (a), the circuit has two inputs, S and R, and two outputs Q and $\bar{Q}$. The memory feature is obtained by feedback connections, from the Q output to one input of G4, and from the $\bar{Q}$ output to an input of G3. The feedback is arranged so that the effect of a previous input is remembered.

When a flip-flop is in the SET state its Q output = 1 ($\bar{Q}$ =0). Conversely, when it is RESET, the Q output =0 ($\bar{Q}$ =1).

The application of a 1 at the S input (while R = 0) will cause the flip-flop to SET. To reset the flip-flop, apply a 1 to the R input (while S = 0).

To analyse the circuit, let us assume that when the flip-flop is switched on, Q = 0 ($\bar{Q}$ =1) and that the signals applied to both input lines are 0; S=0, R=0. With the Q output at 0 and the $\bar{Q}$ at 1, the top input to G4 will be a 0 and the lower input to G3 will be a 1. The S input to G1 is 0, therefore the output from G1 and the top input to G3 will be 1.

The R input to G2, which is also 0, will produce a 1 at the output of G2. G3 now has as its inputs 1-1, so the Q output will be 0. The inputs to G4 are 0-1, which will hold the $\bar{Q}$ output at 1. For the inputs S=0, R=0, the outputs do not change and are stable with Q remaining at 0, $\bar{Q}$ at 1.

If the S input is now changed to a 1 (R still at 0) then G1 output = 0 and the output of G3 will be forced to a 1, making Q = 1. The 1 on the Q output is then fed back to the top input of G4. The other input to G4 is also 1 (the inverse of R) making G4 inputs 1-1, so the output from G4 will become 0. The $\bar{Q}$ output, which is now 0 is fed back to the lower input of G3, making both inputs to G3 = 0. Again

4: Sequential logic elements

the circuit is stable with $Q = 1$ (SET), $\overline{Q} = 0$. If the S input is now returned to 0 the circuit will remain in the SET condition.

Keeping the S input at 0, and applying a 1 to the R input will cause the flip-flop to reset; $Q = 0$, $\overline{Q} = 1$.

With R at 1, G2 output will be 0, which will force the output of G4 to 1 ($\overline{Q} = 1$). The S input is 0, so the output from G1 is 1. The 1 on the $\overline{Q}$ output is fed back to the lower input of G3. G3 has inputs 1-1, making its output 0 ($Q = 0$; RESET). The 0 on the Q output is fed back to the top input of G4. G4 has inputs 0-0. Again the circuit is stable with $Q = 0$, $\overline{Q} = 1$.

If we now make $S = R = 1$ we are attempting to both SET and RESET the flip-flop at the same time. G1 output = G2 output = 0 and $Q = \overline{Q} = 1$. If the Set and Reset inputs are simultaneously returned to zero there is no way of telling what the output will be. The final state of the outputs, which is dependent on the relative switching speeds of the gates, is indeterminate. In practice, the condition $S = R = 1$ must be avoided.

The use and action of an S-R flip-flop may be summarised as follows:

1. At power up the circuit can settle in either the SET (S) or RESET(R) state.
2. S and R are normally held at zero and the outputs remain stable; either $Q=1$, $\overline{Q}=0$ or $Q=0$, $\overline{Q}=1$. $\overline{Q}$ is the complement or inverse of Q.
3. An input sequence 0-1-0 on the S (Set) input will SET the flip-flop; $Q=1$
4. A similar 0-1-0 input sequence at the R (Reset) input will RESET the flip-flop; $Q = 0$
5. The input condition $S=R=1$ is indeterminate and in practice should not be allowed.

Just like combinational logic elements the operation of a flip-flop may be described by means of a truth table. The truth table and logic circuit symbol for both the NAND and NOR versions of the flip-flop are given in Table 4.1

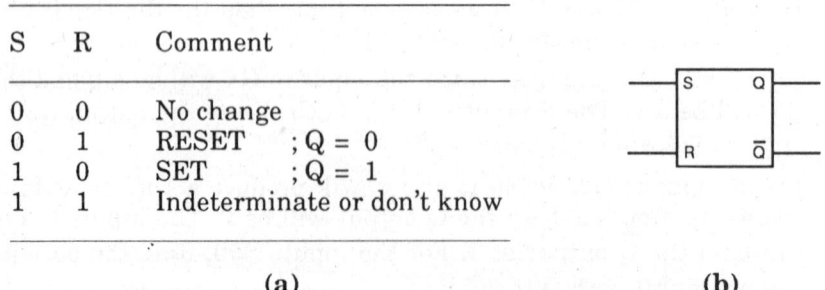

S	R	Comment
0	0	No change
0	1	RESET ; $Q = 0$
1	0	SET ; $Q = 1$
1	1	Indeterminate or don't know

(a) (b)

Table 4.1 S-R flip-flop (a) Truth Table (b) Symbol

As stated previously, the output of a sequential system depends on its past inputs as well as the order in which the present inputs are applied .

4: Sequential logic elements

 Short answer question 4.1

Refer to Fig 4.1 (b). Assume that the flip-flop is in the SET state and that both S and R are 0. If a 0-1-0 sequence is applied to the R (reset) input, analyse the circuit and deduce the state of the Q output.

 Answer to SAQ 4.1

Initially, S=R= 0 and Q =1, $\bar{Q}$ =0. Because the Q output is 1, the input to G3 is 0. The $\bar{Q}$ output is 0, therefore the input to G4 is 1. G1 inputs are 0-1 and its output is 0. The inputs to G2 are 0-0 and its output is 1. With S=R=0, the flip-flop is stable in the SET state.

If the RESET (R) input is taken high, then the inputs to G2 are 0-1 and its output will go LOW. The input to G4 is now 0, therefore its output will go HIGH. The G1 inputs are now 0-0 and its output will be a 1. The input to G3 is HIGH, so its output will go LOW (Q = 0). In effect, the flip-flop has entered the RESET state. When the R input returns to a LOW level the device will remain in the RESET condition.

The basic flip-flop which we have just described is operated directly by the S-R inputs and works in asynchronous mode. However, in practice, it is desirable to be able to SET or RESET the flip-flop, by means of a clock, so that it is possible to set or reset the device at a precise time.

4.3 THE CLOCKED S-R FLIP—FLOP

If the basic S-R flip-flop of Fig 4.1 is modified by the inclusion of a CLOCK (CLK) input, the resulting device, which is shown in Fig 4.2, is the logic diagram of a clocked S-R flip-flop. PRESET and CLEAR inputs have also been included. The clock input is used to change the S-R flip-flop from an element used in asynchronous logic systems to one which may be used in synchronous circuits. **The clock input is the signal which causes the flip-flop to SET or RESET at a precise time.** It may also be used to synchronise all of the flip-flops in a synchronous system.

Both PRESET and CLEAR, work independently from, and have priority over, the clock and data inputs. The preset input is used to set the flip-flop to 1, while the clear input may be used to reset it to 0. Because both of these are inputs to NAND gates, they are active LOW.

4: Sequential logic elements

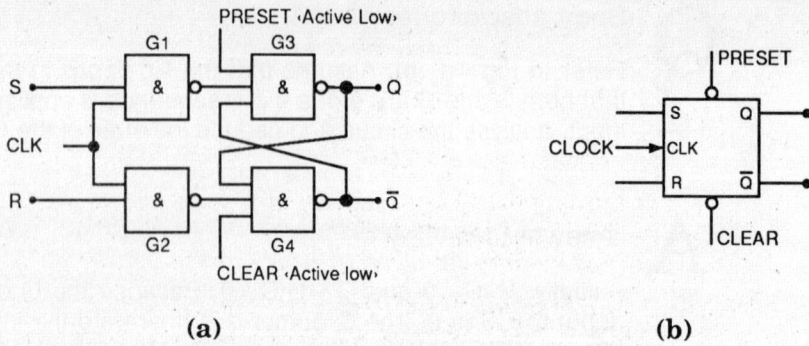

Fig 4.2 Clocked S-R flip-flop (a) Logic diagram (b) Symbol

The clock which is used to synchronise the elements in a system, so that they work together in an orderly controlled manner, is referred to as the system clock, and for an 8-bit microcomputer would typically have a frequency of 1 MHz, 2 MHz or 4 MHz. Because sequential logic systems depend for their operation on the presence of a clock signal it is important that terms associated with clock waveforms are fully understood.

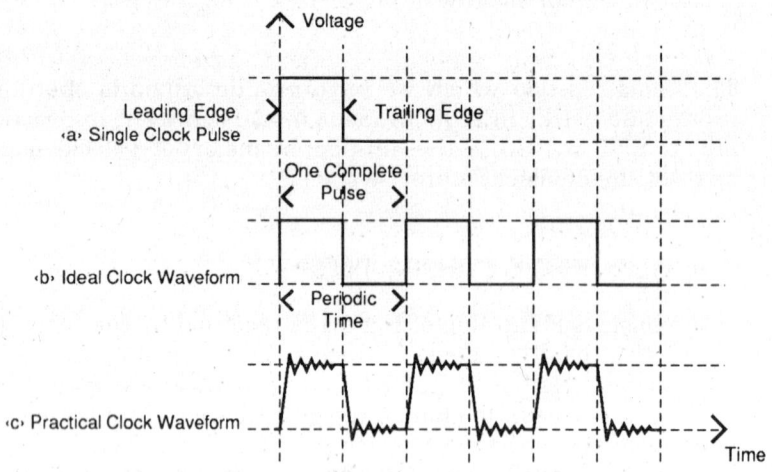

Fig 4.3 Clock waveforms.

A clock pulse – as seen in Fig 4.3 (a) – has two transitions, one from **low to high** level, which is the **leading edge**, and one from **high to low** level – the **trailing edge**. Some flip-flop circuits take data in and store it when the clock pulse is HIGH, while others are triggered by the leading or trailing edge of the clock pulse The data sheet for a particular device provides this information.

The clock signal for a system consists of a continuous wavetrain of rectangular pulses as illustrated in Fig 4.3 (b). The time taken to complete one pulse is the periodic time (T). The frequency (f) = 1/T. If the periodic time is 0.5 microseconds, then,

$$f = \frac{1}{T} = \frac{1}{0.5 \text{ microseconds}}$$

$$= \frac{1}{0.5} \times 10^6$$

$$= 2 \text{ MHz}$$

Practical microcomputer clock signals do not have vertical leading and trailing edges. Examination of the clock signal of a microcomputer, using an oscilloscope, would reveal a waveform like that of Fig 4.3 (c)

The clocked S-R flip-flop is similar to the unclocked version of the device, except, to SET or RESET it a clock pulse must be present. (CLK =1).

Consider the operation of Fig 4.2. Assume that when power is applied to the circuit Q=0, $\bar{Q}$ = 1. With S=R= 0 and no clock present (CLK = 0) the output from G1 and G2 =1. If the PRESET input is disabled with a 1, then the three inputs to G3 are 1-1-1 (don't forget that the $\bar{Q}$ output feeds back a 1 to the bottom input of G3) and its output will be 0 (RESET). If the CLEAR input is also disabled with a 1, the inputs to G4 are 0-1-1 and its output is 1. Under these conditions the flip-flop is stable in the RESET state.

If the SET input is now changed to a 1 and a clock pulse applied (CLK = 1) the output from G1 will be 0, while G2 output stays at 1. Assume that the PRESET and CLEAR inputs are at level 1 and therefore disabled. The LOW output from G1 results in the output of G3 becoming a 1, and the flip-flop enters the SET state. The 1 from the Q output is fed back to the top input of G4, making its inputs 1-1-1, which changes its output to a 0. If the clock is now removed (CLK = 0) the circuit remains stable in the SET state.

Short answer question 4.2

Refer to Fig 4.2 With NO clock signal applied, what will happen to the output if S=0 and R =1 ?

Answer to SAQ 4.2

Because there is no clock signal the output cannot change. It will remain in its previous state.

Short answer question 4.3

Refer to Fig 4.2

If the flip-flop is in the SET state (Q =1) and the SET(S) input is LOW, what will happen if the RESET input is made HIGH and a clock pulse is applied? Assume that the PRESET and CLEAR inputs are disabled.

4: Sequential logic elements

> **Answer to SAQ 4.3**
>
> Initially with S=R=0 the flip-flop is stable in the SET condition; Q =1.
>
> If a HIGH level signal is applied to the R input, and a clock pulse is applied then the inputs to G1 are 0-1, making it's output a 1. The inputs to G2 are 1-1, so it's output is 0. The LOW output from G2 will result in G4 output going HIGH. ($\bar{Q}$ = 1). The $\bar{Q}$ output is fed back to the bottom input of G3, making it's inputs 1-1-1. Therefore the Q output enters the RESET state. After the Clock (CLK) and Reset (R) inputs return to 0, the flip-flop remains stable in the RESET condition.

The operation of the clocked S-R flip-flop is illustrated in the timing diagram of Fig 4.4

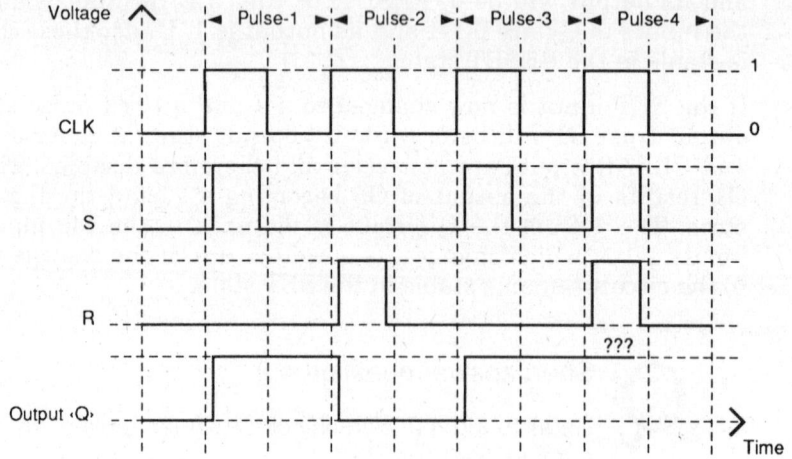

Fig 4.4 Timing diagram for a clocked S-R flip-flop

While the first clock pulse is HIGH (CLK =1), the SET input becomes 1, the RESET remains at 0, and the flip-flop enters the SET state (Q =1).

The flip-flop remains SET until the second clock pulse goes HIGH. It then RESETS itself, because the RESET input is HIGH (SET is LOW).

During the third clock pulse the S input goes HIGH (while the RESET is LOW) to SET the flip-flop.

While the fourth clock pulse is HIGH, S and R are both high, forcing the Q and $\bar{Q}$ outputs to 1. When the clock returns to 0, there is no way of predicting the state of the outputs.

In summary, data at the S and R inputs is only stored when the clock pulse is at logic level 1. Table 4.2 is the truth table for the device.

4: Sequential logic elements

t_n		t_{n+1}	
S	R	Q_{n+1}	Comments
0	0	Q_n	No change in outputs
1	0	1	SET action
0	1	0	RESET action
1	1	?	Indeterminate

Table 4.2 Truth table for a clocked S-R flip-flop.

In table 4.2, $\bar{Q}$ which is the inverse or complement of Q, has been omitted. Note that t_n denotes the time before a clock pulse, and t_{n+1} the time after the clock pulse; Q_n and Q_{n+1} are the logic levels at the Q output corresponding to these times.

Short answer question 4.4

State how the PRESET and CLEAR inputs may be disabled.

Answer to SAQ 4.4

By connecting them to a HIGH level.

4.4 THE D-TYPE FLIP-FLOP (OR LATCH)

A **D**-type flip-flop is a **D**ata element which can be used to temporarily store one bit of data. Modification of an S-R flip-flop, by connecting an inverter (NOT gate) between the S and R inputs, results in a D-type flip-flop. Because R is always the inverse of S, the hazardous condition, S=R=1 cannot occur. Fig 4.5 shows how an S-R flip-flop may be modified to give a D-type device.

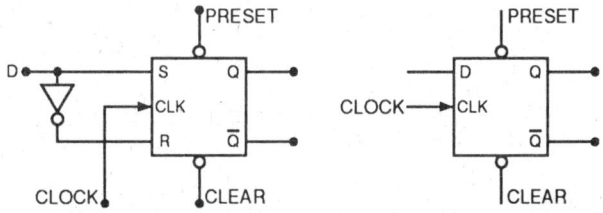

Fig 4.5 D-type flip-flop and logic symbol

When the D input =1, and the clock =1, the data will be transferred from the D input to the Q output.

If D=0 and the clock =1, the 0 will be transferred from the D input to the Q output.

4: Sequential logic elements

If the clock input is at 0 the flip-flop will be disabled or inhibited and no output changes can occur.

The device may be preset to 1(Q=1) by momentarily applying a low level signal to the PRESET input. Likewise, it may be cleared (Q=0) by the application of a similar signal to the CLEAR input. The small circle or bubble on these input pins indicates that they are active LOW; they are enabled by logic level 0.

The operation of the D-type flip-flop is summarised in table 4.3. Like the clocked S-R flip-flop, t_n denotes the time before a clock pulse, and t_{n+1} the time after the clock pulse; Q_n and Q_{n+1} are the logic levels at the Q output corresponding to these times.

	t_n		t_{n+1}	
D	Q_n		Q_{n+1}	Comments
0	0 or 1		0	The 0 on the D input is transferred to the Q output when the flip-flop is clocked.
1	0 or 1		1	The application of a clock pulse transfers the 1 on the D input to the Q output.

Table 4.3 Truth table for a D-type flip-flop

Short answer question 4.5

Refer to Fig 4.5

If the various inputs to the D-type flip-flop are as follows, explain what will happen.

i) PRESET = HIGH

ii) CLEAR = LOW

iii) D = HIGH

iv) A single clock pulse is applied

Answer to SAQ 4.5

Because the CLEAR input is permanently at a LOW level the flip-flop will remain cleared. The CLEAR input has priority over the clock and D inputs.

4.5 MASTER-SLAVE AND EDGE TRIGGERED FLIP-FLOPS.

In our discussions on the S-R and D-type flip-flops, working as synchronous logic circuit elements, we assumed that the data was transferred from the input to the output while the clock pulse was at logic level 1(sometimes called static triggering). In practice, static triggering can lead to difficulties.

For instance, one of the difficulties associated with clocking data from the input to the output of a flip-flop, while the clock pulse is at logic level 1 is illustrated in Fig 4.6

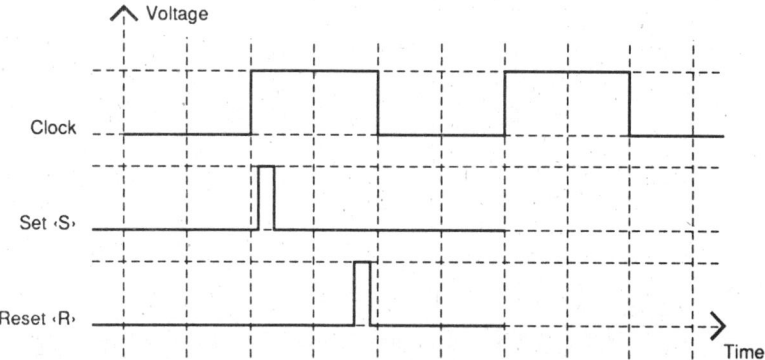

Fig 4.6 Triggering a Flip-flop while the clock is at logic level 1

Here the clock pulse is too wide, and it fails to return to zero, before the inputs change. The original inputs S=1 and R=0 were intended to SET the flip-flop but because the inputs changed while the CLK was still at level 1, the flip-flop responds again during the original clock pulse and RESETS the device. The clock pulse should be short enough to return to zero before the inputs change thus ensuring that the Q output does not change again until the next clock pulse.

The duration of the clock pulse in the HIGH state could be reduced (frequency increased) in an attempt to overcome this problem. However, that could lead to other problems such as, the slowest flip-flop in the system might not be able to respond quickly enough.

These problems are overcome by the use of either **master-slave** or **edge-triggered** devices.

EDGE TRIGGERING

In the quest for higher operating speeds and the need to overcome the problems associated with static triggering, various types of flip-flops were developed. These included edge-triggered and master-slave devices. In the range of devices described as edge-triggered flip-flops, data is transferred to the output on the incidence of either the **leading edge or trailing edge** of the clock pulse. Although edge-triggered flip-flops are faster than master-slave devices the preference is for the master-slave types because with edge triggered flip-flops unsuspecting timing problems can arise.

MASTER-SLAVE TRIGGERING

The master-slave principle may be applied to all types of flip-flops. Unlike the edge-triggered type which uses just a single flip-flop (which makes it faster) the master-slave device uses two flip-flops in series. Fig 4.7 shows the circuit diagram of a master-slave flip-flop constructed from NAND gates. The circuit is basically two clocked S-R flip-flops, connected in a master-slave configuration, with the addition of further feedback, from the $\bar{Q}_s$ output to the top input of G1 and from the Q_s output to the bottom input of G2.

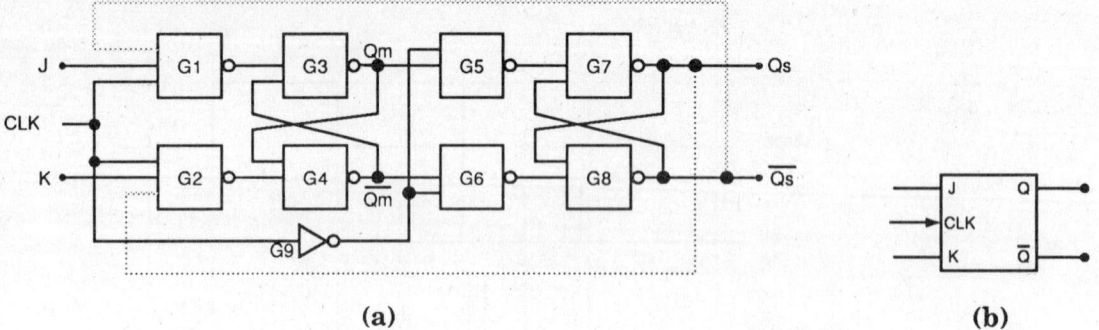

Fig 4.7 (a) The Master-Slave (M-S) J-K Flip-flop (b) Logic symbol

The circuit now has two levels of feedback which makes circuit analysis more difficult, but examination proves that there is no disallowed input condition and a useful 'toggle' action is produced.

The operation of the master-slave J-K flip-flop is summarised Table 4.4

Basically, the J-K inputs affect the master section of the flip-flop when the clock is HIGH, but the output of the master is only transferred to the slave (and hence the Q output) when the clock goes LOW. Therefore a **complete clock pulse**, not just one edge, is required **to operate a master-slave flip-flop**. While data is being taken into the master section, the slave section is isolated, and when data is being transferred from the master to the slave data cannot be taken into the master section.

J	K	ACTION AT NEXT CLOCK PULSE	
0	0	No change	; $Q_{n+1} = Q_n$
1	0	Flip-flop SETS	; $Q_{n+1} = 1$
0	1	Flip-flop RESETS	; $Q_{n+1} = 0$
1	1	The output changes state (Toggles)	; $Q_{n+1} = \bar{Q}_n$

Q_n = Output before the clock pulse is applied
Q_{n+1} = Output after the next clock pulse

Table 4.4 Action table for a master-slave flip-flop

4: Sequential logic elements

From the action table for the master-slave flip-flop we can see that the behaviour of the device, for the first three inputs, is the same as that of an S-R flip-flop. The J and K inputs of this flip-flop correspond to the S and R inputs of the S-R device.

In the case of an S-R flip-flop, if S=R=1 then the output is indeterminate.

However, in a J-K flip-flop, the fourth input combination, J=K=1, yields a useful result, where the output changes state at each clock pulse. This is referred to as the 'toggle' effect and is widely used in counting systems.

Referring to Fig 4.7 G1, G2, G3, G4 make up the master section and G5, G6, G7, G8 the slave part of the device. Before attempting to analyse the circuit when J=K=1, assume that the flip-flop is SET (Q_s =1).

If the clock now becomes a 1, G1 has inputs 0-1-1 and its output is 1, which has no effect on G3 (because the NAND gate is zero sensitive). The inputs to G2 are 1-1-1 and its output is 0. Because of the LOW output from G2, G4 output goes to a HIGH level, producing inputs of 1-1 to G3. G3 output becomes 0 and the master section of the flip-flop has been RESET (Q_m=0). The G4 inputs are 0-0, so it's output is 1. As the clock is still at a HIGH level the output from G9 is 0. The inputs to G5 are now 0-0 so its output is 1. G6 inputs are 1-0, therefore its output is also 1. The G7 inputs of 1-0 will hold the Q output at 1(Q_s=1), while G8 inputs are 1-1, holding the $\bar{Q}$ output at 0 ($\bar{Q}_s$=0). When the clock pulse is at 1, new data is taken into the master section of the flip-flop and the slave section is inhibited because of the action of G9, the inverter.

The clock pulse now falls to zero. This produces a HIGH output from G2. The output from G1 remains HIGH. Because the outputs from G1 and G2 are both HIGH the master section of the flip-flop cannot take in any new data. However, both inputs to G6 are HIGH, which produces a LOW output from G6. G8 responds to the output of G6 and makes $\bar{Q}$ = 1 ($\bar{Q}_s$ =1). This 1 is fed back to the lower input of G7, making it's inputs 1-1 and G7 output goes LOW (Q_s = 0). The output of G7 feeds back a 0 to the top input of G8. G8 inputs are 0-0 and its output remains at 1 ($\bar{Q}_s$=1). We have just seen that when the clock pulse goes LOW data is transferred from the master to the slave but new data cannot be taken into the master section. A single clock pulse changes the state of the output. The master-slave flip-flop toggles with each clock pulse.

Short answer question 4.6

Assume that the master-slave J-K flip-flop is RESET (Fig 4.7). Explain what will happen if one complete clock pulse is applied to the device.

J=K=1.

4: Sequential logic elements

Answer to SAQ 4.6

Initially, with the clock pulse at 0, the flip-flop is stable in the RESET state.

If a clock pulse is then applied the G1 inputs are 1-1-1 and its output is 0. The G2 inputs are 1-1-0 and its output is 1. The LOW output from G1 will make the output from the master section of the device 1 ($Q_m=1$). The output of G3 is fed back to the top input of G4, making it's inputs 1-1 and its output 0. Because of the LOW output from G9, G5 output = G6 output = 1, which has no effect on G7 and G8. In other words, when the clock pulse is HIGH, new data is taken into the master section of the device, while the slave is isolated from the master.

When the clock pulse goes LOW, the outputs from G1 and G2 are HIGH. Therefore no new data can be taken into the master. However, the HIGH output from G9, makes the G5 inputs 1-1 and it's output 0, which forces G7 (the Qs output) to 1. G6 inputs are 0-1 and it's output remains at 1. G8 then has inputs 1-1, producing an output of 0 ($\overline{Q}_s = 0$).

The flip-flop is now stable in the SET state.

4.6 PRACTICAL APPLICATIONS OF FLIP-FLOPS: MECHANICAL SWITCH DEBOUNCING, FREQUENCY DIVISION

Flip-flops are widely used in digital systems and microcomputers. Typical applications include, mechanical switch debouncing, frequency division, counters and registers.

MECHANICAL SWITCH DEBOUNCING

When a mechanical switch is operated, the contacts open and close (bounce) several times instead of making a single contact. Even using high quality switches, switch contact bounce may last for a period of several milliseconds before finally coming to rest.

Consider the circuit of Fig 4.8, which consists of a mechanical switch (S), an inverter (NOT gate) and a resistor (R). It provides an input to a digital system or a microcomputer. At first glance it might appear reasonable to generate an input signal to the microcomputer using a mechanical switch.

With the switch open a HIGH level is fed through the resistor to the input of the NOT gate giving a LOW output and there is no problem. However, if the switch is now closed, it will not make cleanly and will bounce a number of times before settling in the closed position. Instead of the output changing from 0 to 1, it will change between 0 and 1 a number of times giving the output waveform of Fig 4.8 (b). The computer now sees a number of 1s and 0s instead of a single transition from 0 to 1.

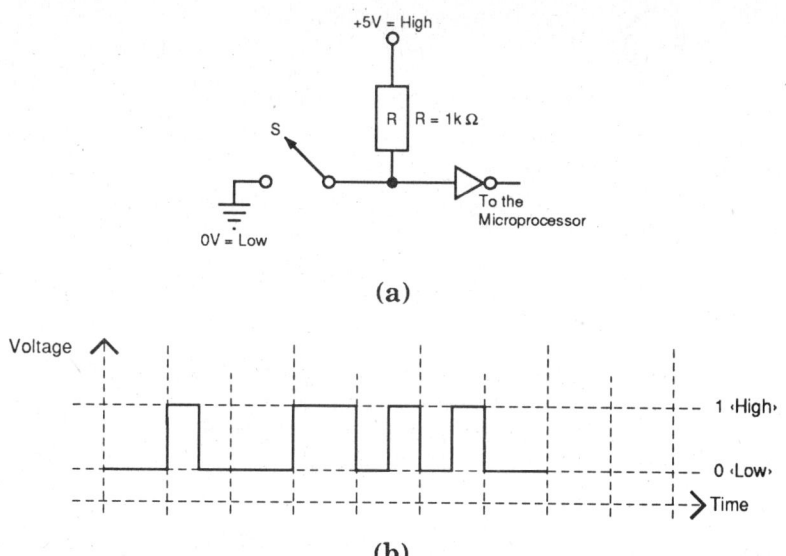

Fig 4.8 Output of an inverter showing the effect of mechanical switch bounce

The circuit of Fig 4.9 which uses a flip-flop can be used to overcome this problem.

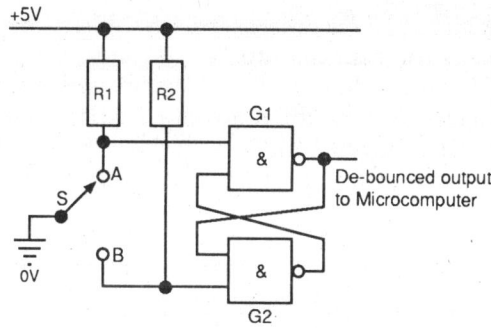

Fig 4.9 Simple switch debounce circuit

NAND gates G1 and G2 operate as an S-R flip-flop to eliminate switch bounce. To illustrate how it operates assume that when the switch (S) is operated it moves to position 'B'. One input to G2 is 0, so its output is 1. G2 output is fed back to one input of G1, making G1 inputs 1-1, which produces a 0 as an input to the microcomputer. Even if contact 'B' is broken, G2 output will still be 1, because of the feedback from G1 output. Both inputs to G1 are still HIGH holding its output at 0. Irrespective of the number of times that the switch bounces the output to the computer will be stable at 0.

4: Sequential logic elements

  Short answer question 4.7

Refer to Fig 4.9 If the switch (S) is now moved to position A explain the operation of the circuit. Will switch bounce be a problem ?

  Answer to SAQ 4.7

When the switch is first moved to position A, the top input to G1 will be 0. This will have the effect of setting the output of G1 at a HIGH level.

The output of G1 is fed back as an input to G2, therefore the inputs to G2 are 1-1 and it's output is 0. The LOW level on the output of G2 feeds back as an input to G1, holding G1 output at 1. Even if contact 'A' is broken, the output will remain at 1, because of the feedback from G2.

FREQUENCY DIVISION

As mentioned previously each microprocessor has a clock circuit which generates a wavetrain of pulses. As well as synchronising all of the circuits within a system it determines the speed at which the system operates. System speed is of course not solely dependent on the clock. For instance, their is a maximum theoretical speed at which a given processor is capable of operating. The system clock is often referred to as the **master clock.** Although the system clock might generate pulses at 4 MHz, not all parts of the system need necessarily operate at that frequency. Some parts of it might require a 2 MHz signal for correct operation. In practice, the 2 MHz signal would be derived from the master clock. Fig 4.10 shows a circuit which is suitable for frequency division. The basis of the circuit is a J-K flip-flop.

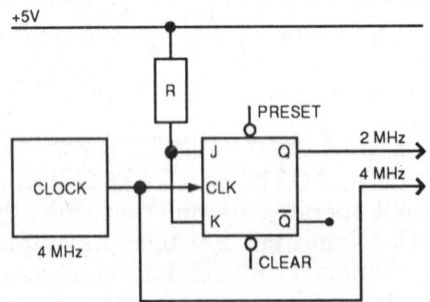

Fig 4.10 Frequency division circuit

The J-K flip-flop is operated in the toggle mode so that its output changes state with each clock pulse. This is achieved by connecting the J-K inputs to logic level 1 through a resister. The timing diagram for the circuit, which shows the logic state of the clock input to the flip-flop and its Q output is given in Fig 4.11

4: Sequential logic elements

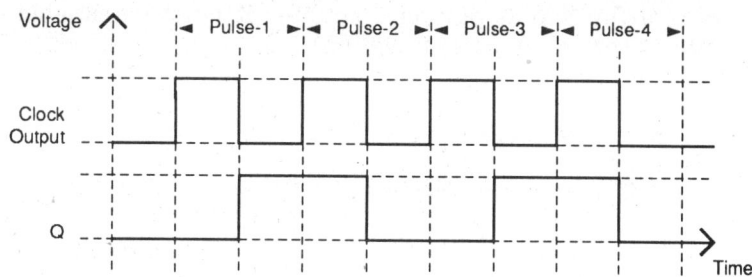

Fig 4.11 Timing diagram for frequency division circuit

The flip-flop is switched as the clock signal falls from 1 to 0. It is initially cleared or RESET (Q=0) by momentarily applying a 0 to the CLEAR input.

Because the device only changes state as the input clock pulse goes from logic level 1 to 0, the Q output is never affected by the leading (rising) edge of pulses. Therefore the first time that the Q output changes is at the trailing edge of the first clock pulse. It then remains at a high level until the trailing edge of pulse 2 when it changes from 1 to 0. On the trailing edge of all subsequent clock pulses it changes state (toggles).

Examination of the waveform reveals that for the four input clock pulses applied to flip-flop, only two appear at its output. In effect, frequency division, by two, has been performed.

4.7 DIGITAL COUNTERS

Counters are fundamental components of digital systems, and can be used in timing, control and sequencing applications. They appear within the microprocessor and in computer circuits. Typical applications of counters include:

a) A special counter (the Program Counter) which is used within a microprocessor and contains the address of the next instruction to be executed by the microprocessor.

b) Direct counting. For instance, it might be necessary to count manufactured objects moving along a motorised conveyor belt, which is part of an industrial process.

c) A number of support chips have been developed to work with microprocessors. For the Zilog Z80 MPU a CTC (Counter Timer Circuit) is available. The CTC is a programmable IC which can, for example, be programmed in the counter mode to divide the frequency of the incoming signal. This chip contains four counters.

d) Time and frequency measurement.

e) Analogue to digital signal conversion systems.

A digital counter is a circuit which is capable of counting the number of pulses applied to one of its inputs. Essentially, a counter consists of a number of flip-flops connected in tandem (in series). J-K or D-type devices may be used. When

4: Sequential logic elements

using a flip-flop as part of a counter it must be capable of changing its output state at each clock pulse (toggling).

Short answer question 4.8

We have already seen that in order to toggle a J-K flip-flop it is necessary to apply a HIGH level to the J, K inputs. To achieve the same effect when using a D-type the $\bar{Q}$ output must be connected to the D input as shown in Fig 4.12.

Assuming that the device operates on the leading-edge of the clock pulse, draw the timing diagram to show how the flip-flop toggles.

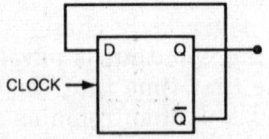

Fig 4.12

Answer to SAQ 4.8

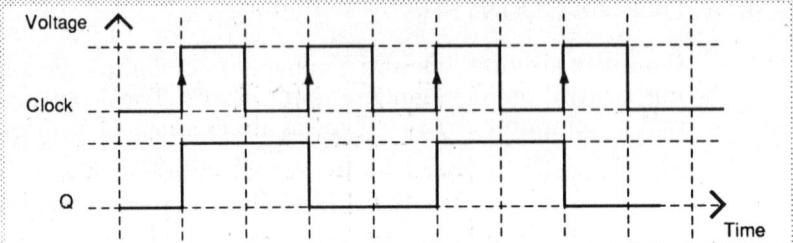

Fig 4.13

As the timing diagram shows the output changes state (toggles) whenever the clock pulse changes from 0 to 1. For four input pulses only two output pulses occur. Hence, the input signal frequency has been divided by 2.

Counters may be operated in synchronous or asynchronous mode. A synchronous counter is one in which all the outputs are directly clocked at the same time by the input clock signal.

In an asynchronous system there is no common control; a change in one section of the system causes further changes in other sections and so on. Examples of both types of system now follow.

4.8 AN ASYNCHRONOUS 4-BIT BINARY UP-COUNTER

Fig 4.14 illustrates a 4-bit asynchronous (or ripple) counter constructed from four master-slave J-K flip-flops. The Q output from each flip-flop is connected to the clock input of the next flip-flop in the chain. With all J-K inputs connected to +5V via a resistor (1kiloOhm recommended) they are held at a HIGH level, which ensures that each flip-flop is capable of toggling. In this mode the flip-flops are sometimes known as T (Toggle) flip-flops. The outputs from the four flip-flops are being monitored by Light Emitting Diodes (LEDs) D1 to D4. Resistors R2 to R5 are current limiting resistors (220 Ohms would suffice).

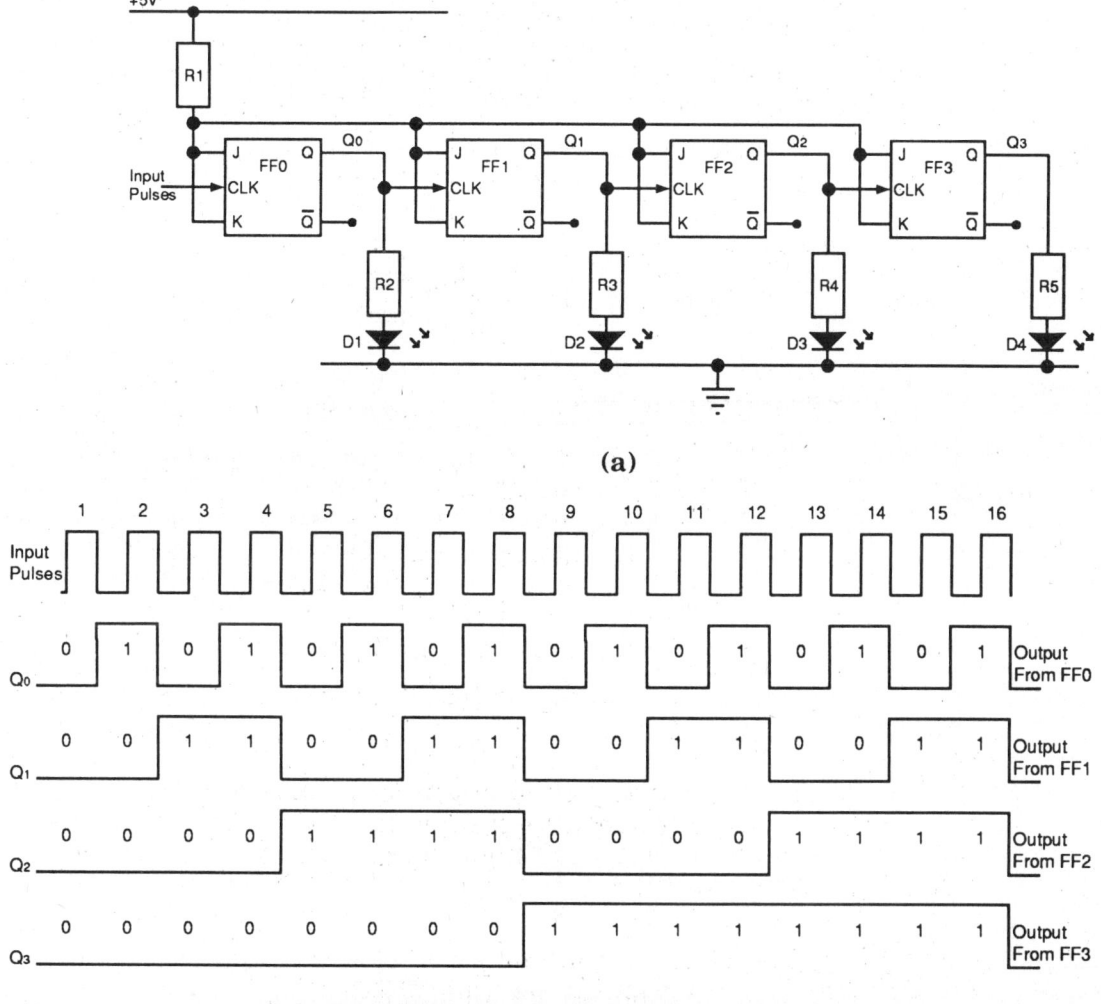

(a)

(b)

Fig 4.14 An asynchronous 4-bit binary counter
(a) Logic diagram (b) Timing diagram

4: Sequential logic elements

Before the count begins all flip-flops are CLEARED (All Q outputs = 0). Because master-slave devices are being used, whenever the signal on the clock input changes from 1 to 0, the flip-flop will toggle.

As the timing diagram shows the first flip-flop (FF0) will toggle as each input clock pulse goes from 1 to 0. For 16 input pulses it will produce 8 output pulses at Q_0. The output of the second flip-flop (FF1) will change whenever Q_0 output goes from HIGH to LOW. For the eight input pulses to FF1 it will produce 4 pulses at its output Q_1. The four pulses at Q_1 output are used to clock FF2. FF2 therefore produces two output pulses which are used to clock FF3. The output from FF3 is a single pulse. Because each stage must wait for a change in the previous one before it can begin to change the circuit is **asynchronous.**

If the binary values, which are written on the timing diagram are read from left to right Table 4.5 is obtained. FF0 provides the first bit of the output and is therefore the Least Significant Bit (LSB)

Examination of Table 4.5 shows that the outputs Q_0, Q_1, Q_2 and Q_3 give the binary representation of the number of pulses fed into the input of the counter.

Input pulse number	Flip-flop outputs			
	Q_0 '1'	Q_1 '2'	Q_2 '4'	Q_3 '8'
0	0	0	0	0
1	1	0	0	0
2	0	1	0	0
3	1	1	0	0
4	0	0	1	0
5	1	0	1	0
6	0	1	1	0
7	1	1	1	0
8	0	0	0	1
9	1	0	0	1
10	0	1	0	1
11	1	1	0	1
12	0	0	1	1
13	1	0	1	1
14	0	1	1	1
15	1	1	1	1
16	0	0	0	0

Up to 16 (2^4) pulses (pulse 0 to 15) may be counted using four flip-flops. The counter resets itself at the sixteenth pulse. (see timing diagram)

In general, a chain of flip-flops counts in binary up to the number 2^N-1 before it resets itself to its original state. N is the number of flip-flop stages in the counter.

Table 4.5 A 4-bit binary counter

Short answer question 4.9

Although the PRESET and CLEAR inputs have not been shown in Fig 4.14 these active low pins are present on the chips. How are they disabled during normal counting operations ?

 Answer to SAQ 4.9

By connecting them to a HIGH level

4.9 A BCD UP-COUNTER

The counter in Fig 4.14 has 16 different states (0000 to 1111). It would be referred to as a MOD-16 counter, where the MOD number is always equal to the number of states which the counter goes through in each complete cycle, before it recycles back to its starting state. In general, if N flip-flops are connected in a chain, the counter will have 2^N different states, so it is a MOD-2^N counter. The basic ripple counter of Fig 4.14 is limited to MOD numbers that are equal to 2^N, where N is the number of flip-flops. This value is actually the maximum MOD number that can be obtained using N flip-flops. The basic counter can be modified to produce MOD numbers less than 2^N by allowing the counter to skip states that are normally part of the counting sequence. For instance, a MOD-10 or binary coded decimal (BCD) counter would count in binary from 0000 to 1001. The minimum number of flip-flops required is four (three would only count from 000 to 111). However, four flip-flops will normally count from 0000 to 1111, so a method of resetting the counter after it has reached 1001 has to be found and outputs 1010 to 1111 must be circumvented. The reset method as shown in Fig 4.15 (a) can be applied. Immediately after receipt of the 10th (1010) pulse, all four flip-flops must be reset to zero. This is achieved by feeding Q_1 and Q_3 to a NAND gate, the output of which is used to clear the flip-flops. At the 10th pulse $Q_1 = Q_3 = 1$ and the output from the NAND gate will be 0. It's output is connected to the CLEAR (CLR) input of all flip-flops, therefore all flip-flops will be cleared. The timing diagram {Fig 4.15(b)} which illustrates the action of the counter indicates the presence of a glitch or spike which is caused by the momentary occurrence of the 1010 state before clearing the counter.

Again, if the binary values which are written on the timing diagram are read from left to right Table 4.6 is obtained. FFO is the least significant bit (LSB) and FF3 the most significant bit (MSB) of the BCD counter.

4: Sequential logic elements

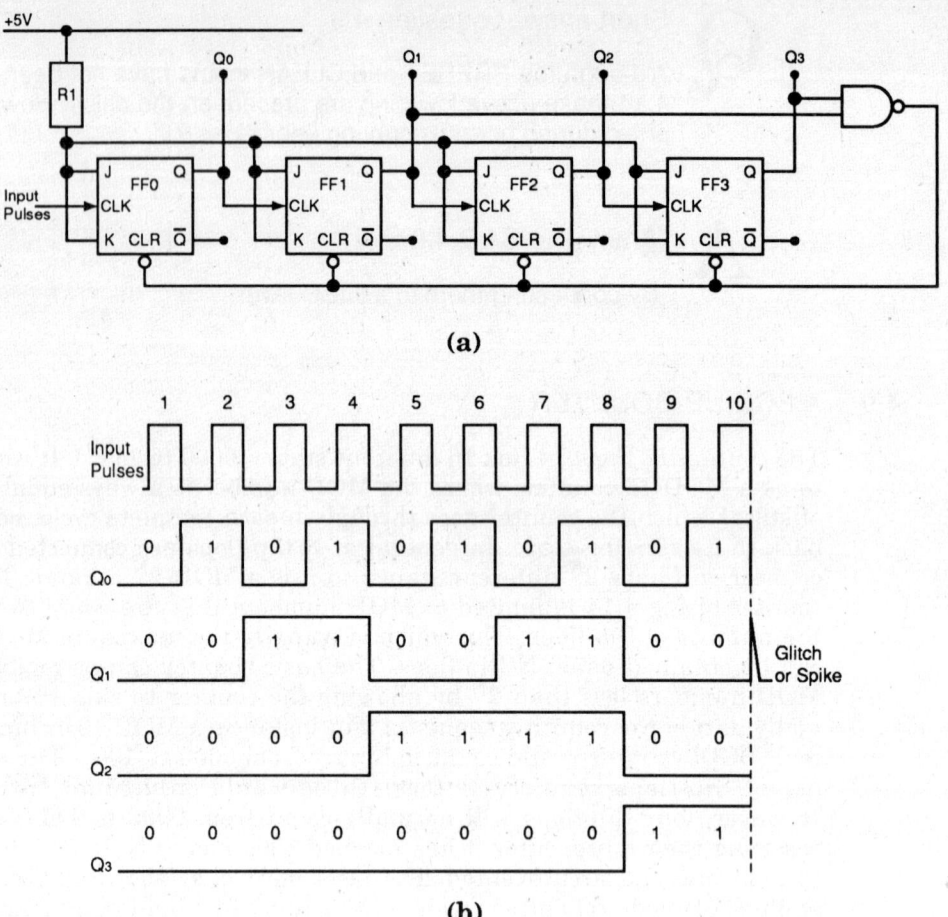

Fig 4.15 BCD counter (a) Logic diagram (b) Timing diagram

4: Sequential logic elements

Input pulse number	Flip-flop outputs			
	Q_0 '1'	Q_1 '2'	Q_2 '4'	Q_3 '8'
0	0	0	0	0
1	1	0	0	0
2	0	1	0	0
3	1	1	0	0
4	0	0	1	0
5	1	0	1	0
6	0	1	1	0
7	1	1	1	0
8	0	0	0	1
9	1	0	0	1
10	0	0	0	0
11	1	0	0	0
12	0	1	0	0

Table 4.6 MOD-10 Asynchronous counter

Q Short answer question 4.10

DESIGN A MOD-6 ASYNCHRONOUS BINARY UP-COUNTER

4: Sequential logic elements

 Answer to SAQ 4.10

A MOD-6 counter will provide outputs as per Table 4.7.

Input pulse number	Flip-flop outputs		
	Q_0 '1'	Q_1 '2'	Q_2 '4'
0	0	0	0
1	1	0	0
2	0	1	0
3	1	1	0
4	0	0	1
5	1	0	1
6	0	0	0

Table 4.7

Immediately after receipt of the 6th pulse all three flip-flops must be RESET.

This is achieved by feeding the Q_1 and Q_2 outputs, both of which are HIGH, as inputs to a two-input NAND gate. The output from the gate can be used to RESET all flip-flops to 0. Fig 4.16 shows the logic diagram.

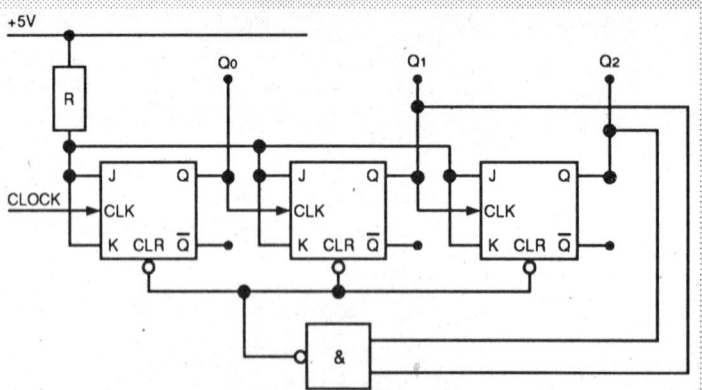

Fig 4.16 A MOD-6 Asynchronous counter

4.10 AN ASYNCHRONOUS 4-BIT BINARY DOWN-COUNTER

The counters considered so far operated as binary up-counters where each flip-flop is triggered by the Q output of the preceding stage. In a down-counter each flip-flop is triggered by the $\bar{Q}$ output of the preceding flip-flop. In both counters the first flip-flop is triggered by the clock. Fig 4.17 shows a four stage down-counter.

Assume that each flip-flop is triggered as the clock changes from 1 to 0 and that they are all initially SET at 1. The output (Q_0) from the first flip-flop (FF0) changes state whenever the input pulse changes from 1 to 0.

FF1 is triggered by $\overline{Q}_0$ (the inverse of Q) therefore it will change state when Q_0 is going from 0 to 1 ($\overline{Q}_0$ will be going from 1 to 0). Flip-flops FF2 and FF3 operate in a similar manner to FF1.

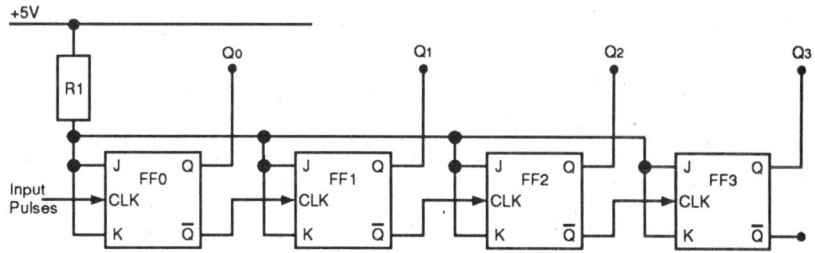

Fig 4.17 An asynchronous 4-bit down counter

Short answer question 4.11

Draw the timing diagram for the 4-bit binary down counter illustrated in Fig 4.17

Answer to SAQ 4.11

The timing diagram of Fig 4.18 shows that the counter operates as a 4-bit down counter; it counts down from 1111_2 to 0000_2 (15_{10} to 0_{10}).

It carries on repeating that count sequence.

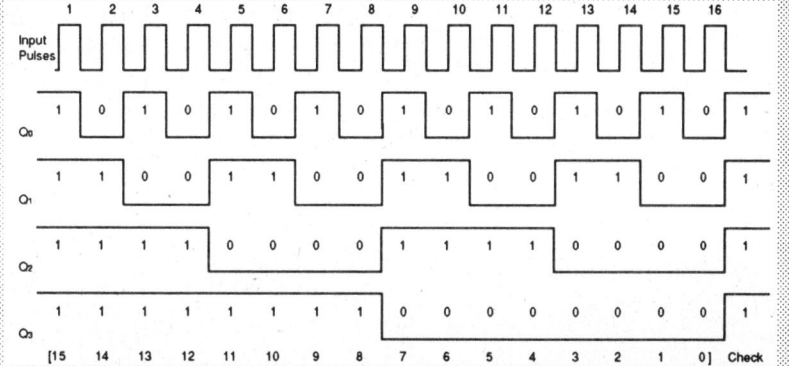

Fig 4.18 Timing diagram for binary down counter

4: Sequential logic elements

4.11 SYNCHRONOUS COUNTERS

The asynchronous counters discussed so far have the advantage of simplicity over synchronous counters; they require fewer components to produce a given counting sequence. However, they have one major drawback, which is caused by their basic principle of operation. Each flip-flop is triggered by the transition at the output of the preceding flip-flop. Because of the inherent propagation delay time, t_{pd}, of each flip-flop, this means that the second flip-flop will not respond until a time t_{pd} after the first flip-flop receives an input pulse; the third flip-flop will not respond until a time equal to $2 \times t_{pd}$ after the clock pulse occurs and so on. In other words, the propagation delays of the flip-flops accumulate so that the Nth device cannot change state until a time equal to $N \times t_{pd}$ after the clock pulse occurs. Because each input pulse essentially 'ripples' through all of the flip-flops in the counter, the time taken for one pulse to 'ripple' through a counter with a large number of flip-flops may be greater than the arrival of the next input pulse to the counter, and false counts may occur. The cumulative effect of the flip-flop delays is to limit the speed of operation of asynchronous counters. These limitations can be overcome with the use of synchronous counters in which all of the flip-flops are triggered by the same clock input pulses.

4.12 A 4-BIT SYNCHRONOUS BINARY UP-COUNTER

Fig 4.19 illustrates a 4-bit synchronous counter made with four master-slave J-K flip-flops. Remember, when the J and K inputs are low on a J-K flip-flop, the output does not change when the flip-flop is clocked. But if J and K are high, the flip-flop toggles when it is clocked. Now you can work your way through a count sequence to see how the counter works.

The counter is initially cleared by applying a LOW pulse at the CLEAR (CLR) input. FF0 which has its J-K inputs permanently ties to a HIGH level will toggle from 0 to 1 when the first clock pulse is applied. Since the J-K inputs of FF1 are now high, the next clock pulse will change Q_1 to 1 and Q_0 back to 0 to give an output count of 0100_2 or 2_{10}. With Q_0 now low, only Q_0 can change on the next clock pulse. This gives an output count of 1100_2 or 3_{10}. Since Q_0 and Q_1 are now both high, gate G1 will put a HIGH on the J and K inputs of FF2 so that on the next clock pulse Q_2 will become 1, while Q_0 and Q_1 will change to 0, giving an output of 0010_2 or 4_{10}. The rest of the count sequence follows a similar pattern. At count 7 when Q_0, Q_1 and Q_2 are all 1s, AND gate G2 will enable FF3 to toggle to a 1, giving a count of 8. At count 15 all of the outputs are HIGH, so they will toggle back to 0 on the next clock pulse.

4: Sequential logic elements

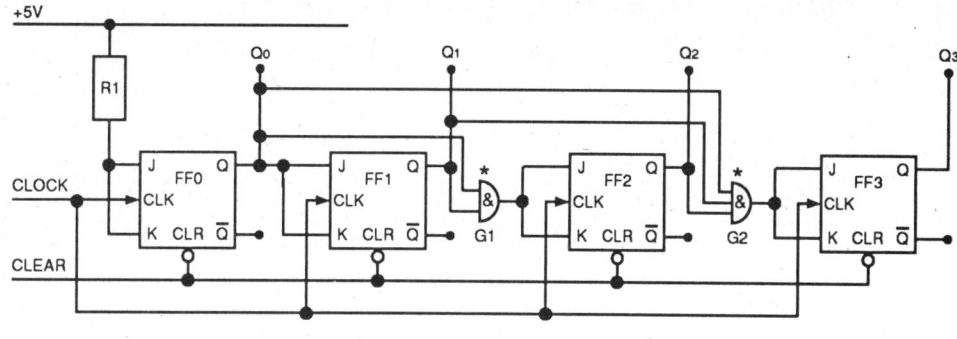

* Old British Standard for AND GATE

Fig 4.19 A 4-bit Synchronous binary up-counter.

Q Short answer question 4.12

Refer to Fig 4.19. Assume that the counter output is 1010_2 or 5_{10}. Explain what will happen if a single clock pulse is applied to the system.

A Answer to SAQ 4.12

With an output of 1010, $Q_0 = 1$; $Q_1 = 0$; $Q_2 = 1$; $Q_3 = 0$

G1 inputs are 1-0 and it's output will be 0. Therefore FF2 will not toggle with the next clock pulse (J=K=0). G2 inputs are 1-0-1 and its output is 0, therefore FF3 cannot toggle (J=K=0) with the next clock pulse. However, both FF0 and FF1 will change with the next pulse. This will give an output count of 0110_2 or 6_{10}. Remember Q_0 is the LSB.

4.13 SHIFT REGISTERS

We have seen that a flip-flop can store one bit of information. A register is a group of flip-flops used for the storage of binary data and a shift register is one which is designed so that the data may be 'shifted' along the register in either direction; left or right. Shift registers have a wide range of applications in digital systems and computers. They can be used for temporary data storage, serial-to-parallel conversion, and vice versa. They are also found within the MPU where they may be used in the processes of multiplication and division.

4.14 SERIAL-IN SERIAL-OUT SHIFT REGISTERS

Two basic circuits for shift registers are shown in Fig 4.20, where (a) uses J-K flip-flops and (b) D-type flip-flops. Although these registers are four bits wide, in practice, a register may be any number of bits wide. In a shift register, the output of each flip-flop is connected to the input of the next flip-flop. Referring to Fig 4.20 (b) if the CLEAR input is momentarily taken LOW all four flip-flops (FFA, FFB, FFC and FFD) will be cleared (all Q outputs = 0). Recall how a D-type flip-flop works; the data on the D input is transferred to the Q output when a clock pulse is applied. Assume that the data word to be input to the shift register is 0101. If a 1 is placed at the input to the first flip-flop and a clock pulse applied that data will be entered into FFA. If the input data is now changed to a zero and another clock pulse applied FFA output will become 0 and FFB 1. On each successive clock pulse the data will shift one place to the right. The movement of data through the shift register is illustrated in Fig 4.21

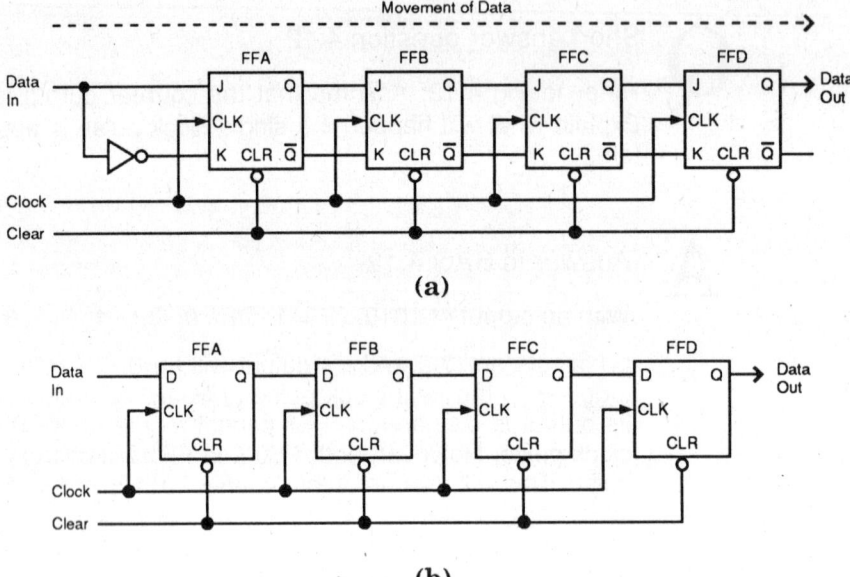

Fig 4.20 A 4-bit shift register using (a) J-K flip-flops (b) D-type flip-flops

4: Sequential logic elements

	FFA	FFB	FFC	FFD
Initially	0	0	0	0
After ONE clock pulse	1	0	0	0
After TWO clock pulses	0	1	0	0
After THREE clock pulses	1	0	1	0
After FOUR clock pulses	0	1	0	1

Note: Before each clock pulse is applied the appropriate data must be applied at the input to FFA

Fig 4.21 Movement of data through a shift-register.

Short answer question 4.13

Refer to Fig 4.20 (a). All Q outputs are cleared initially. The data word to be loaded into the shift register is 0101. Explain how this is achieved.

4: Sequential logic elements

> **A** **Answer to SAQ 4.13**
>
> When using J-K flip-flops if J=0 and K=1 then the device will RESET at the next clock pulse. But if J=1 and K=0 it will SET.
>
> Applying the first 1 to FFA will make J = 1 and K =0 and on receipt of the first clock pulse FFA will store a 1. The J-K inputs to FFB are now 1-0 respectively. The next bit (0) of the input data word is applied to FFA, making its J input =0 and K =1. Hence when the second clock pulse is applied FFA will RESET while FFB will be SET to1. In effect the first bit has been shifted into FFB and the second bit has been taken into FFA. When the third clock pulse is applied the output will be as follows:
>
> FFA= 1; FFB = 0; FFC= 1; FFD = 0.
>
> After the fourth clock pulse all four bits will have been loaded into the shift register.

In the register which we have just described it took four clock pulses to load the four bit word 0101 into the register. In this example the data was fed into, and taken out from, the register one bit at a time, and for this reason it is known as a SERIAL-IN SERIAL-OUT (SISO) shift register. Depending on how the input is applied to, and output taken from, shift registers they are classified as:

1. SERIAL-IN SERIAL-OUT   ; SISO
2. SERIAL-IN PARALLEL OUT   ; SIPO
3. PARALLEL-IN PARALLEL-OUT   ; PIPO
4. PARALLEL-IN SERIAL-OUT   ; PISO

These four classifications are illustrated in Fig. 4.22

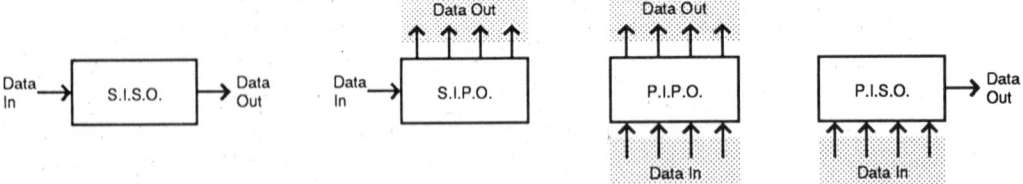

Fig 4.22 Classification of shift registers

Whether applied to the input or output **SERIAL** means that information is either going in to, or coming out from, the flip-flop **one bit at a time**. On the other hand, if data is being loaded into, or being read from, a shift register in **PARALLEL**, all of the data bits are transferred in or out **at the same time**.

4.15 SERIAL-IN PARALLEL-OUT SHIFT REGISTER

The basic circuit of Fig 4.23 can be used as a serial-in parallel-out shift register. The data word is loaded in the usual way (Refer to Fig 4.20 and the accompanying explanation), but instead of taking the output from FFD, it is read out from all four flip-flops simultaneously.

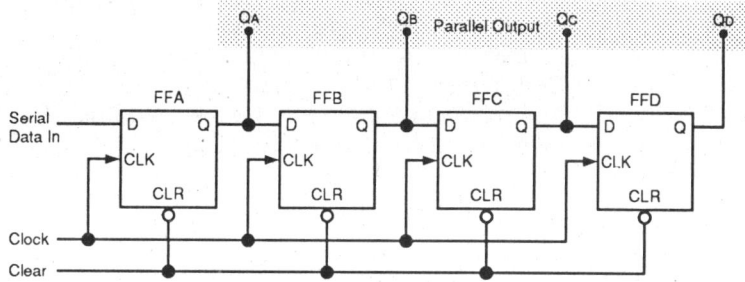

Fig. 4.23 SERIAL-IN PARALLEL-OUT SHIFT REGISTER

4.16 PARALLEL-IN SERIAL-OUT SHIFT REGISTER

Fig 4.24 shows a four-bit parallel-in, serial-out shift register. The operation of the circuit is as follows. A clear pulse is applied to the Clear (CLR) input to initially reset all flip-flops to zero. If the parallel data to be loaded into the register is 0101 and the write enable signal is activated with a HIGH level, FFB and FFD will be set to 1, while FFA and FFC will remain at 0. The PRESET(PS) input to the flip-flops is active LOW. The four-bit data word 0101 is now stored in the shift register.

To read out the stored four-bit word in serial format, clock pulses are applied to shift the stored bits to the right.

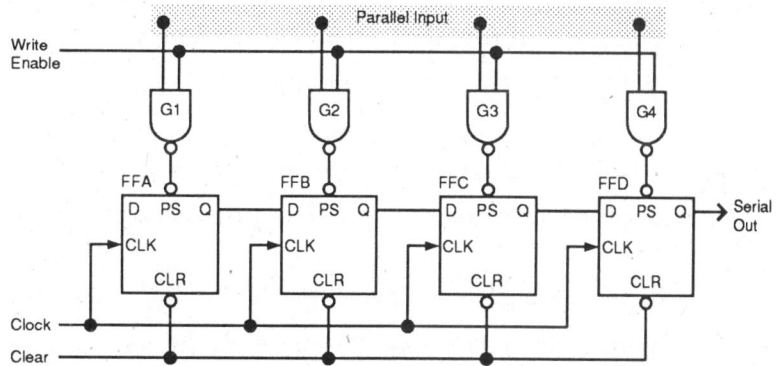

Fig 4.24 Parallel-in serial-out shift register

Q Short answer question 4.14

Refer to the logic diagram of the parallel-in, serial-out shift register and explain how FFA is cleared while FFB is set to 1 when the WRITE signal is enabled with a 1.

4: Sequential logic elements

Answer to SAQ 4.14

Clear all flip-flops initially by applying a LOW pulse to the CLEAR input. The two inputs to G1 are 0 (the data) and 1 (the write enable). Therefore it's output is 1. This has no effect on the PRE-SET input of FFA (because it is active LOW). FFA remains cleared. The inputs to G2 are 1-1, hence it's output is 0. G2 output then presets FFB to a HIGH level.

SUMMARY

- Digital systems can operate in ASYNCHRONOUS or SYNCHRONOUS mode.
- In asynchronous systems, the outputs of logic circuits can change state at any time. For instance, as soon as an input/s change the output may change.
- In synchronous systems, the exact times at which any output can change states are determined by a signal called the CLOCK.
- The clock signal is generally a continuous wavetrain of rectangular pulses. Basically, it is a crystal controlled oscillator.
- A flip-flop is a basic memory device which can store one bit of data.
- In an S-R flip-flop the input condition S=R=1 leads to an indeterminate output.
- D-type and J-K flip-flops are widely used in digital systems.
- Flip-flops may be used to construct counters and shift registers
- A counter is a group of flip-flops arranged so that they indicate the total number of pulses applied to the input.
- A Binary Coded Decimal (BCD) counter counts from 0000_2 to 1001_2 before it recycles.
- A register is a group of memory cells (flip-flops) used to store data.
- A shift register is a register in which the stored data can be moved to the right or the left.
- Depending on how the input is applied to, and the output taken from, shift registers may be classified as follows:

    Serial-In Serial-Out   ; SISO
    Serial-In Parallel Out ; SIPO
    Parallel-In Parallel-Out ; PIPO
    Parallel-In Serial-Out ; PISO

END OF CHAPTER QUESTIONS

Section A: Multiple choice questions (Answers in Appendix A)

1. If the inputs to the NAND latch, shown in Fig 4.25, are X=0; Y=1, the logic levels at Output 1 and Output 2 respectively will be

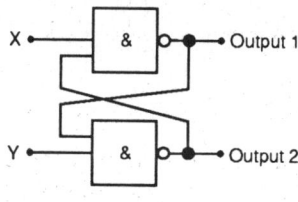

Fig 4.25

   a) 01
   b) 11
   c) 10
   d) 00

2. If a flip-flop is in the SET state, it's Q output will be

   a) 0
   b) 1
   c) tri-stated
   d) indeterminate

3. A 2 MHz signal is applied to the input of a J-K flip-flop which is operating in the 'toggle' mode. The frequency of the signal at the Q output will be

   a) 2 MHz
   b) 4 MHz
   c) 1 MHz
   d) 1 kHz

4. Refer to Fig 4.26

   All flip-flops are initially cleared. How many clock pulses have to be applied to the system before the output from FF3 becomes a HIGH level?

   a) 8
   b) 6
   c) 2
   d) 4

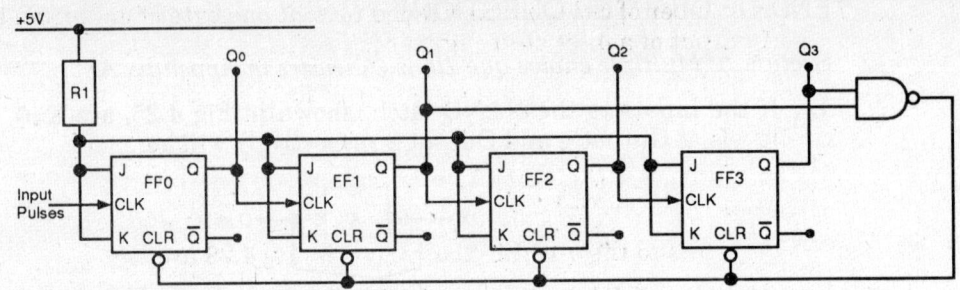

Fig 4.26

5. Refer to Fig 4.27

   The input data is fixed at a LOW level and the outputs are as shown. The number of clock pulses required to give an output of 0000 is

   a) 4
   b) 3
   c) 5
   d) 2

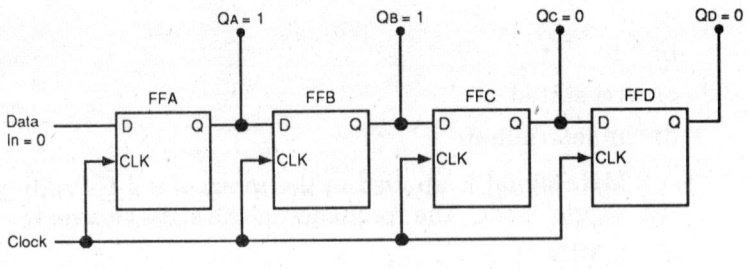

Fig 4.27

6. Refer to Fig 4.28

   This logic circuit operates as a

   a) 4-bit asynchronous counter
   b) 4-bit synchronous counter
   c) BCD counter
   d) Serial-In Serial-Out shift register

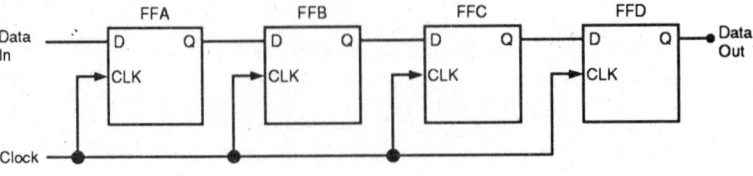

Fig 4.28

7. The number of clock pulses needed to shift one byte of data from the input to the output of a 4-bit shift register is
   a) 32
   b) 16
   c) 11
   d) 12

8. The inputs to the J-K flip-flop, shown in Fig 4.29 are:

   PRESET = CLEAR = 1;   J=K=0

   If a single clock pulse is applied the device will
   a) toggle
   b) set
   c) reset
   d) not change states

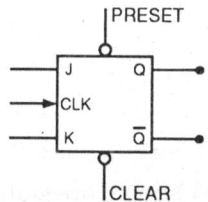

Fig 4.29

9. If the flip-flop, shown in Fig 4.30, is leading edge triggered, which of the following waveforms will appear at the Q output? Assume that the Q output is initially cleared.

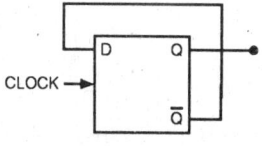

Fig 4.30

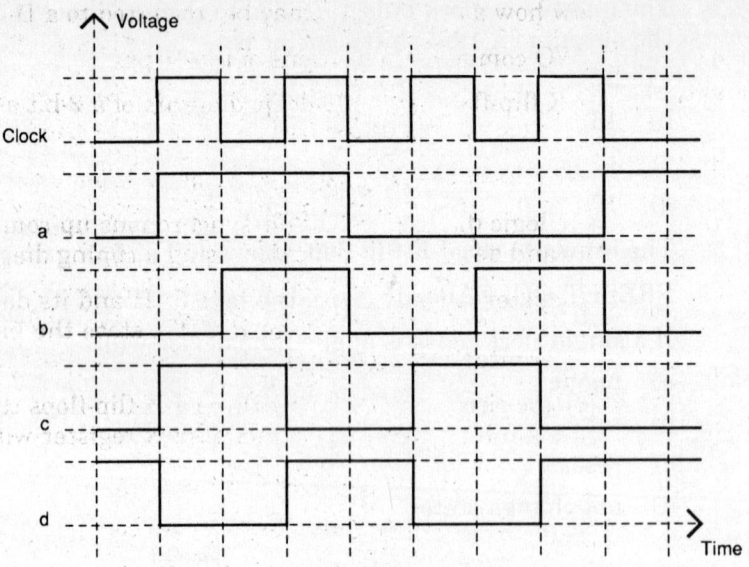

Fig 4.31

10. Refer to Fig 4.32

    The logic circuit shown is a 3-bit
    a) asynchronous binary up-counter
    b) shift register
    c) asynchronous binary down-counter
    d) synchronous binary up-counter

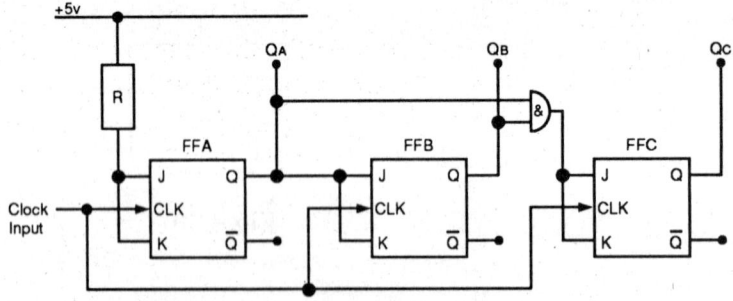

Fig 4.32

Section B: Short answer questions

1. What is the main difference between asynchronous and synchronous systems?

2. Draw the logic diagram of an unclocked S-R flip-flop using four two-input NOR gates. With the aid of a TRUTH TABLE describe its operation.

3. (a) Draw the truth table for a J-K flip-flop

4: Sequential logic elements

(b) Show how a J-K flip-flop may be converted to a D-type flip-flop.

4. State TWO common applications of flip-flops.
5. Using J-K flip-flops draw the logic diagram of a 2-bit asynchronous binary up-counter.
6. Using J-K flip-flops design a MOD-12 asynchronous binary up-counter
7. Draw the logic diagram of a 3-bit synchronous up-counter using master-slave flip-flops and describe its operation using a timing diagram
8. A shift register is loaded with the byte 5AH and its data input is at logic 0. If the data is shifted from LEFT to RIGHT, state the binary code contained in the register after three clock pulses.
9. Draw a logic circuit to show how three J-K flip-flops can be connected together to form a 3-bit, serial-in/serial-out, shift register with a RESET or CLEAR facility

Chapter 5
Logic Families

The two most popular logic families, TTL and CMOS, are introduced in this chapter. The criteria which system designers use for selecting a logic family are outlined. A comparison table for TTL and CMOS logic families and handling precautions for integrated circuits are also included.

5.1 INTRODUCTION

Although digital logic systems and computers could be built using discrete (separate or individual) components, such as, transistors, resistors, capacitors and diodes, modern systems utilise integrated circuits (ICs). The cost of ICs is very low. Besides a substantial reduction in size, they offer other advantages and benefits compared with discrete circuitry. Their reduced power consumption makes the digital system more economical to operate. They have a high reliability against failure, so the digital system needs less repairs. The operating speed is higher, which makes them suitable for high speed applications. The use of ICs reduces the number of external wiring connections because many of the connections are internal to the package. Because of all of these advantages, digital systems and computers are always designed with integrated circuits.

5.2 LEVELS OF INTEGRATION

The first objective in the development of integrated circuits was the fabrication (construction) of a complete logic gate on a single silicon chip and its encapsulation in a suitable package. However, it soon became clear, that several similar gates could be fabricated on a single chip at very little additional cost. In order to obtain the lowest cost per gate as many gates as possible are formed on one chip and encapsulated in a single package. This increasing complexity, coupled with the wide range of logic circuit types, has generated the need for definitions of complexity levels. These are known as levels (or scales) of integration.

The following ranges are approximate and are only intended to give a good guide to the number of gates that may be put down on a single piece of silicon and to the complexity of the various digital ICs.

SSI: Small Scale Integration

A single IC package containing **up to about 10 gates**. Examples are ICs containing 4 AND gates or six NOT (inverter) gates (see Fig 5.2)

MSI: Medium Scale Integration

A single IC package containing **approximately 10 to 100 gates**. Examples of MSI devices include counters and shift registers.

LSI: Large Scale Integration

A single IC package containing from **100 to 10 000 gates.** 8-bit microprocessors are classified as LSI devices.

VLSI: Very Large Scale Integration

A single IC package containing between **10 000 and 100 000 gates**. 16-bit microprocessor chips and high density memories fall into this category.

ULSI: Ultra Large Scale Integration

A single IC package containing **more than 100 000 gates.**

Multiple choice question 5.1

In terms of levels of integration, a single IC containing 50 logic gates, would be classified as:

a) SSI
b) MSI
c) LSI
d) VLSI

Answer to MCQ 5.1

B

5.3 IC PACKAGES

Integrated circuits are made in several different packages. These packages differ in the method used to mount the IC package on the printed circuit board (PCB), the amount of circuitry contained within each chip, and the number of external connections to the chip. Fig 5.1 shows the most common IC packages.

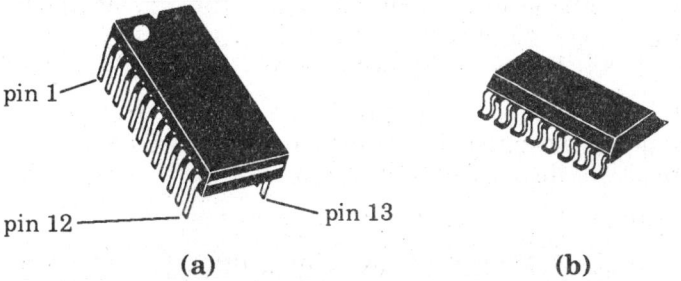

Fig 5.1 Common IC packages:
(a) DIL; (b) Surface mount device (SMD)

The dual in-line (DIL) package, illustrated in Fig 5.1 (a), is at present, the most widely used one. Note the notch on one end. When you orientate the notch to the left, pin 1 is located below the notch. On some packages a small dot (or circle) on top of the package indicates the location of pin 1.

5: Logic families

Fig 5.1 (b) is one of the newest package types. It is designed for surface mounting. In this case, each chip is soldered, using a machine, to the surface of the printed circuit board. This is replacing the traditional method of inserting IC pins through the PCB and soldering on the reverse side. The advantage of this approach is that it makes the PCBs much smaller and cheaper to manufacture. The disadvantage is that it makes them virtually impossible to repair unless you have a sophisticated surface mount device soldering workstation.

Fig 5.2 shows the data sheets for a number of SSI packages. The data sheet for a particular IC is used to indicate:

a. the power supply pins to the chip
b. where the input/s may be applied
c. where the gate output is taken from
d. the number of gates within the chip

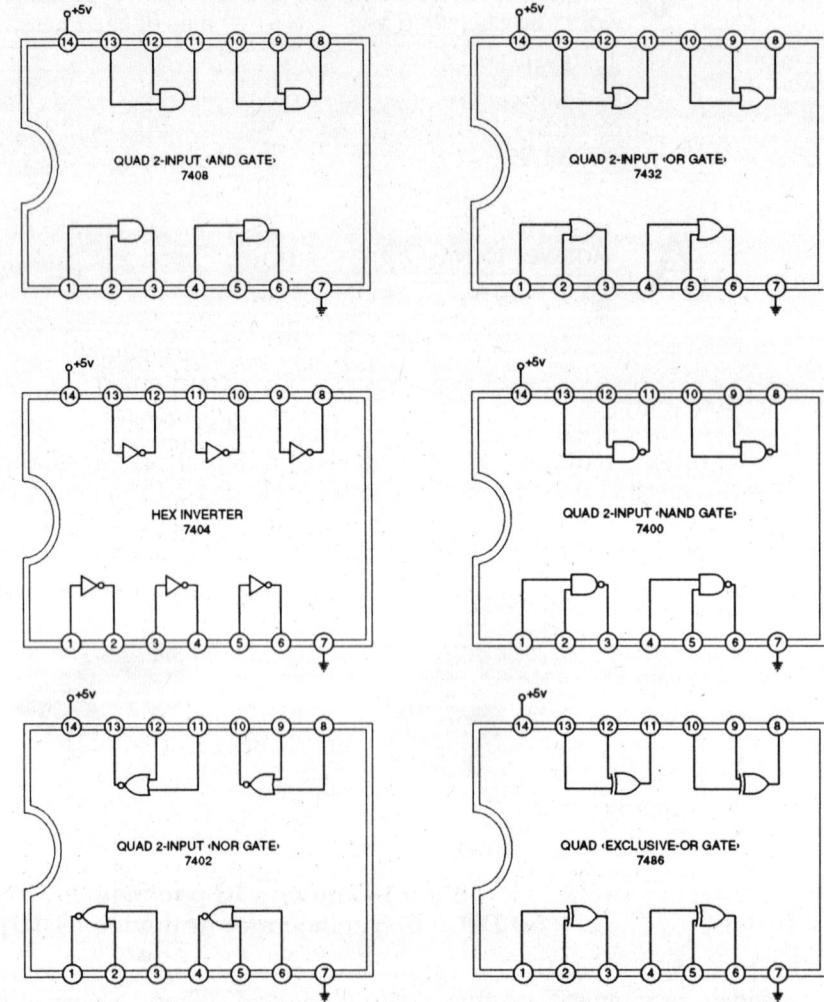

Fig 5.2 Data sheets for 7400 TTL SSI Integrated circuits

5.4 CRITERIA FOR SELECTING A LOGIC FAMILY

With the widespread use of digital logic ICs comes the necessity to understand these devices as system components. All of the logic gates (Chapter 3) and sequential logic elements (Chapter 4) and numerous other devices are available within the TTL (Transistor Transistor Logic) or CMOS (Complementary Metal Oxide Semiconductor) logic families. TTL uses bipolar transistors (NPN and PNP) as the main circuit element whereas CMOS uses unipolar MOSFET (Metal Oxide Semiconductor Field Effect Transistor) transistors.

In order to be able to make an informed choice between logic families it is necessary to understand the main characteristics of each family. For example, it may well be that the most important consideration in a particular system is that minimum power is dissipated; for another system maximum speed of operation might be the overriding factor and so on.

Designers usually select a logic family on the basis of the following criteria:

a. Speed of operation

b. Power dissipation

c. Fan-out

d. Noise margin or noise immunity

e. Availability and Cost

Speed of Operation

The speed of a logic family is measured by the propagation delay time, which is the time delay between the application of an input pulse and the resultant change in the output of that device. Fig 5.3 illustrates propagation delays for a NOT gate (inverter). The difference in nS (nano seconds) from when the input has completed 50% of its transition to the point where the output has completed 50% of its transition is the propagation delay time. Examination of the waveforms shows that there are two propagation delay times. One, called t_{phl}, is the delay time when the input causes the output to change from a HIGH to a LOW level, and the other, t_{plh}, is the delay time when the output goes from a LOW to a HIGH level. For a NAND or NOT gate, t_{phl} is 7nS and t_{plh} is 11nS. Generally the propagation delay for the family is quoted as the average of the two delays; $(7 + 11)/2 = 9nS$.

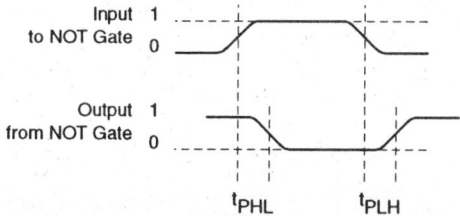

Fig 5.3 Propagation delays for a TTL NOT/NAND gate

5: Logic families

 Multiple choice question 5.2

The average propagation delay, quoted in nano seconds (nS), for a quad two-input TTL NAND gate is approximately:

a) 100 nS

b) 1 nS

c) 5 nS

d) 10 nS

 Answer to MCQ 5.2

D

Power Dissipation

Every IC requires a certain amount of electrical power to operate. This power is supplied by the power supply unit (PSU) which generates the necessary D.C. voltages for the system, from the A.C. mains input. The positive power supply pin on the chip, is labelled V_{cc} for TTL or V_{dd} for MOS devices and the ground pin is generally denoted by GND. (sometimes V_{ss} for MOS).

Generally an IC contains several circuits. Most typical power measurements are made when half of the circuits on the chip are in the 1 state and the others are in the 0 state. Under these conditions let the average current be $I_{cc\,(ave)}$. See Fig 5.4. Then the average power drain from the power supply is:

Power Dissipation = $V_{cc} \times I_{cc\,(ave)}$

$P_{D\,(Ave)}$ $\qquad = V_{cc} \times I_{cc\,(Ave)}$ Watts (W)

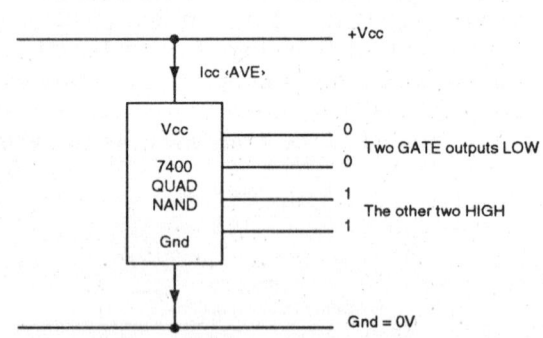

Fig 5.4 IC power dissipation

Power dissipation is important because the heat generated by the chip will increase with power dissipation. Excessive power dissipation:

a. drives up the cost of the power supplies.

b. increases the amount of heat generated within the package and in the vicinity of the device.

c. may lead to component breakdown from excessive heat which is a prime cause of failure in electronic circuits and systems.

For these reasons, it is clear, that the design engineer must pay attention to the power dissipation of the devices which make up the system. Otherwise, the power supply will become over expensive and the cost of repairs and maintenance may escalate.

Compared with TTL, CMOS dissipates very little power at low frequencies, but its dissipation increases as the frequency increases.

Short answer question 5.1

If the average current taken by a package consisting of four NAND gates is 8 mA (milli Amperes) calculate the average power dissipated by (i) the complete package (ii) an individual gate. Express your answers in mW (milli Watts)

Answer to SAQ 5.1

(i) The average power taken by the package is:

$$P_{D\,(ave)} = {}^{8}/_{1000} \times 5$$

$$= 0.008 \times 5$$

$$= 0.040 \text{ W} = 40 \text{mW}$$

(ii) One NAND gate requires an average power of $40/4 = 10$ mW.

Speed-Power Product

There are many versions (or 'series') of the TTL basic gate. The speed-power product is an important parameter for comparing these (also applies to other logic families). This is the product of the propagation delay and the power consumption measured in picojoules (pJ). Clearly, a low value of speed-power product is desirable. Researchers are continually striving to reduce the speed-power product by either increasing the speed of an IC (reducing its propagation delay) or by decreasing its power dissipation. Because of the nature of transistor circuits, it is difficult to do both.

Fan-out

In general, the output from a logic gate is required to drive (supply enough current) for several logic inputs. Usually fan-out is determined for a standard gate in a family, driving other gates in the same family and is defined as the maximum number of standard inputs that a gate output can drive reliably. This means that

5: Logic families

the output voltage from the device must not fall outside the limits for levels 1 and 0 as specified by the manufacturer.

Fig 5.5 illustrates that a standard TTL NAND gate output is driving ten inputs of other similar gates. In this case the fan-out is 10. High fan-out is an advantage, because additional drivers are not needed to supply many loads connected to the same source. CMOS because of its high input impedance, has the largest fan-out capability of any logic family.

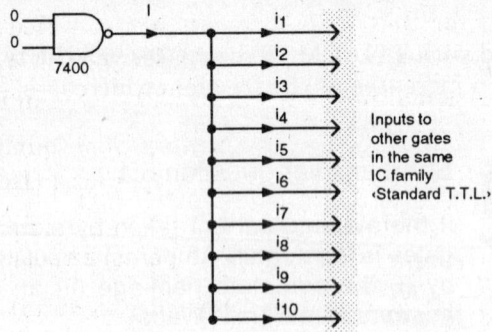

Fig 5.5 Fan-out of a logic gate

Q Short answer question 5.2

When comparing CMOS with TTL which one

a) dissipates less power

b) has a greater fan-out

A Answer to SAQ 5.2

a) CMOS (But power dissipation increases with frequency)

b) CMOS

Q Short answer question 5.3

Briefly describe what is meant by the 'FAN-OUT' of a logic gate.

A Answer to SAQ 5.3

Fan-out specifies the number of standard loads that the output of a gate can drive without impairment of its normal operation. A standard load is defined as the current flowing in the input of another gate in the same IC family.

Noise Immunity or Margin

Because the devices within a system are interconnected via conductors (copper tracks on PCBs etc.) stray magnetic and electric fields can induce a voltage on the connecting tracks and wires between logic circuits. These unwanted or spurious signals are called noise and can sometimes cause the voltage at the input to a logic gate to drop below the minimum for a HIGH input level ($V_{IH\,(min)}$) or rise above the maximum for a LOW input level ($V_{IL\,(max)}$)

The limits for these input signals are specified by the manufacturers who also publish d.c. values of noise margin, giving both typical and worst case values.

The d.c. noise margins for TTL are illustrated in Fig 5.6, where:

$V_{OH\,(min)}$ = HIGH level output voltage (minimum). This is the minimum voltage level at a logic circuit output for a HIGH level.

$V_{OL\,(max)}$ = LOW level output voltage (maximum). The maximum voltage level at a logic circuit output for a LOW level.

$V_{IH\,(min)}$ = HIGH level input voltage (minimum). The voltage level required for a logical 1 at an input. Any voltage below this will not be recognised as a HIGH level by the logic circuit.

$V_{IL\,(max)}$ = LOW level input voltage (maximum). Any voltage above this level will not be recognised as a LOW by the logic circuit.

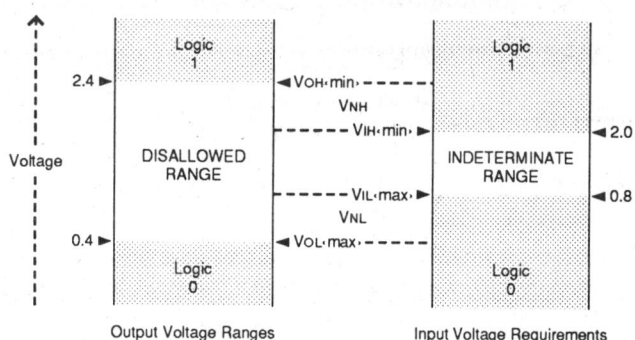

Fig 5.6 DC noise margins for TTL

The noise immunity of a logic circuit is a measure of its ability to tolerate noise voltages on its inputs.

Fig 5.6 shows the voltage levels for a gate output in the HIGH and LOW states. The minimum output voltage for a HIGH level is 2.4V and the maximum for a LOW is 0.4V. The disallowed range must be avoided. On a gate input the minimum voltage to be recognised as a HIGH level is 2.0V and the maximum for a LOW level is 0.8V. Voltages in the indeterminate range should be avoided because they will produce an unpredictable response.

5: Logic families

From the diagram:

The HIGH level noise margin (V_{NH}) = $V_{OH\,(min)}$ − $V_{IH\,(min)}$
= 2.4V − 2.0V
= 0.4V
= 400 mV

& the LOW level noise margin (V_{NL}) = $V_{IL\,(max)}$ − $V_{OL\,(max)}$
= 0.8 − 0.4
= 400 mV

If output voltages enter the disallowed range or input voltages the indeterminate range then the manufacturer does not guarantee satisfactory operation of the logic circuits. Good design practice dictates that the recommended voltage ranges are strictly adhered to.

In summary, noise margin is the limit of a noise voltage which may be present without impairing the proper operation of a logic circuit.

The higher the figure for noise margin the better the device in that respect.

Short answer question 5.4

Write down the formula for HIGH state noise margin.

Answer to SAQ 5.4

V_{NH} = $V_{OH\,(min)}$ − $V_{IH\,(min)}$

Availability and Cost

In addition to the factors discussed previously, availability and cost, must also be considered. Delays in obtaining ICs would retard design progress. Availability also refers to the number of different types of chips available. In a wide series a complex function may be available in a single chip that would have to be built up from a number of less complex chips in another family.

The cost of ICs should be a relatively minor factor affecting the choice of a logic family. Both TTL and CMOS have been mass produced in large quantities and they are available at competitive prices. Other less common logic families would, of course, be more expensive.

5.5 THE TTL LOGIC FAMILY

The Texas Instruments (TI) Transistor Transistor Logic (TTL) logic family was introduced as a standard product line in 1964. Designated semiconductor network (or SN) series 54. The original devices were intended primarily for the military market, where size, power consumption, and reliability requirements were paramount. Soon afterwards TI was able to offer these circuits as Series 74. The latter were lower cost versions with guaranteed operating conditions over a 0° to +70° Centigrade range. Series 54 covers the temperature range −55° to +125°C.

The 74 series will operate reliably over the voltage range 4.75 to 5.25V whereas the 54 series can tolerate a voltage variation of 4.5 to 5.5V. Because of its greater tolerance of voltage and temperature variations, the 54 series is more expensive. It finds wide use in military and space applications where extreme ranges of conditions may be encountered. The 74 series is used in industrial applications.

At the time of writing, the TTL family still enjoys the most widespread use in applications that require SSI and MSI devices.

The original TTL 74 series became known as the STANDARD TTL series. Many semiconductor manufacturers now produce TTL ICs. Fortunately, they all use the same numbering system.

Devices are coded as follows:

p74XXs ; p is a prefix which is unique to a manufacturer.
SN= Texas; N = Signetics; MC = Motorola.
DM = National Semiconductor

XX is a two or three digit number which specifies the device function (e.g. Quad 2-input NAND)

s A suffix which may vary from one manufacturer to another; it specifies the package (e.g. plastic or ceramic) and other mechanical features.

Examples:

N7404 is a Signetics hex inverter.

SN7400 is a Texas Instruments quad 2-input NAND

DM7408 is a National Semiconductor quad 2-input AND gate.

Another letter/s may also appear between the 74 and the XX. These are used to signify other types of TTL ICs which have been developed.

Other TTL Series

In order to make available a wider choice of speed and power characteristics several other TTL subfamilies have been introduced. Each of these will now be described briefly.

Low-Power TTL: 74L Series

This is known as the **74L Series**. This series was developed for applications where minimum power dissipation is required. A typical NAND gate in this series has an average power dissipation of 1mW, compared with 10 mW for standard TTL. However, the 74L series has much longer propagation delay; 33 nS against 9 nS for standard TTL. The 74L series is now obsolete because of other developments that have taken place both in TTL and CMOS.

High-Speed TTL: 74H Series

74H is a high (H) speed TTL series. The average propagation delay for 74H devices is about 6 nS. However, the increased speed is accomplished at the expense of increased power dissipation. The basic NAND gate in this series has an average power dissipation of 23mW. With the development of Schottky TTL the 74H series has become obsolete.

Schottky TTL: 74S Series

The 74, 74H and 74L TTL Series operated with the internal transistors fully saturated, which causes delays when they are being switched, and limits the circuits switching speed.

The German physicist, W.H. Schottky, discovered a way of not allowing the transistors to go as deeply into saturation, which resulted in an increase in switching speed. A 74S00 NAND gate has an average propagation delay of 3nS, which is twice as fast as the 74H00. The average power dissipation is approximately 20mW. Thus, 74S has twice the speed of 74H at about the same power dissipation. This is why the 74H series has become obsolete.

Low-Power Schottky TTL: 74 LS Series

The 74LS series consumes less power than the 74S series. A NAND gate in the LS series has an a typical propagation delay of about 9.5 nS and an average power dissipation of 2mW. Although its switching speed is roughly the same as standard TTL, its power dissipation is much less, so the 74LS series has gradually replaced the 74 series in those applications where relatively high speed operation is required at minimum power consumption. It has become the 'mainstay' of the TTL family, and it can be found in almost all new designs that do not require maximum speed. Its leading position, however, will gradually be taken over by the new improved Advanced Low-Power Schottky series; 74ALS. The latter offers an improvement over the 74LS series in both speed and power dissipation.

Table 5.1 gives typical values for some of the more important characteristics of each of the TTL series. The figures quoted are for a NAND gate in each series. The maximum clock rate is specified as the maximum frequency that can be used to toggle a J-K flip-flop. This gives an indication of the frequency range over which each IC series can be operated.

TTL Series	74	74L	74H	74S	74LS	74ALS
Propagation Delay (nS)	9	33	6	3	9.5	4
Power Dissipation (mW)	10	1	23	20	2	1
Speed-power Product (pJ)	90	33	138	60	19	4
Max clock rate (MHz)	35	3	50	125	45	70
Fan-out	10	10	10	10	20	20

Table 5.1 TTL logic families

Short answer question 5.5

Refer to Table 5.1

i) Which TTL series is best at high frequencies?

ii) Which series have essentially become obsolete?

Answer to SAQ 5.5

i) The 74 Schottky series: 74S, because a flip-flop in that series can toggle at a frequency of 125 MHz.

ii) 74H (high speed) and 74L (low-power)

Unconnected (Floating) TTL Inputs

Any input to a TTL circuit that is left disconnected (not connected to anything else) acts exactly like a logical 1 applied to that input. When an input is left unconnected, it is said to 'float'.

In some applications not all of the gate inputs will be used. The question then arises 'what do we do with the unused inputs?'. For instance, a particular application needs a 2-input NAND gate, but only three input NAND gates are available.

Fig 5.7 shows three possible alternatives.

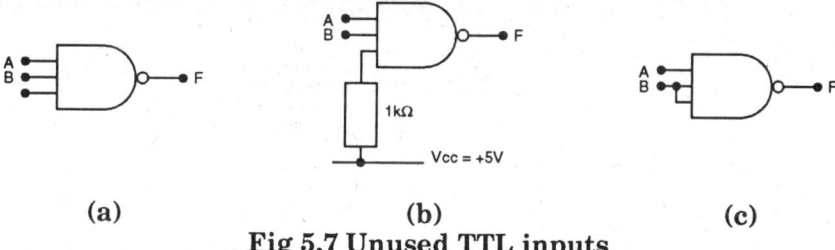

(a)　　　　　　　(b)　　　　　　　(c)

Fig 5.7 Unused TTL inputs

In Fig 5.7 (a) the unused input is left disconnected, which means that it acts as a HIGH level. The NAND gate output is therefore F = NOT (A . B . 1) = NOT (A . B), which is the desired result. Although it gives the correct output, it is highly undesirable to leave an input disconnected, because it is liable to pick up any stray signals caused by magnetic or electric fields and these could cause the gate to malfunction.

A better technique is shown in Fig 5.7 (b), where the unused input is connected to +5V via a 1k Ohm resistor. This ensures a HIGH input on that pin at all times. The resistor is included to prevent power supply spikes from damaging the IC.

A third possibility is illustrated in Fig 5.7 (c), where the unused input is tied to one of the other inputs of the gate. With this technique, there is a danger that the fan-out of the driving gate may be exceeded, because current now has to be supplied for three inputs instead of two. Otherwise it is a satisfactory method.

5.6 MOS LOGIC FAMILIES

MOS (Metal Oxide Semiconductor) technology derives its name from the basic MOS structure in which a metal electrode is insulated from the semiconductor substrate by a very thin layer of silicon-dioxide.

The transistors used in MOS technology are MOSFETs (Metal Oxide Semiconductor Field Effect Transistors).

The chief advantages of MOSFETS are that it is relatively simple and inexpensive to fabricate, it consumes very little power and occupies very little chip space. TTL technology which uses bipolar transistors (NPN and PNP) is more complex to fabricate. One TTL transistor requires about fifty times more space on the piece of silicon than a MOSFET transistor. This in effect means that a MOS IC can accommodate more circuit elements on a single chip than bipolar ICs. Hence MOS technology is more suited to large scale integration (LSI) and very large scale integration (VLSI). Among the devices that use MOS technology are microprocessors and memories.

The principal disadvantage of MOS ICs is their relatively slow operating speed compared with bipolar IC families. In any application where speed is not the prime concern MOS devices are an attractive alternative to bipolar logic.

Digital logic circuits employing MOSFETS fall into three categories:

1. PMOS: (P-channel devices)
2. NMOS: (N-channel devices)
3. CMOS: (Complementary Metal Oxide Semiconductor, which uses both P-channel and N-channel devices)

The first microprocessors from Intel, the 4004 and the 8008, were fabricated using PMOS technology. However, because NMOS is much faster than PMOS the next generations of microprocessors used NMOS.

CMOS LOGIC

CMOS is widely used in MSI and SSI applications. Its main features are:

a. Can operate over the 5-15V range, but some circuits may be operated at 3V or 18V.
b. Its main advantage is low power dissipation. It only uses a fraction of the power needed by TTL low-power or low-power Schottky.
c. It has a high immunity to noise.
d. CMOS is generally slower than TTL, although the new high-speed CMOS series can compete with the 74 and 74LS series.

Most of the available CMOS devices belong to the 4000B series.

UNUSED CMOS INPUTS

The golden rule is 'CMOS inputs should never be left disconnected'. All CMOS inputs have to be tied either to a HIGH level or GND or to another input. An unconnected CMOS input is susceptible to noise (unwanted signals), which could result in malfunction of the device.

OTHER LOGIC FAMILIES

Besides TTL and CMOS a number of other logic technologies are available. Among these are:

a. **ECL: Emitter Coupled Logic**

   Like TTL this also uses bipolar transistors. However, in these devices transistor saturation is prevented, thus increasing switching speed. The propagation delay of these devices is very low; less than 1nS for some versions. **Maximum clock rates of up to 600MHz are possible using ECL.** Therefore it is used for very high speed applications.

b. **I^2L: Integration Injection Logic**

   I^2L also uses bipolar transistors. This type of logic is not used for discrete gate ICs. It is used mainly for LSI/VLSI functions.

   It is **used in digital watches.**

COMPARISON BETWEEN IC LOGIC FAMILIES

The main characteristics of some of the most popular logic families are given in Table 5.2. Typical figures are quoted.

Series	74	74S	74LS	74ALS	4000B	ECL
Propagation Delay (nS)	9	3	9.5	4	50	1
Power Dissipation per gate (mW)	10	20	2	1.2	0.001	40
Maximum Clock Rate (MHz) {For a flip-flop}	35	125	45	70	12	300
Worst-case noise margin (V)	0.4	0.3	0.3	0.4	1.5	0.25
Fan-out	10	10	20	20	50	25

Table 5.2 IC Logic families

Short answer question 5.6

Refer to Table 5.2.

(i) Which series offers the best noise margin?

(ii) Which series dissipates most power?

> **Answer to SAQ 5.6**
>
> (i) CMOS 4000B
>
> (ii) ECL

Remember that the lowest figure for propagation delay and power dissipation is desirable, whereas the highest figure for clock rate, noise margin and fan-out is preferred.

5.7 HANDLING MOS DEVICES

All electronic devices, to varying degrees, are sensitive to damage by static electricity. MOS devices are especially susceptible to damage from static electric charges, while the bipolar logic families like TTL and ECL are much less so. The human body is a great source of static electricity. For example, simply walking across a nylon carpet can generate static charges of up to 30,000 volts in your body. If you then touch the input pin of a MOS IC a sizeable electric charge will be applied to the device and this may result in its destruction.

To prevent accidental damage to MOS ICs (microprocessors, memories, CMOS logic etc.) the following precautions are recommended.

Storage and transport

Store and transport the circuits in their original packing. Alternatively, use may be made of a conductive material (aluminium foil) or special IC carrier that either short-circuits all leads or insulates them from external contact. Store PCB boards in conductive plastic or metallic envelopes.

Testing or handling

1. Connect the chassis of all test instruments, soldering iron tips, and your workbench (if metal) to earth. This prevents the build up of static electric charges on these devices that could be transferred to any printed circuit board or IC that may come in contact with them.

2. Electrically connect the person doing the testing or handling to the conductive surface with a special wrist strap. The wrist strap contains a large resistor that limits current to a non lethal value should you accidentally touch a 'live' voltage while working with the equipment.

3. Signals should not be applied to the inputs while the power supply is off. All unused input leads should be connected to either the supply voltage or ground.

4. Soldering: Soldering iron tips, including those of low voltage irons, or soldering baths should also be kept at the same potential as the MOS circuits and the PCB.

5. Dress personnel in clothing of non-electrostatic material (no wool, silk or synthetic fibres).

6. To prevent permanent damage due to transient voltages, do not insert or remove MOS devices, or printed circuit boards with MOS devices, from test sockets or systems with power on.

SUMMARY

- Chips may be classified by the number of gates fabricated on a single piece of silicon. This leads us to talk of various levels of integration for ICs.
    - SSI : Small Scale Integration
    - MSI : Medium Scale Integration
    - LSI : Large Scale Integration
    - VLSI : Very Large Scale Integration
    - ULSI : Ultra Large Scale Integration

- Common IC package types are DIL (Dual in-line) and SMD (Surface mount device)

- Popular digital IC logic families are:

    TTL : Transistor Transistor Logic. Known as STANDARD TTL and its subfamilies;

    Schottky TTL   : 74S
    Low-Power Schottky   : 74LS
    Advanced Low-Power Schottky :   74ALS

    CMOS: Complementary Metal Oxide Semiconductor
    ECL : Emitter Coupled Logic
    I^2L : Integration Injection Logic

- CMOS ICs dissipate very little power.

- ECL is a very high speed logic family.

- The factors that have to be considered when choosing a logic family are:
    - Propagation delay
    - Power dissipation
    - Maximum clock rate
    - Noise margins
    - Fan-out
    - Range of functions available
    - Operating voltage
    - Cost

- Unconnected or floating TTL inputs act like a HIGH level. Generally, it is best to tie them to +5 volts through a resistor.

5: Logic families

- Unused CMOS inputs must either be tied to a HIGH level or GND or another input.
- Special precautions have to be observed when handling MOS devices or printed circuit boards with MOS components.

CHAPTER REVIEW QUESTIONS

Section A: Multiple choice questions (Answers in Appendix A)

1. An IC containing 8 gates would be classified as:
    a) ULSI
    b) VLSI
    c) MSI
    d) SSI

2. A small dot or circle printed on top of an IC indicates:
    a) V_{cc}
    b) Gnd
    c) Pin 14
    d) Pin 1

3. Generally, the speed of operation of a logic gate is quoted in:
    a) seconds
    b) milli seconds
    c) nano seconds
    d) micro seconds

4. The power supply pin of a TTL chip is generally labelled:
    a) V_{DD}
    b) V_{cc}
    c) Gnd
    d) V_{ss}

5. Which one of the following logic families dissipates least power?
    a) standard TTL
    b) ECL
    c) low-power Schottky TTL
    d) CMOS

6. The main advantages of CMOS when compared with TTL are
    a) higher power consumption with high fan-out
    b) higher speed operation with low power consumption

c) lower power consumption with low fan-out
d) lower power consumption and better noise margins

7. The usual power supply requirements for a 74 Series TTL device is
    a) +5V with a 5% tolerance
    b) +3 to +18V
    c) +5V with a 10% tolerance
    d) +12V

8. SMD on a data sheet for an integrated circuit means
    a) single memory device
    b) serial mode data
    c) surface mount device
    d) synchronous mode device

9. An unused input to a TTL NAND gate will act like
    a) a tri-state input
    b) a low level
    c) a high level
    d) an open circuit

10. When the maximum clock rate is quoted for a logic family, it applies to a
    a) single logic gate
    b) counter
    c) shift register
    d) flip-flop

Section B: Short answer questions

1. Give ONE example of a device which would be classified as
    i) SSI
    ii) MSI
    iii) LSI
    iv) VLSI

2. Briefly describe the meaning of each of the following:
    i) propagation delay
    ii) power dissipation
    iii) noise margin
    iv) fan-out

3. LIST typical values for each of the following in relation to low-power Schottky TTL.
    i) Propagation delay

5: Logic families

   ii) Power dissipation
   iii) Noise margin
   iv) Supply voltage
   v) The voltage level for a high output.

4. Using typical figures complete table 5.3

Logic Family	74 {STD}	4000B
Propagation Delay (nS)		
Power Dissipation (mW)		
Maximum clock rate (MHz)		

Table 5.3

5. Draw a top view of a typical 14-pin DIL package. Label all pin numbers, carefully indicating pin 1.

6. LIST 5 handling precautions for MOS ICs and printed circuit boards with MOS components.

7. Discuss alternative methods for dealing with unused TTL and CMOS inputs.

8. A logic circuit which operates at a frequency of 50kHz is to be used in portable equipment which is powered by a PP9, 9 volt battery. Which logic family would you choose for the design of the circuit?

9. Refer to Fig 5.8
   i) Identify the manufacturer of the ICs
   ii) To which logic family do the ICs belong?
   iii) At what voltage level would these chips operate?
   iv) State the number of similar gate inputs that may be driven by the Sum output.
   v) How much power is dissipated by each gate?

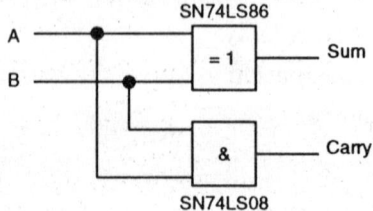

Fig 5.8

10. Refer to Fig 5.9
    i) Which pin is used for the positive power supply?
    ii) Which pin is the ground pin?
    iii) To which logic family does the IC belong?
    iv) Is the function provided by this IC available in another logic technology? If so, state the type number.

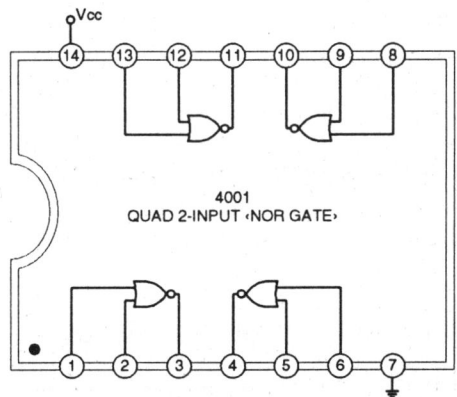

Fig 5.9

Chapter 6

Inside the Microprocessor – A First Look

The microprocessor is the most important component in a microcomputer. As well as generating the necessary control signals for the complete system it also performs all of the processing. Whether your involvement is in programming, system design or troubleshooting a good knowledge of the internal organisation of the microprocessor is essential. Because real microprocessors are fairly complex we will begin our study of the internal organisation of the microprocessor using a simplified functional block diagram. In successive chapters this diagram will be extended to introduce most of the features found in eight bit microprocessors.

6.1 MICROPROCESSOR ARCHITECTURE

The architecture of a building refers to its structure. For example, an office block may be divided into a number of different sections, such as, a reception area, individual office units, washroom facilities and access space linking all parts of the building. Similarly, the architecture of a microprocessor relates to its internal structure or organisation which shows how its internal subsystems interact and how they are linked together.

In summary, **microprocessor architecture** refers to the internal structure or **organisation of a microprocessor.**

For anyone actively involved in microprocessor applications it is important that differences between microprocessors are understood. This would enable an engineer to select the best microprocessor for a particular application. When comparing processors essential questions have to be asked.

1. What is the length of the microprocessor's data word?
2. How much memory can the processor directly address?
3. At what speed does the processor execute instructions?
4. What registers are available to the programmer?
5. How many registers does the processor have?
6. What range of instructions does the processor support?
7. What are the addressing modes?

The first three of these follow next. Details of some of the registers appear later in this chapter, with additional coverage in Chapters 7 and 8. The instruction set and the addressing modes are covered in Chapter 11.

6: Inside the microprocessor – a first look

 Multiple Choice Question 6.1

Select the one microprocessor characteristic which is not an architectural feature.

a) data word length

b) instruction set

c) number of processor registers

d) manufacturer

 Answer to MCQ 6.1

D

6.2 MICROPROCESSOR WORD LENGTHS

Microprocessors are most often compared in terms of the lengths of their data words. The first ever microprocessor was the 4-bit Intel 4004. The length of the data word for this processor was 4-bits. Each microprocessor works on a data word of fixed length. This simplifies the design of the processor. Presently, the most common word lengths are, 8-bit, 16-bit and 32-bit. Data words of these lengths are illustrated in Fig 6.1

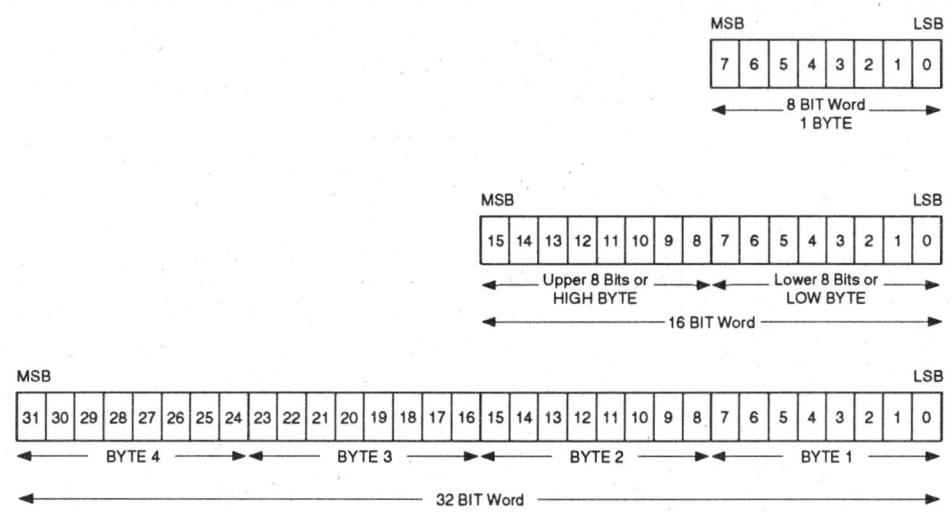

Fig. 6.1   8, 16 and 32-bit words

The 8-bit data word is so common that it has been given the special name **byte**. From Fig 6.1 we can see that the 16-bit word is made up of two bytes. The bits 0 to 7 are called the low byte and the bits 8 to 15 the high byte. The 32-bit word con-

6: Inside the microprocessor – a first look

sists of four bytes. Irrespective of the word length, the digit furthest to the left is referred to as the **Most Significant Bit**, abbreviated to **MSB**, whereas the digit furthest to the right is called the **Least Significant Bit** or the **LSB**.

The majority of Personal Computers i.e. PCs being marketed at present are either 16-bit or 32-bit machines. In relation to PCs the word **byte** is frequently encountered. For example:

i) the storage capacity of disks is quoted in terms of bytes

ii) the amount of Random Access Memory (RAM) in a personal computer system would typically be 1, 2 or 4 million bytes, known as mega bytes (Mb).

Generally, the processor with the longer word length will solve problems faster, but this does not mean that we should always design a product with the latest microprocessor, which has the longest word length. The longer the data word, the more expensive the processor. Cost will have to be considered and so in practice it may be a trade-off between speed and cost.

Short Answer Question 6.1

a) How many bits are there in a byte?

b) How many bits are needed for a word of two bytes?

Answer to SAQ 6.1

(a) 8 BITS   (b) 16 BITS

6.3 DIRECTLY ADDRESSABLE MEMORY

The address bus of the microprocessor is used to transmit the address from the microprocessor to a device, the memory or input/output port involved in a data transfer. Table 6.1 shows the number of memory locations that can be addressed using different numbers of address lines.

6: Inside the microprocessor – a first look

Number of address lines	Number of directly addressable memory locations
1	2
2	4
3	8
4	16
5	32
6	64
7	128
8	256
9	512
10	1024
11	2048
12	4096
13	8192
14	16384
15	32768
16	65536

Table 6.1 Relationship between address lines and memory locations

These figures are derived as follows. Each line of the address bus can be either at logic level 0 or logic level 1; one of two states. So we can use the formula,

No of directly addressable memory locations = $2^{\text{Number of address lines}}$

Ten address lines can address 2^{10} memory locations i.e. 1024 memory locations. In the computer industry it is standard practice to refer to this number of memory locations as one kilo (1k).

Example: Consider the Intel 4004, the original processor which had 14 address lines.

$$\text{No. of directly addressable memory locations} = 2^{14}$$
$$= 16384$$
$$= \frac{16384}{1024} \text{ (kilo memory locations)}$$
$$= 16 \text{ k memory locations}$$

From Table 6.1 you will note that each time an address line is added, the amount of addressable memory is doubled. The 4004 was quickly followed by the eight bit processor which had 16 address lines and could therefore address 64k memory locations.

6: Inside the microprocessor – a first look

Short Answer Question 6.2

Using a microprocessor with a 16-bit address bus, it is possible to directly address 64 kBytes of memory.

How much memory could be directly addressed if the address bus was increased to 20 bits.

Answer to SAQ 6.2

Number of locations = 2^{20}
= 1048576 bytes
= 1024 Kilobytes (kb)
= 1 Megabyte (Mb)

6.4 AN EXAMPLE OF MEMORY ADDRESSING

Consider a hypothetical or imaginary 4-bit microprocessor, which has, for example, a three bit address bus. This is illustrated in Fig 6.2.

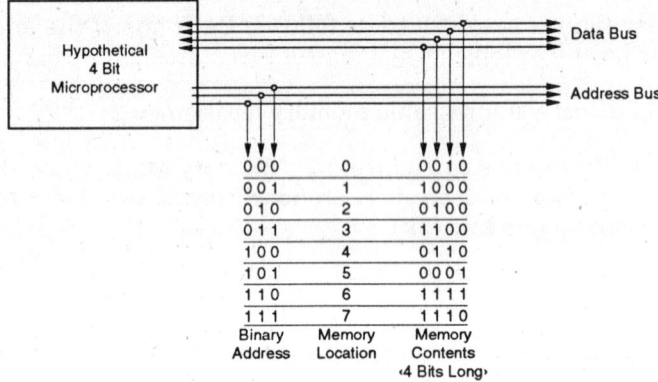

Fig 6.2 Using a hypothetical 4-bit processor to address memory

Each location in memory is identified by a number called the address. In this example, the three bit address can select or address any one of eight memory locations, identified by the numbers 0 to 7. If the processor needs the data word from a memory location it must send its address along the address bus to the memory.

For example, if the processor wishes to read the data word stored at memory location 2, then it must send the address 0 1 0 along the address bus to the memory. The data word 0 1 0 0 is then read out from the selected memory location onto the data bus and taken along the data bus into the microprocessor. This topic will be expanded in Chapter 9 – Microcomputer Memories.

6: Inside the microprocessor – a first look

Short Answer Question 6.3

What is the function of a memory address?

Answer to SAQ 6.3

To identify the memory location involved in a data transfer

6.5 SPEED OF OPERATION OF THE MICROPROCESSOR

Since the first microprocessor became available in 1970 many companies have been striving to improve microprocessor architecture. Every improvement in architecture has resulted in an increase in microprocessor speed and computing power.

Processor speed may be measured in two different ways. The first is the microprocessor's clock frequency. This is the speed at which the microprocessor's clock oscillator operates. Typically this is expressed in megahertz (1 megahertz or 1 MHz equals 1 million cycles per second).

A second method of rating a microprocessor's speed is the number of instructions it can execute in one second. The speed is then stated in terms of **MIPS**; Millions Of Instructions per Second.

Table 6.2 shows the clock frequency and the MIPS rating for a number of common processors.

The speed figures quoted are only intended to indicate a good measure of processor speed because it is difficult to do exact speed comparisons between processors.

Processor	MIPS
4004	0.09
Z80A	0.30 (4 MHz)
Z80B	0.45 (6 MHz)
8088	0.75 (5 MHz)
80286	2.30 (12.5 MHz)
80386SX	3.00 (16 MHz)
i386	7.00 (33 MHz)
i486	25.00 (33 MHz)

Table 6.2 Average processing speed in terms of Millions of Instructions per Second (MIPS)

6: Inside the microprocessor – a first look

Short Answer Question 6.4

When an 8 MHz 8-bit processor is compared with an 8 MHz 80286, the 80286 is approximately twice as fast for simple data transfers. State the reason for this.

Answer to SAQ 6.4

Because the data bus is twice as wide

6.6 INSIDE THE MICROPROCESSOR

The vast majority of all 8-bit microprocessor chips on the market today implement the same **standard** architecture. The two chief functions of any processor are processing and control.

Before examining any particular processor a simplified version of the **standard** model will be presented as a mechanism for understanding some fundamental concepts that apply to all microprocessors.

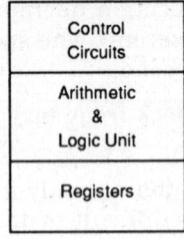

Fig 6.3 The major functional parts of a microprocessor

Fig 6.3 illustrates that the three major functional parts of the microprocessor are:

1. **Registers** (Temporary storage)
2. **The Arithmetic & Logic Unit (ALU)**
3. **Control Circuits**

All three parts work together as a unit to form the microprocessor.

1. **Registers**

   A microprocessor has many registers. Each **register is a group of memory cells** used to provide temporary storage of words within a microprocessor. Each cell is a flip-flop that can store one bit of information. When flip-flops are organised to store a binary word, the arrangement is referred to as a register. See Chapter 4 for full details of flip-flops. Fig 6.4 shows an 8-bit register. At present it is only necessary to understand that the number and type of registers in any particular microprocessor will be different from those in another microprocessor. Some of the main registers within a typical microprocessor will be introduced later in this chapter, with additional **coverage in** Chapters 7 and 8.

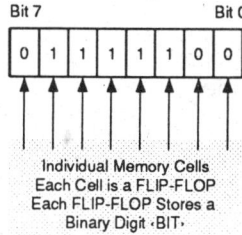

Fig 6.4 An 8-bit microprocessor register

2   Arithmetic & Logic Unit (ALU)

The **ALU** is made up of logic circuits whose function is to **process data**. It performs both **arithmetic** and **logic operations** on words of data which are fed to its inputs.

3   Control circuits

The **control circuits** contain an instruction decoder which can be regarded as the control logic's intelligence which acts like the **brain** of the microprocessor. The instruction decoder works with the timing and control logic.

 Multiple Choice Question 6.2

The ALU's main function is to

a) perform additions

b) logically or arithmetically modify data words

c) perform logical operations on data words

d) control the internal elements of the processor

 Answer to MCQ 6.2

B

 Short Answer Question 6.5

What is a register?

Answer to SAQ 6.5

A group of flip-flops (memory cells) used to store words within a microprocessor

6.7 THE INTERNAL MICROPROCESSOR BUSES

The microcomputer system block diagram presented in Chapter 1 Fig 1.8 illustrates that the microprocessor, memory and input/output integrated circuits are interconnected by a bus. Information is passed between the various units of the computer via the bus. Over it a complete word can be transferred in parallel. The term **bus** is used to denote a **group of wires** or **conduction tracks** on a printed circuit board which act as paths for digital signals that have a common function. As the diagram shows a **microcomputer bus** is divided into **three groups of signals.** The microprocessor has three internal buses – the **address bus**, the **data bus** and the **control bus**, which connect to the external system buses through pins on the integrated circuit.

- **The data bus**

   A set of eight wires for an 8-bit processor which can simultaneously carry 8-bits or 1 byte words. Data can flow in either direction; the bus is **bi-directional.**

- **The address bus**

   A set of wires, (sixteen for eight bit processors) along which is sent the binary code (the address) that identifies the memory location to be used or the input/output port involved in a data transfer. Addresses can only be issued by the microprocessor, so this bus is **unidirectional.**

- **The control bus**

This bus is used to send control signals generated by the microprocessor to the memory and input/output units. For example, if the processor wishes to read a byte of data from the memory it would generate a memory read signal. It should be noted that some control signals (interrupts) enter the processor.

6.8 THE MICROPROCESSOR BLOCK DIAGRAM

The block diagram shows how the internal elements of the microprocessor are interconnected. This diagram makes it simpler to understand its internal architecture. When attempting to understand new microprocessors, reference is always made to block diagrams which are useful when comparing different microprocessors.

In this chapter, the simplified block diagram shown in Fig 6.5, which is a **subset** of the standard commercially available microprocessor, will be used to introduce some of the internal elements of the microprocessor.

6: Inside the microprocessor – a first look

The same basic diagram will then be extended in Chapters 7 and 8 to present a simplified model of a real processor.

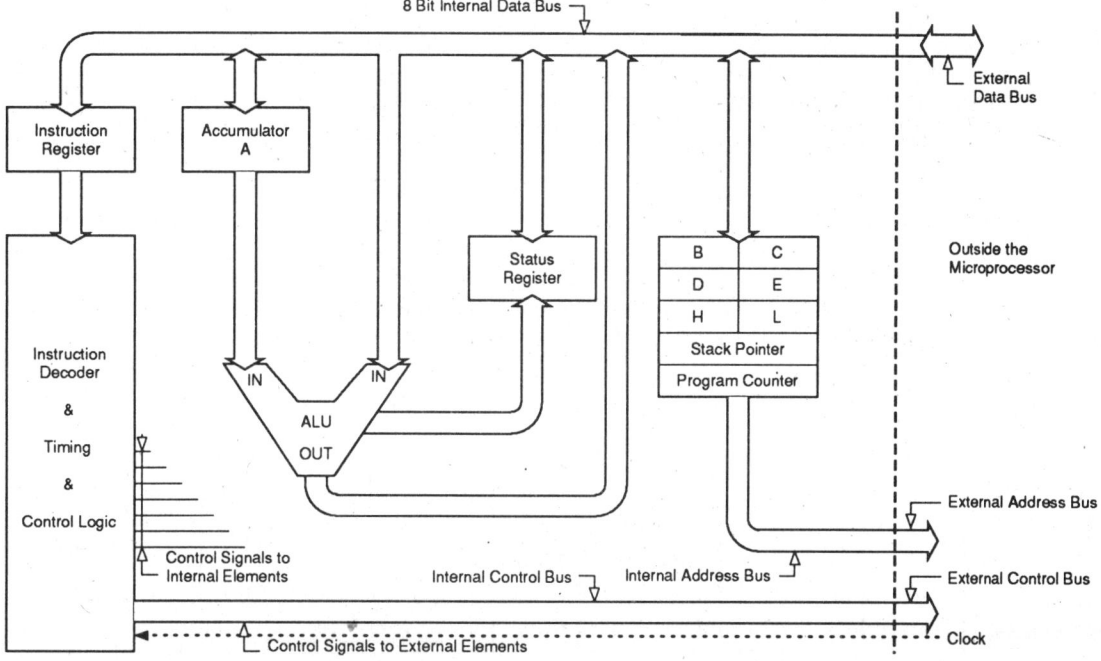

Fig 6.5 Simplified internal architecture of a typical 8-bit microprocessor

Short Answer Question 6.6

What is the symbol used to represent a microprocessor bus?

Answer to SAQ 6.6

Two parallel lines. Thus: _____
_____

6.9 THE MICROPROCESSOR'S REGISTERS

The registers within the microprocessor are highlighted in Fig 6.6. They act as temporary data storage devices within the microprocessor, (not all registers are available to the programmer). A programmer's model of the Z80 MPU is given in Chapter 8 Section 8.9.

From the diagram it is clear that the registers are:

6: Inside the microprocessor – a first look

(a) **B C**
  D E } general purpose registers
  H L
(b) **accumulator**
(c) **status register**
(d) **instruction register**
(e) **program counter**
(f) **stack pointer**

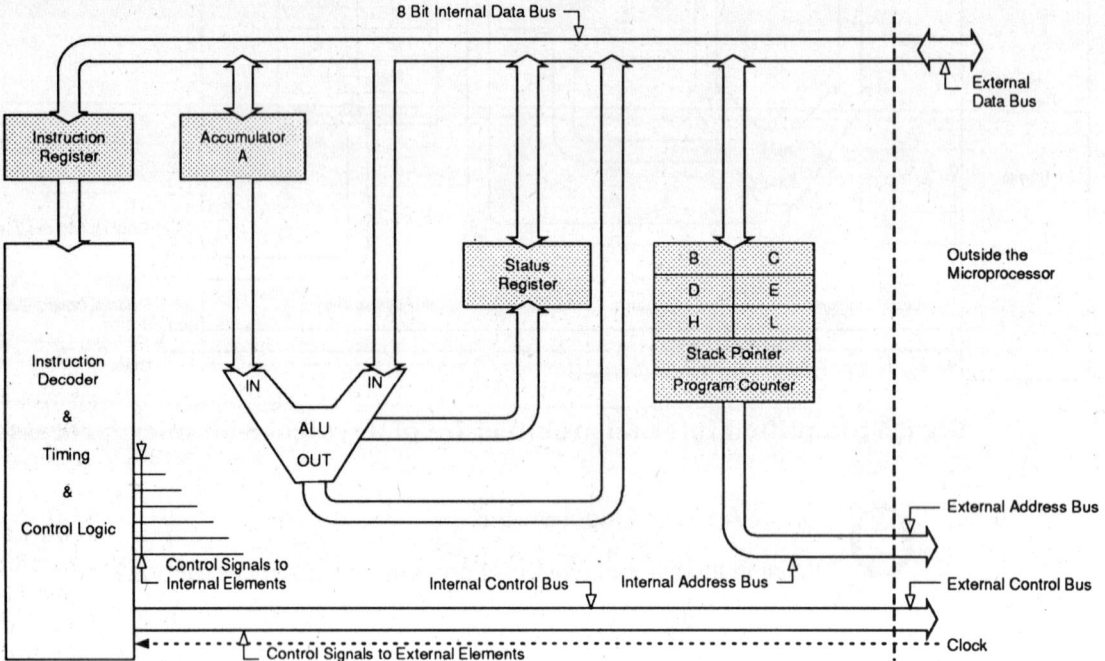

Fig 6.6 The microprocessor's registers

6.10 THE ARITHMETIC AND LOGIC UNIT (ALU)

All microprocessors contain an arithmetic and logic unit, which is often referred to simply as the ALU. The **ALU**, as its name implies, is that portion of the microprocessor hardware which **performs the arithmetic and logical operations** on the binary data.

Fig 6.7 highlights the ALU section of the processor.

6: Inside the microprocessor – a first look

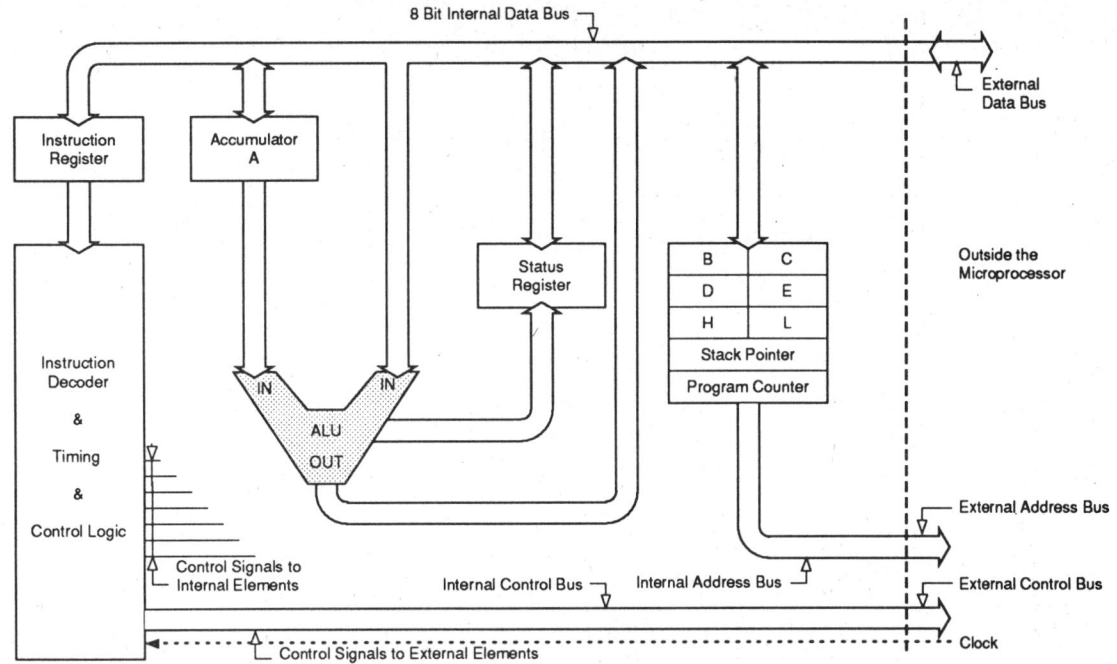

Fig 6.7 The ALU of the microprocessor

The ALU must contain an addition circuit which is capable of combining the contents of two registers in accordance with the logic of binary arithmetic. This provision permits the microprocessor to perform arithmetic manipulations on the data which is applied to its inputs.

In Chapter 2 it was shown that binary subtraction can be implemented using complement arithmetic and that binary multiplication and division can be implemented using the shift-and-add and the shift-and-subtract methods respectively. Consequently, the arithmetic operations of subtraction, multiplication and division can be reduced to a series of complement and addition operations. Therefore only registers (See Chapter 4 for details) and addition circuits are necessary in order to be able to perform addition, subtraction, multiplication and division.

The ALU may have to perform logical operations and thus it has in-built logic networks constructed around registers and logic elements. These circuits perform operations, such as the logical ORing of two bytes. The need for these operations is not immediately apparent. This aspect of the ALU will be dealt with in Chapter 11 Section 11.5 (Traffic Lights).

The type of functions performed by the ALUs of most microprocessors include:

        Add

        Subtract

        Logical AND

        Logical OR

Logical Exclusive OR

Shift left

Shift right

Increment

Decrement

Complement

Fig 6.7 illustrates that the ALU has two inputs, both labelled 'IN' and a single output, identified as 'OUT'.

Examples of specific ALU functions will be given in Chapter 8.

 Short Answer Question 6.7

Name two arithmetical operations which the ALU of every processor is capable of performing.

 Answer to SAQ 6.7

Addition and Subtraction

6.11 THE MICROPROCESSOR'S CONTROL CIRCUITRY

When solving a problem using a computer a set of instructions, called the program has to be written. These instructions are stored in the computer's memory. They tell the computer what steps must be carried out to solve the problem and also in what sequence the microprocessor must carry out the instructions. The control circuitry includes timing/control logic and the instruction decoder. The latter receives its input signal from the instruction register. The control circuitry directs the fetching of instructions from the memory of the system and it is also responsible for the execution of these instructions. It does this by providing timing and control signals that tell the ALU and other circuits what to do and when to do it. In other words the control circuitry of the microprocessor keeps all the other parts working in the right time sequence; it synchronises the entire system.

A crystal controlled oscillator, which is usually referred to as the system clock, provides an external input to the control circuitry of the microprocessor. This clock signal is the reference for all timing operations within the processor. See appendix B for details of a practical clock circuit.

The control circuitry of the processor is highlighted in Fig 6.8.

6: Inside the microprocessor – a first look

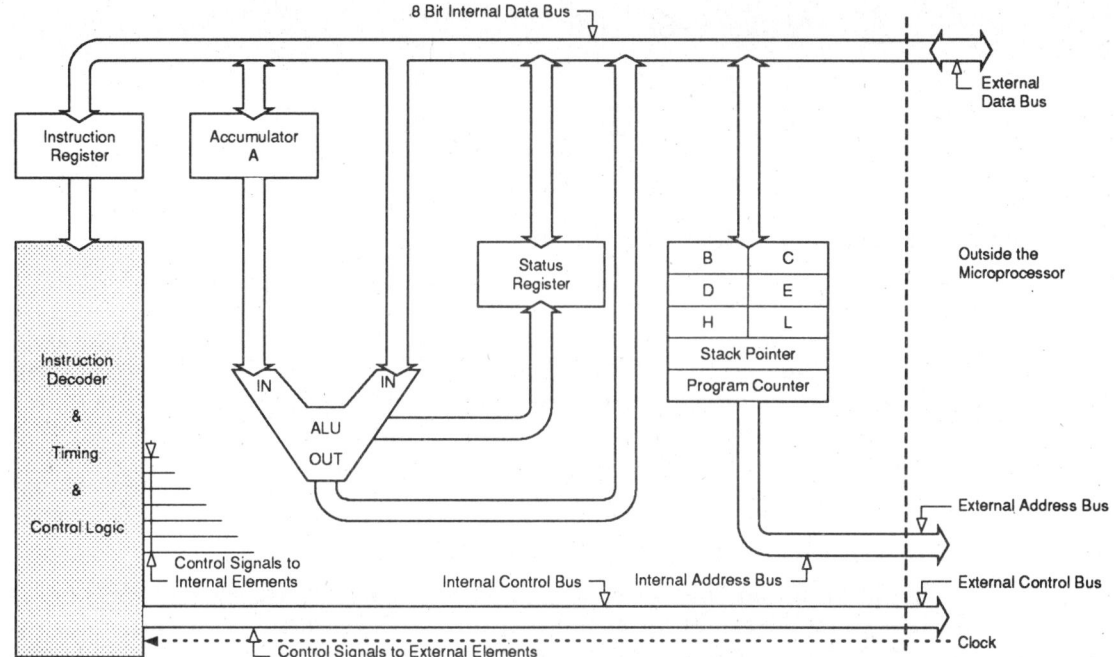

Fig 6.8 The control circuitry of the processor.

This consists of the instruction decoder and the timing and control logic. The diagram shows that two groups of signals stem from this section of the processor.

i. A group of signals that control the various internal elements of the microprocessor, such as, the accumulator, status register, ALU etc.

ii. A set of control signals which are brought out to pins on the integrated circuit and which are used to control external devices, such as, memory and input/output ports. This group of signals would include, for example, a signal for reading data from memory. This signal would be identified by a mnemonic, for example, RD and on the circuit diagram would be shown as an output signal from the microprocessor. Although the block diagram implies that all control signals originate from within the microprocessor, some signals, such as, the interrupt signals, are generated by external devices and therefore act as input signals to the microprocessor. In the interest of clarity these signals have been omitted.

 Short Answer Question 6.8

Refer to Fig 6.8 Which part of the microprocessor controls the ALU? Name any one of the control bus signals.

6: Inside the microprocessor – a first look

> **A** Answer to SAQ 6.8
>
> The timing and control section.
>
> A typical control bus signal would be memory read

6.12 THE GENERAL PURPOSE REGISTERS

These are highlighted in Fig 6.9.

Each of these registers is capable of storing or holding one byte of data and any one of them may be connected to the bi-directional data bus. The byte stored in any of these registers can be transferred simultaneously to or from the data bus. We will see how this achieved in the next chapter. They are called general purpose registers because their role is not defined in advance by the manufacturer. It is up to the programmer to use them in the most appropriate manner. For example, when adding two bytes of data, one of the bytes could be placed in any one of the six general purpose registers.

It should be noted that in some microprocessors, register pairs may be used. Registers may be combined as follows; B with C, D with E, H with L. When combined in this way they are known as register pairs which are then capable of storing a 16-bit word. This facility is provided by microprocessors such as the Intel 8085 and the Zilog Z80. When used in this way the 16-bit word can either be 16 bits of data or a 16-bit address.

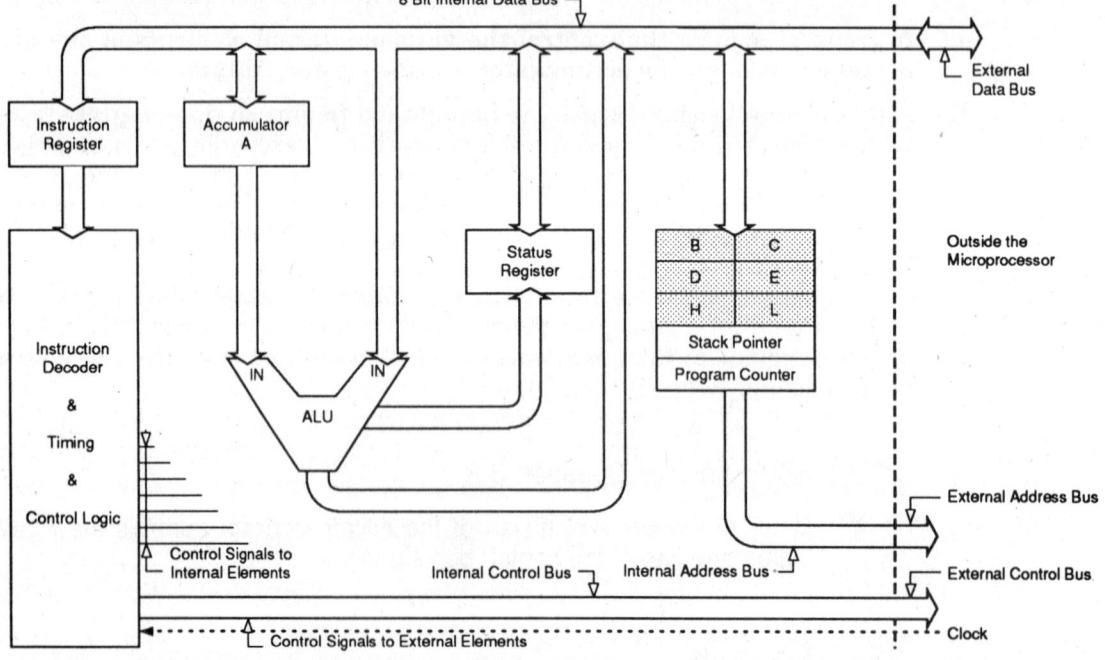

Fig 6.9 The general purpose registers

6: Inside the microprocessor – a first look

 Short Answer Question 6.9

a) Name the six general purpose registers and state the number of bits which each one can store.

b) State one practical application of register 'B'

 Answer to SAQ 6.9

a) B,C,D,E,H and L. Each one can store eight bits
b) It can store a byte of data for arithmetic or logic operations.

 Short Answer Question 6.10

When programming the microprocessor, register pairs may be used. Which registers may be combined?

 Answer to SAQ 6.10

B with C; D with E ; H with L

In Chapter 7 the function of the accumulator, status register, program counter, instruction register and stack pointer will be explained.

SUMMARY

- Microprocessors are now used in a diverse range of applications; pocket calculators, motor cars, and personal computers to name but a few.
- The architecture of a microprocessor refers to its internal organisation.
- The total amount of memory which a processor can directly address is 2^n where n is the number of address lines.
- Generally all 8-bit microprocessor integrated circuits on the market today implement the same architecture.
- The major functional parts of the processor are the: Registers, Arithmetic and Logic Unit (ALU) and Control circuitry.
- The Registers (temporary storage) are used to temporarily store instructions or data within the microprocessor.
- The ALU is an element that can perform several arithmetic and logic functions such as addition or the logical ORing of two byes of data.

❐ The control circuitry generates all the necessary control signals for the internal processor elements and the external system components.

❐ The general purpose registers are B,C,D,E,H and L. Used individually these can store a byte. Register pairs BC, DE and HL can hold a 16-bit word.

CHAPTER REVIEW QUESTIONS

Section A. Multiple choice questions (Answers in Appendix A)

1. Which one of the following is correct?
   a) a byte is a four bit word
   b) the number of bits in a byte is eight
   c) a byte is a sixteen bit word
   d) a byte can take the value 0 or 1

2. The memory addressing capability of a microprocessor which has 24 address pins is:
   a) 16 kb
   b) 16 Gb
   c) 64 kb
   d) 16 Mb

3. When a microprocessor is writing/reading data to/from RAM, each storage location is identified by means of an address which is sent along the:
   a) data bus
   b) control bus
   c) address bus
   d) address and data bus

4. The purpose of the microprocessor clock circuit is to
   a) divide the system clock frequency by 2
   b) generate a variable frequency signal
   c) generate a timing reference for the system
   d) invert the incoming pulses before they reach the clock pin of the processor

5. Which one of the following formulae gives the maximum number of memory locations (including zero) which can be addressed with n bits?
   a) 2^n
   b) 2^{n+1}
   c) 2^{n-1}
   d) $2^n - 1$

6. In relation to digital words the initials MSB stand for:
   a) most significant byte
   b) microprocessor status bit
   c) most significant bit
   d) memory status bit
7. A register is
   a) a group of memory cells used to provide temporary storage of words within the microprocessor
   b) a one bit memory cell
   c) a device where the user's program is stored
   d) always 8-bits long
8. The output from the clock circuit is connected as an input to the
   a) RAM
   b) ROM
   c) data bus
   d) microprocessor
9. The ALU has
   a) one input and two outputs
   b) one input and one output
   c) two inputs and two outputs
   d) two inputs and one output
10. The LSB of a digital word is the
    a) least significant byte
    b) lower significant byte
    c) longest significant bit
    d) least significant bit

Section B: Short answer questions

1. LIST three major architectural features which separate one microprocessor from another.
2. LIST three popular word lengths used in today's microprocessors
3. What is the most common application of 16-bit microprocessors?
4. Explain the term MIPS.
5. Name the three internal buses of a microprocessor.
6. With the aid of a sketch explain what is meant by an 8-bit **register**.

7. Refer to Fig 6.10 Identify the components labelled:

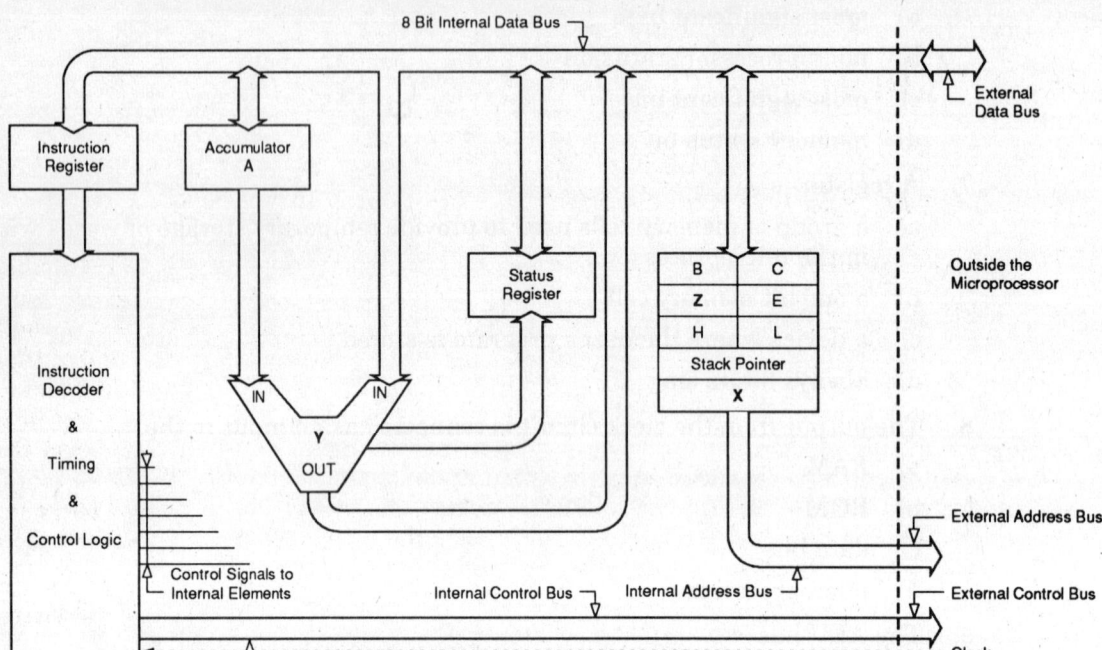

Fig 6.10

    X
    Y
    Z

8. State two practical uses of the six general purpose registers.
9. Briefly explain the function of the address bus within a microprocessor.
10. LIST any four common functions which the ALU is capable of performing.

Chapter 7
Other Microprocessor Registers

7.1 THE ACCUMULATOR

The accumulator is the **8-bit register**, shown highlighted in Fig 7.1 It is connected to the internal data bus via a bidirectional connection. This register works closely with the ALU. Whenever the ALU is manipulating data, for example, adding two bytes or logically ORing two bytes the accumulator holds one of them. The other byte could be stored in any one of the six general purpose registers B, C, D, E, H or L. The result of an arithmetic or logical operation will appear on the output of the ALU. From there it is taken onto the internal data bus and from that bus into the accumulator. In summary, the accumulator is a special storage register associated with the arithmetic logic unit, initially used for holding one of the bytes which is being processed and once the computation has been completed the **result** is **stored** back into the **accumulator**.

In Chapter 8, when dealing with how the microprocessor executes typical instructions, illustrations will be given to show how the accumulator works.

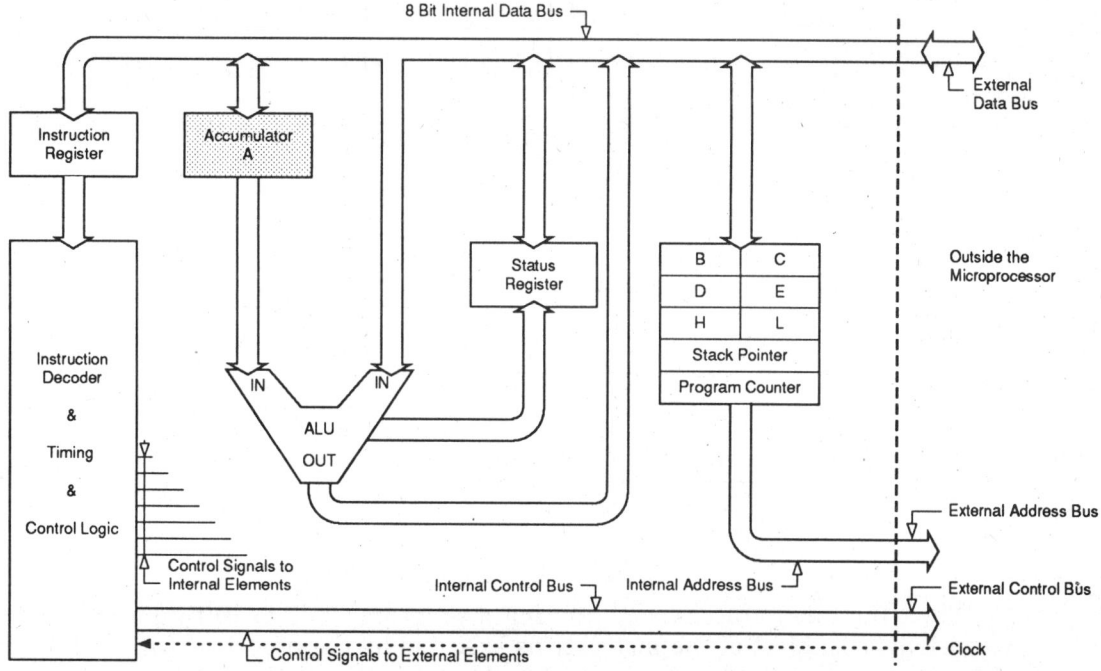

Fig 7.1 The accumulator

7: Other microprocessor registers

Short answer question 7.1

What is the accumulator?

Answer to SAQ 7.1

The accumulator is a special 8-bit storage register associated with the ALU which holds the results of a computation.

7.2 THE STATUS REGISTER

This register is sometimes referred to as the **Flag register** or the **Condition Code Register** (CCR). A flag is an indicator that can be set or reset. A flip-flop is an example of a device which can be set to one or reset to zero. The status register shown highlighted in Fig 7.2, is an 8-bit register.

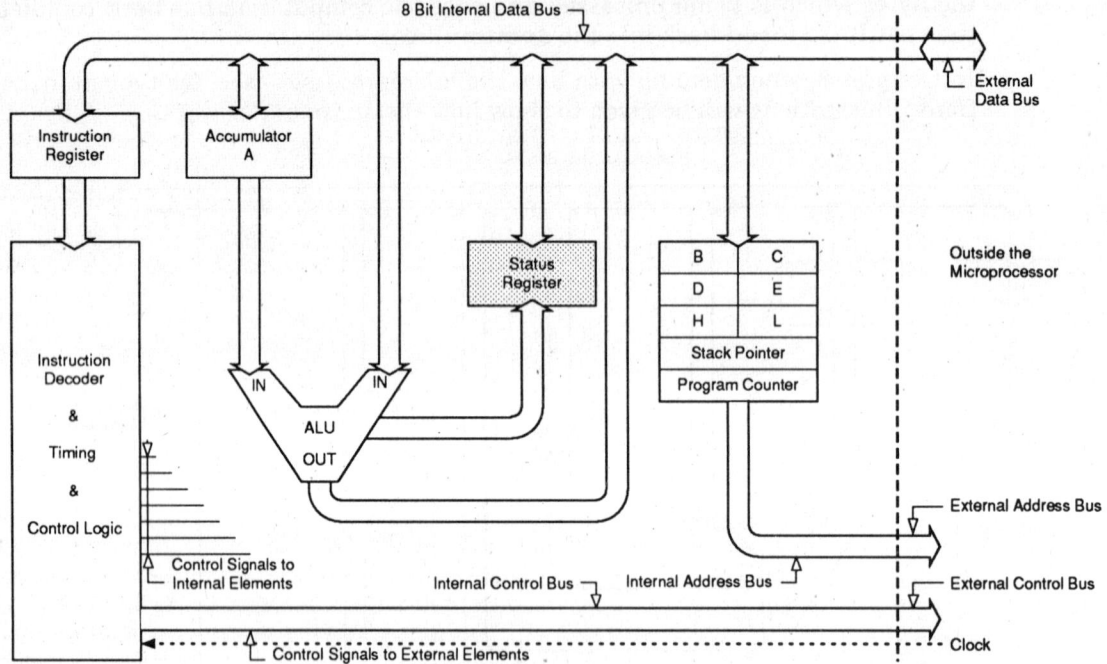

Fig 7.2 The status register

When the microprocessor is running a program, it is executing a sequence of instructions. Most of the instructions executed by the processor will modify some or all of the bits in the status register. ALU operations and certain register operations may set to 1, or clear to 0, one or more of the status bits in this register. It may be asked 'Why store these results' and 'are they of any practical use.'?

7: Other microprocessor registers

Certain bits of the status register may be tested by instructions in the program and decisions made based on whether the bit being tested is set or clear. These bits of the register, may be used as conditions for jump, call and return instructions.

For details of the Z80 flag register and how the flags may be used for practical programming applications refer to Chapter 11 and appendix G.

In order to illustrate how the status register is affected by ALU operations, consider the following examples. The two's complement representation for signed binary numbers is used where the most significant bit (MSB) of the number is the sign bit. The MSB is 0 for a positive number, and 1 for a negative number.

In order to understand the following examples you may find it necessary to read parts of Chapter 2, particularly Sections 2.4 to 2.6.

Example 1 Using two's complement notation ADD the two 8-bit numbers 1 1 1 1   0 0 0 0 and 0 1 1 1   0 1 0 1

$$-16 = 1\,1\,1\,1\,0\,0\,0\,0$$
$$+117 = 0\,1\,1\,1\,0\,1\,0\,1$$

1   0 1 1 0 0 1 0 1 = + 101

Carry   8-bit positive result

The result left in the accumulator (0110 0101) is +101, which is correct. The carry bit of the status register is set to 1.

Example 2 Represent +120 and +105 in two's complement form and then add the two numbers.

$$+120 = 0\,1\,1\,1\,1\,0\,0\,0$$
$$+105 = 0\,1\,1\,0\,1\,0\,0\,1$$

carry   = 0   1 1 1 0 0 0 0 1 = −31
overflow = 1

In this example the carry flag has been cleared to zero, while the overflow flag has been set to one. The overflow flag indicates that the two's complement number in the accumulator is in error since it has exceeded the maximum possible (+127) or is less than the minimum possible (−128) number that can be represented by two's complement notation.

This example illustrates that adding the two positive numbers, +120 and +105, produced a negative result, which is incorrect. The accumulator is in error, since it has exceeded the maximum possible positive number of +127, that may be represented by an 8-bit two's complement number.

7: Other microprocessor registers

 Short answer question 7.2

Add the following 8-bit binary numbers. After adding these numbers, indicate the state of the zero (Z), sign (S) and carry (C) bits of the status register.

1010 1010

1111 1111

 Answer to SAQ 7.2

    1010 1010
    1111 1111
   ————————
 1   1010 1001

The Z (Zero) flag = 0; Z is reset because the answer isn't 0
The S (Sign) flag = 1; S indicates that the answer is negative
The C (Carry) flag = 1; The addition generated a Carry out

7.3 THE PROGRAM COUNTER (PC)

The instructions that make up a program are stored in the system's memory. The microprocessor references the contents of memory in order to determine what action it should take. This means that the microprocessor must know which location contains the next instruction.

Each of the locations in memory is numbered to distinguish it from all other locations in memory. The number which identifies a memory location is called the **address**. The binary word stored at a given address is known as the contents of that memory location. See Fig 7.3 which represents a 1k Byte Random Access Memory (RAM).

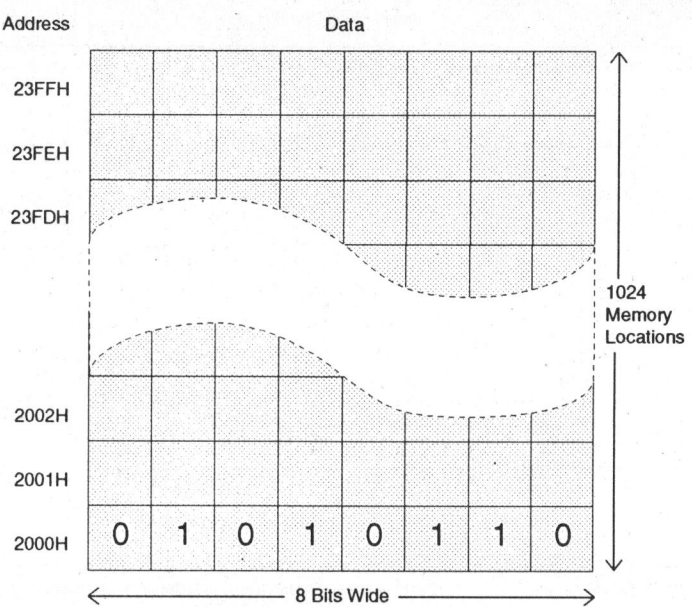

Fig 7.3 A 1k byte RAM

The number which appears on the left hand side of each memory location is its address, expressed in hexadecimal. The memory addresses are generated by the processor and sent along the address bus to the memory. As an 8-bit microprocessor has a 16-bit address bus, the 16 bits that make up the address are conveniently represented by four hexadecimal characters. From Chapter 2 Section 2.2 the total number of memory locations is:

23FFH − 2000H = 03FFH = 1024_{10} (including 0) = 1k Byte of memory.

Each memory location stores an 8-bit word or one byte.

An essential part of any microprocessor is the **Program Counter** which is highlighted in Fig 7.4. The Program Counter or PC contains the **16-bit** address of the next instruction to be executed. If the microprocessor is to deal with the next instruction, it must bring that instruction into itself from memory. It does this by outputting the contents of the program counter, which **holds the address of the next instruction**, to the external system address bus. The address is taken via the address bus to the memory which then releases the contents of the addressed location; the next instruction, onto the data bus and from there it is taken along the internal data bus to the instruction register of the microprocessor.

Basically, the program counter's purpose is to hold the 16-bit memory address of the next instruction to be executed.

7: Other microprocessor registers

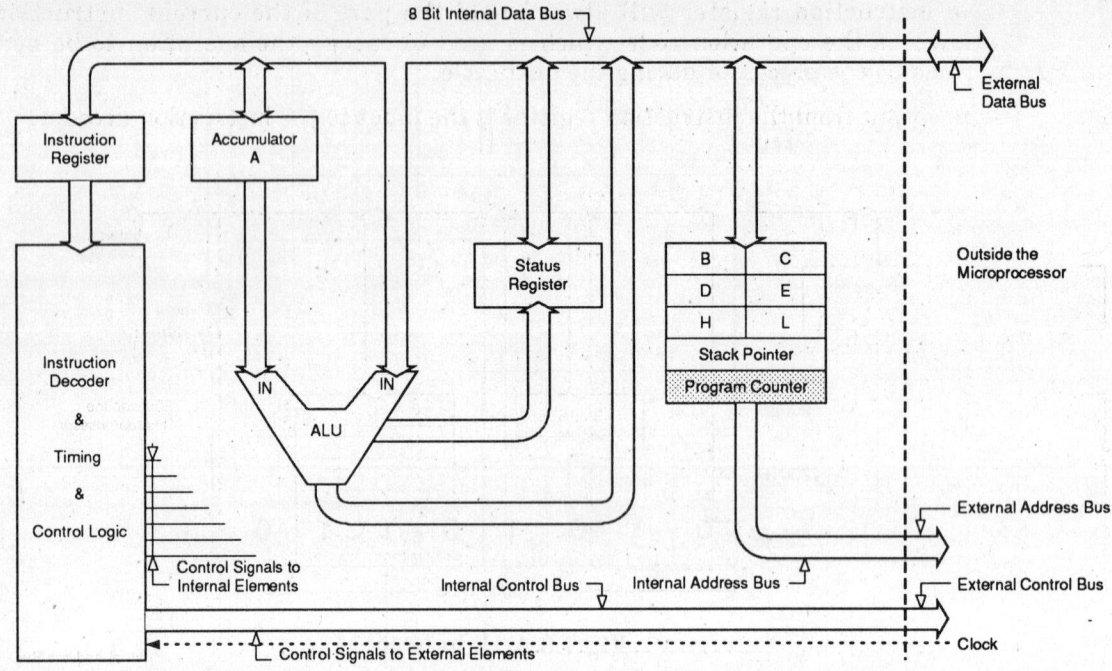

Fig 7.4 The program counter or PC register

 Short answer question 7.3

The address of the next instruction to be executed is 2000H. In which one of the processor's registers is it stored?

When this address is being sent to the memory, by the processor, along which one of the system buses will it travel?

In this example the address is 2000H. What does the letter 'H' mean?

 Answer to SAQ 7.3

The program counter register.

The address bus

The 'H' denotes that the address is expressed in hexadecimal or hex.

7.4 THE INSTRUCTION REGISTER

The instruction register highlighted in Fig 7.5 is eight bits wide and as the diagram shows it is connected to the internal data bus, but can only receive data.

7: Other microprocessor registers

The instruction register will always hold the part of the current instruction known as the operation code which is used to specify the operation to be performed by the processor during the next cycle.

The output from the instruction register is the input to the instruction decoder.

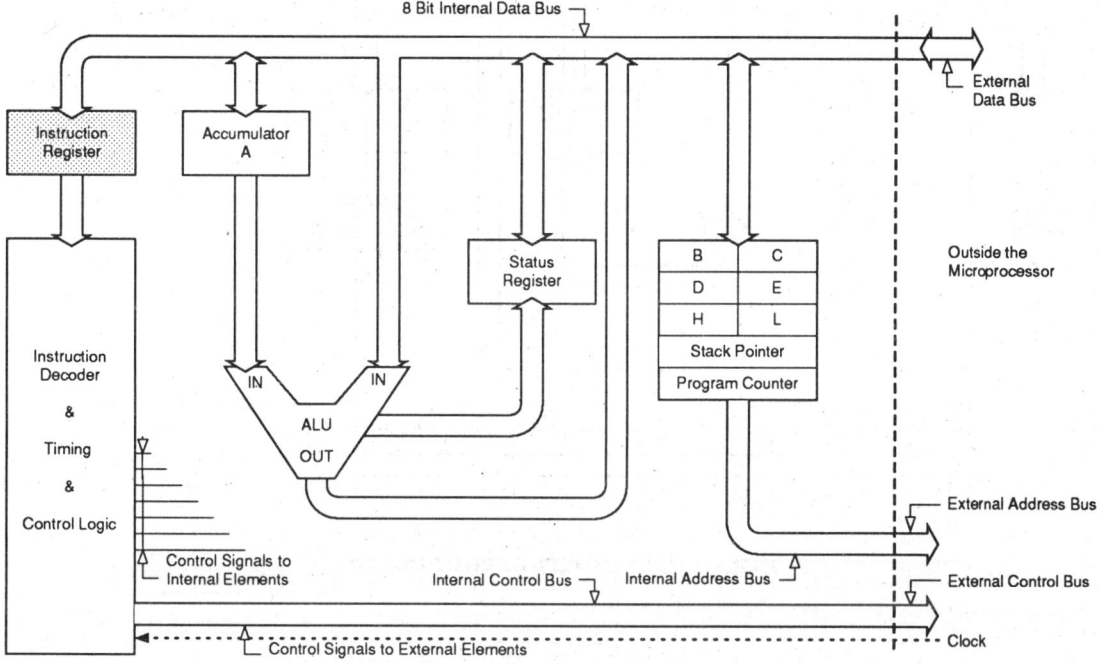

Fig 7.5 The Instruction Register

Q Short answer question 7.4

State the number of bits which the instruction register can store.

Which part of a microprocessor instruction is stored in the instruction register?

A Answer to SAQ 7.4

8 BITS

The operation code (OP-CODE)

7.5 THE STACK POINTER (SP)

The stack pointer is the 16-bit register highlighted in Fig 7.6

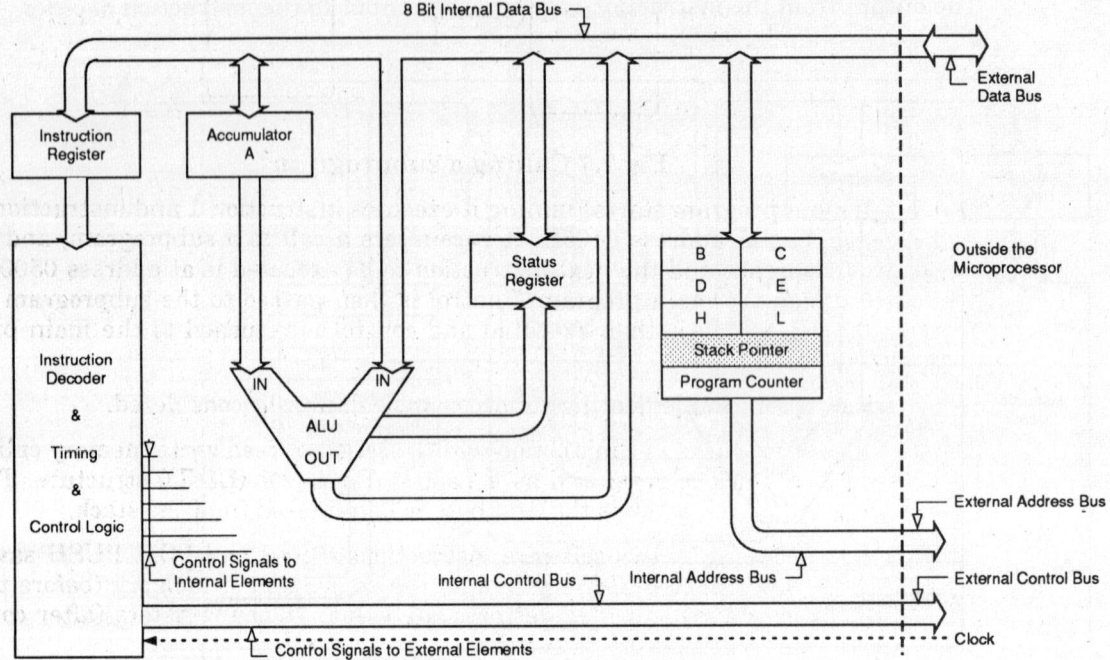

Fig 7.6 The stack pointer

When designing programs it is essential that they are structured. Although this topic is covered in Chapter 11, it is useful to introduce the concept of structured programming now, so that one application of the stack pointer can be described. In section 7.3 we saw that the program counter is the register which holds the address of the next instruction in the program to be executed. However, when executing programs that contain procedures or subroutines it is necessary to load the program counter with a new value. This raises some important questions, such as 'What happens to the address of the next instruction which is stored in the program counter?'.

Structured programming is an orderly approach to programming which emphasises breaking large and complex tasks into distinct sections or modules (subroutines or subprograms). Consider an application where it may be necessary to execute the same block of code many times within a program. Rather than writing the same piece of code wherever it is required in the program, it is far more efficient to write the block of code (subprogram) once outside the main program and then have the main program call that subprogram whenever it is needed. An example of this might be a section of code for printing a menu on the screen.

7: Other microprocessor registers

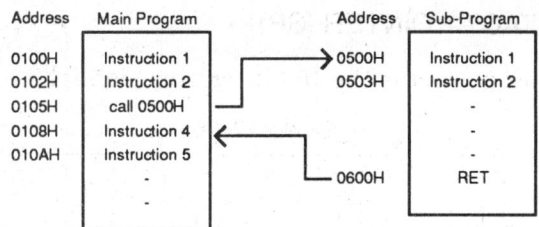

Fig 7.7 Calling a subprogram

When the main program starts running it executes instruction 1 and instruction 2 in sequence, but at address 0105H, it encounters a call to a subprogram, and so goes out of sequence and the next instruction to be executed is at address 0500H, which is outside the main program. Control is then passed to the subprogram at address 0500H, which is then executed and control is returned to the main program as indicated.

The mechanism for implementing subprograms will now be considered.

The stack pointer works in conjunction with a section of read/write memory called the **stack**. The stack is organised as a Last In First Out (**LIFO**) structure. The last byte placed on the stack is the first byte to be removed from the stack.

The stack is accessed by two software instructions PUSH and POP. PUSH saves the contents of microprocessor registers on the stack area of memory (before the subroutine is executed) and POP restores the values to the registers (after completion of the subroutine).

In the above programming example once the sub-program is completed it is essential that the next instruction executed is the one at address 0108H. How can it be guaranteed that this will happen? At the end of instruction 2 the program counter holds the address of the next instruction; 0108H and this is the address which must be stored on the stack, in random access memory, before the program counter is loaded with the address 0500H of the subprogram.

When the microprocessor encounters the CALL instruction in the program it automatically pushes the address stored in the program counter out to the system stack and loads the program counter with the address of the subprogram. This is illustrated in Fig 7.8.

Assume that the stack pointer has been initialised at address 2390H.

7: Other microprocessor registers

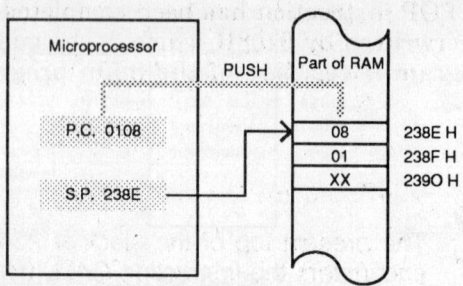

Fig 7.8 PUSHing the program counter contents onto the stack

The steps involved in PUSHing the address 0108H onto the stack are:
i) Decrement the SP by 1 i.e. to 238FH
ii) Save the high order PC byte, 01, at address 238FH
iii) Decrement the SP; SP = 238EH
iv) Save the low order PC byte, 08, at address 238EH

The stack pointer is currently pointing to the top of the stack; 238EH.

The PC is then loaded with the address of the subprogram; 0500H.

The last instruction in the subprogram is a RET (urn) instruction and this causes the address 0108H to be POPped off the stack and back into the program counter within the microprocessor. This is illustrated in Fig. 7.9. As soon as the PC has been loaded with the address 0108H, sequential execution of the program continues.

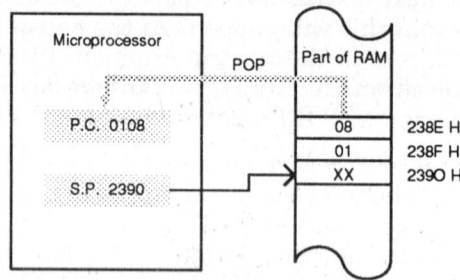

Fig 7.9 POPing the address 0108H from the stack back into the PC.

The POP operation is completed as follows:
i) The SP currently points to the top of the stack ; 238EH. The byte at this location, 08H, is loaded into the low byte of the PC.
ii) The SP is incremented to address 238FH
iii) The high byte of the PC is loaded with the byte stored at 238FH; 01H
iv) The SP is incremented to address 2390H

After the POP instruction has been completed the contents of the PC i.e. 0600H will be overwritten by 0108H which is the address of the next instruction in the main program. Execution of the main program can then continue from that address.

Short answer question 7.5

The present top of the stack is 2360H. Assuming that the processor encounters the instruction CALL 0400H draw a diagram which shows how the PC contents are pushed onto the stack in random access memory. The CALL instruction is at location 200AH.

Answer to SAQ 7.5

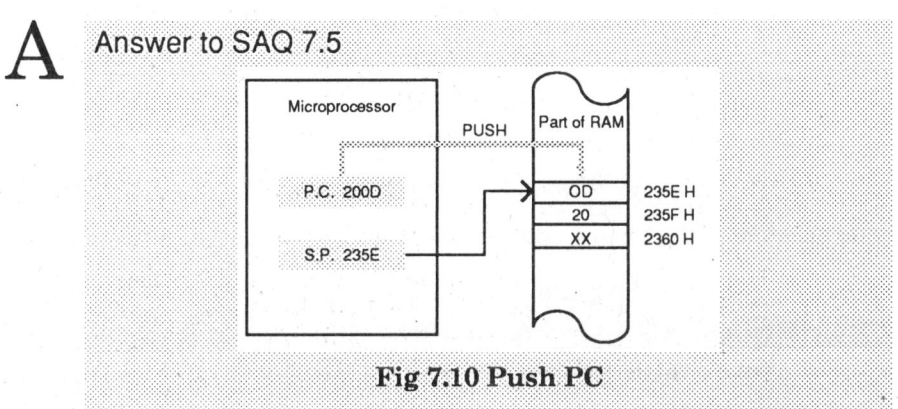

Fig 7.10 Push PC

SUMMARY

In this chapter the role of the following microprocessor registers was explained.

- Accumulator (A)
- Flag register (F)
- Program Counter (PC)
- Instruction Register (IR)
- Stack Pointer (SP)

❏ Accumulator

The accumulator is an 8-bit register which holds one of the bytes during arithmetic and logical operations. After computation it stores the result.

❏ Flag register
Also known as the STATUS or CONDITION CODE REGISTER.

This is another 8-bit register which contains information about the present state of the microprocessor, in particular the accumulator; did the last calculation in the ALU produce a carry etc.

7: Other microprocessor registers

❏ Program Counter

This is a 16-bit register which holds the address of the next instruction to be executed by the processor.

❏ Stack Pointer

A 16-bit register which is used to implement subroutines in programs. It is used in conjunction with the STACK which is a read/write space in memory. It is also used when peripherals interrupt the processor.

❏ To PUSH means to save the contents of microprocessor registers on the stack. See programming examples in Chapter 11.

❏ To POP means to restore the contents of various registers in the processor on completion of a subroutine or interrupt service routine.

CHAPTER REVIEW QUESTIONS

Section A: Multiple choice questions (Answers in Appendix A)

1. When an operation code is fetched into the microprocessor, it is transferred from memory into the
   a) accumulator
   b) flag register
   c) ALU
   d) instruction register

2. Which one of the following registers is dedicated to indicating the status of the microprocessor?
   a) program counter
   b) stack pointer
   c) condition code register
   d) accumulator

3. When a microprocessor is transferring data to and from memory, the unique identifying label given to each storage location is called the
   a) address
   b) operation code
   c) operator
   d) word

4. In a microcomputer the STACK is
   a) a read/write space in RAM
   b) one of the registers within the processor
   c) a section of ROM
   d) used to hold the operation code

5. The 2's complement of the 8-bit binary number 1101 1011 is
   a) 0010 0100
   b) 0010 0101
   c) 1010 0100
   d) 1010 0101
6. One use of the stack is to store the
   a) starting address of the main program
   b) monitor program
   c) user's program
   d) return address when using subroutines
7. The ALU is that part of the microprocessor hardware which
   a) controls the internal elements of the microprocessor
   b) only performs logic operations
   c) only performs arithmetic operations
   d) performs both arithmetic and logical operations.
8. An 8-bit microprocessor is adding two bytes. One of the bytes must reside in the
   a) instruction register
   b) flag register
   c) program counter
   d) accumulator
9. The function of the program counter in a microprocessor is to
   a) preserve the status of the ALU
   b) decode the instructions
   c) hold the address of the next program instruction to be executed
   d) count the number of clock pulses
10. The stack pointer is part of the
    a) MPU
    b) ROM
    c) PIO
    d) RAM

Section B: Short answer questions

1. Draw a block diagram which shows how the ALU, Accumulator and Flag register are connected to the internal data bus of a microcomputer.
2. State one practical application of the accumulator.

3. Name one of the flags found within the status register and with the aid of an example explain its purpose.
4. Explain the difference between PUSH and POP.
5. 1111 1111 is a two's complement number. Is the number positive or negative? What is its magnitude?
6. The following signed numbers are added in the ALU of a microprocessor,

   0000 1111

   1111 1110

   How will this addition affect each of the following flags?

   Z (Zero)

   S (Sign)

   C (Carry)
7. State why the connection between the general purpose registers and the internal data bus is bidirectional.
8. Name one register within the microprocessor which has unidirectional communications with the internal data bus.
9. State the number of BITS that can be stored in the:
   a) accumulator
   b) instruction register
   c) flag register
   d) general purpose register 'B'
   e) program counter
   f) stack pointer
10. Assuming two bytes of data are to be added. Suggest suitable registers for storing the bytes before the addition takes place.

    Where will the result be held?

Chapter 8

Other Features of Real Microprocessors: The Fetch-Execute Cycle

A simplified functional block diagram of a microprocessor was introduced in Chapters 6 and 7. Many components found in real microprocessors were omitted in the interest of clarity. However, in order to explain how practical microprocessors carry out program instructions it is necessary to look at the inside of the MPU in more detail. The additional features introduced in this chapter are emphasised in Fig 8.1. The microprocessor fetch-decode-execute cycle, and the Z80 MPU are also included in this chapter.

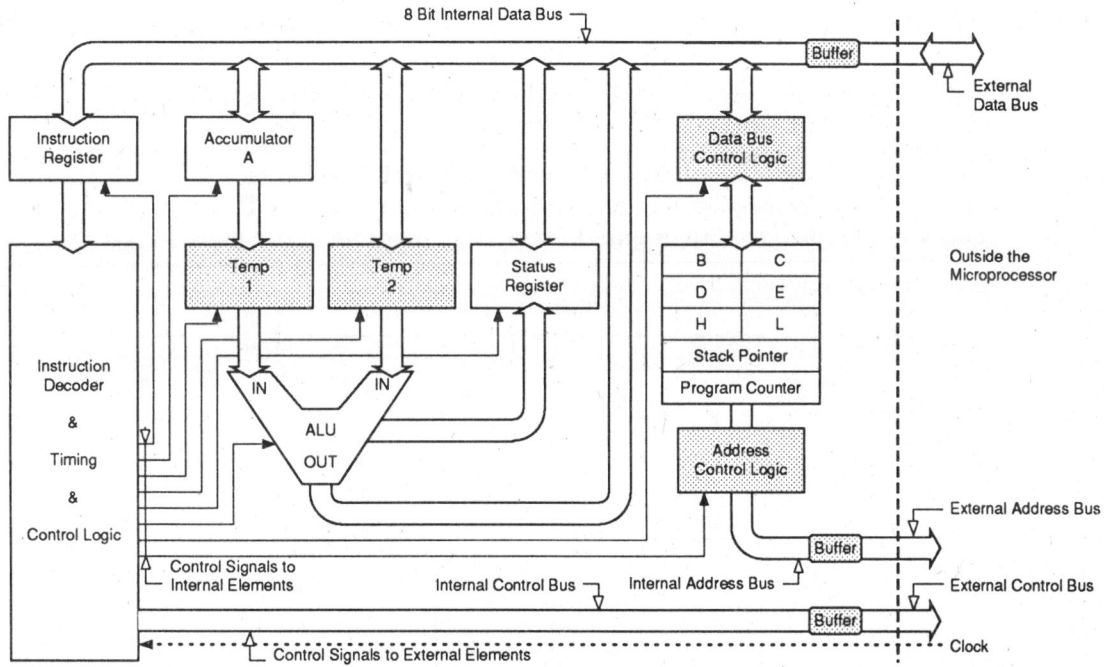

Fig 8.1 Additional microprocessor features

 Short answer question 8.1

Compare Fig 8.1 with the diagram used throughout Chapters 6 and 7 and make a list of the additional components.

8: Other features of real microprocessors – the fetch-execute cycle

> **A** Answer to SAQ 8.1
>
> The additional components are:
> * Temporary registers Temp 1 and Temp 2
> * Data bus control logic
> * Address bus control logic
> * Address/data/control bus buffers
>
> Also the internal control signals are shown going to each of the internal components.

8.1 DATA BUS CONTROL LOGIC

The data bus control logic shown in Fig 8.2, forms a two-way connection with the internal data bus. Like the other internal elements of the microprocessor, it too is controlled by the control logic. The data bus control logic performs the necessary switching between the data bus and a particular register. To illustrate how it works, assume that a byte of data is being read in from memory to register B. The data bus control logic forms a channel into register B, so that the data on the internal data bus is fed into the selected register; register B. The data bus control logic is capable of switching data to or from any one of the general purpose registers, the stack pointer or the program counter and the internal data bus.

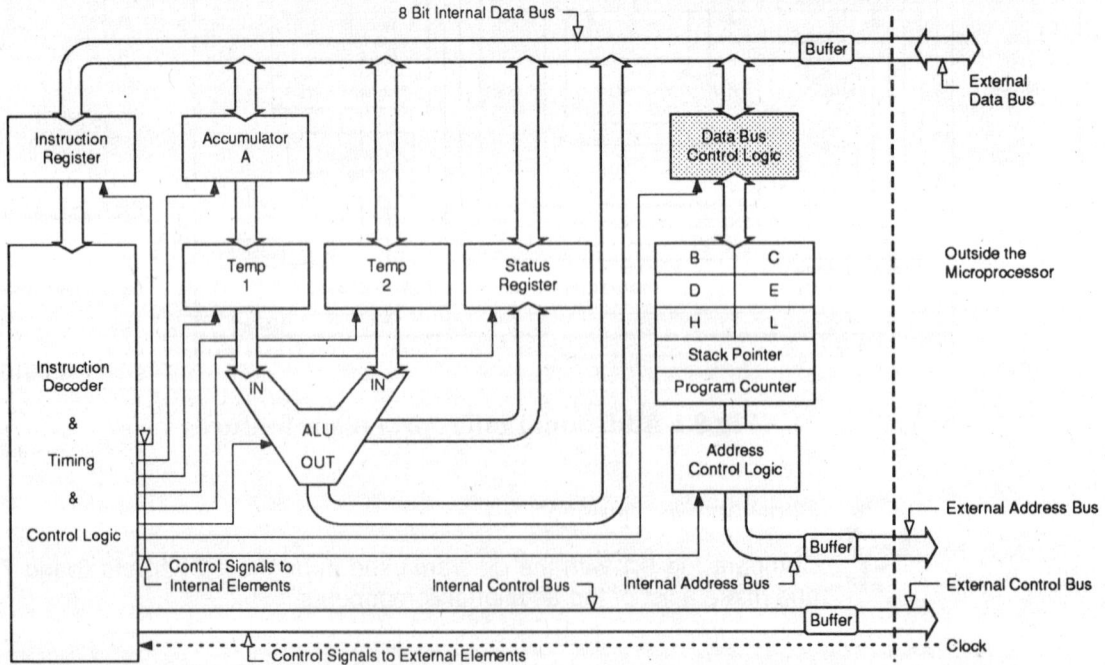

Fig 8.2 The data bus control logic of the processor.

8: Other features of real microprocessors – the fetch-execute cycle

Q Short answer question 8.2

Refer to Fig 8.2 How many bits can be transmitted simultaneously along the connection between the data bus and the data bus control logic?

A Answer to SAQ 8.2

8

8.2 ADDRESS CONTROL LOGIC

The address control logic shown in Fig 8.3, forms a one-way connection with the internal address bus, and its function is similar to the data bus control logic. Depending on the instruction being executed, the next address to appear on the address bus, could originate from a number of different registers, such as, the PC or SP or a general purpose register pair. The address control logic connects the current address register to the internal address bus.

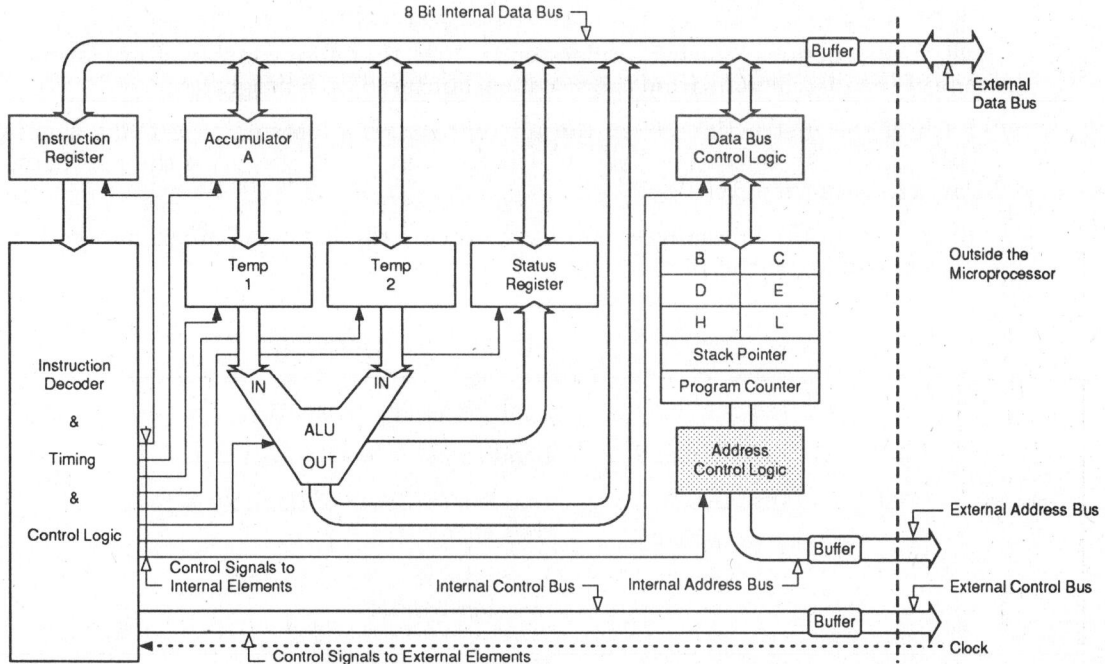

Fig 8.3 The address control logic of the processor.

8: Other features of real microprocessors – the fetch-execute cycle

 Short answer question 8.3

Is the address control logic a bidirectional or unidirectional device? Explain.

 Answer to SAQ 8.3

Unidirectional, because addresses are always generated by the microprocessor.

8.3 DATA/ADDRESS/CONTROL BUS BUFFERS

The purpose of these buffers is to drive the external system buses and to provide isolation between the external and internal buses under certain conditions, such as, Direct Memory Access (D.M.A.).

8.4 THE MICROPROCESSOR FETCH – DECODE – EXECUTE CYCLE

In Chapter 11 we will see that each microprocessor has a unique instruction set; a set of instructions which it understands. It is therefore capable of executing any one of the instructions from the set, if encountered, in a program.

Each of the instructions from the microprocessor's instruction set has a unique code, called the Operation Code, which specifies which operation the microprocessor is to perform next.

Imagine that the microprocessor has to execute the following program, which consists of five instructions.

Instruction No.	Effect of the Instruction
Instruction 1	Load register A with 4BH
Instruction 2	Load register B with 55H
Instruction 3	Add the contents of Register B to that of register A
Instruction 4	Store the result at memory location 2100H
Instruction 5	Halt the processor

When the processor starts to execute this program it will go through the following sequence for the first instruction:

i   FETCH the operation code for the first instruction from the memory, and place it in the instruction register.

ii DECODE the instruction ; the instruction decoder determines which operation from the instruction set of the microprocessor is to be carried out.

iii EXECUTE the instruction, or carry out the operation requested by the programmer in that instruction.

Having gone through the three cycles, FETCH, DECODE, EXECUTE for the first instruction, it then moves to the second instruction, and again performs these three cycles. In fact, it goes through the same three cycles for every instruction in the program. When the microprocessor encounters the HALT instruction it halts the processor.

The process of FETCHING, DECODING and EXECUTING instructions within a program is illustrated in Fig 8.4

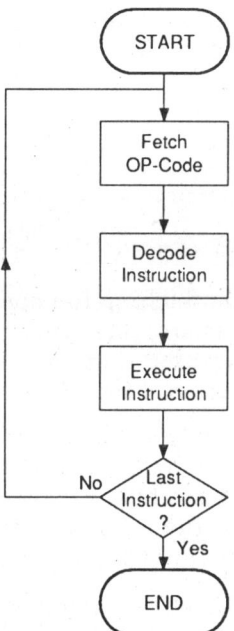

Fig 8.4 Flowchart illustrating the FETCH-DECODE-EXECUTE cycle which a microprocessor goes through while running a program.

 Short answer question 8.4

In the fetch-decode-execute flowchart what is meant by 'FETCH OP–CODE'?

Answer to SAQ 8.4

It indicates that the processor is reading in an instruction (op-code) from memory into the control unit of the microprocessor (instruction register)

8.5 HOW THE MICROPROCESSOR EXECUTES AN INSTRUCTION

Consider an instruction which is to load the Accumulator with the byte of data 6CH.

This instruction may be formally written as:

LD A,6CH (This topic is covered in Chapter 11.)

The three cycles for this instruction will now be examined; the FETCH – DECODE – EXECUTE cycle.

FETCH CYCLE

Fig 8.5 shows that the operation code 3EH for this particular instruction is stored in random access memory at location 2000H, and the byte of data, 6CH, which is to be loaded into register A, is stored in the next consecutive memory location, 2001H.

The steps involved in fetching the operation code from the RAM into the instruction register of the microprocessor are summarised below, and are clearly illustrated in Fig 8.5. Assume that the program counter (PC) has been loaded with 2000H; the start address of the instruction.

1. The control circuitry sends a signal to the Address Control Logic, which then selects the PC and switches the address 2000H which is held in the PC onto the internal address bus. From the internal address bus, the address 2000H is taken through the address buffer to the external system address bus. The RAM now knows that the memory location being selected is 2000H.

2. The control logic now activates the memory read (RD) signal. This is necessary because the operation code 3EH has to be read out from the RAM onto the data bus.

3. After a short delay, known as the memory access time, the operation code (OP-CODE) 3EH appears on the external data bus.

4. The operation code is then transmitted back along the external data bus, to the data pins of the processor, and from there it is taken via the data bus buffer to the internal data bus.

5. The control logic then activates the internal control signal which is connected to the instruction register, and the OP-CODE 3EH is placed in the instruction register.

8: Other features of real microprocessors – the fetch-execute cycle

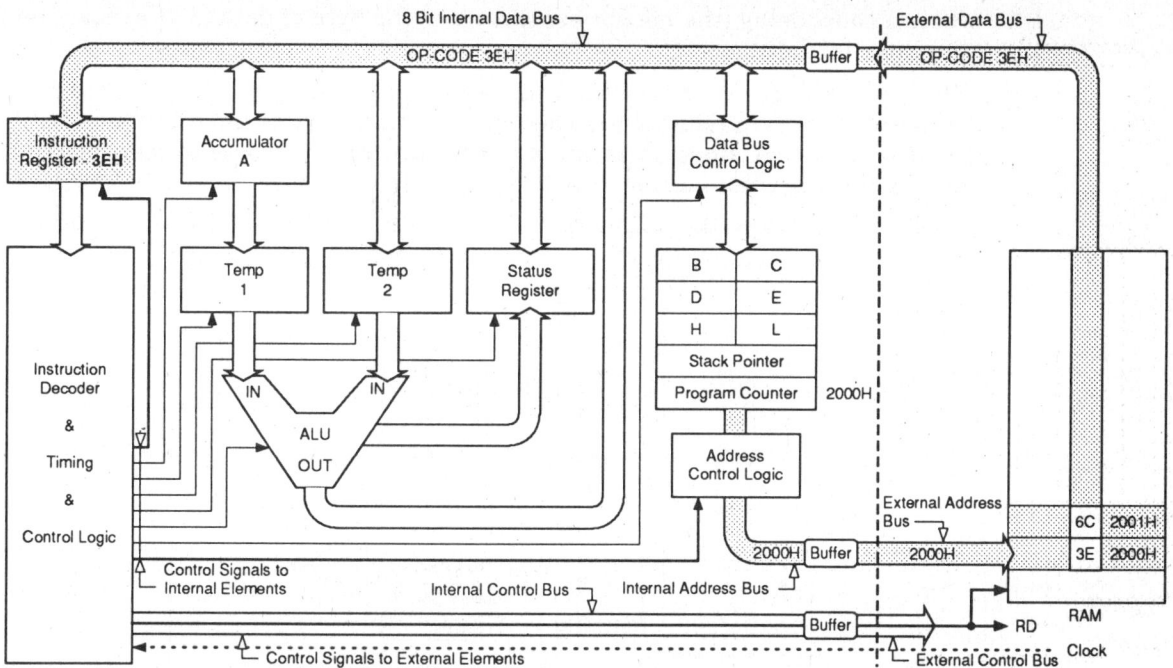

Fig 8.5 OP-CODE FETCH for the instruction LD A, 6CH

DECODE CYCLE

Once the instruction is in the instruction register, the instruction decoder can establish which operation is to be performed, and together with the timing/control logic, manipulates the internal registers and buses, so that the instruction is carried out during the execute cycle.

EXECUTE CYCLE

While the operation code was being fetched from memory, the PC was incremented (by 1) so it now holds the address 2001H, which is the address of the byte of data, 6CH, in random access memory, which has to be loaded into the accumulator.

During the EXECUTE cycle the microprocessor carries out the steps listed below, which are illustrated in Fig 8.6

1. The control circuitry sends a signal to the Address Control Logic, which then selects the PC and switches the address 2001H, stored in the PC, onto the internal address bus. This address is then transmitted through the address buffer, to the external address bus. The RAM now knows that memory location 2001H is being selected.

2. The control logic activates the memory read (RD) signal. This is necessary in order to read out the byte of data, 6CH, from the RAM to the external data bus.

8: Other features of real microprocessors – the fetch-execute cycle

3. After a short delay (the memory access time) the byte of data 6CH appears on the external data bus.

4. The byte of data on the external data bus is then taken via the data bus buffer to the internal data bus. The control logic activates the internal control signal, which is connected to the accumulator, and the byte of data 6CH is placed in the accumulator.

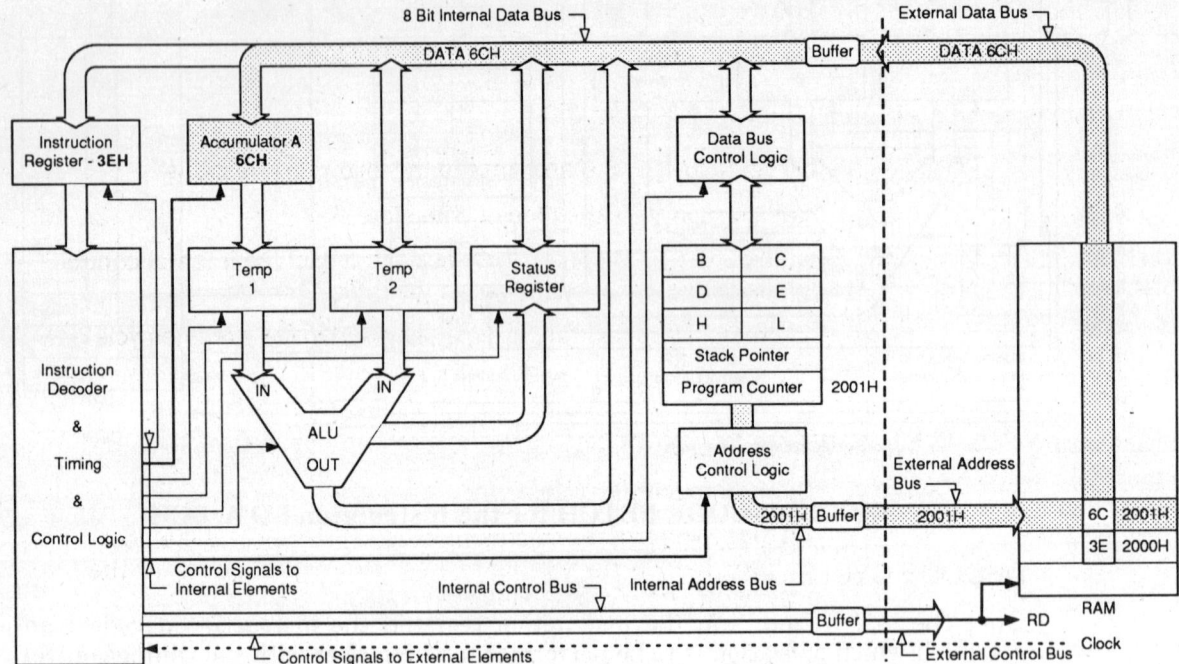

Fig 8.6 LD A,6CH EXECUTE CYCLE

Short answer question 8.5

For the op-code fetch part of the instruction LD A,6CH answer the following questions.

a) In which RAM location was the op-code stored?

b) Along which of the three microprocessor buses was the op-code transmitted?

c) In which microprocessor register was the op-code stored?

d) At the end of the op-code fetch what value was stored in the PC?

8: Other features of real microprocessors – the fetch-execute cycle

Answer to SAQ 8.5

a) 2000H
b) Data bus
c) Instruction register
d) 2001H

Short answer question 8.6

Carefully examine Fig 8.6 and answer the following questions

a) In which register is the byte of data stored?
b) Did the timing and control logic activate any of the internal control signals during the execute part of the cycle?
c) Did the data bus control logic play any part in the execute cycle?

Answer to SAQ 8.6

a) The accumulator or register A
b) Yes, for example, the internal control signal going to the accumulator had to be enabled. Also, the signal going to the address control logic had to be activated.
c) NO

8.6 ANOTHER EXAMPLE OF THE FETCH – DECODE – EXECUTE CYCLE

In this example, register B, one of the general purpose registers will be loaded with the byte of data 5FH. As with the previous example, this instruction is stored at memory locations 2000H and 2001H. The operation code for this instruction is 06H. Due to the similarity with the previous example only a brief explanation is given.

FETCH CYCLE

The main activities are illustrated in the block diagram of Fig 8.7.

1. The microprocessor outputs the address 2000H from the PC to the address bus.
2. The memory read (RD) signal is activated by the processor.
3. The byte of OP-CODE, 06H, is read from memory location 2000H onto the external data bus.

8: Other features of real microprocessors – the fetch-execute cycle

4. The op-code is transmitted from the external data bus to the internal data bus.

5. The internal control signal going to the instruction register (IR) is activated by the control circuitry and it places the OP-CODE 06H in the IR.

During the OP-CODE FETCH the PC is incremented, by 1. It now stores the address 2001H.

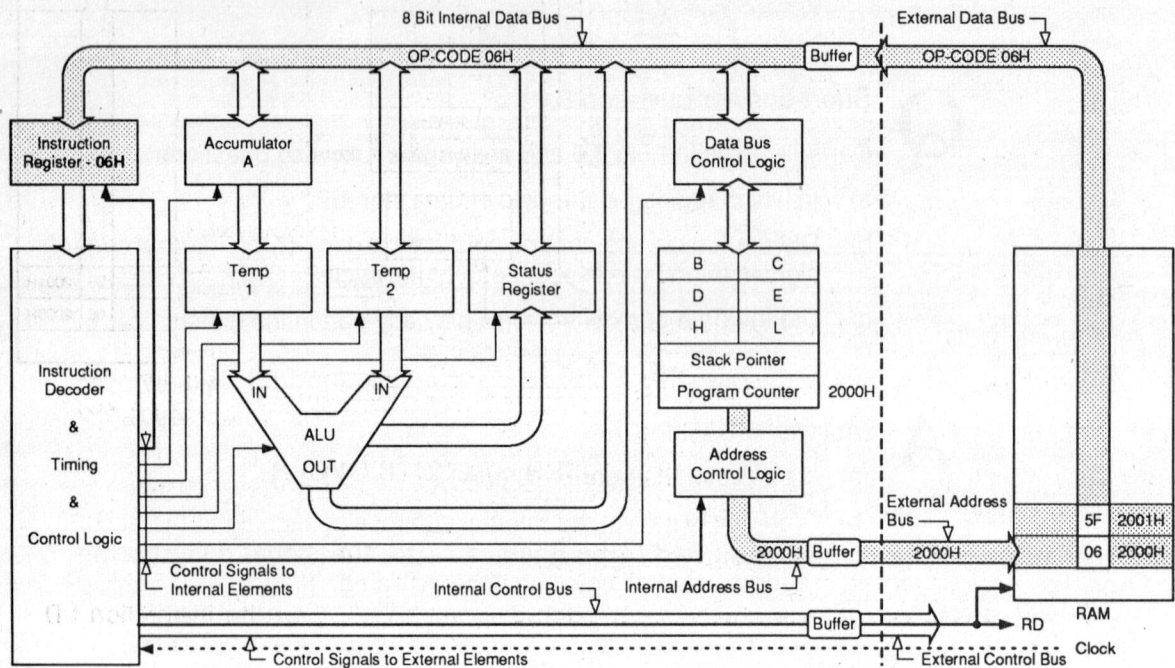

Fig. 8.7 LD B, 5FH OP-CODE FETCH cycle

EXECUTE CYCLE

The registers and main signals involved in this cycle are shown in Fig 8.8. The execute cycle involves the following steps.

1. The microprocessor outputs the address 2001H from the PC to the address bus.

2. The memory read (RD) signal is activated by the processor.

3. The byte of data, 5FH, is read from memory location 2001H, onto the external data bus

4. The data is transmitted from the external data bus to the internal data bus.

5. The control circuitry sends a signal to the data bus control logic which makes a connection between the internal data bus and the general purpose register B. The byte of data is then placed in register B.

The PC is incremented to 2002H where it expects the next instruction to start.

8: Other features of real microprocessors – the fetch-execute cycle

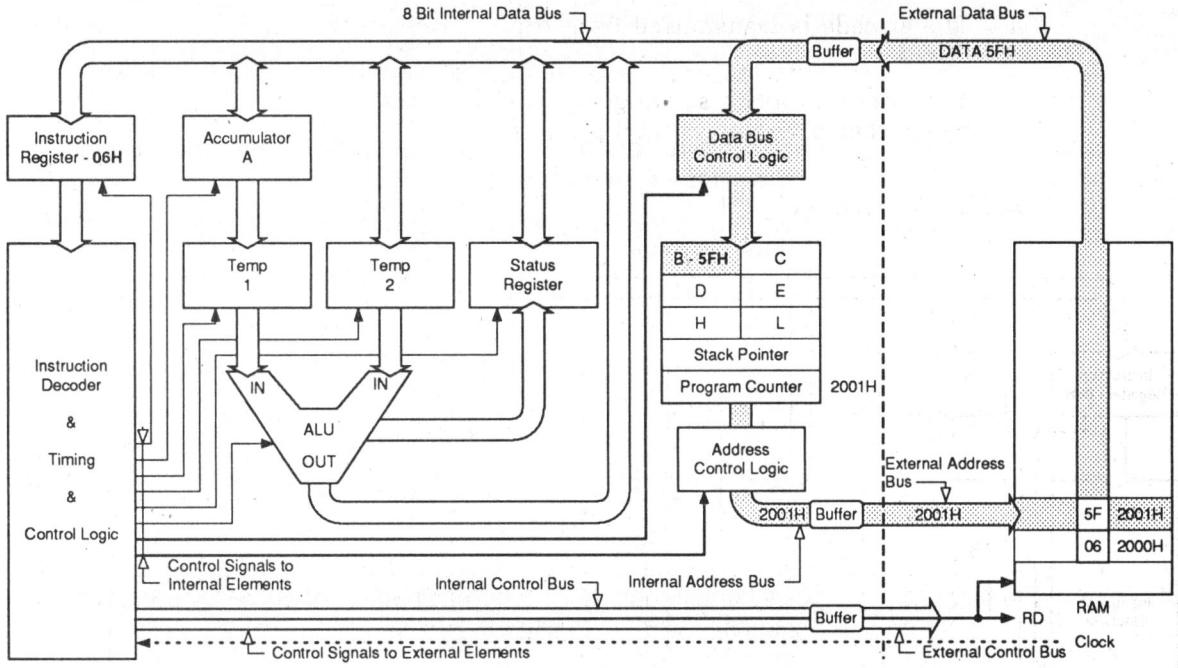

Fig. 8.8 LD B,5FH EXECUTE CYCLE

Short answer question 8.7

Refer to the op-code fetch diagram, Fig 8.7, for the instruction LD B,5FH and explain.

a) Why did the PC initially hold the address 2000H?

b) During the op-code fetch cycle what happens to the program counter?

c) Did the address control logic play any part in the op-code fetch cycle?

Answer to SAQ 8.7

a) Because the op-code for the instruction was stored at memory location 2000H in RAM.

b) It was incremented, by 1, to 2001H

c) Yes, because the address 2000H had to be output from the program counter to the address bus.

189

8: Other features of real microprocessors – the fetch-execute cycle

Short answer question 8.8

Refer to the execute cycle diagram, Fig 8.8, for the instruction LD B,5FH and answer the following questions.

a) Which component of the microprocessor activated the RD signal and what is it's purpose?

b) Were any of the internal processor control signals enabled during this cycle?

c) State the contents of register B in binary

Answer to SAQ 8.8

a) The timing/control logic of the processor. The function of the memory read (RD) signal is to enable the data to be read out from the RAM to the system data bus.

b) Yes. For instance, the internal control signal going to the data bus control logic had to be enabled, so that the byte of data could be stored in register B.

c) 5FH = 0101   1111 in binary

8.7 USING THE ALU TO PERFORM ARITHMETIC OPERATIONS

For this example, it is assumed that registers A and B have been loaded with the bytes of data 06H and 04H respectively. Remember, that whenever the ALU manipulates two bytes of data, the accumulator must hold one of them. When the operation is completed the accumulator will hold the result.

FETCH CYCLE

The operation code for this instruction 80H is stored at memory location 2000H in random access memory. Refer to Fig 8.9 which illustrates the OP-CODE FETCH cycle.

A summary of the steps involved during this cycle is:

1. The microprocessor outputs the contents of the PC 2000H to the address bus.
2. The processor activates the memory read (RD) signal.
3. The op-code, 80H, is read from memory location 2000H onto the external data bus.
4. The op-code is transmitted from the external data bus to the internal data bus.
5. The control logic activates the signal going to the instruction register and the byte of OP-CODE is placed in the instruction register.

8: Other features of real microprocessors – the fetch-execute cycle

During the OP-CODE FETCH cycle the PC is incremented to address 2001H.

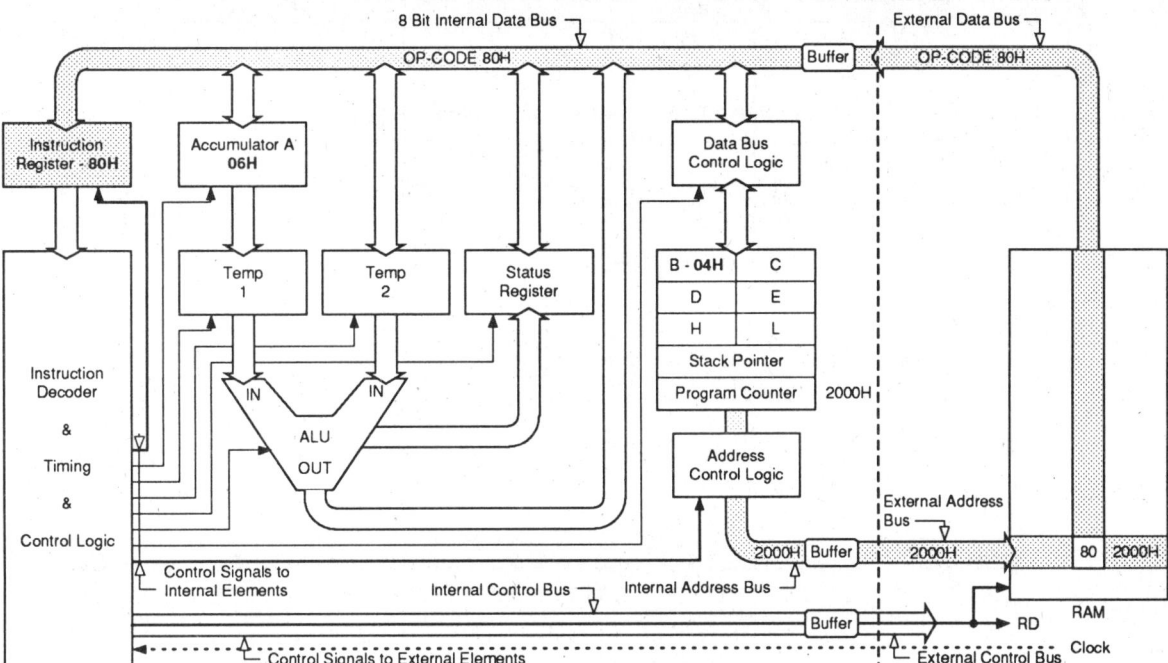

Fig 8.9 ADD A,B OP-CODE FETCH cycle

EXECUTE CYCLE Part I

In this part of the cycle two transfers will be carried out simultaneoulsy. Firstly, the contents of register B will be transferred to the temporary register, Temp 2. At the same time the contents of the accumulator are transferred into the other temporary register, Temp 1. By inspecting Fig 8.10 it can be ascertained that these transfers can occur in parallel, as they use different paths within the system. Parallel transfers speed up the operation.

8: Other features of real microprocessors – the fetch-execute cycle

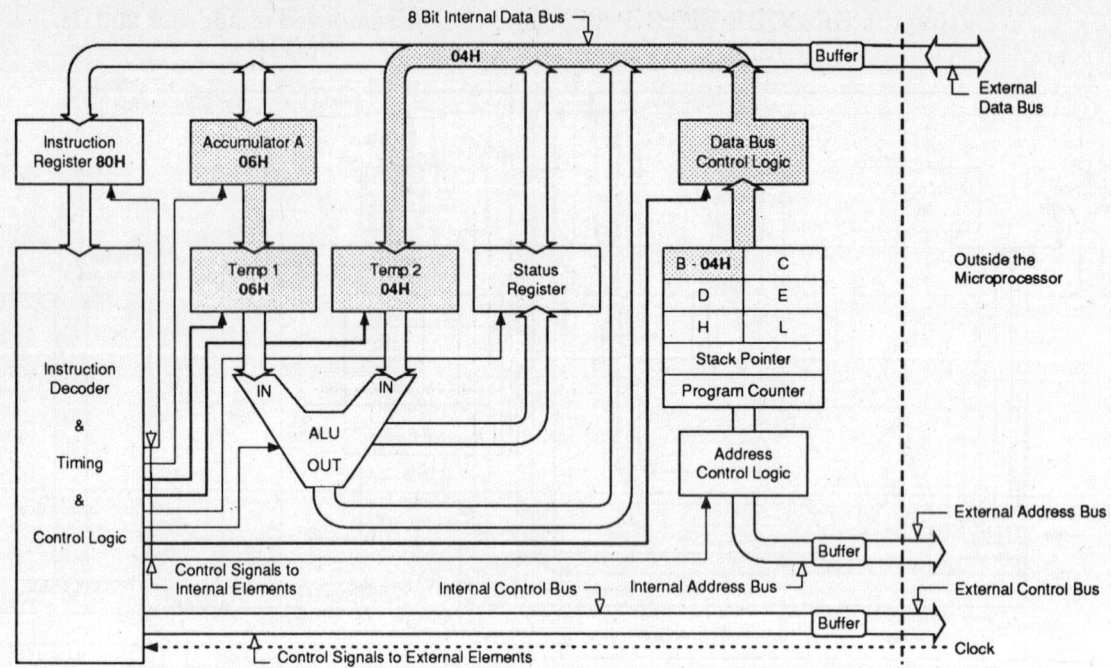

Fig 8.10 ADD A,B EXECUTE CYCLE Part I

EXECUTE CYCLE Part II

Now both inputs of the ALU are correctly conditioned and the addition may be performed. Fig 8.11 shows that Temp 1 and Temp 2 provide the two inputs to the ALU. On receiving the signal from the control circuitry the ALU adds the two bytes and generates the result 0AH, which is taken from the output of the ALU, to the internal data bus, and from there it is clocked into the accumulator by the control signal from the control logic. The main activities that occur during the execute cycle part II are illustrated in Fig 8.11

8: Other features of real microprocessors – the fetch-execute cycle

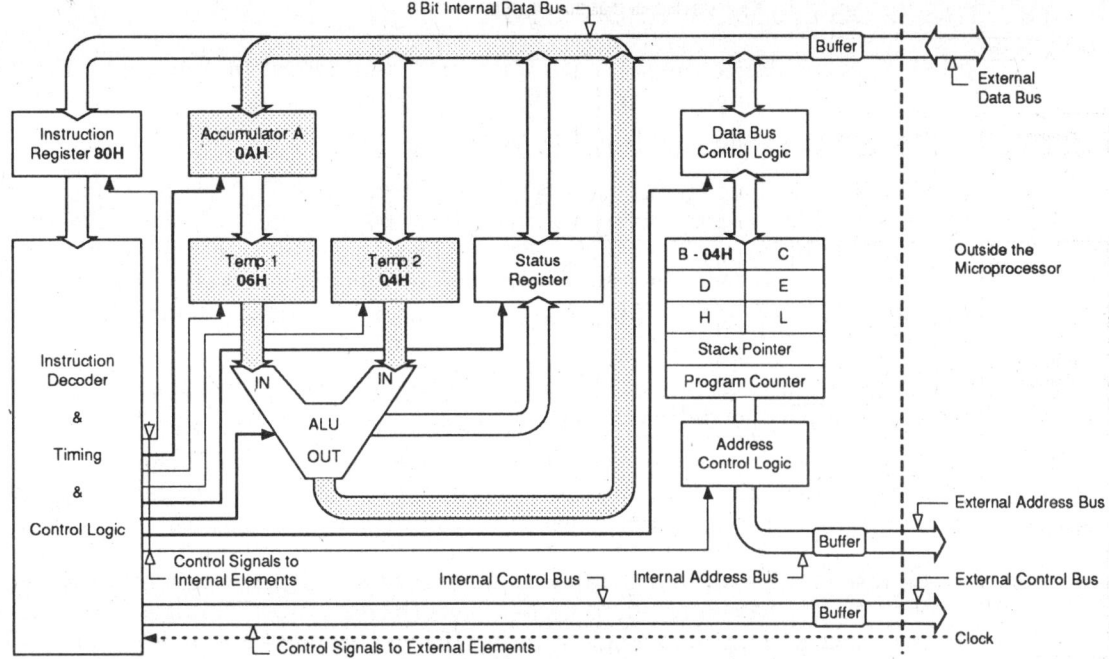

Fig 8.11 ADD A,B EXECUTE CYCLE Part II

Short answer question 8.9

Refer to Fig 8.11 and explain

a) Why does the accumulator now contain 0AH?

b) What happened to the 06H which was originally stored in the accumulator?

c) What is the present contents of the program counter?

Answer to SAQ 8.9

a) Because the result of adding 04H and 06H is stored in the accumulator; 04H + 06H = 0AH

b) It was overwritten by the result of the computation

c) 2001H

8.8 THE ZILOG Z80 MICROPROCESSOR

This is very similar to the standard microprocessor described previously. Fig 8.12 shows a simplified block diagram of the Zilog Z80 microprocessor.

The Z80 has two additional features. These are:

i) Two independent 16-bit index registers (IX and IY). The Z80 provides a large number of instructions for use with these two registers. These registers are used for indexed addressing. The addressing modes will be examined in Chapter 11. At this stage it is only necessary to appreciate that the use of the index registers by the programmer can greatly simplify many types of programs, especially where tables of data are used.

ii) An alternate register set not shown on the diagram. (For details refer to the programmer's model given in Section 8.9)

At any one time the programmer can select either set of registers to work with through a single exchange command for the entire set of general purpose registers. In systems where fast interrupt response is required, one set of general purpose registers may be reserved and an accumulator/flag register may be reserved for handling this very fast routine. Only a simple exchange command need be executed to go between the routines. This greatly reduces interrupt service time by eliminating the requirement for saving and retrieving register contents in the external stack during interrupt or subroutine processing.

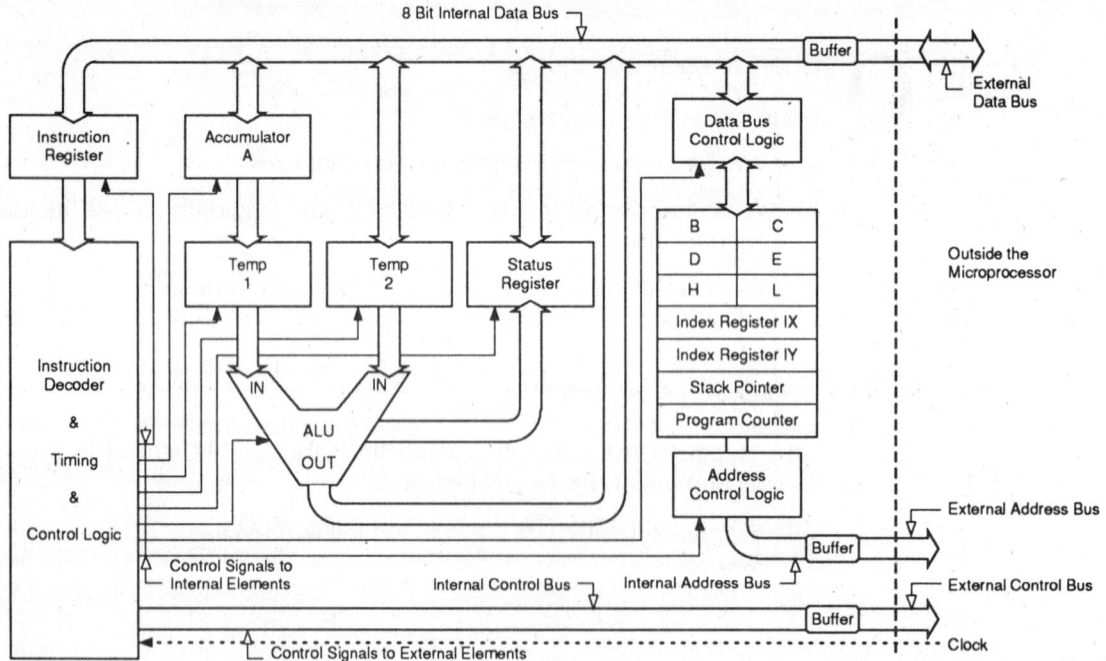

Fig 8.12 Simplified Z80 microprocessor architecture

8.9 PROGRAMMING MODEL OF Z80 MPU

The programming model of a microprocessor indicates those parts of the microprocessor which are accessible to the programmer. It only shows the **registers** of the microprocessor **which may be used by the programmer**. The value stored in any of the registers shown in the programming model may be changed under program control. Fig 8.13 shows a simplified programming model of the Z80 processor

Note the alternate register set, which was referred to in Section 8.9

Main Register Set		Alternative Register Set		
Accumulator A	Flags F	Accumulator A1	Flags F1	
B	C	B1	C1	General
D	E	D1	E1	Purpose
H	L	H1	L1	Registers

Index Register IX	
Index Register IY	Special
Stack Pointer SP	Purpose
Program Counter PC	Registers

Fig 8.13 Z80 register configuration

SUMMARY

- ❐ The data bus control logic is capable of switching data to or from any one of the general purpose registers, the stack pointer or the program counter and the internal MPU data bus.
- ❐ The address control logic connects the current address register to the internal address bus.
- ❐ When the microprocessor is executing an instruction it proceeds in three cycles:
  - I   FETCH the operation code from RAM and store it in the instruction register within the MPU.
  - II DECODE the instruction. The decoder works out which instruction has to be carried out.
  - III EXECUTE the instruction. The control logic generates all of the necessary signals in order to carry out the instruction.
- ❐ The programming model of a microprocessor shows which registers are available to the programmer.

CHAPTER REVIEW QUESTIONS

Section A: Multiple choice questions (Answers in Appendix A)

1. The function of the microprocessor clock circuit is to
    a) tell the processor when to start the program
    b) provide a basic timing reference
    c) invert incoming signals
    d) act as a counter

2. When a microprocessor is reading data from memory the $\overline{RD}$ line is at
    a) logic 1
    b) logic 0
    c) half way between logic 1 and logic 0
    d) either logic 0 or logic 1

3. The memory read signal is part of the
    a) data bus
    b) address bus
    c) I/O bus
    d) control bus

4. The memory read signal within a microprocessor based system is activated by the
    a) RAM
    b) ROM
    c) Input/output device
    d) Microprocessor

5. When the microprocessor is executing a program it goes through three cycles for each instruction, these are
    a) fetch the op code
       execute the instruction
       decode the instruction
    b) execute the instruction
       decode the instruction
       fetch the op code
    c) decode the instruction
       fetch the op code
       execute the instruction
    d) fetch the op code
       decode the instruction
       execute the instruction

8: Other features of real microprocessors – the fetch-execute cycle

6. The function of the microprocessor is to
   a) store the user's applications package
   b) store the system software
   c) process data and generate the signals necessary to control the system
   d) run a memory self-test program when the system is switched on

7. The first byte of every machine code instruction is the
   a) operand
   b) address
   c) location
   d) operation code

8. During the operation code fetch cycle, the MPU must
   a) save the contents of all of its registers on the stack
   b) perform a POP operation
   c) output the contents of the program counter to the address bus
   d) generate a memory write signal

9. When an operation code is read from memory it is released onto the
   a) control bus
   b) address bus
   c) data bus
   d) the address, data and control buses

10. The programmer's model of a microprocessor is
    a) never published by the manufacturer
    b) of no use whatsoever
    c) the same for all 8-bit microprocessors
    d) used by assembly language programmers

Section B: Short answer questions

1. Describe the meaning of the following terms:
   i) Address
   ii) Memory location

2. With the aid of an example describe the difference between a memory READ and WRITE signal.

3. Draw the block diagram of a typical 8-bit microprocessor.

   Your answer must include:
   i) the accumulator
   ii) status register
   iii) ALU

8: Other features of real microprocessors – the fetch-execute cycle

iv) instruction register
v) instruction decoder
vi) timing and control logic
vii) the six general purpose registers
viii) any necessary buffers
ix) data and address bus control logic
x) any necessary temporary registers.
xi) the stack pointer
xii) the program counter
and the internal buses.

4 For a Zilog Z80 microprocessor briefly explain the function of each of the registers which are available to the programmer.

5 Draw a flowchart to illustrate how a microprocessor executes a program

6 With the aid of a diagram explain how the MPU would perform the op-code fetch cycle for the instruction LD B,A. This instruction copies the contents of the accumulator into register B, and the operation code, 47H, is stored at memory location 2100H.

7 Having performed an op-code fetch the MPU now knows that it has to load the byte of data, CFH, which is stored at memory location 2200H into the general purpose register D. With the aid of a diagram describe the EXECUTE cycle for this instruction.

Chapter 9
Microcomputer Memories

Microcomputers and microprocessor-based products such as, the logic analyser (Chapter 13) require memory for storing digital data and programs in the form of binary-coded instructions. In Chapter 8 we saw that when a microcomputer is running a program the MPU is in constant communication with the random access memory (RAM) where the user's program is stored. When your Personal Computer (PC) is first switched on it performs a RAM self-test before loading the operating system into it. Some of the system software for a PC is stored in Read Only Memories or Erasable Programmable ROMs (EPROMs) while in the case of small single board microcomputer systems all of the system software is generally stored in some type of ROM. Hence a good understanding of computer memories is desirable.

This chapter is devoted to semiconductor RAM and ROM memory. Functional block diagrams for both will be examined. Illustrations of how to connect memories to the address and data buses will be given. Memory decoding will be introduced with the aid of practical examples illustrating how to connect ROM and RAM to the microprocessor.

9.1 INTRODUCTION

We will begin our study of memories with a summary of the following key words associated with memories.

- Memory cell
- Memory word
- Storage capacity
- Address
- Read operation
- Read access time
- Write operation
- Random Access memory
- Read Only Memory
- Static and dynamic memories
- Main store
- Backing store

Memory cell

The basic unit of semiconductor memory is the memory cell which is a device or electrical circuit capable of storing a single binary digit; 0 or 1. The memory cell may be constructed from either bipolar (NPN/ PNP) or MOS (MOSFETs) transistors. In Chapter 4 we saw that a flip-flip is a 1-bit memory cell. Another example of a memory cell is a charged capacitor. The presence of an electric charge on the plates of a capacitor represents bit 1: no stored charge corresponds to bit 0.

Memory word

If memory cells are organised in groups they can be used to store a number of bits. For instance, a register (See Chapter 6) consisting of eight flip-flops can be considered to be a memory that is storing an 8-bit word (a byte). In this case the memory word size (or width or length) is 8 bits. Popular word sizes for microcomputers are 8, 16 and 32 bits.

Storage capacity

This is a way of specifying the total number of bits stored in a particular memory device or complete memory system. The organisation of a memory chip may be expressed as:

Memory organisation = Number of words × number of bits per word

For example, a RAM may be organised as 1024 × 8 or 2048 × 8 or 16384 × 4, to name just a few types of memory organisations. The first number in the specification indicates the total number of words contained within a single IC. The second indicates the number of bits per word (word size). Generally, the number of words in a memory is a multiple of 1024. It is common to use the designation '1k' to represent 1024 (2^{10}) when referring to memory storage capacity. Thus, a memory with a storage capacity of 2k bytes = 2 × 1024 × 8 = 16384 bits. For larger memories the storage capacity may be expressed in Mega bytes (Mb). One Mb = 2^{20}.

Short answer question 9.1

Calculate the number of words and the total number of bits stored in a 1Mbyte memory IC.

Answer to SAQ 9.1

Total words = 2^{20} = 1,048,576

Hence total number of bits = 1,048,576 × 8 = 8,388,608 bits

Address

The address is a number that identifies the location of a word in memory. Each word stored in memory has a unique address. Addresses are always expressed as binary numbers, although as we saw previously (Chapter 2) they are frequently represented in hexadecimal or octal for convenience. Fig 9.1 illustrates a small 8 word memory. Each of these words has a specific binary address. For example, the binary address code for word 4 is 100. In a microcomputer the addresses are issued by the microprocessor. In this example we see that three address bits are required to address any one of the eight memory locations. A memory consisting of 16 words would require a 4-bit address and so on.

Short answer question 9.2

A computer memory is capable of storing 1024 words. Calculate the number of address lines needed in order to be able to address any one of its locations.

 Answer to SAQ 9.2

No. of memory locations = 2^x where x = number of address lines

$1024 = 2^x$ Hence number of address lines = 10.

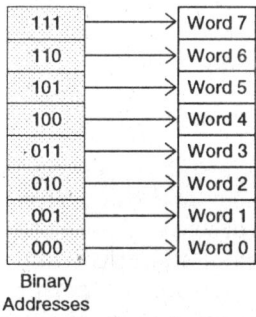

Fig 9.1 Memory addresses

Read operation

When the microprocessor wishes to perform a memory read operation it issues the binary address of the word it wants to select in memory. It also activates **control signals** such as, memory read. After a short delay the selected data word is released from the memory onto the data bus. It is taken via the data bus to the MPU. Basically, the read operation consists of taking data out from a specific memory location. Reading data from memory does not affect the stored information in any way.

Access time

After the MPU has issued the address and other signals which are necessary to perform a memory read operation, the system has to wait for a certain length of time, called **read access time.** This is the time between the memory receiving a new input address and the data becoming available at the output. Access time is a measure of the devices operating speed. The faster the speed (the lower the access time) the more expensive the device.

Write operation

Write is the operation whereby a new word is placed into a particular memory location. It is also referred to as a **store** operation. The results of arithmetic calculations that take place within the MPU may be written into random access memory. Whenever a new word is written into a memory location it overwrites (replaces) the original word stored at that location.

Random Access Memory: RAM

Random access memory, universally known as RAM, but more realistically described as any memory that **can have information both written into it and also read out of it**. The term random access is used to define memory in which the actual physical location of a memory word has no effect on how long it takes to read from or write into that memory location. In this sense ROM semiconductor memories could be described as being random access memories.

Random access memory is **volatile** (assuming no back up power supply) which means that as soon as the power to it is switched off all information in the memory is lost.

Read Only Memories: ROM

The program stored in the ROM part of a microcomputer system is a computer program that needs no alterations. Since RAM is a volatile memory, turning power off and on again destroys the binary information stored in it. The ROM is **non-volatile** memory and the program stored in it is available every time power is turned on. The process of entering data is called **programming** or **burning** the ROM. The part of the operating system which handles the communications between the computer and its peripherals, known as BIOS, (Basic input-output system) is programmed into ROM chips. In small single board microcomputer systems the complete operating system (the monitor) may be stored in ROM.

Static and Dynamic memories

Static **R**andom **A**ccess **M**emories, commonly known as **SRAMs**, store data for as long as the power is left switched on, without the need for periodically rewriting the data into memory (refreshing). SRAM memory cells are essentially flip-flops which will hold their stored information provided the power supply is not interrupted. For applications where speed and reduced complexity are more critical than space and power considerations, static RAMs are still the best. They are generally faster than dynamic RAMs and require no refresh operation. Although they are simpler to design with, they cannot compete with the higher capacity and lower power requirement of dynamic RAMs.

Dynamic **R**andom **A**ccess **M**emories or **DRAMs** are fabricated using MOS (Metal Oxide Semiconductor) technology. The capacitive effect between the gate and the source of the MOS transistor can be used to hold charges which represent 1s and 0s.

Basically, the presence of a charge on the capacitor may be used to represent one logic state and its absence the other logic state. Because these charges leak off after a period of time, dynamic RAMs require periodic charging of the memory cells; this is called **refreshing** the dynamic RAM. Typically, each cell must be refreshed about every 2mS or its data will be lost. Where large amounts of random access memory are required in personal computers DRAMs are used. For a given amount of memory they occupy much less space than SRAMs. The cost per bit of dynamic RAMs is typically $\frac{1}{5}$ to $\frac{1}{4}$ that of static RAMs.

9: Microcomputer memories

The need for refreshing is a disadvantage of DRAM as compared to SRAMs because it adds a requirement to the memory system design.

Main store

This is the computers internal memory which stores the instructions and data that the MPU is currently working on. The chief requirement of the main store is to provide fast response to microprocessor read and write requests. It usually consists of semiconductor memory devices.

Backing store

This is used to store large amounts of information external to the computer's main (internal) store. It is generally slower than internal memory and is always non-volatile. Modern backing stores use magnetic tape and disk. (See Chapter 12).

Short answer question 9.3

Briefly explain the difference between SRAM and DRAM.

Answer to SAQ 9.3

Static random access memory (SRAM) uses flip-flops to store information which is retained as long as the power is not interrupted.

Dynamic random access memory (DRAM) relies on storing an electric charge on a capacitor. Because the charge leaks away the memory cells must be refreshed periodically.

9.2 READ ONLY MEMORIES.

ROMs are semiconductor memories used to provide a microprocessor system with non-volatile internal (main) memory. Information in ROM can be read out but not altered. There are several types of non-volatile memory that can be used in microcomputer systems. These are:

Read Only Memory: ROM
Programmable Read Only Memory: PROM
Erasable Programmable Read Only Memory: EPROM
Electrically Erasable Programmable Read Only Memory: EEPROM

Irrespective of the type of ROM used, data can only ever be read out from the device. (See Fig 9.2.)

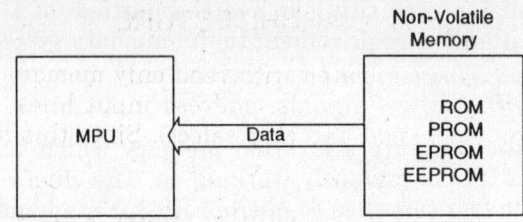

Fig 9.2 Reading data from ROMs

ROM

The ROM is programmed by the manufacturer. Once data has been entered into the device it cannot be altered subsequently. ROMs are used to store programs and data that are not to change during the operation of a system. A major use for ROMs is the storage of programs in microcomputers. Since all ROMs are non-volatile, these programs are not lost when the microcomputer is turned off. At switch on the microcomputer can immediately begin executing the program stored in ROM.

PROM

A PROM may be programmed by the manufacturer or the user. Once programmed the contents of the PROM cannot be altered.

EPROM

The main disadvantage of the PROM device is the fact that it cannot be reprogrammed. An EPROM may be programmed by the manufacturer or the user. Data is programmed into an EPROM by applying high voltage signals. Data is erased by shining ultraviolet light onto a transparent window that covers the IC. This process takes about 20 to 30 minutes. These devices are often used in development work where the program may undergo several changes. In personal computers a firmware upgrade may be performed by replacing the EPROMs with new ones supplied by the manufacturer. EPROMs have two major disadvantages. First, they have to be removed from their sockets in order to be erased and reprogrammed. Furthermore, erasure removes the complete memory contents; this necessitates complete reprogramming even when only one memory word has changed. The EEPROM was developed as an improvement to the EPROM.

EEPROM

Electrically erasable programmable read only memory, also known as electrically alterable programmable read only memory (EAPROM) can be programmed and erased in circuit by the application of suitable electrical pulses. Unlike the EPROM it may be selectively reprogrammed.

No matter which non-volatile memory you are using in your system application, the operating characteristics are all very similar. In the next section a functional block diagram of ROM will be examined.

9.3 ROM SIGNALS AND ARCHITECTURE

Typical signals associated with read only memory (ROM) are given in Fig 9.3 (a). It has three sets of signals: address input lines, data output lines, and control inputs (memory read and chip select). Since this memory stores 1024 (1k) words, it has 1024 different storage locations and therefore 1024 different binary addresses ranging from 00 0000 0000 to 11 1111 1111 (0 to 1023 in decimal). Thus there are 10 address inputs (2^{10} = 1024), A_0 to A_9. The memory addresses which the MPU would issue in order to select locations 0,1 and 2 are:

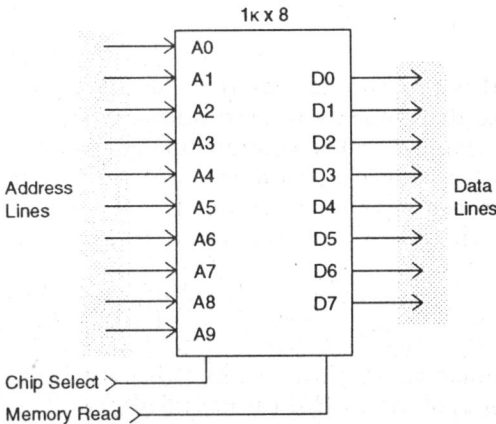

Fig 9.3(a) ROM signals

A_9	A_8	A_7	A_6	A_5	A_4	A_3	A_2	A_1	A_0	
0	0	0	0	0	0	0	0	0	0	Location 0
0	0	0	0	0	0	0	0	0	1	Location 1
0	0	0	0	0	0	0	0	1	0	Location 2

The data outputs of the ROM are tristate outputs which permits the connection of many memory ICs (and other devices) to the same data bus.

The control input 'chip select' is usually abbreviated to either CS or CE (chip enable). The control line memory read (RD) is a signal from the control bus.

The internal architecture (organisation or structure) of a ROM is very complex, and we need not be familiar with all its detail. We will limit our discussion to a functional block diagram of the device, such as that shown in Fig 9.3(b).

9: Microcomputer memories

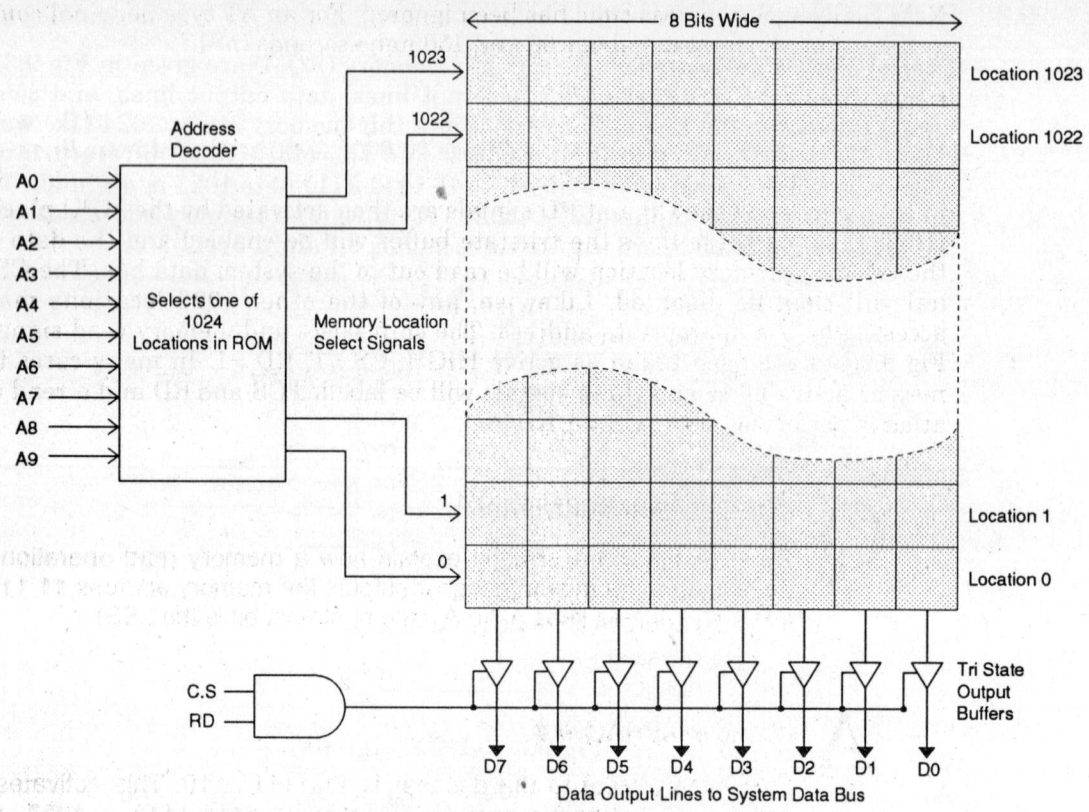

Fig 9.3(b) Read only memory. Functional block diagram of the inside of the chip.

A sequence of electrical events (listed below) occurs each time data is to be read from the device. Keep in mind that this general sequence must be followed regardless of the type of MPU or ROM used in the application. In section 9.9 we will see how the Z80 microprocessor may be connected to an EPROM and how it reads out data from the device.

1. The microprocessor outputs the address of the word which it wants to read from memory. This address acts as an input to the ROM address decoder.

2. The address decoder works out which one of the 1024 memory locations has to be selected for the read operation.

3. The chip select (CS) and memory read (RD) are made active. This produces a HIGH output from the AND gate which enables the active high tri-state buffers. See Fig 9.3 (b)

4. The data is taken out from the selected memory location through the buffers to the system data bus.

5. The chip select is made inactive to remove the ROM from the system data bus.

Note that memory access time has been ignored. For an AT type personal computer this would lie between about 60 and 150 nano seconds (nS).

Example:

If the microprocessor outputs the address 00 0000 0000 on the address lines, A_0 to A_9, the address decoder will activate its 0 output line thereby selecting location 0 in the memory. If the CS and RD signals are then activated by the MPU placing a HIGH level on these lines the tri-state buffer will be enabled and the data from the selected memory location will be read out to the system data bus. The CS signal will then be disabled. Likewise, any of the other 1023 locations may be accessed by the appropriate address. The chip select and memory read signals in Fig 9.3(b) have been taken as active HIGH; CS =1, RD =1. In many cases these may be active LOW and these signals will be labelled $\overline{CS}$ and $\overline{RD}$ and a read operation is performed when $\overline{CS}$ =0, $\overline{RD}$ =0.

Short answer question 9.4

Refer to Fig 9.3(b). Briefly explain how a memory read operation is performed if the microprocessor outputs the memory address 11 1111 1110 on address lines A_9 to A_0 (the rightmost bit is the LSB).

Answer to SAQ 9.4

The binary input to the decoder is 11 1111 1110. This activates output 1022 from the decoder (because 11 1111 1110_2 = 1022_{10}) which selects memory location 1022 for a read operation. If the chip select (CS) and memory read (RD) signals are both taken HIGH by the MPU then the output from the AND gate will be HIGH. This enables the tri-state buffers and the byte of data may be read out from the memory to the system data bus.

9.4 POPULAR EPROMS

Due to the widespread use of EPROMs in personal computers we will now take a more detailed look at these devices. Various size, organisation and speed options are available to suit a wide range of applications. Both NMOS and CMOS types are readily available. Some typical examples of NMOS devices are:

EPROM	2716	2732	2764	27128	27256	27512
Organisation	2048 × 8	4096 × 8	8192 × 8	16384 × 8	32768 × 8	65536 × 8
Access time (nS) Max.	450	450	250	250	250	250
Program Voltage (V)	+25	+21	+12.5	+12.5	+12.5	+12.5

9: Microcomputer memories

For design work and troubleshooting it is necessary to understand typical EPROM signals. As an example consider the 2716 in Fig 9.4.

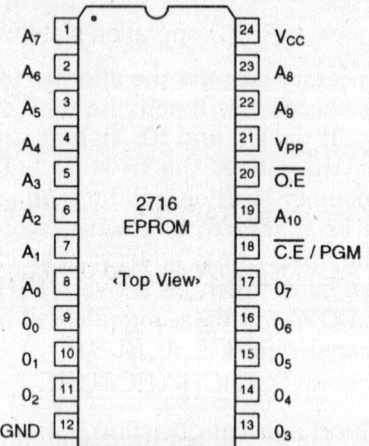

Fig 9.4 2716 EPROM signals

Table 9.1 gives a summary of the pins on the device.

PIN LABEL	DESCRIPTION
A_0 to A_{10}	The 10 address input lines
O_0 to O_7	The 8 data output pins corresponding to D_0 to D_7
V_{cc} & GND	+5V and 0V respectively
$\overline{CE}$/PGM	When the chip is being programmed this pin is pulsed with HIGH and LOW signals. Otherwise it acts as the chip enable.
$\overline{OE}$	Output enable. Held HIGH during programming. For reading data from the device it is brought LOW.
V_{PP}	+25V for programming. Under normal use it is tied to +5V

Table 9.1 2716 EPROM signals.

Short answer question 9.5

Refer to Fig 9.4

During a READ operation state whether the following pins are HIGH or LOW.

i) Pin 18   ii) Pin 20   iii) Pin 21

 Answer to SAQ 9.5

i) LOW ii) LOW iii) Tied permanently to a HIGH level

9.5 RAM SIGNALS AND ARCHITECTURE

As with the ROM, a simplified functional diagram will be used. Just like the ROM it consists of a number of memory locations, each having a unique address, an address decoder and tri-state buffers. However, one fundamental difference is that both READ and WRITE operations may be performed with RAM. Random access memories are available with a wide range of capacities and word sizes of 1, 4 or 8 bits.

Fig 9.5 shows the simplified structure of a RAM which has 64 locations in which it stores 64 words of 4 bits each; a 64×4 memory.

9: Microcomputer memories

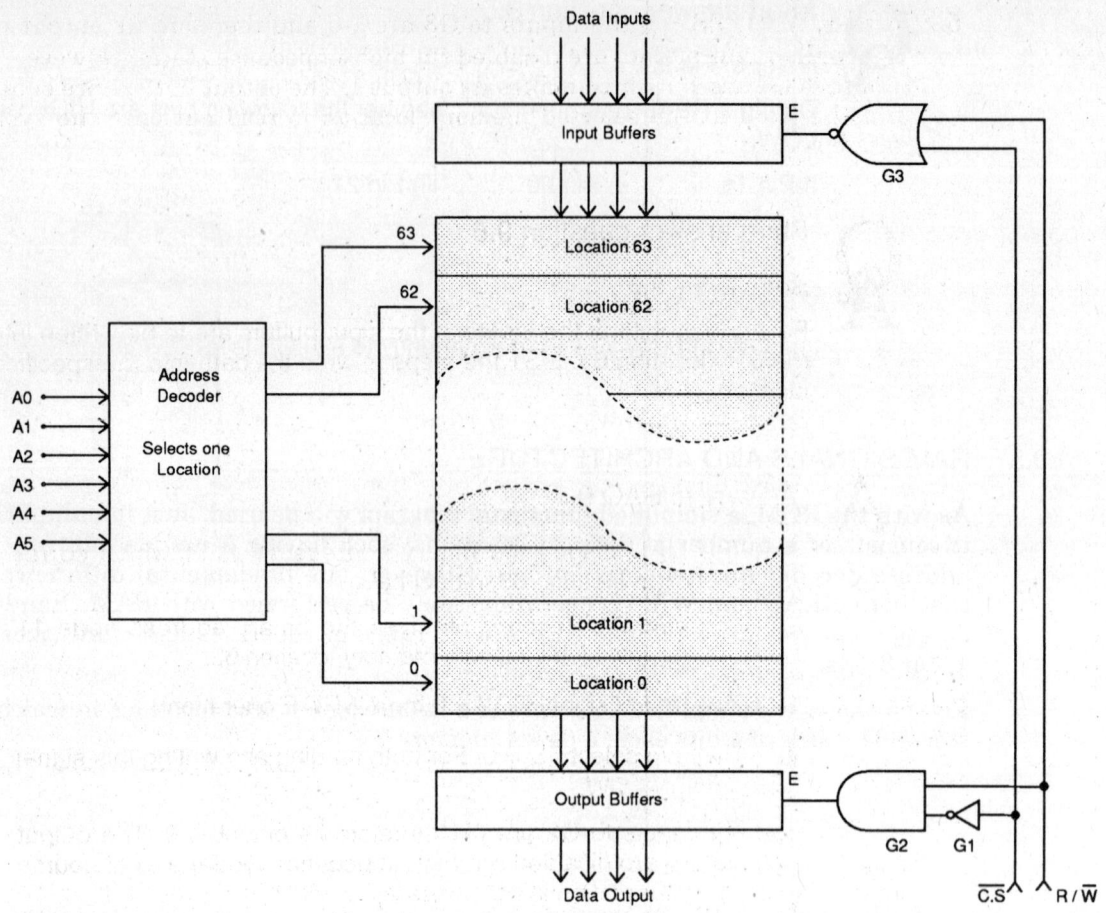

Fig 9.5 Internal organisation of a 64 × 4 RAM

In order to select one of the 64 memory locations for reading or writing, the microprocessor outputs the binary address which is applied to the input of the address decoder. Since $64=2^6$ the decoder requires six inputs. Each address code activates one particular decoder output, which in turn selects its corresponding memory location.

Reading from the RAM

A READ operation is summarised in the following steps.

1. The MPU issues the address of the memory location which it wants to read.
2. The memory address decoder selects one of the 64 locations.
3. The read/write ($R/\overline{W}$) signal = 1, because this line is HIGH for reading and LOW for a write operation.
4. The chip select ($\overline{CS}$) is brought low because this signal is active LOW.

5. With R/$\overline{W}$ =1, $\overline{CS}$ = 0 the inputs to G3 are 1-0 and therefore its output is 0. Hence the input buffers are disabled (in high impedance state). However, the inputs to G2 are 1-1 which makes its output 1. The output buffers are enabled and the word at the selected memory location is read out onto the system data bus.

Short answer question 9.6

Refer to Fig 9.5.

Four bits of data at the inputs of the input buffers are to be written into memory location 63. LIST the steps to write the data into the specified location.

Answer to SAQ 9.6

1. The MPU issues the binary address 11 1111 which corresponds to location 63 in decimal.
2. The address decoder receives the binary address code 11 1111 from which it selects memory location 63.
3. The control signal R/$\overline{W}$ = 0 for a WRITE operation
4. The chip select $\overline{CS}$ = 0. For both reading and writing this signal is active LOW.
5. The inputs to G2 are 0-1 therefore its output is 0. The output buffers are disabled. (in high impedance mode) and of course a read operation is not possible.
6. However, the inputs to G3 are 0-0 and the output from NOR gate G3 will be 1. The input buffers are now enabled and the data may be written into location 63 which the address decoder has selected.

9.6 AN EXAMPLE OF A POPULAR SRAM CHIP

Let's now examine a typical RAM memory that is widely used in industry. The 6116 static ram is illustrated in Fig 9.6. The RAM we have chosen for this discussion is a 2048-word × 8-bit high speed static CMOS RAM.

9: Microcomputer memories

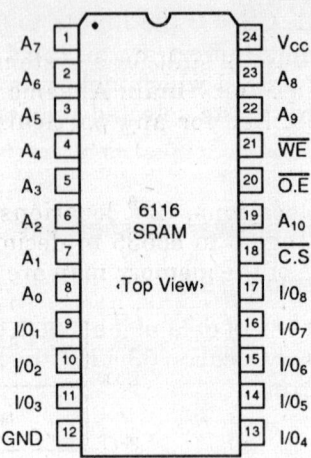

Fig 9.6 6116 SRAM

The signals associated with this chip are summarised in Table 9.2

PIN LABEL	DESCRIPTION
A_0 to A_{10}	The address bus input signals
I/O_1 to I/O_8	The data input/output pins. These correspond to data lines D0 to D7 respectively
V_{CC} and GND	Power supply pins
$\overline{CS}$	Chip select
$\overline{WE}$	Write enable
$\overline{OE}$	Output enable

Table 9.2 6116 SRAM signals

Short answer question 9.7

Refer to table 9.2. State the logic levels on the following pins of the 6116 SRAM when the microprocessor is performing a memory read operation.

i) $\overline{CS}$ ii) $\overline{OE}$ iii) $\overline{WE}$

A   Answer to SAQ 9.7

i) LOW ii) LOW iii) HIGH

9.7 MEMORY MAPS

Before any hardware is built for a system, the design development engineer must first construct a **memory map.** A memory map is used to indicate which address locations are specified for any particular ROM or RAM (or INPUT/OUTPUT) device. Fig 9.7 shows a typical memory map for an 8-bit microcomputer. Because the microprocessor chip has 16 address lines it can directly address any one of 65536 memory locations. (2^{16} locations). The MPU can therefore output any address in the range 0 to 65535 in decimal. The addresses which are written on the left hand side of the memory map are derived as follows:

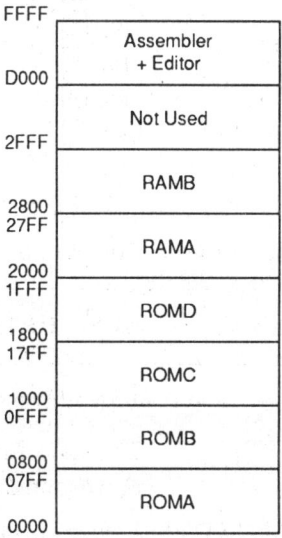

Fig 9.7 Memory map for an 8-bit microcomputer

If we represent the addresses of locations 0 and 65535 in binary this gives:

A_{15}	A_{14}	A_{13}	A_{12}	A_{11}	A_{10}	A_9	A_8	A_7	A_6	A_5	A_4	A_3	A_2	A_1	A_0
0	0	0	0	0	0	0	0	0	0	0	0	0	0	0	0
1	1	1	1	1	1	1	1	1	1	1	1	1	1	1	1

Representing these binary addresses in hexadecimal we get 0000H and FFFFH. Therefore the memory location labelled 0000H is memory location 0 and FFFFH is location 65535.

We can see that the entire memory map of 65536 address locations is divided into functional blocks. These blocks indicate the address locations that are reserved for specific ROMs and RAMs etc.

Short answer question 9.8

Refer to Fig 9.7

Calculate the number of words that may be stored in ROM A

9: Microcomputer memories

> **A** **Answer to SAQ 9.8**
>
> Number of memory locations = 07FFH − 0000H = 7FFH and
>
> $$7FFH = 7 \times 16^2 + F \times 16 + F \times 1$$
> $$= 7 \times 16^2 + 15 \times 16 + 15 \times 1$$
> $$= 1792 + 240 + 15$$
> $$= 2047$$
>
> Hence number of memory locations = 2048 (including 0).

9.8 MEMORY DECODING

We have already seen that both ROM and RAM have internal address decoders. Their function is to select one memory location from many, within the chip. The binary address input to the decoder dictates which address location will be selected. The function of a decoder can be summed up with the aid of Fig 9.8 which shows a three line to eight line decoder.

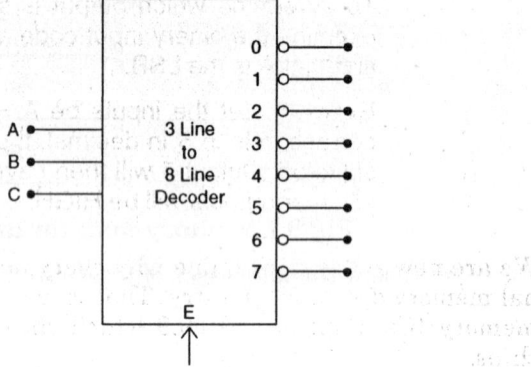

Fig 9.8 3-line to 8-line decoder

The device has three input lines A, B and C where A is the least significant bit (LSB) of the binary input. The eight outputs are labelled 0 to 7. Note that the outputs are active LOW (denoted by the small circle on the output lines) which means that the selected output will go LOW while the other 7 will assume a HIGH (disabled) value. The enable (E) is active HIGH.

The operation of the device is quite simple. If the chip is enabled and the binary input code is A=0, B=0 and C=0 then the output labelled 0 will be selected and go LOW, while outputs 1 to 7 will remain HIGH. If the input code is A=1, B=0 and C=0 then output 1 will be activated while outputs 0,2,3,4,5,6 and 7 will remain HIGH. The complete operation of the decoder can be described by the use of a truth table.

9: Microcomputer memories

 Short answer question 9.9

Draw the truth table for the decoder shown in Fig 9.8

 Answer to SAQ 9.9

Inputs			Outputs							
C	B	A	0	1	2	3	4	5	6	7
0	0	0	0	1	1	1	1	1	1	1
0	0	1	1	0	1	1	1	1	1	1
0	1	0	1	1	0	1	1	1	1	1
0	1	1	1	1	1	0	1	1	1	1
1	0	0	1	1	1	1	0	1	1	1
1	0	1	1	1	1	1	1	0	1	1
1	1	0	1	1	1	1	1	1	0	1
1	1	1	1	1	1	1	1	1	1	0

To determine which output is selected and therefore goes LOW, examine the binary input code and change it to decimal-not forgetting that A is the LSB.

Example: Let the inputs be A = 1 ; B= 0; C= 1. The binary input corresponds to 5 in decimal, therefore the output labelled 5 will be selected. Output 5 will then have a LOW level signal on it whereas all other outputs will be HIGH.

We are now ready to examine why every microcomputer system must have external memory decoding circuitry. That is, a circuit placed between the MPU and the memory ICs. Consider Fig 9.9 which shows a microprocessor and two memory chips.

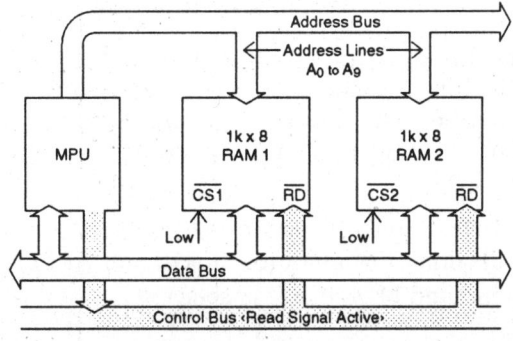

Fig 9.9 The need for memory decoding

Both of the RAM chips, RAM 1 and RAM 2, are 1kilo-byte devices. This means that each one has 1024 memory locations. In order to be able to select one memory location from the 1024 locations ten address lines are needed so bits A_0 to A_9 of the address bus are used.

To illustrate the need for external memory decoding consider the following scenario.

a. The byte of data in RAM 1 at memory location 03FFH is 01H.

b. The byte of data in RAM 2 at memory location 03FFH is 00H.

c. The chip select signals for RAM 1 and RAM 2, $\overline{CS1}$ and $\overline{CS2}$, are both at a LOW level.

If the microprocessor now issues the address 03FFH both of the chips will receive this address. Their internal address decoders will select location 1023 (3FFH = 1023 in decimal) in each IC and their outputs to the system data bus will be:

	D_7	D_6	D_5	D_4	D_3	D_2	D_1	D_0
RAM 1 = 01H =	0	0	0	0	0	0	0	1
RAM 2 = 00H =	0	0	0	0	0	0	0	0

In this example it is clear that there will be **bus conflict** or **bus contention** because it is impossible for data line zero, D_0, to be at two different logic levels simultaneously (0 and 1). If fact, the large resultant current would probably damage the system and render it inoperative. Bus conflict, where two or more devices try to access shared bus lines, must therefore be avoided at all costs. The problem is circumvented by using external (outside the memory devices) decoding logic which ensures that only one of the chip select signals will ever be active at a given time.

9.9 PRACTICAL DECODING SYSTEMS

A full treatment of decoding techniques and system design is beyond the scope of this book. The decoding logic can be designed in a variety of ways. The general principle of address decoding is illustrated in Fig 9.10, where some of the upper address bus bits which are not being used by the memory devices are used as inputs to the decoding circuitry which generates the chip select signals for the memory chips. The four memory devices, MD0 to MD3, are 1k byte chips therefore the address bus bits A_0 to A_9 are connected to each of them. The address bus bits A_{10} and A_{11} are used as inputs to the address decoding logic. If A10 and A11 are both LOW then output '0' is selected so that the chip select signal to MD0 ($\overline{CS0}$)is activated. To determine which chip select is active convert the decoder binary input to decimal. For instance, if A10 and A11 are both HIGH, this corresponds to 3 in decimal and MD3 ($\overline{CS3}$) is selected.

9: Microcomputer memories

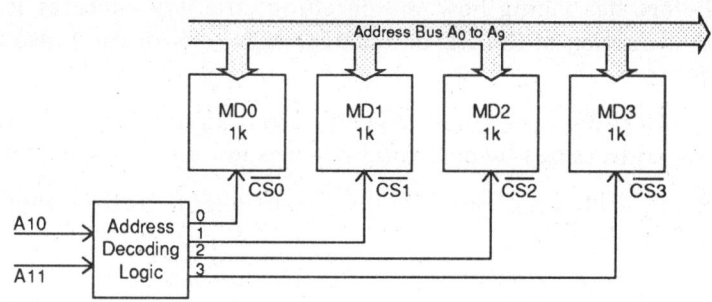

Fig 9.10 Memory decoding

Memory (and port) decoding circuitry may be designed using:

a. LOGIC GATES

b. SPECIAL DECODING CHIPS (like 74LS138)

c. EPROMS

An example of memory decoding

The system shown in Fig 9.11 uses a Zilog Z80 microprocessor (IC1), two erasable programmable read only memories – EPROMs 1 and 2 (IC2, IC3), a low-power Schottky TTL 3-line to 8-line decoder, 74LS138, (IC5) and a two input OR gate, $\frac{1}{4}$ of 74LS32, (IC4).

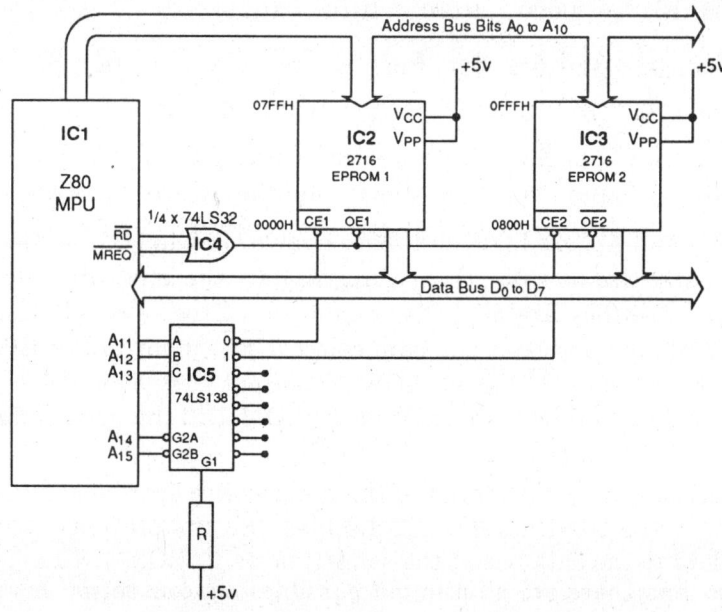

Fig 9.11 Practical memory decoding circuit

EPROM 1 has been placed on the system memory map between addresses 0000H and 07FFH while EPROM 2 appears between 0800H and 0FFFH.

Before describing how the decoding circuitry operates it is necessary to explain the function of the $\overline{RD}$ and $\overline{MREQ}$ MPU signals and also G1, $\overline{G2A}$ and $\overline{G2B}$ of the decoder.

$\overline{MREQ}$ (memory request) is an output signal from the MPU which indicates that the address bus holds a valid address for a memory read or write operation.

$\overline{RD}$ indicates that the MPU wants to read data from memory or an Input/Output (I/O) device.

G1, $\overline{G2A}$ and $\overline{G2B}$ are enable inputs for the decoder chip. G1 is active HIGH while $\overline{G2A}$ and $\overline{G2B}$ are active LOW.

For the microprocessor to perform a read operation with one of the chips it must ensure that the relevant chip select signal, $\overline{CE1}$ or $\overline{CE2}$, is active and that both memory read ($\overline{RD}$) and memory request ($\overline{MREQ}$) are LOW in order to enable the EPROM output enable ($\overline{OE}$) lines.

We are now ready to consider the operation of the circuit. Any address in the range 0000H to 07FFH should result in EPROM 1 being selected – with a LOW signal at $\overline{CE1}$, while EPROM 2 is disabled with a HIGH level signal at $\overline{CE2}$.

Suppose the MPU outputs an address which lies within the range of EPROM 1, say 06ABH.

From the hexadecimal representation of the address bus we can work out the binary value of each of the address bus bits;

06ABH = 0000 0110 1010 1011_2;

A_{15}	A_{14}	A_{13}	A_{12}	A_{11}	A_{10}	A_9	A_8	A_7	A_6	A_5	A_4	A_3	A_2	A_1	A_0
0	0	0	0	0	1	1	0	1	0	1	0	1	0	1	1

Address lines A_0 to A_{10} are wired directly to the two memory ICs. A_{11} to A_{15} are used as inputs to the decoder IC and they are all at a LOW level.

A_{14} and A_{15} are LOW and these enable $\overline{G2A}$ and $\overline{G2B}$ of the decoder (G1 is permanently tied to +5V= 1). A_{11}, A_{12}, A_{13} are the select line inputs to the decoder and because they are all LOW output '0' will be selected. Therefore, output '0' goes LOW and activates the chip select ($\overline{CE1}$) input pin of EPROM 1. Provided that both $\overline{RD}$ and $\overline{MREQ}$ are LOW the output enable pin ($\overline{OE1}$) will become active and the data will be read out from EPROM 1 to the system data bus. From the data bus the data is taken into the MPU.

Because only one output of the decoder can ever be active at a given time output '1' is at a HIGH level which disables $\overline{CE2}$ and prevents EPROM 2 from outputting data to the data bus at the same time as EPROM 1. The memory decoding circuitry has therefore eliminated possible bus contention between the two memory devices.

9: Microcomputer memories

Short answer question 9.10

Pick any address in the range 0800H to 0FFFH and prove that the MPU can read from EPROM 2 but not 1.

Answer to SAQ 9.10

Consider the address 0800H. First of all represent the address in binary.

0800H = A_{15} A_{14} A_{13} A_{12} A_{11} A_{10} A_9 A_8 A_7 A_6 A_5 A_4 A_3 A_2 A_1 A_0

            0   0   0   0   1   0   0   0   0   0   0   0   0   0   0   0

Again A_0 to A_{10} are wired directly to the address pines of the ICs. A_{15} and A_{14} are both LOW and these enable $\overline{G2A}$ and $\overline{G2B}$ of the decoder. G1 is permanently tied to a HIGH level. Hence, the decoder is correctly enabled. The decoder input select lines are A_{11} (LSB), A_{12} and A_{13} and their binary values are 1-0-0 respectively. This corresponds to 1 in decimal so the '1' output line of the decoder will go LOW and enable the chip select ($\overline{CE2}$) of EPROM 2. If memory read ($\overline{RD}$) and memory request ($\overline{MREQ}$) are LOW the MPU can then read out the data from EPROM 2 onto the system data bus. From the system data bus the data can be taken into the MPU. While output '1' of the decoder is active at a LOW level output '0' is HIGH and the chip select for EPROM 1 is disabled.

9.10 SIMMS AND SIPS

All personal computers have ROM (or EPROM) and RAM memories fitted. To run modern applications a considerable amount of RAM is needed. Nearly all mother boards have at least some memory fitted. Generally one area of the motherboard is dedicated to holding the RAM ICs. This can usually be identified by the large number of rows of IC holders/chips of the same type device.

Memory is available in two types of packaging.

1. Dual In-Line (DIL). These have 16,18 or 20 pins and are fitted into sockets. See Chapter 5 Section 5.3.

2. More recently, several small versions of these memory chips have been developed onto miniature circuit boards and these fit into special slots or rows of sockets. These come in two types; SIPs (Single In-line Packages) and SIMMs (Single In-line Memory Modules). The SIPs have lots of small pins along one edge whereas the SIMMs have an edge connector. See Fig 9.12.

9: *Microcomputer memories*

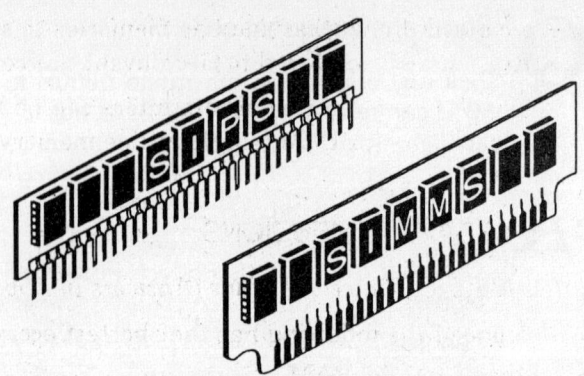

Fig 9.12 Memory devices

SUMMARY

- The two major semiconductor technologies used to build integrated circuit memories (and other digital ICs) are bipolar (NPN/PNP) and MOS (metal oxide semiconductor).

- MOS memory is the most common one for microprocessor systems.

- Volatile memory loses its data when there is a power failure or if the power is switched off accidentally. RAM (assuming that it is not battery backed etc) is volatile.

- Non-volatile memory does not need power to keep the data which is stored in it. All types of ROMs are non-volatile.

- Static memories are constructed by using a flip-flop to store each bit of data. They are generally faster than dynamic RAM. Because of cost they are only used where small amounts of memory are required.

- MOS dynamic memories will hold a charge for only a few milliseconds and they must be refreshed.

- DRAMs typically have four times the density of SRAMs.

  Compared with SRAMs, board space for the same amount of memory is reduced by a factor of four (approx).

- The cost per bit of dynamic RAM storage is typically $\frac{1}{5}$ to $\frac{1}{4}$ that of static RAM.

- The main internal memory of most personal computers uses dynamic RAM because of its high capacity, low power consumption and cost.

- Memory organisation is specified in terms of the number of words which the device can store and the number of bits per word.

- A functional block diagram of RAM or ROM consists of memory cells, an internal address decoder and tri-state buffers.

- The range of addresses employed and the type of memory used (RAM or ROM) is indicated pictorially by a diagram known as a memory map.

☐ When connecting devices such as memories to shared lines (a BUS) decoding circuitry must be employed to circumvent bus conflict or bus contention.

☐ Memory devices for personal computers can be DIL (dual in-line), SIP (single in-line package) or SIMM (single in-line memory module) type packages.

CHAPTER REVIEW QUESTIONS

Section A: Multiple choice questions (Answers in Appendix A)

1. Which one of the following has the shortest access time?
   a. bipolar (static) RAM
   b. NMOS EPROM
   c. NMOS RAM
   d. CMOS RAM

2. Each cell within a semiconductor memory can
   a. store one byte
   b. store two bits of data
   c. be tri-stated
   d. store one bit of data

3. In order to read data from a random access memory the $\overline{CS}$ pin must be
   a. tri-stated
   b. high
   c. low
   d. high impedance

4. Which one of the following devices is electrically erasable?
   a. SRAM
   b. DRAM
   c. PROM
   d. EEPROM

5. A random access memory is located between addresses 0800H and 0FFFH on the memory map of an 8-bit microcomputer system. The storage capacity of this RAM, expressed in kbytes, is
   a. 1
   b. 2
   c. 4
   d. 8

6. Refer to Fig 9.13.

9: Microcomputer memories

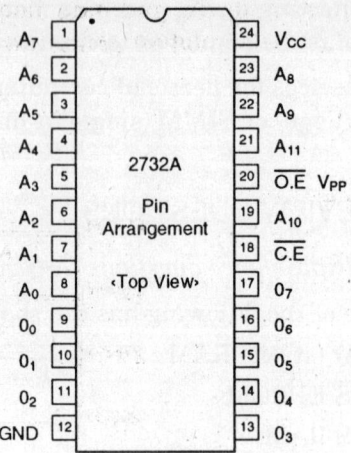

Fig 9.13

The organisation of this chip may be described as

    a.   1024 words × 8 bits

    b.   1024 words × 4 bits

    c   2048 words × 8 bits

    d   4096 words × 8 bits

7.   Refer to Fig 9.14

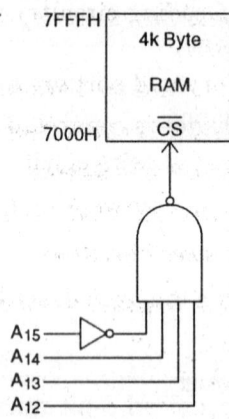

Fig 9.14

In order to activate the memory chip select ($\overline{CS}$) the binary signals on address lines A_{15} to A_{12} respectively, must be

    a.   0111

    b.   0000

    c.   1111

    d.   1110

9: Microcomputer memories

8. Address lines A_0 to A_9 and data lines D_0 to D_7 of a microprocessor are connected to a static random access memory. The total storage capacity of the device is
   a) 8kb
   b) 4kb
   c) 2kb
   d) 1kb

9. Refer to Fig 9.15

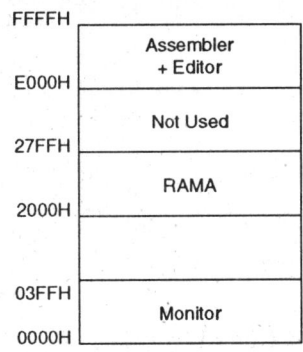

Fig 9.15

The memory map shown is for a single board 8-bit microcomputer. The amount of space occupied by the system software (monitor) is
   a) 1kb
   b) 2kb
   c) 4kb
   d) 8kb

10. The memory decoding circuitry which is used to generate the chip select signals ensures that
    a. both memory and port are activated at the same time
    b. only one device is connected to the data bus at a given time
    c. bus contention will happen
    d. both RAM and ROM are selected simultaneously

Section B: Short answer questions

1. With the aid of a diagram describe each of the following:
   a) memory cell
   b) memory word
   c) address

2. What is the difference between volatile and non-volatile memory. Give one example of each type of memory.

3. State one main difference between static and dynamic memories.

4. Draw a simplified functional block diagram of a 2048 × 8 ROM. Your answer must include storage locations, an address decoder and tri-state buffers.

   Assuming that the device is connected to a microprocessor LIST the steps for performing a READ operation from the ROM.

9: Microcomputer memories

5. Draw a simplified functional diagram of a 256 × 4 random access memory.

    LIST the steps which a microprocessor would go through in order to
    a) WRITE to memory location FFH
    b) READ from memory location 00H

6. With the aid of a diagram consisting of a microprocessor, one ROM and one RAM chip show how bus contention or bus conflict could occur.

7. Refer to Fig 9.16

    If the MPU issues the address 0600H explain why EPROM 1 will be selected but not EPROM 2.

8. Refer to Fig 9.16

    If the MPU issues the address 0900H explain why EPROM 2 will be selected but not EPROM 1

9. Refer to Fig 9.16

    If the microprocessor issues the address 1000H which output of IC5 will be active. How will this affect the two EPROMs?

10. Refer to Fig 9.16

    Amend the diagram to include a third 2716 EPROM which derives its chip select signal from output '2' of IC5. Also ensure that the output enable pin ($\overline{OE}$) of the device is correctly activated. Work out the lower and upper addresses on the memory map for the additional EPROM.

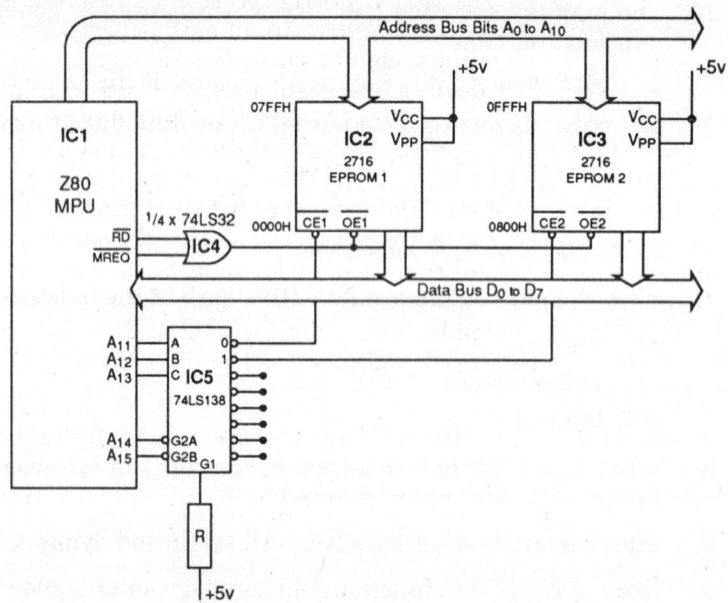

Fig 9.16

Chapter 10

Microprocessor input/output ICs Interfacing and Peripherals

In this chapter, we examine the ports through which the microprocessor outputs or inputs data to/from external devices. These LSI integrated circuits are called Input/Output (I/O) ports. For parallel I/O they are known as parallel input/output ports. Devices such as Zilog's Z80 PIO (Parallel Input Output) and Motorola's PIA (Peripheral Interface Adapter) are examples of programmable parallel I/O chips. Serial communication takes place via devices which are generally known as UARTs (Universal Asynchronous Receiver Transmitters). Block diagrams of both parallel and serial port ICs are given, plus details of how to program the Zilog PIO.

The need for interface circuits placed between the I/O port and peripherals is examined as well as standard interfaces for peripherals. An overview of peripherals such as printers, keyboards, video displays and mice is also included in this chapter.

10.1 PARALLEL I/O

Two major operations that a microprocessor performs are reading data from an input peripheral, and writing data to an output peripheral. All devices which are used for input or output, connected to the I/O ports, are known as peripherals. Examples of input devices are keyboards, disk drive units and transducers plus analogue-to digital converters (ADCs). Typical output devices are printers, visual display units (VDUs), disk drives and digital-to-analogue converters (DACs). An 8-bit microprocessor such as the Z80 has an 8-bit data bus for transferring data throughout the system. Data transfers between the MPU and a PIO or a PIA take place in parallel. The device in Fig 10.1 is called a parallel I/O device because data is written to and read from it in eight simultaneous parallel bits. When it is performing a WRITE operation to a port chip, data is being transferred from the MPU to the I/O port along the 8-bit parallel system data bus. However, if an I/O READ operation is taking place then the data transfer is from the input/output port to the MPU.

As shown in Fig 10.1 the microprocessor can input (read) one byte of data from an input device and output (write) one byte of data to an output device. Both WRITE and READ operations are performed under program control.

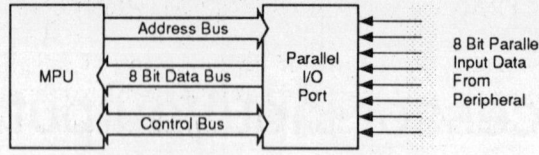

(a) **A port read operation**

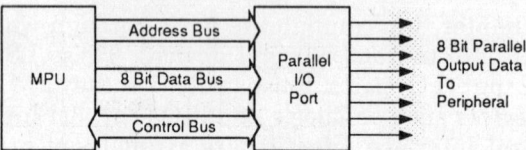

(b) **A port write operation**

Fig 10.1 Port I/O operations

 Short answer question 10.1

What is meant by parallel data transfer?

 Answer to SAQ 10.1

All the bits of data are transferred simultaneously from one part of a system to another. For instance, from an I/O port to the MPU along the 8-bit system data bus.

A single port I/O chip can be programmed for input or output. The Z80 PIO is Zilog's parallel interface device.

The Peripheral Interface Adapter (PIA) is a general purpose, parallel I/O device, designed for use with Motorola microprocessors.

Both of these port I/O devices are implemented using NMOS technology. They are 40-pin DIL packages which use a single +5V power supply. All of their inputs and outputs are TTL-level compatible.

These I/O ports are often called interface ICs. An interface chip is a LSI component that provides the communication link between a microprocessor and devices external to the microcomputer. An interface consists of a number of registers, internal selection logic and control circuits that implement the required transfers. Whilst some simple devices such as, switches and light emitting diodes (LEDs) may be connected directly to the microcomputer I/O port chip, generally an interface, external to the microcomputer, placed between the I/O port and the external device is necessary. See section 10.9

10.2 BLOCK DIAGRAM OF A PARALLEL PORT

The internal architecture or organisation of parallel port ICs varies considerably in complexity. However, the same general principles apply to all of these devices. We will consider the Zilog PIO which contains two nearly identical 8-bit ports, called 'A' and 'B'. A simplified block diagram of side 'A' of the PIO is illustrated in Fig 10.2. Because the two sides of the port are almost identical any general comments regarding side 'A' also apply to side 'B' of the port.

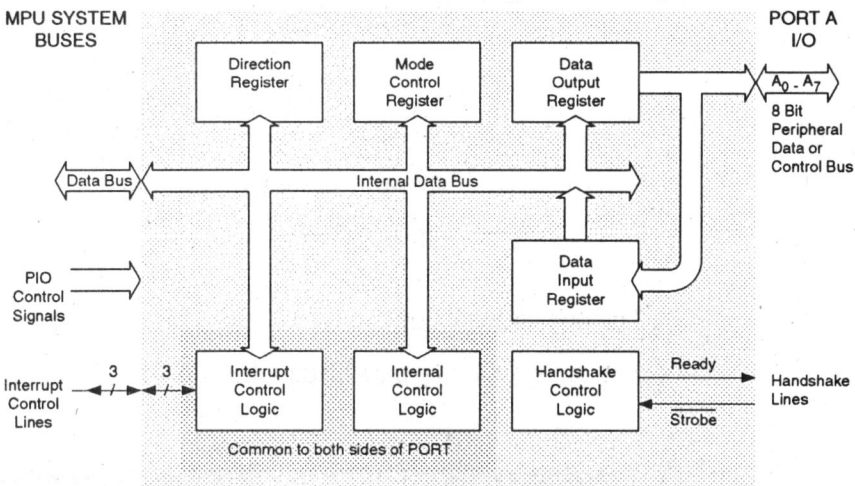

Fig 10.2 Functional block diagram of the Z80 PIO

A brief description of the function of each element in the port will be followed by a programmer's model of the device.

Data input register

The data input register stores data which is being transferred from the peripheral to the MPU. This register holds the data until the microprocessor is ready to read it. The peripheral device may determine when data is transferred to the port input register by means of the strobe ($\overline{STB}$) input as shown in Fig 10.3.

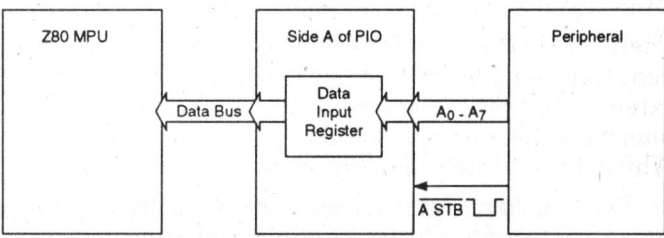

Fig 10.3 Data input to a PIO

Data output register

The data output register is used to store MPU generated output data until the peripheral device is ready to accept the data. The ready (RDY) signal may be used to indicate to the peripheral that new data is available. See Fig 10.4.

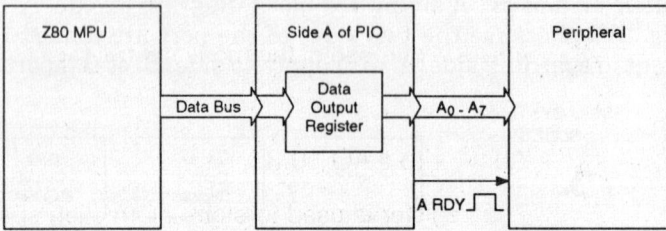

Fig 10.4 Data output to a PIO

 Short answer question 10.2

State the function of the data input and output registers in a PIO.

 Answer to SAQ 10.2

The data input register stores data which is being transferred from a peripheral to the MPU. When the microprocessor is sending data out to a peripheral it is stored in the output data register awaiting collection by the peripheral device.

Mode control register

This register indicates whether the port is in **input, output, bi-directional,** or **control mode**. These four modes are called modes 0 to 3 respectively. The operating modes are explained in section 10.4.

Direction register

When the PIO is being used in mode three, the control mode, input/output lines in either Port A or Port B may be used as individual input or output lines. The direction register determines whether the corresponding data pins are inputs (1) or outputs (0) in the control mode.

Internal control and interrupt logic

The interrupt and internal control logic is common to both side 'A' and 'B' of the port. The **internal control logic** routes the internal data of the device to the correct internal register at the right time. The **interrupt control logic** allows the PIO to correctly request interrupts and handle the interrupt acknowledge from the Z80 MPU. An **interrupt** may be generated by a peripheral device to indicate that it requires attention. The MPU then temporarily transfers control from the main program to a separate **interrupt service routine (ISR)** to deal with the peripheral device that initiated the interrupt. On completion of the ISR the processor returns control to the main program and continues with its execution.

Short answer question 10.3

State the purpose of the mode control register.

Answer to SAQ 10.3

This register is used to store information specifying programmable options for the PIO. It indicates whether the port is in input, output, bi-directional or control mode.

Short answer question 10.4

State the function of the direction register in a PIO.

Answer to SAQ 10.4

When the PIO is programmed in Mode 3 the eight bits of Port A or Port B can be used as individual input or output lines. For instance, four lines in Port A could be used for input while the other four could be used as outputs. The word stored in the direction register will logically define how the eight bits of the port are to be used. A logical 1 in the bit position will set the data line as an input. A logical 0 will set it as an output.

10.3 A PROGRAMMER'S MODEL OF THE Z80 PIO

To the programmer, a PIO will be accessed as four addressable registers. This is illustrated in Fig 10.5

10: Microprocessor input/output ICs interfacing and peripherals

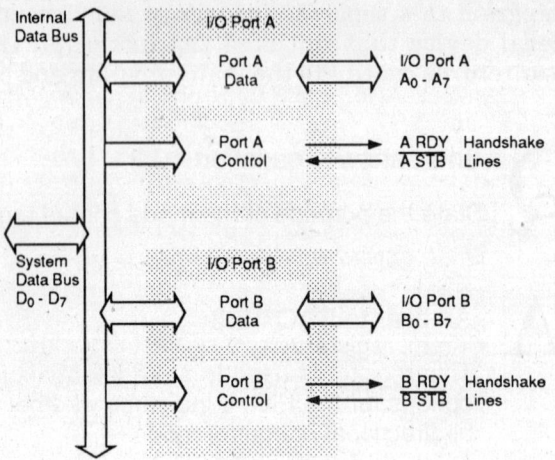

Fig 10.5 A programmer's model of the Z80 PIO

The input control line, $C/\overline{D}$, to the port selects either a control or data register within the PIO. If this line is a logical 1 then the information on the data bus is destined for a control register. However, if it is LOW a data register is being selected. The PIO input signal $B/\overline{A}$ selects either Port B or Port A. If this line is HIGH then Port B is selected, but if it is LOW then Port A is selected. Table 10.1 gives a summary of PIO addresses.

Control or Data Select ($C/\overline{D}$)	Port B or A Select ($B/\overline{A}$)	Register addressed	Port address (Starting with PIO address)
0	0	Data Register A	PIO address
0	1	Data Register B	PIO address +1
1	0	Control A	PIO address +2
1	1	Control B	PIO address +3

Table 10.1 PIO addresses

The port addresses assume that address line A_0 of the MPU is connected to $B/\overline{A}$ and that the PIO input line $C/\overline{D}$ is tied to address line A_1.

The port addresses for the system which we will program in Chapter 11 are:

    PORT A DATA register: 80H
    PORT B DATA register: 81H
    PORT A CONTROL register: 82H
    PORT B CONTROL register: 83H

The port addresses are system dependent, but will always lie in the range 00H to FFH because the lower eight bits of the address bus are used for port addressing for Z80 systems.

10: Microprocessor input/output ICs interfacing and peripherals

 Short answer question 10.5

As far as the programmer is concerned the Z80 PIO consists of four addressable registers. Name these registers.

 Answer to SAQ 10.5

Data register A
Data register B
Control register A
Control register B

 Short answer question 10.6

Assume that you are programming a microcomputer which has a Z80 programmable input/output port (PIO) how would you establish the port addresses?

 Answer to SAQ 10.6

Consult the handbook for the system. The addresses are set by the hardware design engineer.

10.4 Z80 PIO PROGRAMMING MODES

The Z80 PIO is a programmable I/O interfacing chip, specially designed for the Z80. Ports A and B can be used in three different modes: byte output (Mode 0), byte input (Mode 1), and bit input/output (Mode 3) as shown in Fig 10.6. In addition, Port A can be configured in the bi-directional mode (Mode 2). In summary:

>   MODE 0 = BYTE OUTPUT
>   MODE 1 = BYTE INPUT
>   MODE 2 = BI-DIRECTIONAL – Port A only
>   MODE 3 = BIT INPUT/OUTPUT (Control)

10: Microprocessor input/output ICs interfacing and peripherals

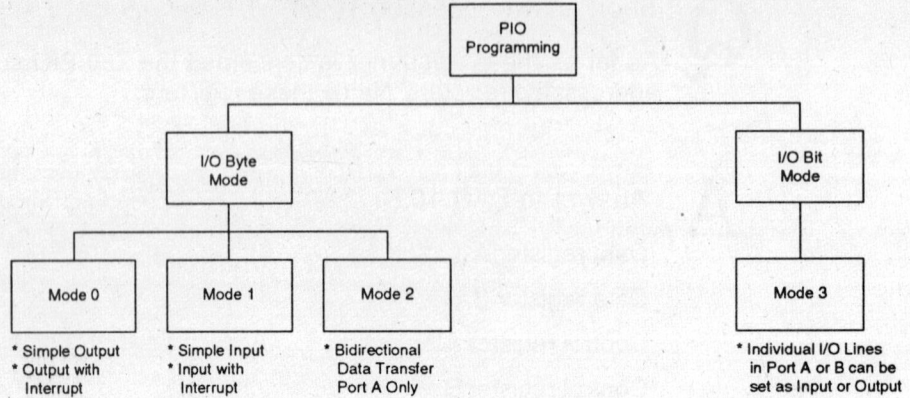

Fig 10.6 Z80 PIO modes

HOW A PIO OPERATING MODE IS SELECTED

The mode of operation must be established by writing a control word to the PIO in the following format:

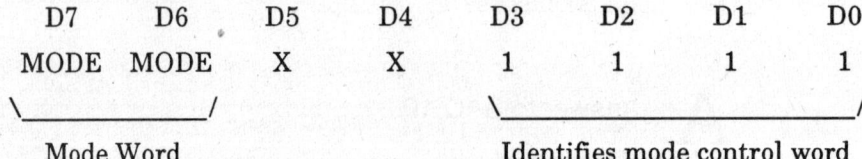

Fig 10.7 Mode control for the Z80 PIO

X = unused bit or don't care.

The lower four bits of the control word are set to logical 1. This indicates that the mode for the port is being set.

Bits D7 and D6 form the binary code for the desired mode according to the following table:

D7	D6	MODE
0	0	0 (Output)
0	1	1 (Input)
1	0	2 (bi-directional)
1	1	3 (control)

Table 10.2

Notes:

i) The mode of operation of a PIO is established by writing a control word to the PIO. The control word is deduced from Fig 10.7 and Table 10.2.

ii) **Mode 0** is for **output** and **mode 1** is for **input.** In these modes, Ports A and B can be used in two ways: simple input/output without handshake signals or interrupt I/O with handshake signals. For details of the handshake mechanism refer to Section 10.9

iii) **Mode 2** uses all four handshake lines, so it is allowed only on Port A

iv) **Mode 3** does not use the handshake signals. It is intended for control applications in which each bit has an individual meaning. When mode 3 is selected, the next control word sent to the PIO defines the directions of the port data bits. A '1' in a bit position makes the corresponding bus line an input, while a '0' makes it an output.

In Chapter 11 we will see how to set up some of these operating modes for a range of practical interfacing problems.

Short answer question 10.7

When mode 3 is selected, the next control word sent to the PIO must define which of the port data bus lines are to be inputs and which are outputs. Assume that Port A is to be used in mode 3 and that the least significant four bits of the Port A data bus are to be used as inputs and the rest of the bits as outputs. Which control word will be sent to the direction register in side 'A' of the PIO?

Answer to SAQ 10.7

The control word sent to Port A direction register will be 0000 1111_2 The four least significant bits are set to 1 because the corresponding data pins are to be used as inputs, whereas the remaining bits are outputs and are therefore set to zero. Hence, the control word is 0FH.

Short answer question 10.8

The control word for side A of a PIO is FFH. In which mode is the port being set?

Answer to SAQ 10.8

MODE 3: FFH = 1111   1111, therefore bits 6 and 7 of the control word are 1s. Using Fig 10.7 in association with table 10.2 we can establish that mode 3 is to be used.

10.5 SERIAL INPUT OUTPUT

To reduce the number of connecting wires required to send digital information over long distances, usually the data is sent in serial form. In other words, one bit of a word is sent after another on a single wire. Most microprocessor manufacturers produce serial programmable I/O controllers, each performing similar functions but known by different names. Common serial I/O devices are:

a) **UART** — Universal **A**synchronous **R**eceiver **T**ransmitter
b) **USART** — Universal **S**ynchronous **A**synchronous **R**eceiver **T**ransmitter
c) **DART** — **D**ual **A**synchronous **R**eceiver **T**ransmitter
d) **SIO** — Serial Input Output
e) **ACIA** — **A**synchronous **C**ommunications **I**nterface **A**dapter

Before attempting to describe the features of a typical serial input/output port a basic understanding of serial communication is necessary.

What is serial communication?

Serial communication is the transmission of data one bit at a time along a single wire. Parallel communication, on the other hand, is the opposite of serial communication, all bits of the data transfer are transmitted or received at the same time. A good example of parallel communication is an I/O read or write operation, in which all eight data bits are written (transmitted) or read (received) at the same time. In fact, all of the data transfers we have seen so far have taken place in parallel.

To further illustrate what serial communication is and how it differs from parallel communication, consider this example. Suppose we wish to send one byte (8 bits) of data from one piece of hardware in a microcomputer system to another. Fig 10.8 (a) and (b) shows how data appears when transmitted in serial and parallel.

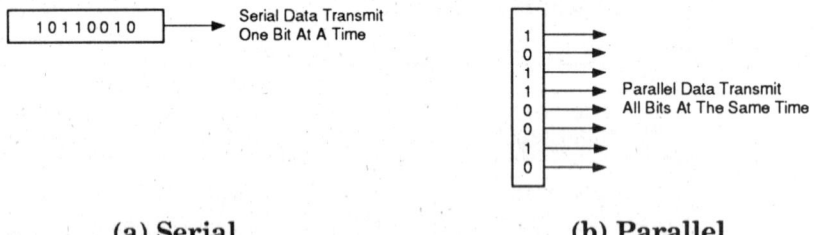

(a) Serial   (b) Parallel

Fig 10. 8 Transmission of data

Notice that the parallel transmission needs 8 separate lines for the communication-one for each parallel bit to be transferred. In the serial transmission, only one physical line is required, the eight bits of data are sent over the single wire, one bit at a time.

A basic arrangement for serial data communications is shown in Fig 10.9 where data is being transmitted serially from MPU 1 to MPU 2. The parallel data to be transmitted from MPU 1 must be converted to a serial bit stream. At the receiving end the reverse process must take place: at MPU 2 a serial to parallel conversion will be necessary. You will recall from Chapter 4 that shift registers are capable of performing either parallel to serial or serial to parallel conversions. It is common practice to use the abbreviation Tx for Transmit and Rx for Receive.

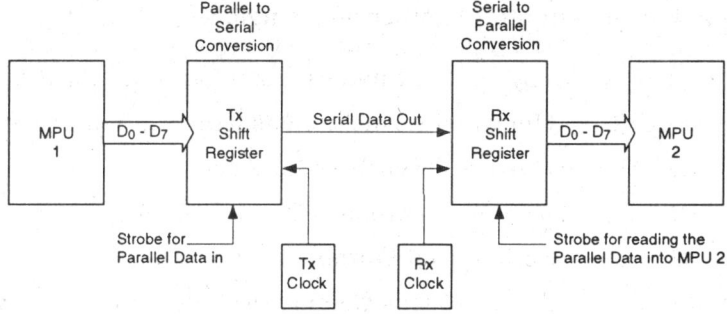

Fig 10.9 A basic serial communication system

One of the critical points of serial communication is the frequency of the transmitted data bit stream. This frequency is called the **Baud rate** which is defined as:

$$\text{Baud rate} = \frac{1}{\text{bit time}}$$

Thus at a transfer rate of 2400 Baud, the bit time is $\frac{1}{2400}$ or 417 micro seconds. Therefore the amount of time required to transmit one byte of data is 8×417 or 3336 micro seconds. The same eight bits would normally take less than 1 micro second for a parallel transfer.

In Fig 10.9 the transmit rate depends on the frequency of the Transmit (Tx) clock which is called the Baud rate clock.

Serial data format

Data transfers usually take place asynchronously so that it is not necessary for the MPU and peripheral to have a common clock signal. In effect, each transmitted data word carries its own synchronisation signal in the form of **start** and **stop** bits. Additionally a **parity** bit is appended, for error checking. The waveform generated by the complete transmission bit stream with start, stop and parity bits which is in accordance with the RS-232 standard for serial communication is shown in Fig 10.10

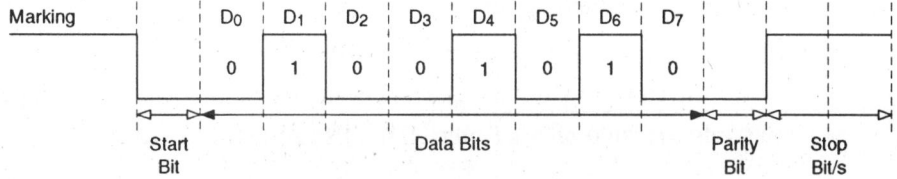

Fig 10.10 Serial data format

When no characters are being sent the line is at a HIGH level and it is in a state called **marking.** The beginning of a character is indicated by a **start** bit which is always low. After the start bit, the data bits are sent out in order, with the least significant bit first. A parity bit may follow the data bits. The end of the character is indicated by one or more always-high stop bits.

The parity bit which is used for error checking is inserted by the transmitter and used by the receiver. Here is an explanation of how the parity bit works. When a word is to be transmitted it contains a certain number of 1s. The number of logical 1s in the word may be odd or even. For instance, the byte 6AH has four 1s in it and therefore has an even number of 1s; the data word 79H has five which is an odd number of 1s. The receiving hardware is set up to receive the data and to encounter either an even or odd number of 1s.

Suppose that the receiving hardware is set up to receive an odd number of 1s in every serial bit stream. The number 79H would be alright, but the number 6AH would not. Therefore the transmitter would insert an additional 1 into the bit stream with the 6AH, prior to the data being sent.

Short answer question 10.9

The character A5H is being transmitted over a serial line. What is the value of the parity bit if EVEN parity is being used?

Answer to SAQ 10.9

A5H = 1010 0101$_2$. This character has an even number (4) of 1s hence the parity bit will be a 0.

10.6 OVERVIEW OF SERIAL PROGRAMMABLE ICS

Microcomputers work with data in parallel form. Thus, to interface with serial devices such as modems, the data must be converted to and from the serial form. Large scale integrated circuits for use in serial data transmission have been available for a number of years. They are connected between the microprocessor and the peripheral. They are generally known as **UARTs** – **U**niversal **A**synchronous **R**eceiver **T**ransmitters. Generally, these devices may be programmed:

- to send 5,6,7 or 8 data bits
- for odd, even or no parity
- to send 1,1.5 or 2 stop bits

A simplified block diagram of a UART is illustrated in Fig 10.11. Table 10.3 gives a brief description of the function of each pin on the UART.

10: Microprocessor input/output ICs interfacing and peripherals

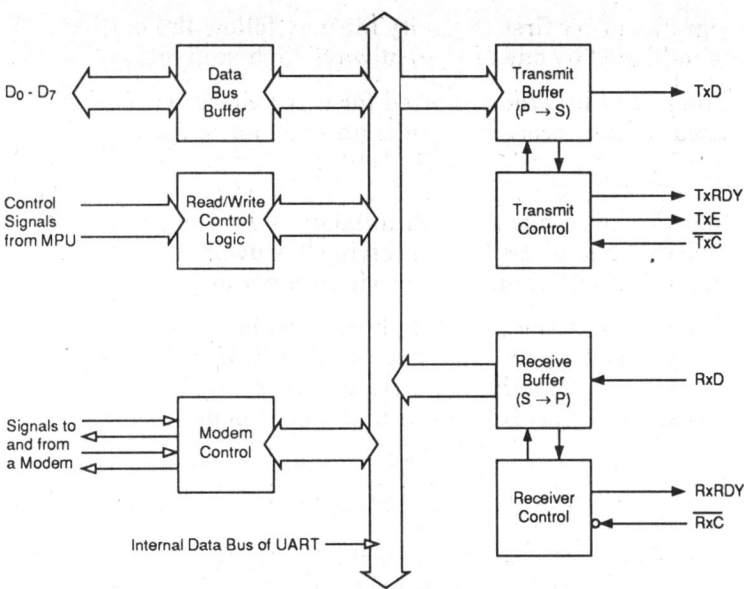

Fig 10.11 Block diagram of a UART

Pin Name	Pin Function	
D_0-D_7	Microprocessor system data bus	
TxD	Transmit Data	This is the output line that serial data will be transmitted from.
RxD	Receive Data	This is the input line that data will be received on.
TxRdy	Transmitter Ready	This output signal tells the MPU that the UART is ready to accept another character to be transmitted
TxE	Transmitter Empty	This output line indicates that the transmit buffer register is empty.
TxC	Transmitter Clock	Transmit Baud rate clock input
RxRDY	Receiver Ready	It is ready to transfer a character to the MPU.
RxC	Receiver Clock	Receive Baud rate clock input

Table 10.3 UART signals

The block labelled **modem control** is used to simplify the interface between the UART and a MODEM (stands for MOdulator DEModulator). For those readers who are not familiar with a modem, it is a device that is used to enable serial transmissions over long distances via the telephone line. The most common standard for serial communication lines is the EIA RS-232 (see section 10.10) When using this standard, typically peripheral devices may be located at distances of about 15 metres from the microcomputer. Basically the modem overcomes the distance limitation and allows information to be transmitted over long distances.

Fig 10.12 shows how a modem fits into a serial communication system which uses a telephone line.

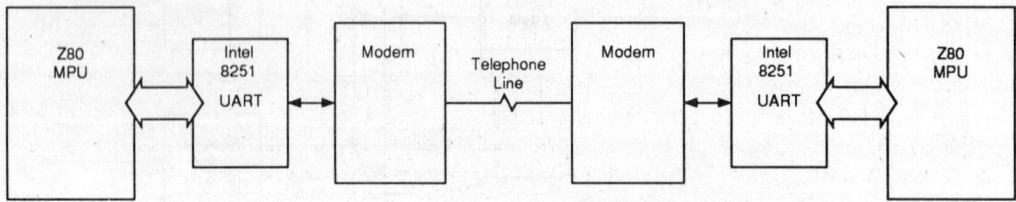

Fig 10.12 Serial communication via telephone line

Q Short answer question 10.10

Name two programmable features of a UART

A Answer to SAQ 10.10

The number of data bits to be transmitted, and odd/even or no parity.

10.7 MEMORY MAPPED AND I/O MAPPED PORTS

Microprocessor input and output ports may be classified as either:

i) **Memory mapped**

ii) **Input/output mapped**-often referred to as **I/O mapped** or **isolated port I/O.**

All microprocessors may be designed with memory mapped ports, but only those microprocessors equipped with the appropriate hardware and input/output instructions may operate with I/O mapped ports.

In memory mapped I/O, the input and output devices are identified by 16-bit addresses. The microprocessor communicates with an I/O device as if it were one of the memory locations. A typical microprocessor-based system using **memory-mapped I/O** is illustrated in Fig 10.13 Note that the chip select signals ($\overline{CS}$) are derived from the same decoding logic for both the memories and the I/O port.

10: Microprocessor input/output ICs interfacing and peripherals

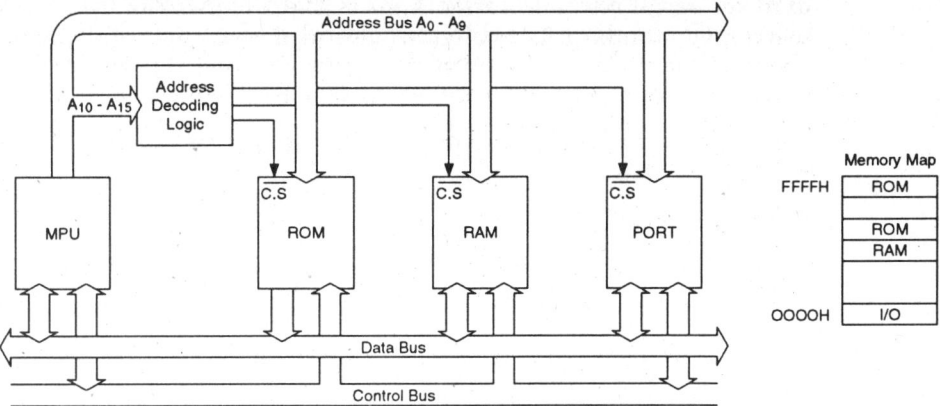

Fig 10.13 Memory mapped I/O

However, in a microcomputer system which is designed to operate with I/O mapped input/output the low byte of the address bus (A_0 to A_7) is used to address up to 256 input/output ports. In order to differentiate between memory and input/output operations, the microprocessor is equipped with special control lines. The Z80 microprocessor has the control signals memory request ($\overline{MREQ}$) and input/output request ($\overline{IORQ}$). When the MPU is transferring data to or from memory then $\overline{MREQ}$ becomes LOW while $\overline{IORQ}$ is held HIGH. For communication with the input/output port $\overline{IORQ}$ is enabled while $\overline{MREQ}$ is disabled. I/O mapped systems also have special instructions for input and output. For the Z80 microprocessor, the input and output instructions are **IN** and **OUT**. Examples of these instructions are given in the next chapter where a number of simple input/output devices are interfaced to the Z80 PIO. A typical system using I/O mapped ports is illustrated in Fig 10.14

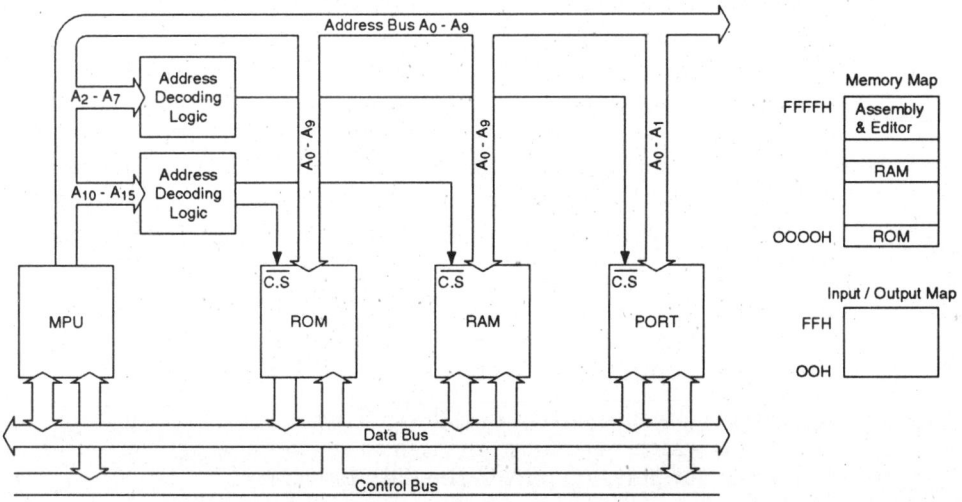

Fig 10.14 I/O mapped input/output

An advantage of memory mapped I/O is that the I/O port may be placed anywhere between 0000H and FFFFH in memory. However, some of the address space must be dedicated to I/O. This may be important for 8-bit microprocessors but is of little significance for processors such as the MC68000 which has a large memory space. In an I/O mapped system the port devices must be placed between 00H and FFH. This may be regarded as a disadvantage since only 256 ports may be addressed (from 00H to FFH). This may also reduce the flexibility of programmers during software development.

Short answer question 10.11

State ONE main difference between memory mapped and I/O mapped input output ports.

Answer to SAQ 10.11

In a memory mapped system the memory and I/O ports are placed on the same map. All devices are addressed using a 16-bit address and the same instructions may apply to a memory or a port.

In an I/O mapped input/output system the memories and the port ICs are kept isolated, with separate instructions for memory and port devices.

10.8 METHODS USED TO TRANSFER DATA BETWEEN A MICROCOMPUTER AND ITS PERIPHERALS

There are many ways in which data transfer between a microcomputer system and external devices can be accomplished, but they all fall into the following three categories:

i) **Programmed I/O** in which all data transfers between the microcomputer system and external logic or peripherals are completely controlled by the microcomputer, or more precisely, by a program which the microprocessor executes. The key characteristic of programmed I/O is that external logic does as it is told by the program which the MPU executes.

ii) **Interrupt I/O.** In this case, peripheral devices force the microcomputer system to suspend whatever it is currently doing in order to attend to the needs of the external logic.

iii) **Direct Memory Access (DMA).** This is a specialised form of I/O data transfer in which peripheral devices take over the system buses, and the microprocessor plays no part in the data transfer.

A full treatment of all three methods is beyond the scope of this book. Practical examples of programmed I/O are given in Chapter 11.

10: Microprocessor input/output ICs interfacing and peripherals

 Short answer question 10.12

Data transfers between a microcomputer and its peripherals fall into three general categories. Name them.

 Answer to SAQ 10.12

Programmed I/O;   Interrupt I/O;   DMA transfers

10.9 INTERFACING EXTERNAL DEVICES TO A MICROCOMPUTER

All microcomputers must be able to transfer information between themselves and various peripherals. The peripheral can vary from a Visual Display Unit (VDU) to a transducer measuring temperature or liquid level in a chemical plant. I/O ports such as the PIO cannot handle all aspects of data transfer between a microprocessor and its external devices, called peripherals. For instance, the I/O port normally operates at TTL levels whereas the voltage needed for a peripheral may be far in excess of the +5V TTL level. In order to make a microcomputer compatible with its peripherals it may be necessary to connect additional circuits, called interfaces, between the I/O port of the microcomputer and its peripheral device as shown in Fig 10.15. Computer interfacing is more specifically defined as the synchronisation of digital information transmission between the computer and its external peripherals.

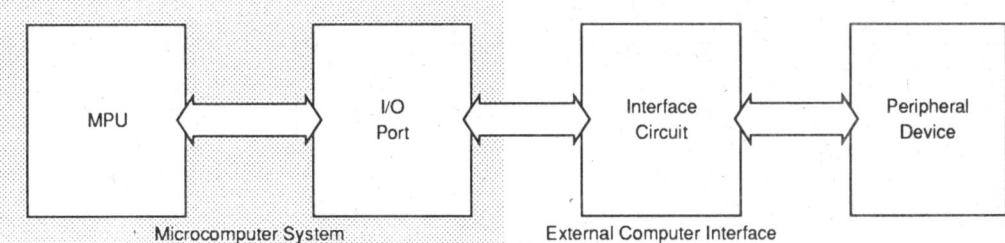

Fig 10.15 Microprocessor interfaces

Many external devices are not directly compatible with the microcomputer, therefore additional circuits may be necessary to deal with the following aspects of interfacing:

i) Differences in voltage levels

ii) Changes in current levels

iii) Electrical isolation

iv) Signal conversion. Analogue to digital and vice versa

v) Differences in operating speed between the microcomputer and its peripherals.

Differences in voltage levels.

For example an external device may operate at +12V whereas the computer works at +5V. In this case the interface will contain an electrical buffer connected as shown in Fig 10.16. Refer to the stepper motor interface in Chapter 11 for a practical illustration of voltage buffering.

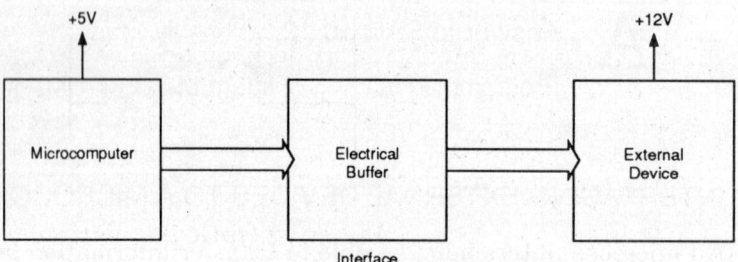

Fig 10.16 Voltage buffering

Changes in current levels

For instance, the current supplied by the I/O port of the computer may be too small to drive a particular peripheral. Again this problem may be solved by using a buffer which amplifies the small electric current supplied by the I/O port of the computer to a level which is capable of driving the peripheral. This is illustrated in Fig 10.17

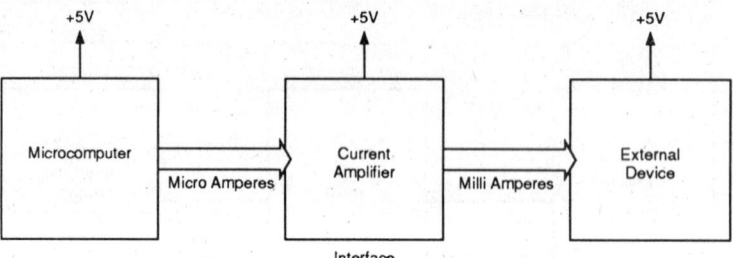

Fig 10.17 Electrical buffer (current amplifier)

Electrical isolation

A common requirement is to be able to interface microcomputer systems to mains operated equipment or other high voltage equipment. Direct connection of a microcomputer to this type of equipment must be avoided otherwise the high voltage levels would damage the computer. Operator safety should also, of course, be taken into account.

The desired isolation may be achieved using an **opto-isolator** which works on the principle of coupling wanted signals by means of a light beam (generally infrared). Because light is not a conductor of electricity, this provides the desired isolation between input and output. Opto-isolators containing a light emitting diode (LED) and a photo-transistor are available in IC form. When a signal is applied to the input terminals, the LED conducts emitting infra-red light which switches the transistor on to produce an output current. The principle of opto-isolation is illustrated in Fig 10.18

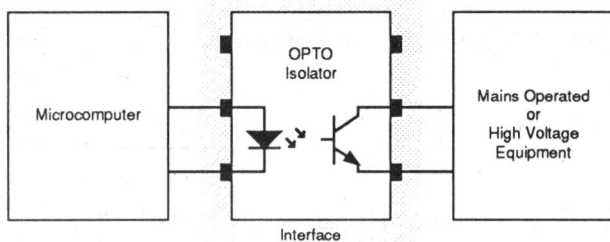

Fig 10.18 Optical isolation

Analogue-to-digital and digital-to-analogue converters

Often the signals in the equipment or transducers to be connected to the computer are in analogue form. Before these signals are applied to the computer they must be converted to digital signals using an analogue-to-digital converter (ADC). Once the input signals have been processed it may be necessary to output the results in the form of an analogue signal, in which case, the digital signals have to be converted to analogue signals using a digital to analogue converter (DAC). A digital quantity will have a value that is specified by the bits 0 or 1. In practice, however, each of these bits is represented by a voltage range. For instance, for TTL logic we know that:

    0V to 0.8V   =   logic 0

    2V to 5V   =   logic 1

Any voltage falling in the range 0 to 0.8V is given the digital value 0, and any voltage in the range 2 to 5 V is assigned the digital value 1. The exact voltage values are not significant because digital circuits respond in the same way to all voltage values within a range. By contrast, an analogue quantity can take on any value over a continuous range of values and its exact value is significant. For example, the output of an analogue temperature-to–voltage converter might be measured as 1.7 V, which may represent a specific temperature of 17°C. If the voltage was measured as something different, such as 1.23V or 2.53V, this would represent a completely different temperature. In other words, each possible value of an analogue quantity has a different meaning. Most physical variables, such as temperature, pressure and flow rate are analogue in nature. When a computer is to be used to monitor and/or control a physical process ADCs and DACs are an essential part of the system. Fig 10.19 gives a general overview of such a system.

10: Microprocessor input/output ICs interfacing and peripherals

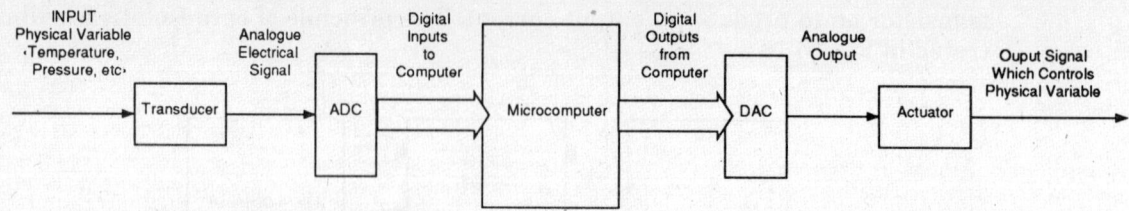

Fig 10.19 Using a computer to monitor and control a physical variable.

Notes:

i) The transducer is a device that converts the physical variable being measured to an electrical variable. Some common transducers include thermistors, photocells, strain gauges and flow meters.

ii) The transducer's electrical analogue output serves as an input to the ADC. The ADC converts this analogue input signal to a digital output. The digital output consists of a number of bits that represent the value of the analogue input. For example, the ADC might convert the transducer's 900 to 1200mV analogue values to binary values ranging from 0101 1010(90) to 0111 1000(120). The binary output from the ADC is proportional to the analogue input voltage. In this example, each unit of the digital output represents 10mV. The analogue input and digital output signals for a 3-bit ADC are illustrated in Fig 10.20.

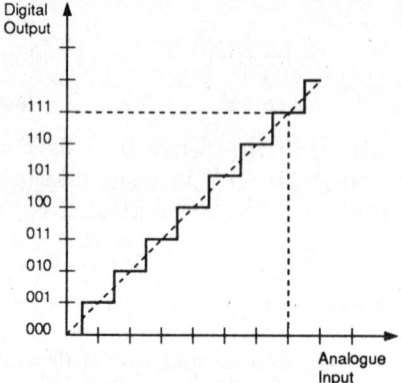

Fig 10.20 Input/output signals for a 3-bit ADC

iii) The digital output from the computer is connected to a DAC, which converts it to a proportional analogue voltage or current. For example, the computer output might produce a digital output ranging from 0000 0000 1111 1111, which the DAC converts to a voltage ranging from 0 to 10V. The digital input and analogue output signals for a 3-bit DAC are shown in Fig 10.21

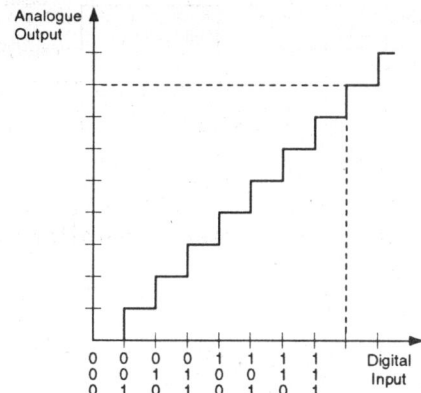

Fig 10.21 Input/output signals for a 3-bit DAC

iv) The analogue output signal from the DAC is often connected to some device or circuit that serves as an **actuator** to control the physical variable. For instance, the DAC signal could serve as an input to a current amplifier which is used to drive a D.C. electric motor.

Operating speed

Generally, peripherals operate at much slower speeds than the microprocessor. Therefore some form of timing control is necessary for applications where the data transfer rates between the computer and the peripheral are different and they are not operating in synchronism. I/O port chips are usually provided with extra signals, called **handshake lines**, which may be used to synchronise the computer to the slower peripheral. These handshake signals can, of course, be used for transferring data either into or out from the computer. We will illustrate the use of these signals where the peripheral is transferring data to the microcomputer. The handshake lines, for the Z80 PIO, shown in Fig 10.22, are RDY (ready) and $\overline{\text{STB}}$ (strobe).

The steps for transferring data from the peripheral to the microcomputer are:

a) The peripheral checks that the ready (RDY) output signal is active at a HIGH level. This indicates that the PIO data input register is empty and is ready to accept data from the peripheral.

b) The peripheral transfers the data into the data input register of the PIO by bringing the $\overline{\text{STB}}$ input signal LOW.

c) The PIO, in response, drops the RDY line to a low level to indicate to the peripheral that its input register is full, and no further data can be accepted until the byte of data has been sent to the microprocessor.

d) Once the MPU reads the contents of the PIO input register, the RDY output signal becomes high again to indicate to the peripheral that more data may be accepted.

10: Microprocessor input/output ICs interfacing and peripherals

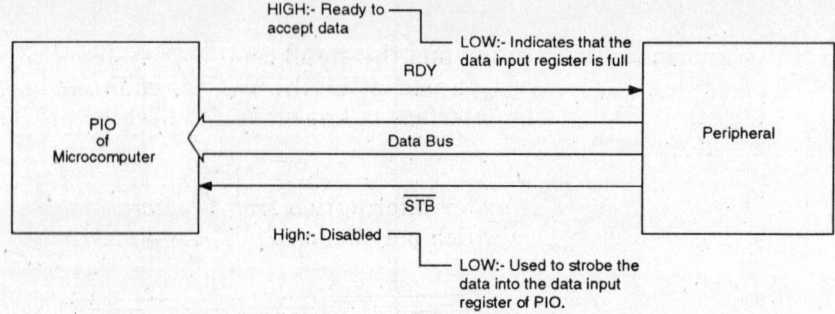

Fig 10.22 Using the HANDSHAKE lines for data output.

 Short answer question 10.13

State FOUR reasons why interfaces may be required between a computer and its peripherals.

Answer to SAQ 10.13

Incompatibility may exist between a computer and its peripherals because of:

i) different operating voltage levels

ii) changes in current levels

iii) the need for electrical isolation

iv) different operating speeds

10.10 INTERFACING STANDARDS AND BUSES

The standard for a.c. power in the United Kingdom, 240V a.c. at 50 Hz, makes it possible to just plug in appliances from most manufacturers without concern for compatibility. When transferring information from one computer to another or to a peripheral, it is also desirable to have a standard format to ensure compatibility between devices.

A standard may include such items as voltage levels, assignment of pin positions for signals, speed of data transfer, maximum length of cables and mechanical specifications.

In this chapter we will concentrate on the standards which are widely used for interfacing microcomputers to peripherals such as printers, modems and terminals.

Parallel interfaces

These are the **Centronics** and the small computer systems interface (**SCSI**). The Centronics interface is named after the printer manufacturer who originally designed it. Today this interface is known as the parallel printer or **Centronics-type interface.** It uses a 36 pin connector like that shown in Fig 10.23. A full signal description of this interface is given in Appendix C. Typically, a Centronics interface is used to transfer information from a microcomputer to a printer. The maximum cable length which may be used is about 3 metres.

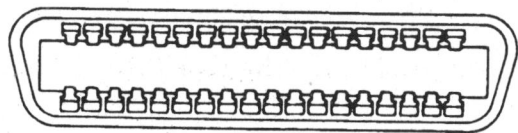

Fig 10.23 36-pin Centronics connector

The **SCSI** interface is mostly used to connect microcomputers to mass storage peripherals such as hard disk (Winchester) drives, floppy disk drives and **tape streamer drives.** This interface uses a 50-pin connector.

The RS232 serial interface

Serial I/O is commonly used to interface a computer to peripherals such as terminals, modems and printers. Peripherals and computers, are of course, designed by many different manufacturers. Hence a common interface standard is desirable to ensure compatibility. The standard for serial communication is the Electronic Industries Association (EIA) Recommended Standard (RS) 232.

The maximum cable length for this standard is about 15 metres. In order to increase the noise immunity for the serial data stream the RS-232 standard specifies voltage levels of between +3V and +25V for logical 0, and between -3V and -25V for logical 1. Most practical implementations use +12V to represent bit 0 and -12V for logic 1.

The RS-232 standard specifies a 25 pin D-type connector which is illustrated in Fig 10.24. The signal definitions for the RS-232C standard are given in Appendix D.

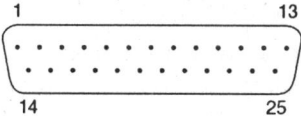

Fig 10.24 An RS-232 D-type connector

Short answer question 10.14

State the name of the standard parallel printer interface and the approximate maximum distance between the computer and the printer.

> **A** Answer to SAQ 10.14
>
> Centronics. About 3 metres.

10.11 PERIPHERAL EQUIPMENT

All devices attached to the I/O ports of a computer are known as peripherals. Examples of peripherals include keyboards, mice, display monitors, disk drives and printers. All of these devices must be connected to the computer via an appropriate interface. Common terms associated with printers and display monitors are presented in this section. The floppy disk drive interface is examined in Chapter 12.

PRINTERS

The printer which is used to produce **hardcopy** of text and graphics on paper is an essential peripheral for most microcomputer systems. Printers are categorised according to the method used to produce the final output. Generally, they may be classified as **impact** or **non-impact** devices. In impact printers a print head strikes an inked ribbon, placed in front of a sheet of paper, leaving an imprint of the print head on the paper. The dot matrix printer is an example of an impact printer. In non-impact printing, the character is formed on the paper by what is, essentially, a non-mechanical process. Laser and ink-jet printers are non-impact devices.

Dot-matrix printer

The dot matrix is the most common type of printer currently in use. This printer creates characters by striking pins against an inked ribbon. Each pin makes a dot, and combinations of dots form characters and illustrations. The majority of dot-matrix printers have either 9 or 24 wires (pins) in the print head, covering a vertical distance of 1/6 inch, and are known as 9 or 24 pin printers. For a 9 pin printer the vertical distance between dots is 1/54 inch (54 dots per inch) and for a 24 pin the distance is 1/144 inch (144 dots per inch). The higher the figure for the dots per inch (DPI) the better the quality of the print output. However a price has to be paid for quality – 24 pin printers are more expensive than 9 pin ones. The speed of dot-matrix printers can vary from 50 to over 500 characters per second (CPS).

A 24 pin dot matrix printer is capable of producing near letter quality (NLQ). Although some dot-matrix printers operate at higher speeds and less cost per page than inkjets or lasers they are notorious for the noise generated while printing.

Inkjet printers

These printers work by spraying tiny dots of ink on the paper rather than firing pins at a ribbon. Magnetised plates in the ink's path direct the ink onto the paper in the desired shapes. Inkjet printers are capable of producing very high quality print (letter quality;LQ), approaching that produced by laser printers. A typical inkjet printer has a resolution of 300 DPI. Resolution may be regarded as the sharpness or clarity of the print.

In general, the price of inkjet printers is lower than that of laser printers. However, they are also considerably slower, printing between one and three pages per minute (PPM). Another drawback of inkjet printers is that they tend to smudge.

Laser printers

Laser printers produce higher quality output than any other type of printer. Although at present they are more expensive than either dot-matrix or inkjet printers prices are falling rapidly and so we can expect laser printers to become the most commonly used form of output printing device. As the name suggests this type of printer utilises a laser beam to produce the image.

For laser printing the output from the computer is converted by an interface into a raster feed, similar to the impulses that a TV picture tube receives. The impulses cause the laser beam to scan a drum that carries a positive electrical charge. Where the laser hits the drum, the drum is discharged. A toner (a fine black powder), which also carries a positive charge is then applied to the drum. The toner, sticks only to the areas of the drum that have been discharged electrically. (A fundamental law of electricity is that like charges repel while unlike charges attract) The toner is then transferred onto the paper through a combination of heat and pressure.

The printing speed of lasers varies from about 4 to 20 pages of text per minute (PPM). A rate of 6 PPM is equivalent to about 40 characters per second (cps).

VIDEO DISPLAYS

During the early years of personal computing the video system (monitor) choice was simply monochrome or colour. Since then, many adapter and display options have been produced. A video sub-system consists of:

i) an adapter which fits into an expansion slot or is built into the motherboard

ii) a video display, known as the monitor, which is compatible with the video adapter.

Some of the common IBM display systems standards are:

> **CGA**   Colour Graphics Adapter
>
> **EGA**   Enhanced Graphics Adapter
>
> **VGA**   Video Graphics Array
>
> **SVGA**   Super Video Graphics Adapter

An important measure of the quality of a monitor is its **resolution**. This term is often used to describe monitors and printers. For monitors, the resolution refers to the size of the pixels used in graphics. In medium resolution graphics, pixels are large, whereas in high resolution graphics, pixels are small. Monitors are often classified as high, medium or low resolution. It should be noted that the actual resolution ranges for each of these grades is constantly shifting as the technology improves.

Table 10.4 gives specifications for CGA/EGA/VGA/SVGA graphics adapters.

Video Standard	Resolution	No. of colours	Mode Type	Character Format	Character Box
CGA	640 × 200	16	Text	80 × 25	8 × 8
	640 × 200	2	Graphics	80 × 25	8 × 8
EGA	640 × 350	16	Text	80 × 25	8 × 14
	640 × 350	16	Graphics	80 × 25	8 × 14
VGA	720 × 400	16	Text	80 × 25	9 × 16
	640 × 480	16	Graphics	80 × 30	8 × 16
SVGA	1024 × 768	256	Graphics	146 × 51	7 × 15

Table 10.4 Video display adapter standards.

Notes:

i) Table 10.4 does not list every possibility for each of these standards.

ii) The resolution figure is a quality indicator.

iii) An SVGA colour monitor provides, 80 × 25 characters with 16 colours in text mode.

Keyboards

The keyboard is a device that enables you to enter information into the computer. Computer keyboards are similar to electric typewriter keyboards but contain additional keys. The keys on a keyboard can be grouped in the following categories:

- Alphanumeric keys: upper and lower case letters, numbers, and punctuation marks.
- Cursor control and direction keys
- The numeric keypad
- Function keys: <F1>etc
- Control keys: <Shift>,<Ctrl> and so on...

There is no standard computer keyboard, although many manufacturers imitate the keyboards of IBM Personal Computers. There are three different IBM PC keyboards: the 83-key PC and XT keyboard; the 84-key AT (Standard) keyboard and the 101-key AT (Enhanced) keyboard. These types of keyboards are sometimes called ASCII keyboards because a key press generates an ASCII code for input to the computer.

Mouse

The mouse is another means of communicating with the computer. It is a small hand-held object with at least one button and sometimes as many as three, which is used to control the movement of the cursor or pointer on a display screen. You can roll the mouse along a hard, flat surface or a mouse pad. As you move the mouse, the pointer on the screen moves in the same direction. The mouse is very useful for graphics programs and allows you to draw diagrams or pictures by using the mouse like a pen, pencil or paintbrush. It is widely used for menu driven applications – you simply point to your command choice and click a mouse button.

SUMMARY

- Data transfer between a microprocessor and its peripherals takes place through its input/output (I/O) ports.
- Examples of programmable parallel I/O ports are the PIO and PIA.
- General purpose programmable serial I/O chips are usually called UARTs.
- Each side of the Zilog PIO contains the following registers:

    data input; data output; mode control and direction.

- To a programmer, a PIO will be accessed as four addressable registers; data and control registers for side A and side B of the port.
- The Z80 PIO programmable I/O interfacing chip may be programmed in FOUR modes:

    | MODE | 0 | Output |
    | MODE | 1 | Input |
    | MODE | 2 | Bi-directional – Port A only |
    | MODE | 3 | Bit input/output (control) |

- Serial communication is the transmission of data one bit at a time along a single wire.
- The data transfer rate for a serial line is measured in BAUD:

$$\text{Baud rate} = \frac{1}{\text{bit time}}$$

- Generally, each serial communication character contains a start bit, a number of data bits, parity bit (for error checking) and a stop bit/s
- A modem is a device that is used for serial communications over long distances.
- The I/O ports may be memory mapped or input/output mapped

- ☐ I/O ports such as the PIO or UART are unable to handle all aspects of data transfer between an MPU and its peripherals, therefore additional circuits, called interfaces, may be necessary.
- ☐ A transducer is a device that converts physical variables, such as, temperature, pressure and flow rate into an electrical variable (resistance, current, voltage).
- ☐ An ADC converts signals from analogue to digital.
- ☐ A DAC converts signals from digital to analogue
- ☐ Centronics is the standard interface for parallel printers. The maximum distance between the computer and the printer should not exceed about 3 metres.
- ☐ The RS-232 serial interface is widely used to interface the computer to terminals, printers and modems. This interface is intended for fairly short cables, about 15 metres.
- ☐ Generally, printers may be classified as impact or non-impact devices. A dot-matrix is an example of an impact printer, while lasers and inkjets are non-impact printers.
- ☐ The speed of dot-matrix printers can vary from 50 to 500 cps. They are capable of producing NLQ. However, they are notorious for the noise generated while printing.
- ☐ Inkjet printers produce near laser quality and are generally capable of printing between 1 and 3 pages per minute (PPM).
- ☐ Laser printers produce the best quality output at speeds of between 4 and 20 pages of text per minute.
- ☐ The quality of a video display (monitor) may be judged by its resolution.
  Quality in descending order is SVGA —>VGA—>EGA—>CGA.

END OF CHAPTER QUESTIONS

Section A: Multiple choice questions (Answers in Appendix A)

1. The main purpose of a PIO in a microcomputer system is to
   a) act as a serial input/output port
   b) interface a modem to the MPU
   c) act as a parallel I/O port
   d) interface to a serial printer

2. A serial data stream contains a parity bit. The reason for this is to
   a) provide a form of error checking
   b) inform the receiving equipment that a character is about to be sent.

c) inform the receiving equipment that the end of the character has been reached.
d) switch off error checking

3. Which one of the following devices contains a data direction register?
   a) ROM
   b) RAM
   c) UART
   d) PIA

4. The mode control word for a PIO is 4FH. In which mode is it to be programmed?
   a) input
   b) output
   c) control
   d) bi-directional

5. Which one of the following devices would be most suitable as part of the interface, between a microcomputer and a mains operated D.C. motor?
   a) DAC
   b) ADC
   c) PIO
   d) Opto-isolator

6. The maximum distance, measured in metres (m), between a Centronics parallel printer and a computer is about
   a) 20m
   b) 15m
   c) 3m
   d) 1m

7. Which one of the following is a serial standard?
   a) Centronics
   b) SCSI
   c) IEEE488
   d) RS-232

8. Which one of the following printers produces the best quality output?
   a) Daisywheel
   b) Dot-matrix
   c) Inkjet
   d) Laser

9. All of the resolution figures quoted are for monitors working in graphics mode. Which one has the best resolution?
   a) 640 × 200
   b) 640 × 350
   c) 640 × 480
   d) 1024 × 768

10. A PIO is using handshaking to transfer data to a peripheral. Which of the following signals is a handshake signal?
    a) Read
    b) Write
    c) Strobe
    d) Clock

Section B: Short answer questions

1. Draw the block diagram of a Z80 PIO and briefly explain the function of its data input/output registers.
2. LIST the four PIO programming modes.
3. The mode control word for a PIO is CFH. In which mode is it being programmed?
4. Draw a simplified block diagram of a UART. LIST three programmable features of UARTs.
5. With the aid of a timing diagram describe the format of a serial data bit stream.
6. What is an interface?
7. State FOUR reasons why interfaces may be needed between a computer and its peripherals
8. With the aid of a simple diagram explain why interfaces frequently contain digital-to-analogue and analogue-to-digital converters.
9. Discuss some of the main features of the RS-232 interface standard.
10. Compare dot-matrix, inkjet and laser printers in terms of speed and quality of output.
11. Name FOUR common IBM display system standards and state with reason which one you would select if highest quality image is the prime concern.

Chapter 11

Microcomputer Programming

A microcomputer is a general purpose system designed around a programmable microprocessor chip. The microprocessor is responsible for processing data and controlling the other elements of the system. To carry out a given task a program of instructions has to be produced and entered into the memory of the computer. Once the instructions are in memory the user can issue the relevant command to the processor to execute the program. This chapter provides a brief introduction to software development. We will also examine the microprocessor's instruction set and addressing modes before presenting a number of simple programs. Various practical programming examples, with details of the required interface, are included in the latter part of the chapter. Chapter 1 covered some aspects of programming languages, so it may be useful to read Section 1.7 before you continue.

11.1 SOFTWARE DEVELOPMENT

If we are using a computer to solve a problem a program has to be designed. The starting point for the design of any computer program must be a specification which details exactly what the program is going to do. The inputs to and outputs from the program must be clearly specified. The job of the programmer is to take the given inputs and write a program to produce the required outputs. In a program specification the definitions of the inputs and outputs must include a description of their meaning. For instance, it may be required to compute the area of a rectangle given its length and breadth. Such a description of the problem is almost a complete specification, and the programmer needs only to know the formula for calculating the area of a rectangle. The problem as specified only has meaning if the terms length, breadth and rectangle and their interrelationships are known. For example, if the specification was given as $A = L \times B$ then the programmer should fully qualify the meaning of A, L and B. For all problems, from simple to complex, the programmer should ensure that the specification is complete and unambiguous before attempting to design the program.

The stages involved in software development are illustrated in Fig 11.1 This type of figure is known as a flowchart. The rectangle symbol is used to indicate that a specific action is to be taken (a process) and the diamond symbol denotes that a decision has to be made.

11: Microcomputer programming

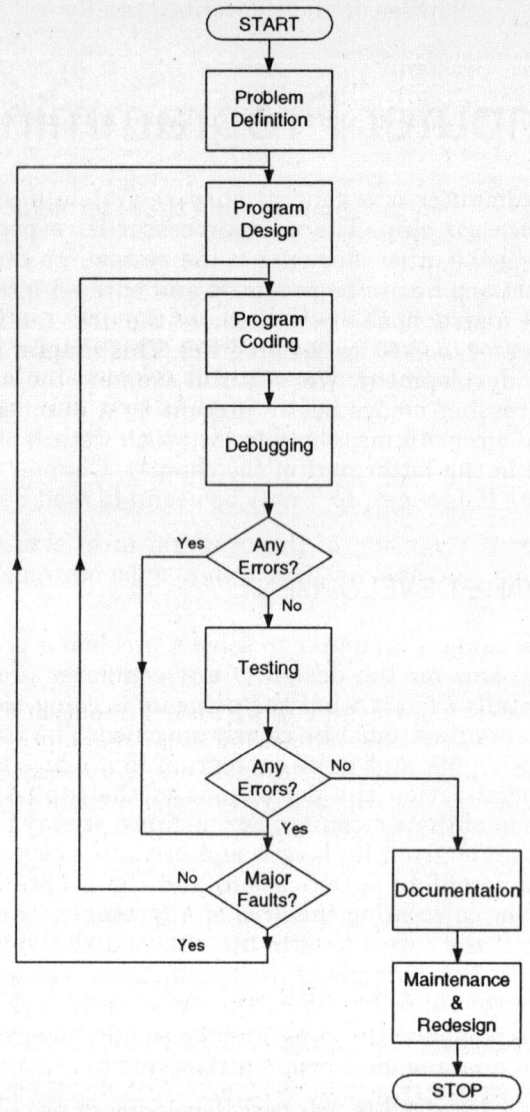

Fig 11.1 Software development flowchart

The stages involved in the software development process are:

- **Problem specification**
- **Program design**
- **Program coding**
- **Debugging**
- **Testing**
- **Documentation**
- **Maintenance and redesign**

Each of these phases are now described briefly:

Problem definition

For example, what is necessary to make a microcomputer control a set of traffic lights or an electrical stepper motor? This stage involves qualifying the system inputs and outputs fully and considering any other relevant details such as, the interface between the computer and the external device to be controlled.

Program design

Program design is the outline of the computer program which will perform the tasks that have been defined. At the design stage, the tasks to be carried out are described in a way that can easily be converted into a computer programming language. Among the useful techniques that may be used at this stage are algorithms, flowcharts, pseudo-code, top-down design, structured programming etc.

Coding

Coding is the writing of the program in a form that the computer can either directly use or translate. The form may be machine code, assembly language, or a high level language.

Debugging

This refers to the tracking down and elimination of errors (bugs) in the program. For the machine code and assembly language programs which are our main concern in this chapter the techniques used for debugging are trace tables and breakpoints. Other tools which may be used include logic analysers, in-circuit emulators and simulators.

Testing

Testing, is ensuring that the program does what it is supposed to do.

Documentation

This will include the problem definition and details of the program design aid (algorithm/flowchart/pseudo-code/structure diagram) used. Coding sheets, details of test results and a user's guide should also be included. Good documentation is important because it will aid future maintenance of the program.

Maintenance and redesign

Maintenance and redesign refer to the servicing, improvement or upgrading and extension of the program. Maintenance of the program may be necessary in order to meet new requirements or handle new tasks as specified by the customer. Bear in mind that a program may have a life of many years.

11.2 PROGRAM DESIGN

Program design is the stage in which the problem definition is formulated as a program. If the program is small and simple, the design stage may involve little more than writing the steps of the solution on a piece of paper. However, if the program is larger or more complex the programmer should consider other recommended methods. We will briefly discuss algorithms, flowcharts, pseudo-code, top-down programming and structured programming.

Algorithms

When first starting to program most people have the impression that the hard part of solving a problem on a computer is translating your ideas into the specific language that will be entered into the computer. This most definitely is not the case. The most difficult part of solving a problem using a computer is coming up with the method of solution. After you come up with the method of solution, it is a simple routine task to translate your method into the required language, be it Pascal, Cobol, Z80 assembly language or some other programming language. When solving a problem with a computer, it is therefore helpful to ignore temporarily the computer programming language and to concentrate instead on formulating the steps of the solution and writing them down in plain English, as if the instructions were to be given to a person. A set of instructions expressed in this way is frequently called an algorithm. To be an algorithm, a sequence of instructions must satisfy two important properties. First of all, each instruction must be taken from a basic set of 'primitive operations' available in the machine carrying out the algorithm. Thus the algorithm for multiplying 15 by 20 may be just one instruction in a machine with multiplication as a primitive, whereas a machine which is only capable of addition and counting would entail 20 successive additions of 15. Secondly an algorithm must produce a result in a finite (limited) number of steps. We will use algorithms as the method of solution for some of our simple machine code/ assembly language programs later in the chapter. In summary, a computer requires a precise sequence of actions to solve a particular problem; such a sequence is called an algorithm.

Flowcharts

A flowchart is a graphical description of a program or system. They may also be used for other purposes, for instance, to indicate the steps to be carried out for troubleshooting a piece of electronic equipment. The flowchart is made up of graphical symbols which are connected together by straight lines which indicate the sequence of operations or flow of data. A selection of commonly used flowchart symbols is given in Appendix E. Flowcharts will be used as the design method for a number of programming exercises that appear later in the chapter.

Top-down design

One of the most successful ways of designing computer programs is to break down the task to be accomplished into a few subtasks, then decompose each big subtasks into smaller subtasks, then replace the smaller subtasks by even smaller subtasks and so forth. Eventually the subtasks become so small that they are trivial to implement in whatever programming language you are using. As well as being a good design method it also aids subsequent modifications of the program. This is very important as most programs are changed at some time. The basic principle of top-down design is illustrated in Fig 11.2 This method is often called stepwise refinement.

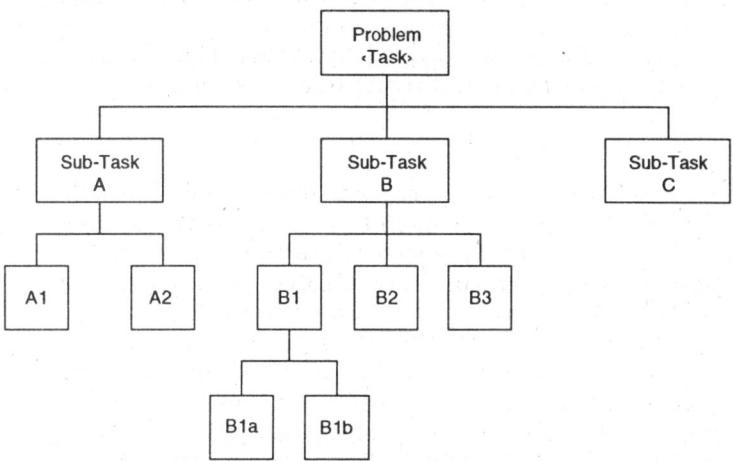

Fig 11.2 Top-down design

A top-down approach such as that just outlined will help to simplify the programming task but the programmer should also use techniques which help to ensure error-free and clear programs. For instance, how do you keep the subtasks (modules) distinct (separate) and stop them from interacting? How do you write a program that has a clear sequence of operations so that you can isolate and correct errors? One answer is to use the method known as structured programming whereby each part of the program consists of elements from a limited set of structures and each structure has a single entry and a single exit. The three basic control structures used in **structured programming** which have a single entry point and a single exit point are **sequence, selection** and **iteration**. These are illustrated in Fig 11.3. All structured programming design methods are based upon the two fundamental principles of stepwise refinement and the three basic control structures sequence, selection and iteration. So it should be noted that top-down programming does not necessarily mean the same as structured programming.

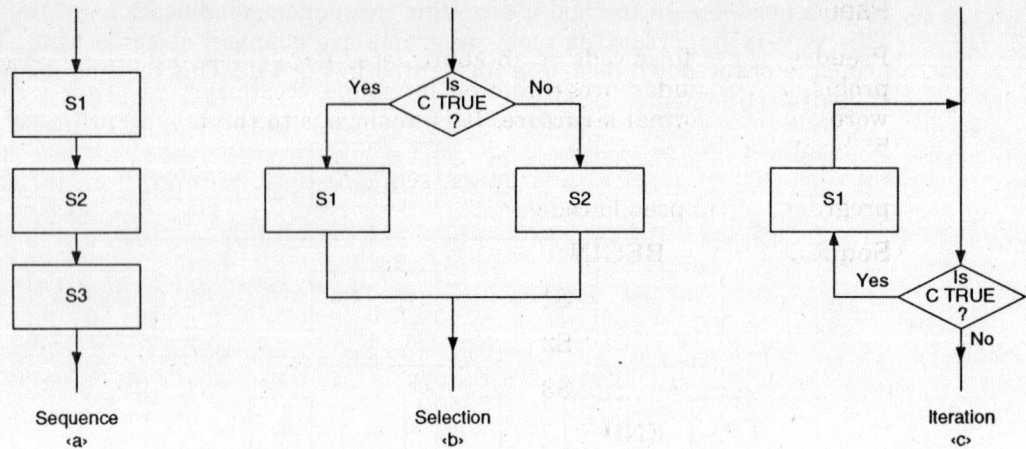

Fig 11.3 Control structures

Sequence

In a sequence, statements are executed consecutively or one after the other. In Fig 11.3 (a) the sequence is:

>S1
>S2
>S3

This means that the computer executes S1 first, S2 second and S3 third. Note that S1, S2 and S3 may be single instructions or program segments consisting of many instructions. Note the single-entry and single-exit points.

Selection

On entry to the selection structure in Fig 11.3 (b) the computer checks whether a condition (c) is TRUE or FALSE. If it is true then S1 is executed otherwise (else) S2 will be executed. S1 and S2 are statements or sequences of statements. Again note that the structure has single-entry and single-exit points.

Iteration

The structure shown in Fig 11.3 (c) is known as a program loop (a sequence of instructions that is executed repeatedly until some specified condition is met). On entry to the iteration structure the computer checks a condition (c) to find out whether it is TRUE or FALSE. If the condition is TRUE then S1 (a single instruction or a sequence of statements) will be executed. As soon as the condition becomes FALSE the iteration terminates. Like the sequence and selection structures this too has a single-entry and single-exit.

Pseudo-code

Pseudo-code or 'false code' is an abbreviated form of a solution to a programming problem. It includes programming language vocabulary together with English words in an informal structure. It is analogous to the broad outline of an essay; both are used to organise and refine the respective final products. We will now express the three basic structures, sequence-selection-iteration, for structured programming in pseudo-code.

Sequence: **BEGIN**
                       S1
                       S2
                       S3
                  END

Selection: **IF** the condition (c) is true   **THEN** do S1
                                                     ELSE do S2

Iteration: **WHILE** the condition (c) is true **DO** S1

These pseudo-code statements can easily be translated into programming languages such as Pascal. In the examples given the highlighted words are part of the programming language vocabulary.

Short answer question 11.1

LIST the stages involved in program development.

Answer to SAQ 11.1

Problem specification; Program design; Program coding; Debugging; Documentation; Testing; Maintenance and redesign.

Short answer question 11.2

Name the three basic control structures for use in structured programming.

Answer to SAQ 11.2

Sequence, selection and iteration.

11.3 THE MICROPROCESSOR'S INSTRUCTION SET

Within a microcomputer instructions are represented by binary words. Each instruction has its own unique binary code which corresponds to one particular operation. When the microprocessor is running a program it executes the program instructions one-by-one.

A microprocessor is only capable of performing a limited number of instructions. When we speak of its instruction set we are talking about all of the instructions which the microprocessor can execute. For instance, the Zilog Z80 MPU can execute 158 different instruction types. The instruction set is designed by each of the individual manufacturers and because there is little or no standardization the instruction set is unique to a particular MPU. This means that the machine/assembly code for one type of microprocessor will not run on another MPU. However, there are exceptions to this, for example, all of the Intel 8080A instructions can be executed by the Z80 MPU. The difficulty of transferring code from one MPU to another can be overcome by the use of a cross assembler if necessary.

In Chapter one we saw that a microprocessor instruction may be represented in three different forms. For example, the instruction to load the accumulator (Register A) of the Z80 MPU with a byte of data may be written as:

>0011 1110   Machine code in binary form
>
>3E   Machine code in HEXadecimal form
>
>LD A   Assembly code mnemonic form

At machine level the binary form of the instruction is used. The instruction is stored in the memory in binary and when the MPU fetches it from there it is taken as a group of bits via the system data bus to the MPU. The hex code is used for the convenience of the programmer. Each hex symbol represents four bits (Chapter 2). Even though the programmer works in hexadecimal for writing and entering the program into the system, it must be converted into binary for the machine. This conversion may be accomplished using either software or hardware. Assembly code represents a half-way position between machine code and a high-level language such as Pascal. Generally, the assembly code is a mnemonic (mnemonic = an aid to memory) derived from the instruction itself. In the above example, **LD A** is a kind of shorthand which stands for '**LoaD** the **A**ccumulator'. Because the instruction mnemonics have been carefully devised assembly code is easy to use and remember.

Programming in assembly language requires that the code is translated into machine code for the microprocessor. This translation may be achieved in two ways. Firstly, you can convert from assembly code to machine code by looking up the instruction set for the processor, which lists the instruction mnemonic and the corresponding machine code expressed in hexadecimal. This technique is known as hand assembly. Secondly, an assembler (a separate program) may be used for this conversion.

Short answer question 11.3

State two methods of converting from assembly language code to machine code.

 Answer to SAQ 11.3

Either look up code in the instruction set for the microprocessor (hand assembly) or use a program called an assembler.

All microprocessors have a relatively large number of instructions in their full instruction set. If you consult the technical manual for any microprocessor and check the sheer number and apparent complexity of the available instructions you may feel that understanding the instruction set is almost an impossible task. Console yourself, because it becomes much more manageable once it is realised that the instructions may be grouped into subsets which perform similar functions. Although different microprocessors have different instructions, there are general requirements for all microprocessors and these are that they must have the following classes of instruction.

1. Data transfer
2. Arithmetic operations
3. Logical operations
4. Program flow control (Test and branch)
5. Input-output
6. Miscellaneous operations.

Data transfer instructions

These are the instructions that transfer data between microprocessor registers, or between a microprocessor register and a memory location. The instruction set contains numerous data transfer instructions and they have a very high frequency of usage in all programs.

Assembly code	Explanation
LD A,n	Load the accumulator (A) with the 8-bit number (n)
LD A, (nn)	Load the accumulator with the byte of data stored in memory at address nn
LD (nn),A	Load the contents of the accumulator into memory location nn
LD B,C	Load register B with the data in register C
LD C,B	Load register C with the data in register B

Table 11.1 Examples of data transfer instructions

Arithmetic operations

Most microprocessors have a variety of arithmetic instructions. They may be divided into two classes. There are those instructions which involve two separate bytes of data, one of which is usually placed in the accumulator. After the ALU has performed an arithmetic operation on the two bytes of data the result is returned to the accumulator. The second class of arithmetic instructions are those which operate on a single byte of data.

Assembly code	Explanation
ADD A,B	Add the contents of register B to the accumulator (A)
ADC A,B	Add, with carry, the contents of register B to A
INC A	Increment register A ; increase its contents by 1
DEC HL	Decrement register pair HL; decrease its contents by 1

Table 11.2 Typical arithmetic instructions

Logical operations

The other class of instructions which may be executed by the ALU of the microprocessor is the set of logical instructions.

Assembly code	Explanation
AND B	Logically AND register B with the accumulator
OR D	Logically OR register D with the accumulator
XOR A	Clear the accumulator

Table 11.3 Logical operations

Jump & branch (Program flow control) instructions

Various instructions allow the programmer to change the program counter (PC) contents. These instructions are usually called either 'jump' or 'branch'. The jump instructions simply change the PC value. A jump instruction may be either unconditional or conditional. An unconditional jump is an instruction which, when encountered in a program, simply loads the program counter with an address which is specified within the instruction. See table 11.4 for examples. The second type of jump instruction, the conditional jump, tests the status or flag register for certain conditions. If the condition exists, the jump happens. If the condition does not exist, the jump does not happen. Examples of this type of instruction are given in table 11.5 A special unconditional jump instruction, the subroutine jump (call) is also available. For the Z80 MPU this is known as the CALL instruction. However, when a subroutine call instruction is encountered in a program, the contents of the PC (and maybe other registers) are PUSHed onto the stack before control is passed to the subroutine. On completion of the subroutine, control is returned to the main program, and the saved PC contents are POPped off the stack and placed back in the program counter. Refer back to Chapter 7, Section 7.5 for details of subroutine calls. Some of the subroutine jump instructions are shown in table 11.6

Assembly code	Explanation
JP nn	Jump to the address nn
JP (HL)	The contents of the HL register pair are loaded into the PC. The next instruction is fetched from this new address

Table 11.4 Unconditional jump instructions

Assembly code	Explanation
JP NZ, nn	Jump on the non-zero condition to address nn
JP Z, nn	Jump on the zero condition to address nn
JP P, nn	Jump on plus to address nn

Table 11.5 Conditional jump instructions

Assembly code	Explanation
CALL nn	Call the subroutine at address nn
RET	Return from the subroutine to the main program

Table 11.6 Subroutine jump (CALL) instructions

Examples of unconditional, conditional and subroutine jump instructions will be given in the programs that follow in this chapter.

Input-output instructions

In Chapter 10 we saw that for memory mapped systems the same instructions may be used for memory and port operations, whereas, an I/O mapped system has special instructions for input/output operations. The most widely used Z80 input-output instructions are those which transfer data between the accumulator (register A) and a specified port. I/O instructions are also examples of data transfer instructions. Table 11.7 shows the syntax for the Z80 IN/OUT instructions.

11: Microcomputer programming

Assembly code	Explanation
IN A, (N)	Transfer data from input port N to the accumulator.
OUT (N),A	Output the contents of the accumulator to port N

Table 11.7 Z80 I/O instructions

Miscellaneous instructions

Examples of these are MPU control instructions such as, **NOP** and **HALT**. NOP stands for No OPeration and may be used to create time delays which are a common requirement in programming. You will see examples of time delays in our practical interfacing problems.

When the MPU encounters a HALT instruction in the program it halts and executes NOPs so as to continue memory refresh cycles for dynamic RAM.

Short answer question 11.4

Into which category of instructions do each of the following belong?

i. LD B,H
ii. LD A, (nn) ; nn = a 16-bit address
iii. SUB C
iv. OR B
v. JP C; C refers to the CARRY bit in the status (flag) register

Answer to SAQ 11.4

i and ii Data transfer; iii Arithmetic; iv Logical and v Jump or program control flow.

Short answer question 11.5

What is the effect of the following instructions?

i   LD A,H
ii LD A, (nn) ; where nn = a 16-bit address

Answer to SAQ 11.5

i   The contents of register H will be copied into the accumulator (register A)

ii The byte stored at address nn, in memory, will be loaded into A

 Short answer question 11.6

Write down the assembly code mnemonic for transferring the contents of the accumulator to memory location 2200H.

 Answer to SAQ 11.6

LD (2200),A

11.4 ADDRESSING MODES

Most of the Z80 instructions operate on data stored in internal registers (A, F, B, C, D, E, H, L, SP, etc), external memory or in the input/output ports. For all of these data movement operations the instruction must contain information relating to the source of the data (is it in an MPU register, a memory location or a port?) and the destination of the data (is it to be moved to a register, memory location or input/output port?). Instructing the MPU as to the data source and destination is called addressing. All microprocessors are equipped with a variety of addressing modes. In order to be an efficient programmer a knowledge of the addressing modes is essential. The Z80 has a total of ten addressing modes, however a full treatment of all of these is beyond the scope of this book.

Before considering the addressing modes a review of the format of a machine-level instruction may be necessary. The majority of instructions consist of two different parts, the operation code (OP CODE) and the operand or address part as shown in Fig 11.4

OPERATION CODE	OPERAND
This specifies the operation to be performed	This specifies either 1. The actual data value, or 2. The address of the data

Fig 11.4 A machine-level instruction

As an example consider the instruction,

    LD A,B
        B = Source address (symbolic)
        A = Destination address (symbolic)
        LD = Operation mnemonic = 47H (See Appendix F)

Similarly, in the instruction LD (nn), A; LD is the operation mnemonic; Register A is the source address and (nn), where nn represents a 16-bit address is the destination address.

Table 11.8 gives a summary of some of the most widely used Z80 addressing modes.

Z80 Addressing Mode	Example	Explanation
Immediate	LD C,5DH	The byte following the op-code in memory is the operand. This mode is used to load 8-bit data into a register.
Immediate Extended	LD HL,2100H	This mode is merely an extension of immediate addressing in that the two bytes following the op-code in memory are the operand.
Register	LD B,A	This mode is used to copy data from one MPU register into another register.
Register Indirect		This is used to copy data between an MPU register and a memory location.
	LD r, (HL)	If, for instance, HL holds the address 2100H then the contents of memory location 2100H will be loaded into one of the MPU registers (r)
	LD (HL),r	Load the contents of the MPU register (r) into the memory location whose address is in HL
Extended	JP 2007H	Extended addressing provides for two bytes (16 bits) of address to be included in the instruction. This data can be an address to which a program can jump or it can be an address where the operand is located.
Implied	AND B	This addressing mode refers to operations in which the op code implies one or more Z80 registers as containing the operands. For example, instructions for logical operations imply that the accumulator holds one of the operands and that the result will be stored in the accumulator.

11: Microcomputer programming

Relative	JR e	In this mode, the byte following the op code specifies a displacement value (e) in 2's complement notation. The value of 'e' is added to the PC so as to enable forward and backward jumps in a program. For example, JR 0AH would cause a jump forward 10 locations from the address of the next instruction.
Indexed	LD r, (IX + d)	The contents of the memory location addressed by the IX register plus the given offset value (d) are loaded into the specified MPU register (r). This is a useful addressing mode for dealing with tables of data.

Table 11.8 Z80 Addressing modes

Short answer question 11.7

State the addressing mode to which each of the following instructions belong?

   i   AND B
   ii   LD r,n ; n = 8-bit data
   iii LD r, (HL)

Answer to SAQ 11.7

i Implicit;   ii Immediate;   iii Indirect

11.5 PROGRAMMING EXAMPLES

Before attempting these programming examples it is worth noting that there is no unique solution to any given problem. Throughout these exercises we will vary the design technique to illustrate the use of algorithms, flowcharts and pseudocode.

Program 1: ADDITION

Write a machine code program to add the two bytes of data, 01H and 02H, stored at memory locations 2100H and 2101H respectively. Store the result at memory location 2102H.

Algorithm

1. Load the accumulator with the number stored at memory location 2100H
2. Load register B from A
3. Load the accumulator with the second number
4. Add the byte in register B to the byte in A
5. Store the result at location 2102H
6. Stop

The algorithm may be translated to pseudo-code thus:

			Explanation
1.	LD A with (2100H)	;	Read the brackets as 'the contents of''
		;	Therefore (2100H) means the contents of memory location 2100H
2.	LD B from A	;	Load B from A
3.	LD A with (2101H)	;	Load the accumulator with the number stored at location 2101H
4.	ADD B to A	;	Add the two numbers
5.	LD (2102H), A	;	Store the result at location 2102H
6.	HALT		

From the pseudo-code we can easily write the assembly language program (source code)

Assembly language program

Assembly language program (Mnemonics)	Comment
LD A, (2100H)	Load A with contents of 2100H
LD B,A	Load B from A
LD A, (2101H)	Load A with contents of 2101H
ADD A,B	Add B to A
LD (2102H),A	Store the result at location 2102H
HALT	Halt the MPU

As mentioned earlier, the assembly language source code can be translated to machine code either by hand assembly or using a program called an assembler. We will hand assemble all of our programs by looking up the operation codes for the instructions in Appendix F.

If the source is now assembled, the following machine code listing is obtained.

11: Microcomputer programming

Memory Address (HEX)	Machine Code	Assembly Code	Comment
2000	3A		Load A with contents of memory location 2100H
2001	00	LD A, (2100H)	
2002	21		
2003	47	LD B,A	Load B from A
2004	3A		Load A with the contents of memory location 2101H
2005	01	LD A, (2101H)	
2006	21		
2007	80	ADD A,B	Add B to A
2008	32		Store the result at memory location 2102H
2009	02	LD (2102H),A	
200A	21		
200B	76	HALT	Halt the MPU

Notes:

i) The memory addresses are expressed in Hexadecimal.

ii) The OP-CODES have been obtained directly from the instruction set in Appendix F.

iii) For arithmetic and logical operations one of the operands must be stored in the accumulator (A).

iv) The result of arithmetic and logical operations is stored in A.

v) When entering instructions which contain an address the low byte of the address must be entered first.

vi) Read () as 'the contents of'. For instance, (A) means the contents of register A and (2102H) means the contents stored at memory location 2102H.

Short answer question 11.8

i How many bytes of memory does the program occupy?

ii Why does the second instruction in the add two bytes program begin at memory location 2003H?

Answer to SAQ 11.8

i 12 bytes. From 2000H to 200BH inclusive.

ii Because the first instruction occupied three memory locations from 2000H to 2002H inclusive.

11: Microcomputer programming

Short answer question 11.9

What alterations are required to program 1 to subtract the number stored at 2100H from the number at 2101H. The result is to be stored at 2102H.?

Answer to SAQ 11.9

Replace the assembly code ADD A,B with SUB B. Change the corresponding machine code from 80H to 90H.

Program 2: TWOS COMPLEMENT

The number 04H is stored in memory at location 2100H. Using the instruction 'Complement the accumulator; CPL' which obtains the one's complement of the number in the accumulator obtain the two's complement of the number and store the result at 2101H.

Pseudo-code

1. LD A with (2100H)
2. Using the instruction CPL obtain the one's complement of the number
3. ADD 1 to the accumulator (2's complement = 1's complement +1)
4. Store the result at location 2101H
5. HALT

From the pseudo code we can write the program code thus:

Memory address	Machine code	Assembly code	Comment
2000	3A 00 21	LD A, (2100H)	Load A with the number at 2100H
2003	2F	CPL	Obtain the 1's complement
2004	3C	INC A	Add 1 to A
2005	32 01 21	LD (2101H),A	Store the result at 2101H
2008	76	HALT	Halt the MPU

Program 3: USING THE HL REGISTER PAIR

In Chapter 6 we saw that the register pairs BC, DE and HL may be used to hold a 16-bit memory address. Generally HL is used for this purpose because it is supported by more instructions than BC or DE for data transfers between the MPU registers and memory.

To illustrate the use of HL as a memory address register (MAR) we will write an assembly language program to add the four bytes of data 01H,02H,03H and 04H which are stored at four consecutive memory locations starting at 2100H. The result of the addition is to be stored at location 2104H.

Algorithm

1. Set up the HL register pair as a memory address register (MAR), initially holding the address 2100H.
2. Load the accumulator (A) with the byte stored at location 2100H
3. Increment the MAR by 1
4. Load register B with the byte stored at location 2101H
5. Increment the MAR by 1
6. Load register C with the byte stored at location 2102H
7. Increment the MAR by 1
8. Load register D with the byte stored at location 2103H
9. Add B to A
10. Add C to A
11. Add D to A
12. Increment the MAR by 1
13. Store the result at 2104H
14. Stop.

Converting each step of the algorithm to assembly language gives:

Memory address	Machine code	Assembly code	Comment
2000	21 00 21	LD HL,2100H	Point HL register to 2100H
2003	7E	LD A, (HL)	Load register A with the first byte
2004	23	INC HL	Increment HL by 1
2005	46	LD B, (HL)	Load register B with the second byte
2006	23	INC HL	Increment HL by 1
2007	4E	LD C, (HL)	Load register C with the third byte
2008	23	INC HL	Increment HL by 1
2009	56	LD D, (HL)	Load register D with the fourth byte
200A	80	ADD A,B	Add B to A
200B	81	ADD A,C	Add C to A
200C	82	ADD A,D	Add D to A
200D	23	INC HL	Point HL register at 2104H
200E	77	LD (HL),A	Store the result at location 2104H
200F	76	HALT	Halt the MPU

11: Microcomputer programming

Short answer question 11.10

Assuming that HL holds the address 2104H, what is the difference between the instructions LD (HL),A and LD A, (HL)?

Answer to SAQ 11.10

If LD (HL),A is executed the byte of data in A will be stored at memory location 2104H, whereas LD A, (HL) will have the effect of loading the byte of data stored at memory location 2104H into the accumulator.

Program 4: PROGRAM LOOPS

There is often a requirement in a program to perform a given task several times. Later when we interface the stepper motor to the computer you will be given an example of this. The program loop is the basic structure that forces the MPU to repeat a sequence of instructions. The principle of program loops is illustrated in Fig 11.5 which has three sections.

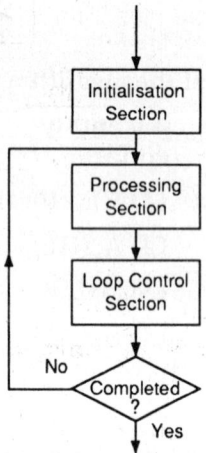

Fig 11.5 Program loop flowchart

i The **initialisation section**, which establishes the starting values of counters, memory address registers and other variables.

ii The **processing section** is where the actual data manipulation occurs. In other words, this is the section that does the work.

iii The **loop control section,** which updates the value of the loop counter.

As an example of a program loop consider the following problem. The ten numbers, 01H, 02H, 03H, 04H, 05H, 06H, 07H, 08H, 09H and 0AH are stored in ten consecutive memory locations, starting at location 2100H which holds the first number 01H. Write an assembly language program using a program loop to add the ten numbers and place the result at 210AH.

11: Microcomputer programming

The flowchart is given in Fig 11.6

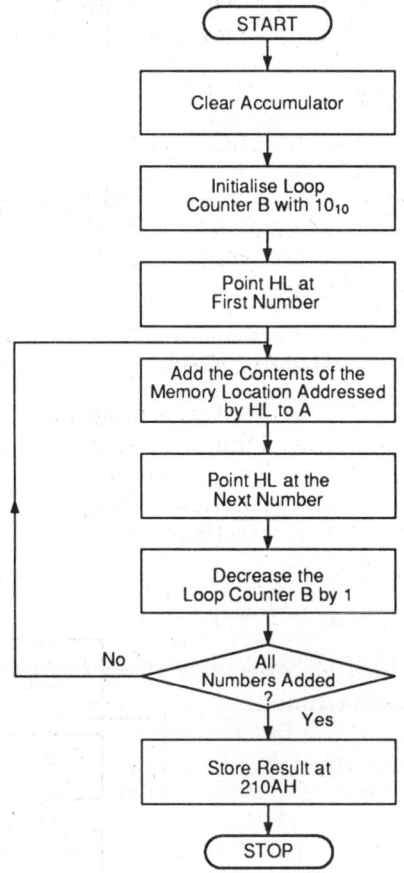

Fig 11.6 Flowchart, showing addition with a loop

The program code is:

Memory address	Machine code	Assembly code	Comment
2000	AF	XOR A	Clear the accumulator
2001	06 0A	LD B,0AH	Initialise the loop counter B with 10 decimal
2003	21 00 21	LD HL,2100H	Point HL at 2100H
2006	86	ADD A, (HL)	Add the contents of the memory location addressed by HL to A
2007	23	INC HL	Point HL at next location
2008	05	DEC B	Decrease loop counter by 1

11: Microcomputer programming

```
2009      C2 06 20    JP NZ, 2006H    If not zero jump back to 2006H
200C      77          LD (HL),A       Store the result at location 210AH
200D      76          HALT            Halt the MPU
```

Short answer question 11.11

In the above program explain how the instruction JP NZ works.

Answer to SAQ 11.11

After each pass through the processing section of the loop the MPU tests the zero flag in the status register. If this flag is not zero, it means that all 10 numbers have not yet been added, and the loop counter is not yet 0 and so the processing section will be repeated until the loop counter B reaches zero.

Time delays

One problem that we will face throughout our discussion on interfacing in the next section is the generation of time delays. These are needed in many practical applications of computers. For instance, the problem of mechanical switch debouncing which we encountered in Chapter four, and solved by simple hardware, can also be eliminated by means of a software delay loop. Traffic light systems and robotics are but two more examples of the need for software delay routines. The flowchart of Fig 11.7 shows one method of obtaining variable amounts of delay. The basic principle of time delays is to use the microprocessor as a counter. This is possible since the processor has a stable clock reference, but it clearly under-utilises the processor. However, delay routines require no additional hardware and often use processor time that would otherwise be wasted.

11: Microcomputer programming

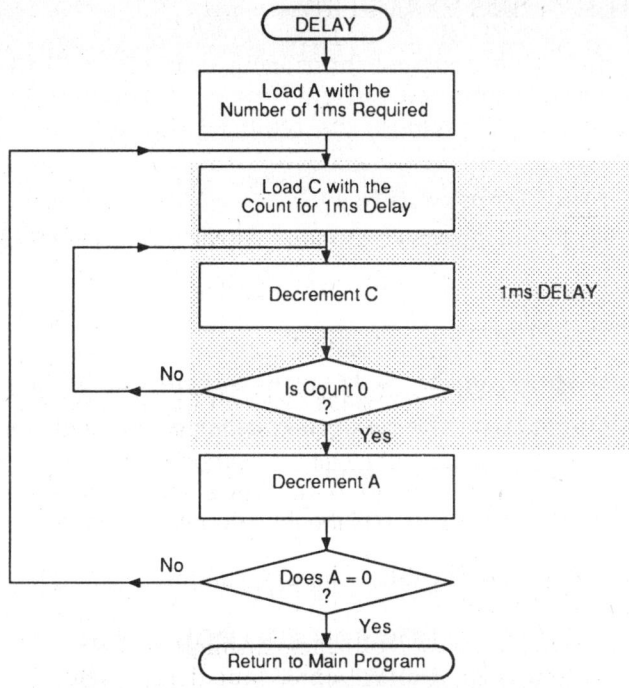

Fig 11.7 Flowchart for variable delay routine

The subroutine for the variable delay assumes a 4 MHz Z80 clock. Load register A with the number of mS delay required.

Memory address	Machine code	Assembly code	Comment
2150	3E 05	LD A,05H	Load A with the number of 1mS required. In this example we are making it 5mS.
2152	0E F9	LD C,F9H	Get count for 1mS delay
2154	0D	DEC C	Decrease counter C by 1
2155	C2 54 21	JP NZ, 2154H	If not zero jump to location 2154H
2158	3D	DEC A	Decrement number of remaining mS
2159	C2 52 21	JP NZ, 2152H	Continue until number of mS =0
215C	C9	RET	Return to main program

This routine will be used later for the stepper motor interface.

11: Microcomputer programming

11.6 INTERFACING EXAMPLES

The following practical interfacing examples will illustrate how to program the I/O port for input/output operations. Each example is provided with either an algorithm or flowchart, the required interface and the assembly language program.

P1. Input from switches

P2. Output to LEDs

P3. Combining switches and LEDs

P4. Pure binary up-counter

P5. Displaying the BCD count outputs on a 7-segment display

P6. Outputting the hex characters to a 7-segment display

P7. A traffic light system

P8. A stepper motor project

Note: For all of the following programming examples:

$$\begin{aligned}
\text{PORT A CONTROL} &= \text{82H} \\
\text{PORT A DATA} &= \text{80H} \\
\text{PORT B CONTROL} &= \text{83H} \\
\text{PORT B DATA} &= \text{81H}
\end{aligned}$$

If you are in any doubt about setting up the PIO programming modes read Chapter 10, section 10.4

P1: INPUT FROM SWITCHES

Fig 11.8 shows a group of eight switches connected to side A of the input/output port. Switch S1 is connected to PA0, switch S2 to PA1 and so on. The byte of data set up at the switch inputs is read into the accumulator when the program is executed.

11: Microcomputer programming

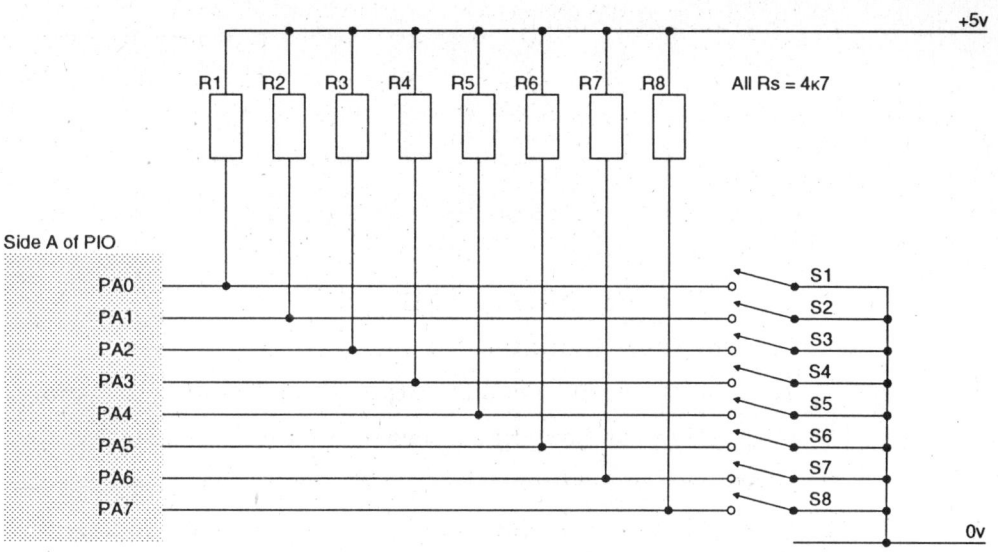

Fig 11.8 Input from switches

Algorithm

1. Set up side A of the port for input mode.
2. Read the byte of data into the accumulator
3. Halt the processor

Program code

Memory address	Machine code	Assembly code	Comment
2000	3E 4F	LD A,4FH	Set side A of port
2002	D3 82	OUT (82),A	to Mode 1 for input
2004	DB 80	IN A,(80)	Read in byte of data
2006	76	HALT	Halt the processor

P2: OUTPUT TO LIGHT EMITTING DIODES

This program outputs a byte of data from the accumulator to eight light emitting diodes (LEDs). The required interface, an electrical buffer, is connected as shown in Fig 11.9

11: Microcomputer programming

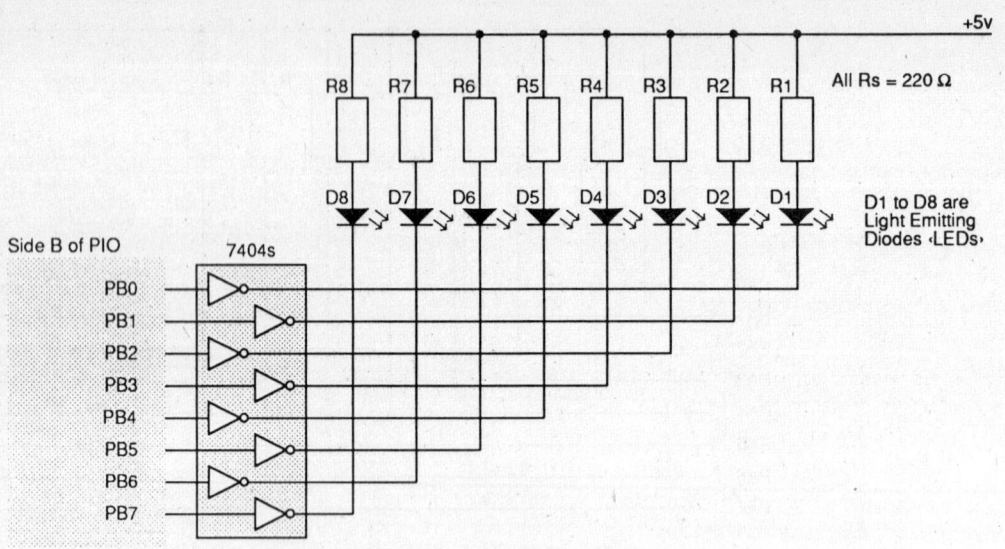

Fig 11.9 Output to LEDs

Algorithm

1. Set up port B for output
2. Place byte of data which is to be output to LEDs in A
3. Output byte to port B
4. Halt the processor

Program code

Memory address	Machine code	Assembly code	Comment
2000	3E 0F	LD A,0FH	Set Port B to
2002	D3 83	OUT (83),A	Mode 0 for output
2004	3E FF	LD A, FFH	Put byte which you want to output into A. In this example it is FFH.
2006	D3 81	OUT (81),A	Output the byte
2008	76	HALT	Halt the processor

 Short answer question 11.12

Explain how the mode control word is derived so as to set Port B in output mode for the last program (P2)

11: Microcomputer programming

> **A** Answer to SAQ 11.12
>
> The mode control word is worked out as follows:
>
> | D7 | D6 | D5 | D4 | D3 | D2 | D1 | D0 |
> |----|----|----|----|----|----|----|----|
> | M | M | X | X | 1 | 1 | 1 | 1 |
>
> X = don't care and M = mode. For output D7 = D6 = 0. Hence control word is 0FH. See Chapter 10, Section 10.4

P3: SWITCHES & LEDs

We are now going to combine the switches and the LEDs so that the **byte of data** which is set up on the input switches is read into the MPU and then sent **back out** to the LEDs. As Fig 11.10 shows Side A of the port is used for input and B output.

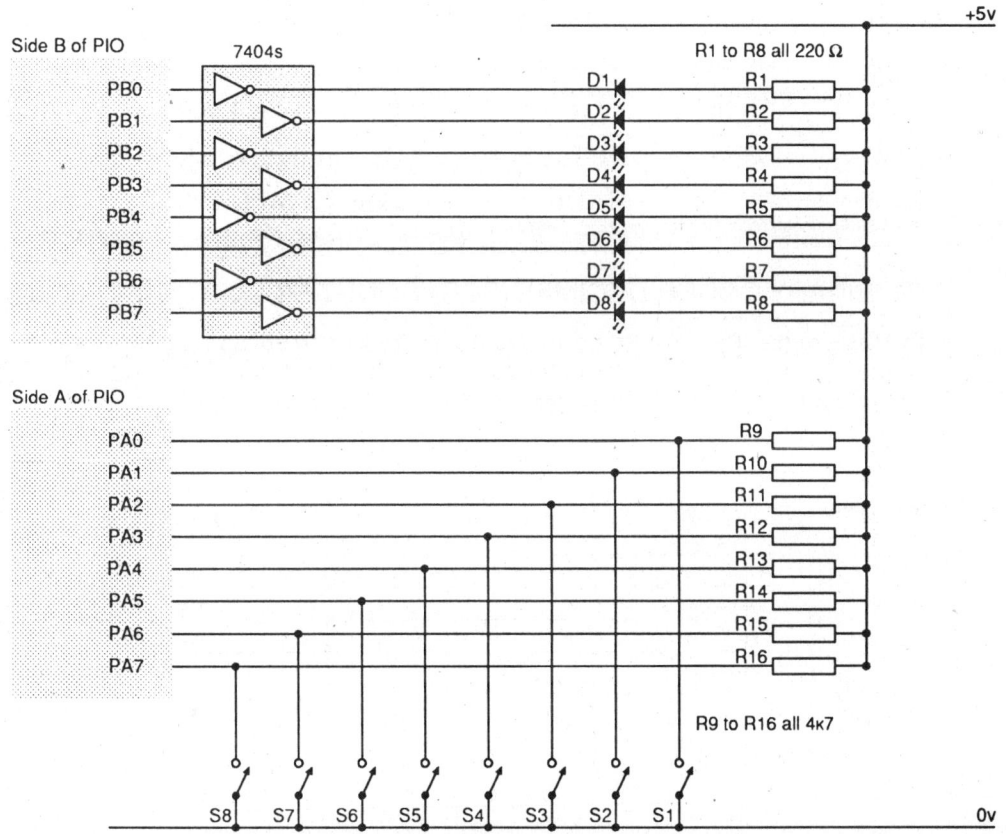

Fig 11.10 Input from switches/output to LEDs

11: Microcomputer programming

Algorithm

1. Set port A for input
2. Set port B for output
3. Read in data from switches
4. Output data to LEDs
5. Halt the processor

Program code

Memory address	Machine code	Assembly code	Comment
2000	3E 4F	LD A,4FH	Set port A to
2004	D3 82	OUT (82),A	Mode 1 for input
2006	3E 0F	LD A,0FH	Set port B to
2008	D3 83	OUT (83),A	Mode 0 for output
200A	DB 80	IN A,(80)	Read in switch data
200C	D3 81	OUT (81),A	Output data to LEDs
200E	76	HALT	Halt the MPU

P4: BINARY CODED DECIMAL (BCD) COUNTER

In this program we are going to get the processor to output the binary codes corresponding to the decimal numbers 0 to 9 with about a one second delay between each number. For test purposes the circuit should be connected as shown in Fig 11.11

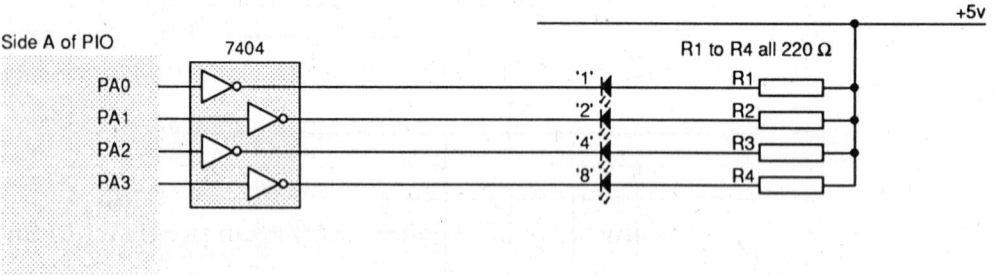

Fig 11.11 BCD Counter

Flowcharts

These are shown for both the main program and the delay subroutine in Fig 11.12

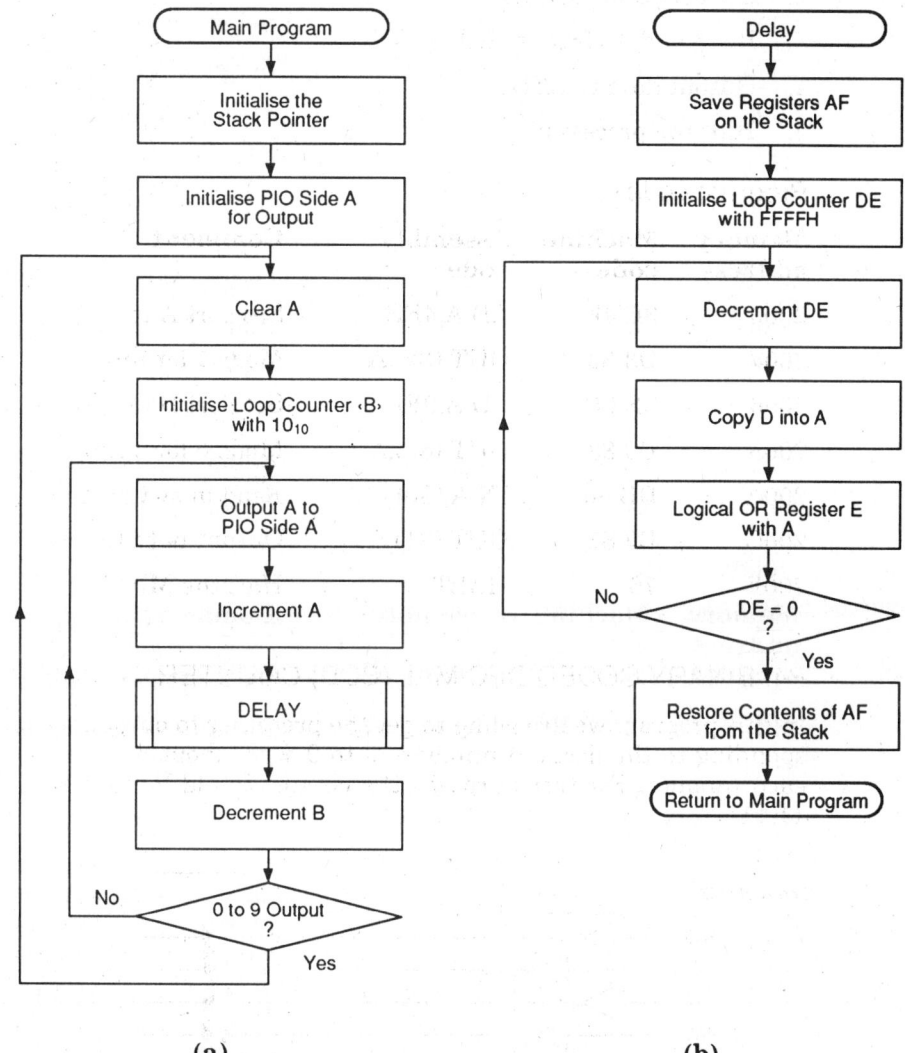

(a)   (b)

Fig 11.12 Flowchart for BCD counter: (a) Main program (b) Subroutine

11: Microcomputer programming

Code for main program

Memory address	Machine code	Assembly code	Comment
2000	31 90 23	LD SP,2390H	Set stack pointer to 2390H
2003	3E 0F	LD A,0FH	Set port A to
2005	D3 82	OUT (82),A	Mode 0 for output
2007	AF	XOR A	Clear the accumulator
2008	06 0A	LD B,0AH	Initialise the loop counter B with 0AH=10 decimal.
200A	D3 80	OUT (80),A	Output A to port
200C	3C	INC A	Add 1 to A
200D	CD 50 21	CALL 2150H	Call the delay at 2150H
2010	05	DEC B	Decrement B by 1
2011	C2 0A 20	JP NZ,200AH	Jump non-zero to 200AH
2014	C3 07 20	JP 2007H	Repeat

Delay subroutine

Memory address	Machine code	Assembly code	Comment
2150	F5	PUSH AF	Save AF on the stack
2151	11 FF FF	LD DE,FFFFH	Initialise loop counter DE with FFFFH
2154	1B	DEC DE	Decrement loop counter
2155	7A	LD A,D	Load A with D
2156	B3	OR E	Decrementing a register pair does not affect any flags. We can overcome this problem by ORing register E, which will affect the zero flag.
2157	C2 54 21	JP NZ,2154H	Jump back to 2154H until the zero flag becomes set; Jump on non-zero to 2154H.
215A	F1	POP AF	Restore AF
215B	C9	RET	Return to main program

P5: DISPLAYING THE BCD COUNT OUTPUTS ON A 7-SEGMENT DISPLAY

Fig 11.13 shows how to display the BCD counter outputs on a 7-segment display. They are connected as inputs to a TTL 7447 BCD to 7-SEGMENT DECODER DRIVER. To test this interface use the program from the last project P4.

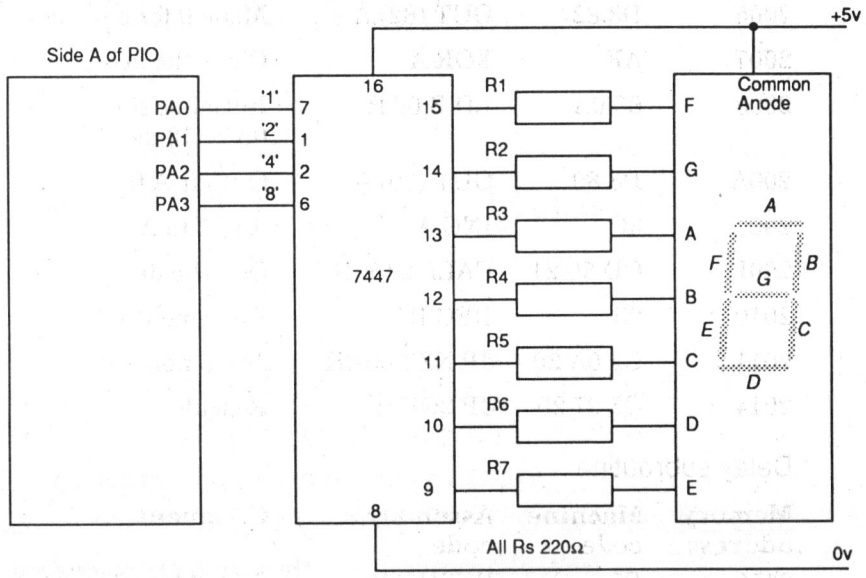

Fig 11.13 BCD output to 7-segment display

P6: OUTPUTTING HEX CHARACTERS TO A 7-SEGMENT DISPLAY

The 7-segment display code for the HEX symbols 0 to F is to be stored in 16 consecutive memory locations starting with 0 at 2200H. Each number will be displayed for about one second (one second delay). The required interface is given in Fig 11.14.

11: Microcomputer programming

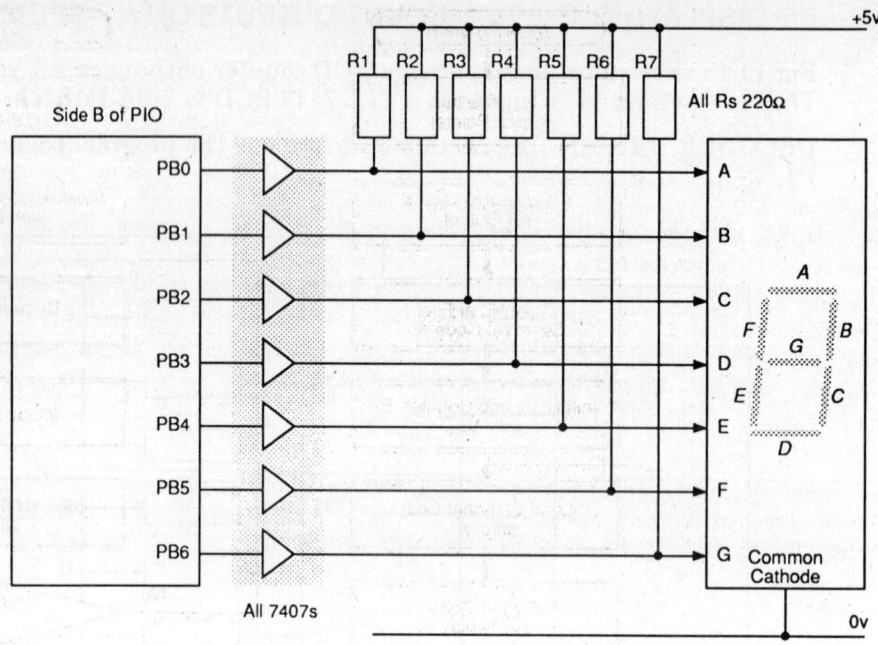

Fig 11.14 Displaying HEX characters

The display codes are:

HEX character	Data to be transferred to the output port
0	3F
1	06
2	5B
3	4F
4	66
5	6D
6	7D
7	07
8	7F
9	6F
A	77
b	7C
C	39
d	5E
E	79
F	71

11: Microcomputer programming

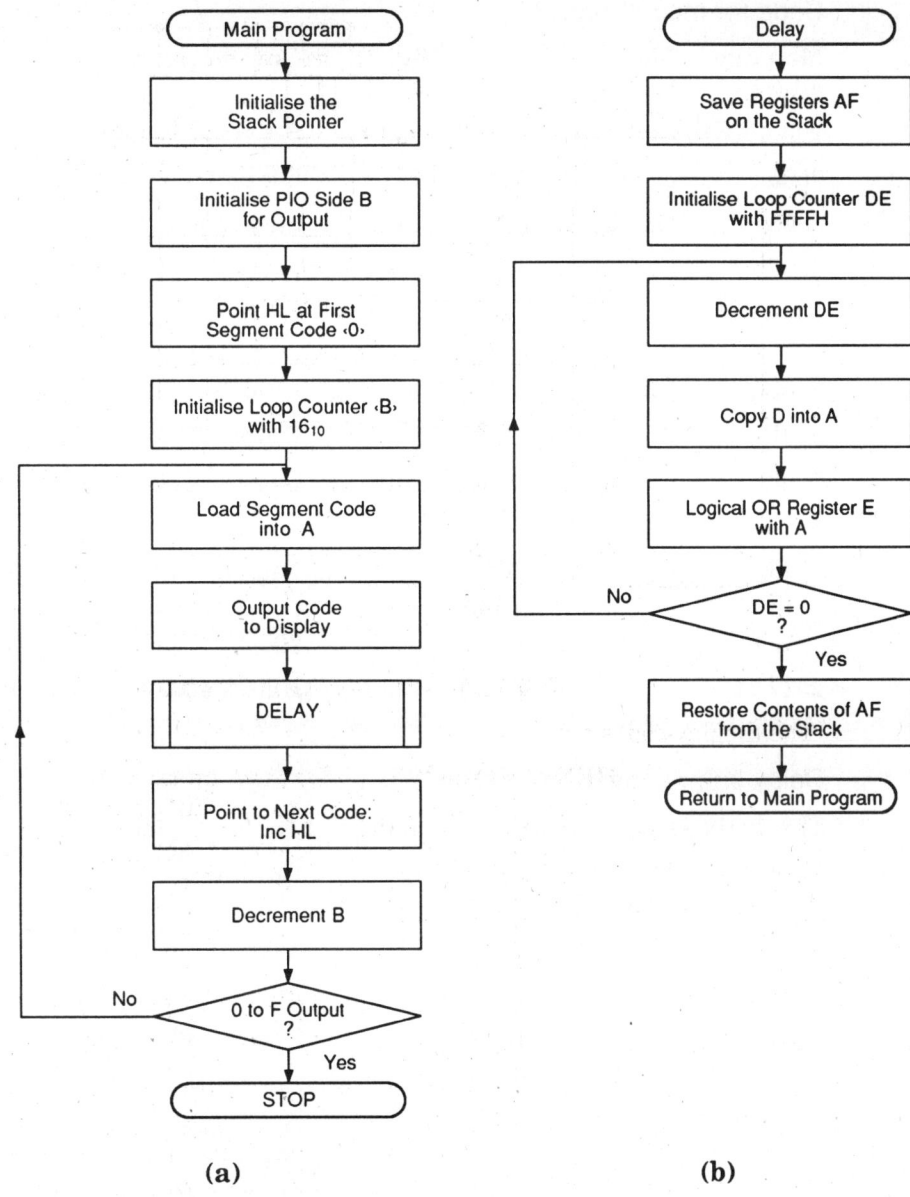

Fig 11.15 Flowchart: displaying HEX characters

11: Microcomputer programming

Code for main program

Memory address	Machine code	Assembly code	Comment
2000	31 90 23	LD SP,2390H	Set stack pointer to 2390H
2003	3E 0F	LD A,0FH	Set port B to
2005	D3 83	OUT (83),A	Mode 0 for output
2007	21 00 22	LD HL,2200H	Point HL at 2200H
200A	06 10	LD B,10H	Initialise the loop counter B with 10H=16 decimal
200C	7E	LD A,(HL)	Load 7-segment code into A
200D	D3 81	OUT (81),A	Output the code to the display
200F	CD 50 21	CALL 2150H	Call the delay subroutine at 2150H
2012	23	INC HL	Point to next code
2013	05	DEC B	Decrement the loop counter
2114	C2 0C 20	JP NZ,200CH	Unless the zero flag is set jump back to 200CH; Jump non-zero to 200CH
2017	76	HALT	Halt the MPU

Delay subroutine

This is the same delay as P4. Reproduced here for convenience

Memory address	Machine code	Assembly code	Comment
2150	F5	PUSH AF	Save AF on the stack
2151	11 FF FF	LD DE,FFFFH	Initialise loop counter DE with FFFFH
2154	1B	DEC DE	Decrement loop counter
2155	7A	LD A,D	Load A with D
2156	B3	OR E	Decrementing a register pair does not affect any flags. We can overcome this problem by ORing register E, which will affect the zero flag
2157	C2 54 21	JP NZ,2154H	Jump back to 2154H until the zero flag becomes set; Jump on non-zero to 2154H.
215A	F1	POP AF	Restore AF
215B	C9	RET	Return to main program

P7: TRAFFIC LIGHTS

This program may be used to control one traffic light only. We will drive three LEDs from the PIO lines PA0, PA1 and PA2 as shown in Fig 11.16

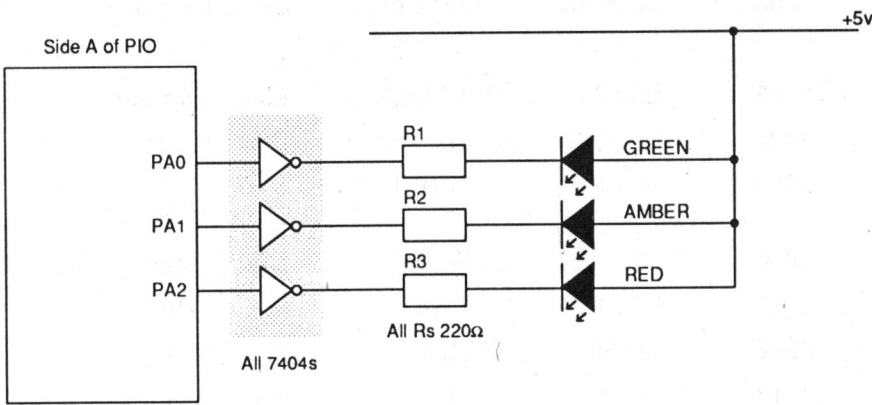

Fig 11.16 Traffic lights

11: Microcomputer programming

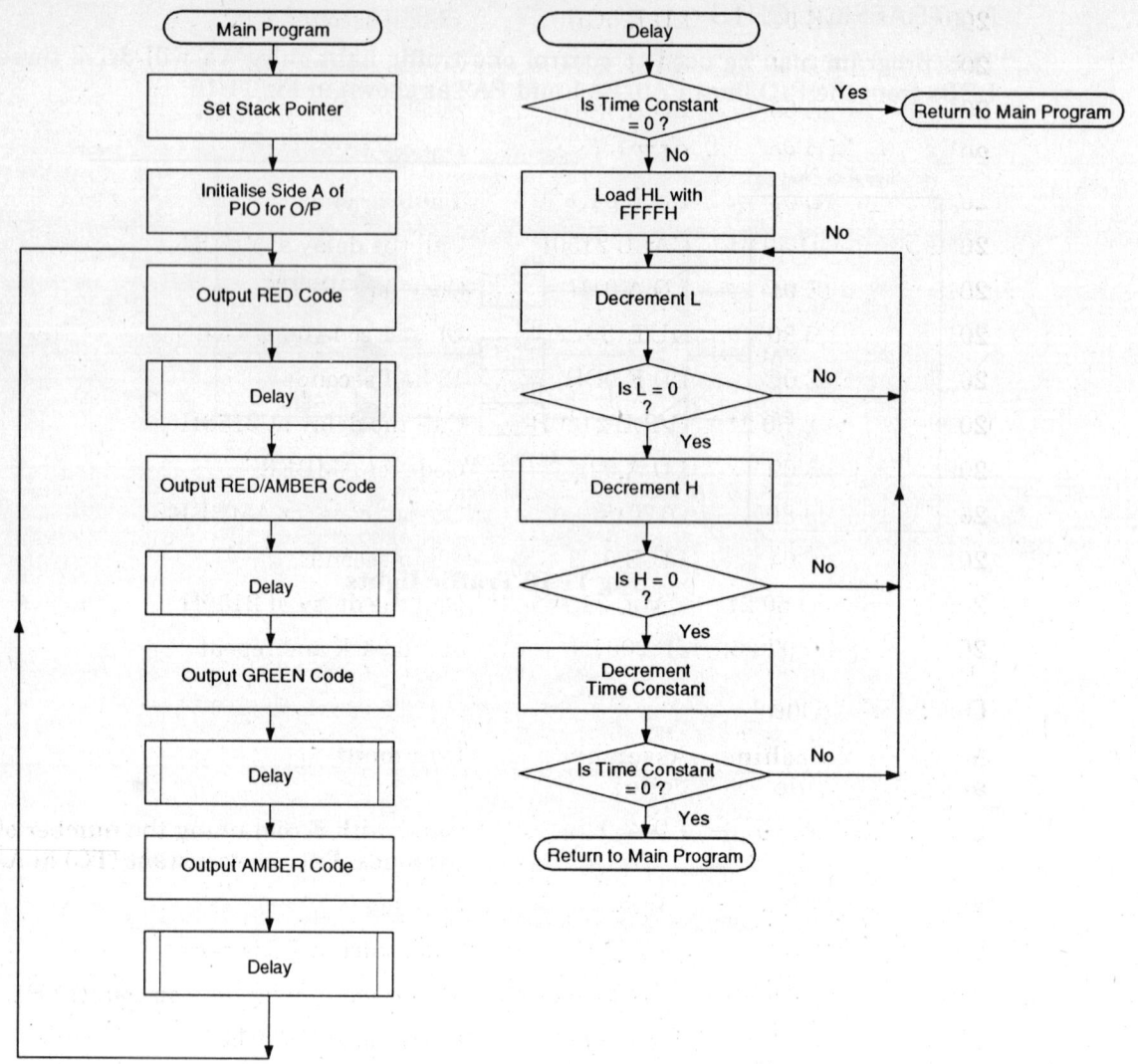

Fig 11.17 Flowchart for traffic lights

Main program

Memory address	Machine code	Assembly code	Comment
2000	31 90 23	LD SP,2390H	Stack set to top of RAM
2003	3E 0F	LD A,0FH	Set PIO
2005	D3 82	OUT (82),A	to output mode
2007	3E 04	LD A,04H	Code for RED
2009	D3 80	OUT (80),A	Output RED

11: Microcomputer programming

Memory address	Machine code	Assembly code	Comment
200B	1E 0C	LD E,0CH	12 half seconds
200D	CD 50 21	CALL 2150H	Call the delay at 2150H
2010	3E 06	LD A, 06H	Code for RED/AMBER
2012	D3 80	OUT (80),A	Output RED/AMBER code
2014	1E 04	LD E,04H	4 half seconds
2016	CD 50 21	CALL 2150H	Call the delay at 2150H
2019	3E 01	LD A,01H	Code for GREEN
201B	D3 80	OUT (80),A	Output code for GREEN
201D	1E 0C	LD E,0CH	12 half seconds
201F	CD 50 21	CALL 2150H	Call the delay at 2150H
2022	3E 02	LD A,02H	Code for AMBER
2024	D3 80	OUT (80),A	Output code for AMBER
2026	1E 04	LD E,04H	4 half seconds
2028	CD 50 21	CALL 2150H	Call the delay at 2150H
202B	C3 07 20	JP 2007H	Jump back and repeat

Delay subroutine

Memory address	Machine code	Assembly code	Comment
2150	7B	LD A, E	Enter with E containing the number of $\frac{1}{2}$ seconds. Put time constant (TC) in A.
2151	B7	OR A	Set flags
2152	C8	RET Z	and return if TC is zero
2153	21 FF FF	LD HL,FFFFH	Maximum number in loop counter HL
2156	2D	DEC L	Count down for delay
2157	C2 56 21	JP NZ, 2156H	Jump non-zero to 2156H
215A	25	DEC H	Decrement H
215B	C2 56 21	JP NZ, 2156H	Jump non-zero to 2156H
215E	1D	DEC E	Decrement E
215F	C2 56 21	JP NZ, 2156H	Jump non-zero to 2156H
2162	C9	RET	Return to main program

P8: STEPPER MOTOR

Fig 11.18 shows how to interface a 4-phase stepper motor to a microcomputer. The SAA1027 generates the four phase signals for the motor. Pulses applied to the step input cause the motor shaft to rotate.

11: Microcomputer programming

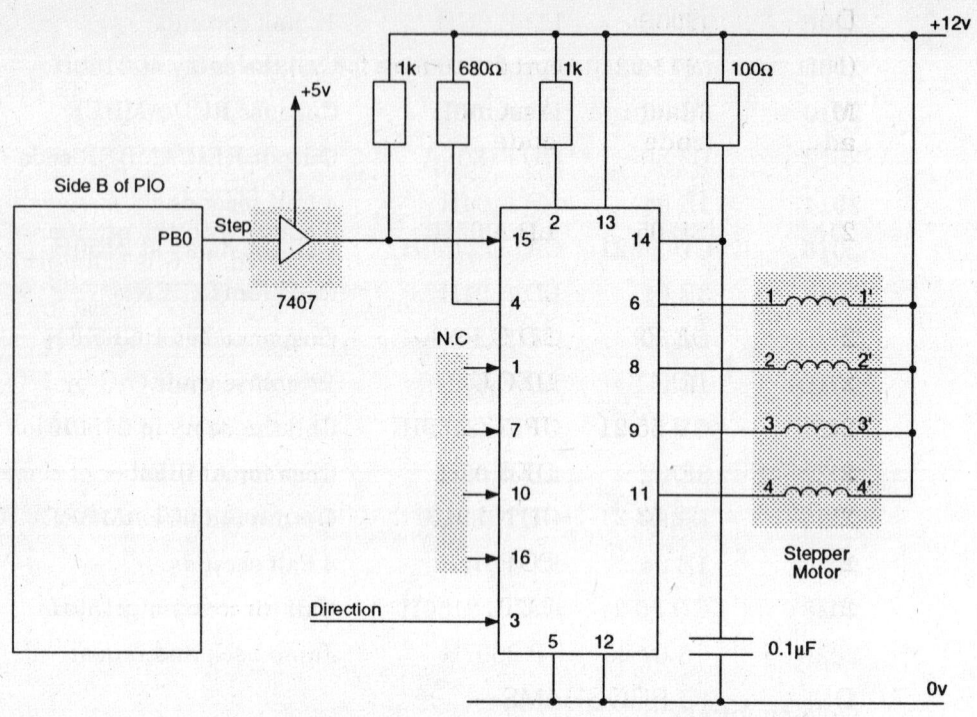

Fig 11.18 Stepper motor interface

Main program

Memory address	Machine code	Assembly code	Comment
2000	31 90 23	LD SP,2390H	Set stack to top of RAM
2003	3E 0F	LD A,0FH	Set port B to
2005	D3 83	OUT (83),A	Mode O for output
2007	3E 01	LD A,01H	Load A with a HIGH signal
2009	D3 81	OUT (81),A	Output the signal
200B	CD 50 21	CALL 2150H	Call the delay subroutine at 2150H
200E	AF	XOR A	Load A with a LOW signal
200F	D3 81	OUT (81),A	Output the signal
2011	CD 50 21	CALL 2150H	Call the delay
2014	C3 07 20	JP 2007H	Jump back to 2007H and REPEAT

11: Microcomputer programming

Delay subroutine

(From section 11.5 but reproduced here for convenience.)

Memory address	Machine code	Assembly code	Comment
2150	F5	PUSH AF	Save AF on the stack
2151	3E 05	LD A,05H	Load A with the number of 1mS required. In this example we are making it 5mS.
2153	0E F9	LD C,F9H	Get count for 1mS delay
2155	0D	DEC C	Decrease counter C by 1
2156	C2 55 21	JP NZ,2155H	If not zero jump to location 2155H
2159	3D	DEC A	Decrement number of remaining mS
215A	C2 53 21	JP NZ,2153H	Continue until number of mS =0
215D	F1	POP AF	Restore AF
215E	C9	RET	Return to main program

11.7 DEBUGGING PROGRAMS

Various errors may occur during software development. For instance, in translating from pseudo-code to assembly language an instruction mnemonic which does not belong to the microprocessor which you are programming may inadvertently be entered on the coding sheet. The assembler will detect it as an error. These errors are commonly referred to as **bugs** and the process of tracking down and eliminating these errors is called **debugging**.

A program may be checked for possible errors by constructing a **trace table**. This is a table which shows the contents of relevant registers and memory locations before and after the execution of each instruction.

Breakpoints may also be used for debugging. A breakpoint is a temporary halt inserted in a program. For example, a breakpoint could be inserted at the beginning of the sixth instruction. This would allow the programmer to inspect the contents of registers and storage locations to check whether or not the first five instructions produced the correct results.

11.8 THE MONITOR

Small single board microcomputer systems are usually equipped with a keyboard consisting of the sixteen hexadecimal keys and a few monitor command keys. The **monitor** refers to the **firmware** or **operating system**. The monitor allows programs to be loaded into the memory and executed via this keyboard. Monitor programs contain not only facilities for loading and executing users' programs, but also aids for debugging programs such as single stepping (executing instructions one-by-one) or tracing and breakpoints. Memory and/or processor registers may also be examined/changed.

SUMMARY

- The stages involved in software development are:

  Problem specification
  Program design
  Program coding
  Debugging
  Testing
  Documentation
  Maintenance and redesign

- Program design aids include:

  Algorithms
  Pseudo-code
  Flowcharts
  Top-down design
  Structured programming

- For structured programming the three basic control structures are:

  Sequence – selection – iteration

- The MPUs instruction set may be divided into the following classes of instructions:

  1. Data transfer
  2. Arithmetic operations
  3. Logical operations
  4. Program flow control (Test and Jump)
  5. Input/output
  6. Miscellaneous

- Instructing the MPU as to the data source and destination is called addressing. All microprocessors are equipped with a variety of addressing modes.

- The HL register pair is very useful as a memory address register (MAR) because it is supported by a number of instructions.

- Program loops are used to repeat a sequence of instructions in a program.

- Time delays are a common requirement when interfacing external devices to a microcomputer. The basic principle of time delays is to use the microprocessor as a counter.

- Debugging refers to tracking down and eliminating errors (bugs) in programs.

- The microcomputer's operating system has facilities for single-stepping (tracing) and breakpoint insertion.

END OF CHAPTER QUESTIONS

Section A: Multiple choice questions (Answers in Appendix A)

1. Which one of the following is a data transfer instruction?
    a) XOR A
    b) SUB B
    c) LD A, (HL)
    d) JP NZ, LOOP

2. Register A contains 04H and B 40H. The result of the instruction AND B is:
    a) 44H
    b) 40H
    c) 04H
    d) 00H

3. The CALL instruction is used to
    a) Jump forward in the program
    b) Jump to the end of the program
    c) Call a subroutine
    d) Call back to the beginning of the program

4. The mode control word for side A of a PIO is 04H. Which of the following modes is it being programmed in?
    a) Bit control
    b) Bidirectional
    c) Output
    d) Input

5. To which addressing mode does the Z80 instruction LD B,A belong?
    a) Immediate
    b) Relative
    c) Indexed
    d) Register

6. The HL register pair holds the address 2200H. What is the effect of the instruction LD (HL),A?
    a) It loads the accumulator with the byte of data stored at 2200H
    b) It transfers the contents of A into HL
    c) It stores the contents of A at 2200H
    d) It transfers the contents of HL into A

11: Microcomputer programming

7. Register B is being used as a loop counter and has been initialised with the value 12H. The number of repetitions required is
   a   12
   b   18
   c   21
   d   28

8. In order to set side B of the PIO in INPUT mode, a suitable mode control word would be
   a   F0H
   b   0FH
   c   F4H
   d   4FH

9. The diamond symbol on a flowchart indicates a
   a   subroutine
   b   process
   c   start or stop
   d   decision

10. The test instruction for deciding whether a program loop should terminate or continue is JP NZ, REPEAT. The loop will terminate when the
    a   carry flag is 0
    b   plus (P) or negative (N) or Zero flags are 0
    c   zero flag is 1
    d   zero flag is 0

Chapter 12

Mass Storage

In this chapter, we look at the ways microprocessor-based systems store large quantities of data and programs. A microcomputer has a limited amount of volatile main memory (storage) which is used to store the program currently being executed, together with temporary data and results. When power is removed from the main store the information in memory is lost, hence a non-volatile backing store is necessary. The media most commonly used to provide this storage for microprocessor and microcomputer systems are Winchester disks, floppy disks and magnetic tape.

12.1 AN INTRODUCTION TO MASS STORAGE

You will already be aware that your personal computer has mass storage facilities because it is probably fitted with hard and floppy disk drives. The reasons for providing microcomputer systems with some type of backing storage media are,

1. There is a need to have long-term non-volatile storage. Programs take a great deal of time and effort to write. Because we cannot afford to lose them they must be stored on some non-volatile medium called backing storage.

2. Even though semiconductor memory is now available at low cost and RAM memory may be battery-backed the storage cost per bit is much more than that for the mass storage media. Backing storage media provide a cheap form of non-volatile storage.

The mass storage devices which we discuss in this chapter are all magnetic media. Like all other peripherals, they must be interfaced to the microcomputer. See Fig 12.1

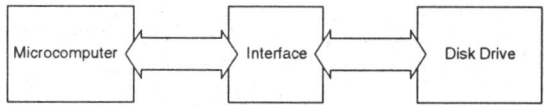

Fig 12.1 Interfacing mass storage media to the microcomputer.

 Short answer question 12.1

Name three backing storage devices used with microcomputer systems.

12: Mass storage

> **A** Answer to SAQ 12.1
>
> Floppy disk; Hard disk; Magnetic tape

12.2 HOW BINARY DATA IS STORED IN MAGNETIC MEDIA

Before examining specific magnetic mass storage devices such as floppy disks, Winchester (hard) disks or tape systems, it is necessary to have a basic understanding of how magnetic media store binary data.

Materials containing iron are known as ferrous materials (or ferromagnetic materials) and they may be magnetised. This means that any material with a high iron content will be attracted to a magnet. If the iron is left in close contact with a strong magnet for long enough, the material also becomes magnetised. The question we then have to ask ourselves is 'How does magnetisation occur?' Fig 12.2 shows a piece of magnetic material which has not been magnetised. As you can see from the diagram the magnetic dipoles act like thousands of tiny little magnets, scattered randomly around the material. If the magnetic material is subjected to a magnetic field such as that produced by the poles of a permanent magnet, the south (S) poles of the magnetic dipoles will be attracted to the north (N) pole of the permanent magnet. Likewise, the north poles of the dipoles will be attracted to the south pole of the magnet. The net result is that the magnetic dipoles within the material align themselves as shown in Fig 12.3. When the external magnetising force (the magnet) is removed the magnetic dipoles stay lined up. The material is then magnetised. The piece of material now has its own north and south poles: the left hand side is now behaving like the south pole of a magnet, while the right side is like a north pole. The direction of the north and south poles depends on the direction of the magnetising force. It is this principle which allows us to write digital information to a magnetic disk or tape. We write a logic 1 as magnetisation in one direction and a logic 0 as magnetisation in the opposite direction.

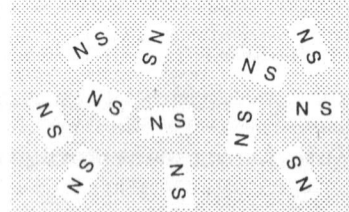

Fig 12.2 An unmagnetised magnetic material

12: Mass storage

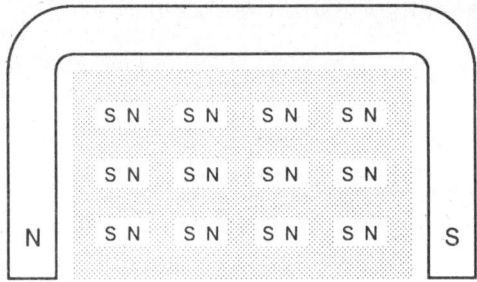

Fig 12.3 Magnetised ferromagnetic material

Magnetic tape is made up of a very fine layer of magnetic material (Metal-oxide) deposited on thin plastic. See Fig 12.4

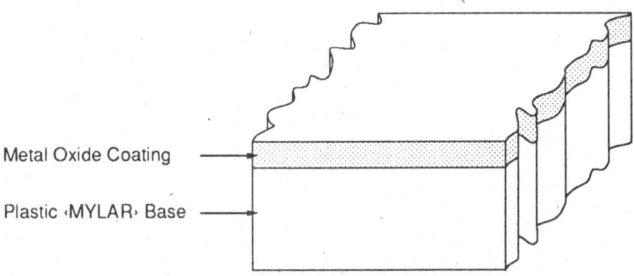

Fig 12.4 Magnetic tape

The mechanism for writing to and reading from magnetic tape is illustrated in Fig 12.5. In normal use the tape moves across the READ/WRITE head. The READ/WRITE heads are constructed by winding copper wire around a soft metal core, making it an electromagnet. The write signal is an electric current which is applied to the input terminals A-B. One direction of electric current (say from A to B) will result in a logic 1 being recorded on the tape. A reversal of the current direction (from B to A) will place a logic 0 on the tape.

To read stored data the tape is passed over a read head. This generates tiny electrical signals in the read head. Although for the purpose of explanation separate READ/WRITE heads were shown in Fig 12.5 it should be noted that in practice a double-sided floppy disk drive has two READ/WRITE heads. A head exists for each side of the floppy disk, and both heads are used for recording (writing) and reading on their respective disk sides.

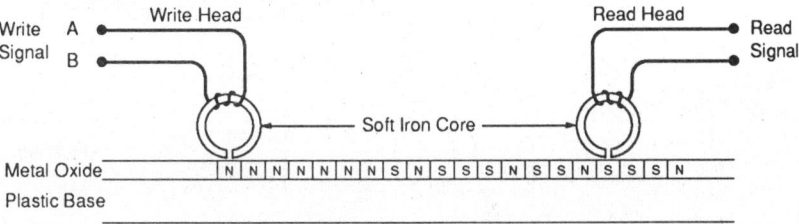

Fig 12.5 Magnetic tape READ/WRITE

Short answer question 12.2

State how bits of data are stored in a magnetic tape.

 Answer to SAQ 12.2

An electric current, called the write current, is passed through the READ/WRITE head, which results in a small area of the surface becoming magnetised. The direction of magnetisation, which depends on the direction of the current, determines whether it is a 1 or a 0.

12.3 FLOPPY DISKS

Floppies are available as $5\frac{1}{4}$ inch and $3\frac{1}{2}$ inch disks. The name 'floppy' disk is derived from the fact that the disk itself is made of a soft material. $5\frac{1}{4}$ inch disks are enclosed in a square cardboard envelope which is lined internally with a low friction material. When in use, the floppy disk rotates at a constant speed of either 300 or 360 RPM (revolutions per minute) inside its cover. The read/write heads are spring loaded and physically grip the disk with a small amount of pressure. Because of the contact between the heads and the disks, a buildup of the oxide material from the disk eventually forms on the heads. As part of preventative maintenance the heads should be cleaned periodically.

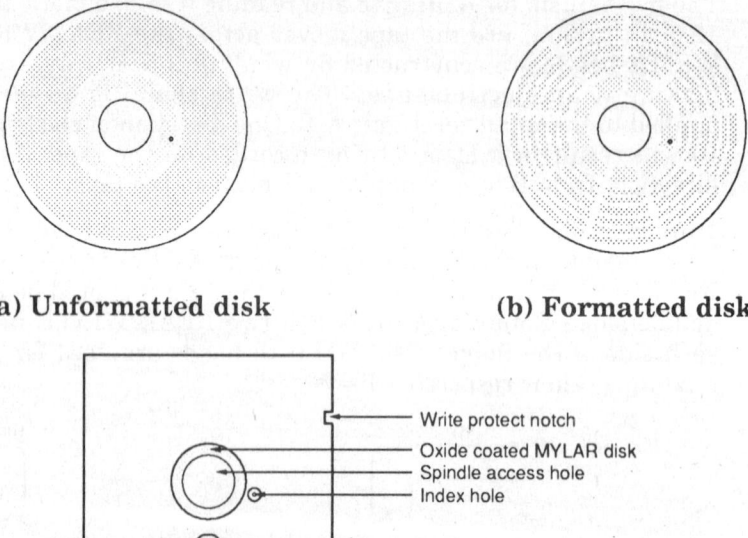

(a) Unformatted disk   (b) Formatted disk

(c) Disk inside protective envelope

Fig 12.6 Floppy disk

Before a disk can be used it must be formatted by running the operating system disk **format** utility which prepares a disk so that the computer can read from it or write to it. Formatting the disk organises it into tracks and sectors as shown in Fig 12.6. Table 12.1 summarises the standard disk formats for $3\frac{1}{2}$ inch disks supported by DOS version 5.0 and higher.

	Double-density (DD)	High-density (HD)	Extra-high density (ED)
Bytes per sector	512	512	512
Sectors per track	9	18	36
Tracks per side	80	80	80
Number of sides	2	2	2
Capacity	720 kilobytes (kb)	1.44 Mb	2.88 Mb

Table 12.1 $3\frac{1}{2}$ **inch floppy disk drive formats**

When you look at a typical $5\frac{1}{4}$ inch floppy disk (Fig 12.6 (c)) you see several things. Most prominent is the large round hole in the centre. When you close the disk drive's 'door', a cone-shaped clamp graps and centres the disk through the centre hole. On the right side just below the spindle-access hole, is a smaller hole, called the **index** hole. This hole is the reference for the first sector on the disk. The oblong cutout, called the head aperture is where the read/write head comes into contact with the disk surface. The write protect notch is used to prevent information from being written onto the disk. If the write protect notch is taped over the disk is write protected and information cannot then be written to it. For instance, you could write protect programs purchased from software houses (and other programs), so ensuring that they are not inadvertantently overwritten.

$3\frac{1}{2}$ inch disks

Because $3\frac{1}{2}$ inch disks use a much more rigid plastic case, which helps stabilise the disk, the disks can record at track and data densities greater than $5\frac{1}{4}$ inch disks. Fig 12.7 illustrates a typical disk. A metal shutter protects the media-access hole. The shutter is manipulated by the drive, and remains closed whenever the disk is not in the drive. Unlike the $5\frac{1}{4}$ inch disk it does not have an index hole, it uses a metal centre hub with an alignment hole. The hole in the hub enables the drive to position the disk correctly.

The write protect mechanism is also different. On the lower left part of the disk is a square hole with a plastic slider. When the slider is positioned to cover the hole, writing is enabled and you can record on the disk. If the disk is high density (HD) it has another hole in the lower right hand corner.

12: Mass storage

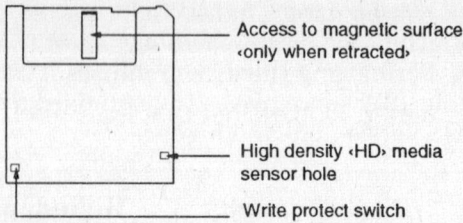

Fig 12.7 3½ inch floppy disk

 Short answer question 12.3

What is meant by formatting a floppy disk?

Answer to SAQ 12.3

Preparing a disk so that the computer can read from it and write to it. During formatting the disk is divided into tracks and sectors

12.4 INTERFACING A FLOPPY DISK DRIVE TO A MICROCOMPUTER

In order to appreciate how a microcomputer may perform write (store) and read (retrieve) operations with a floppy disk it is necessary to take a closer look at how the disk is initialised during the format process. We have already seen that the disk is organised into tracks (concentric circles) and sectors and that the outside track is identified as track 00 and the track closest to the centre of the disk is track 79. The sectors are numbers from 1 upwards.

To access information within the disk, it is necessary to identify the sector on which information is stored and then transfer information to or from that sector. The head must be positioned mechanically over the desired track, and when the appropriate sector comes under the head, information may be transferred serially.

A track is too large an area to manage effectively as a single storage unit. Most disk tracks can store 8,000 or more bytes of data, which would be inefficient for storing small files. For that reason a disk track is divided into several numbered divisions known as sectors. Each sector on a floppy disk is organised as shown in Fig 12.8

Gap	ID Address Mark	Track Number	Side Number	Sector Number	Sector Length	CRC Bytes‹2›	Gap	Data Address Mark	User Data	CRC Bytes‹2›

Fig 12.8 Sector organisation

As Fig 12.8 shows when a disk is formatted, additional areas are formed on the disk for the floppy disk controller to use for sector numbering and the identification of the start and end of each sector. Basically each sector consists of a number of fields separated by gaps. An ID field is used to identify the sector, while a data field contains the user's data. Although some of the terms associated with the sector information are self explanatory, others require a brief explanation.

ID Address mark: This defines that identification (ID) field data follows.

CRC (Cyclic Redundancy Check). The two bytes between the sector length and the gap are used to verify the ID data, while the two bytes following the user data are used to verify the user data. During the read/write process, many hundreds of millions of bits of information are read from or written to the magnetic media by using the techniques we described in Section 12.2. There is a relatively high probability that some bits will not be written or read back properly. This causes errors in the data or program information. Errors may occur during read/write operations for many different reasons. For instance, if there is a small speck of dust on the magnetic medium and it forces the disk away from the head, the bit is either not written or not read. One common method used for error checking is called CRC (Cyclic Redundancy Check).

The **Data address mark** defines that the user data field follows.

In order to interface a floppy disk drive to a microcomputer a number of chips are available commercially. They are generally referred to as floppy disk controllers (FDCs). It is not the intention of this book to deal with any specific FDC nor to cover the complete range of signals available on these devices, but to give a general overview of some of the main signals associated with floppy disk controllers. A floppy disk controller may be used to interface a disk drive to the buses of a microcomputer as shown in Fig 12.9

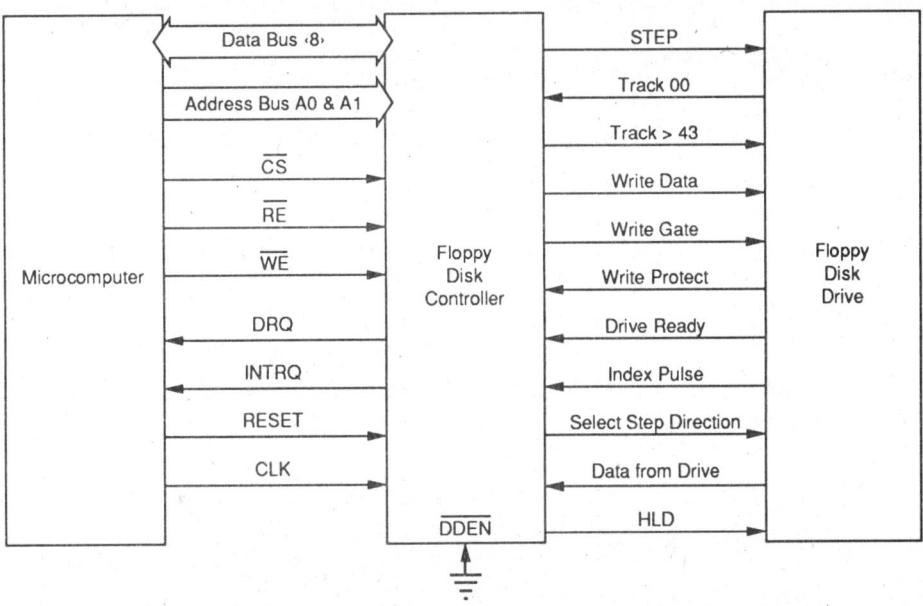

Fig 12.9 The floppy disk controller interface

The signal lines are divided into two groups which interface:

1. The floppy disk controller (FDC) chip to the microcomputer, which we will call the processor interface.
2. The disk drive to the FDC: the floppy disk interface.

Short answer question 12.4

What is the purpose of the CRC bytes on each sector of a floppy disk?

Answer to SAQ 12.4

They are used for error checking the sector identification and user data

The Processor Interface

You are already familiar with many of these signals, hence only a brief description is given.

Data bus

This parallel data bus carries information between the microcomputer and the FDC.

Address bus

Bits A0 and A1 of the address bus are connected to the device and are used to select various registers within the FDC such as, track, sector, data, status and command

$\overline{CS}$

Chip select. This signal is derived from the address decoding logic

$\overline{RE}$

Read enable input. Whenever $\overline{CS}$ and $\overline{RE}$ are active (LOW) data is being read from the FDC.

$\overline{WE}$

Data is being written to the FDC when $\overline{CS}$ and $\overline{WE}$ (Write Enable) are LOW

DRQ

The data request line indicates that the data register within the FDC contains assembled data during disk read operations. Data is read serially from the disk, so the FDC has to assemble it into parallel format. This is done using a shift register. The DRQ signal may also be used to indicate that the data register is empty during disk write operations.

INTRQ

The INTRQ signal indicates an 'interrupt request' and is activated by various combinations of conditions within the FDC

RESET

An input to the FDC which resets it

CLK   The clock input signal.

Short answer question 12.5

What is the function of a floppy disk controller?

Answer to SAQ 12.5

To interface a disk drive to the buses of a microcomputer

Floppy disk interface

The floppy disk interface lines appear on the right side of Fig 12.9.

HLD

This is the 'head load' output from the FDC which is used to energise a solenoid in the disk drive which allows the read/write head to make light contact with the disk surface.

STEP

In order to perform a disk read or write operation the microcomputer must be able to step the read/write head from track to track (and identify sector positions on the disk.). The step signal is activated by the step command and is used to control the stepper motor which moves the read/write head from one track to another.

Select step direction

An FDC output signal which determines the direction of stepping of the read/write head. A HIGH signal on this line causes the signal read/write head to step in towards the centre of the disk, while a LOW signal causes it to step out towards track 00.

Data from drive

This is the serial data which is being read from the disk into the FDC. It is sometimes called the RAW READ data input.

Track 00

This input from the disk drive informs the FDC that the read/write head is positioned over track 00, the outermost track.

Track > 43

This line notifies the disk drive that track 44 or greater is selected. It is used to enable compensation for the lower velocity while recording data on the tracks closest to the centre of the disk.

Write data

The serial data to be written to the disk appears on this output pin.

Write Protect

This input signal from the disk drive is sampled whenever a write command is received. If this line is found to be active the write command is aborted and an appropriate message displayed on the screen. If the disk is write protected this signal will become active.

Write Gate

This line must become active before data can be written to the disk. Basically it allows electric current to flow into the read/write head of the drive. Writing is inhibited if the write protect input is active.

Drive ready

This FDC input signal indicates that the disk is ready for a read or write operation.

Index pulse

The disk drive generates this signal to indicate the start of the first record on each track.

$\overline{DDEN}$

This selects either single or double density. A HIGH level selects single density (SD) and a LOW level double density (DD). Nearly all disks are now double density, hence this input is tied LOW.

Short answer question 12.6

Data is being read in from a floppy disk to a microcomputer. Is the data read from the surface of the disk in serial or parallel? Can the data which is being read be transferred directly to the data bus between the microcomputer and the FDC?

Answer to SAQ 12.6

Data is read from the disk in serial. A data shift register within the FDC converts it to parallel format because the data bus is parallel.

 Short answer question 12.7

In relation to a floppy disk controler (FDC), state the function of the following signals.

i) $\overline{\text{CS}}$

ii) STEP

iii) Write data

 Answer to SAQ 12.7

i) Before the microcomputer can communicate with the FDC it must be selected. $\overline{\text{CS}}$ is the chip select signal which is generated by an address decoder.

ii) The STEP signal is activated by the step command and is used to control the stepper motor which moves the read/write head by one track position for each pulse.

iii) This output from the FDC provides data for writing to the disk.

12.5 HARD DISKS

The second form of disk drive is the hard disk or Winscester drive. A hard disk contains rigid, disk shaped platters usually constructed of aluminium or glass. Unlike floppy disks, the platters cannot bend or flex, hence the term hard disk. The basic physical operation of a hard disk drive is similar to that of a floppy disk drive. A hard disk stores a much larger quantity of data and operates much faster than a floppy drive. Most hard disks spin at 3600 RPM, approximately 10 times faster than a floppy drive. The heads on a hard disk do not touch the platters during normal operation. High rotational speed combined with a fast head-positioning mechanism and more sectors per track makes hard drives so much faster than floppy drives at storing and retrieving data.

Machines containing hard disks should be handled carefully. Hard disks are fragile and sensitive to shock. Sudden movement could result in the heads coming in contact with the platter spinning at full speed. When contact with the platters is hard enough to do damage, it is called a head crash, and the results will vary from the loss of a few bytes of data to a totally damaged disk.

12.6 HARD AND FLOPPY DISKS COMPARED

In order to make a comparison it is necessary to understand certain terms such as, storage capacity, average access time and data transfer rate.

Storage capacity

The capacity of a disk is the number of bytes of information that may be stored on the disk. Storage capacity may be quoted in kilobytes (kb) or megabytes (Mb).

Average access time

Average access time is a measure of the time it takes, on average, to move the head from the current position to the track you want to read.

Transfer rate

The transfer rate is the speed at which the bits are read from or written to the disk.

Table 12.2 shows a comparison of some of the important features of hard and floppy disks, in terms of storage capacity, average access time and transfer rate.

Disk type	Storage capacity Mb	Average access time mS	Transfer rate in megabits per second	Rotational speed of disk in RPM
Floppy $3\frac{1}{2}$ inch ED	2.88	100 – 200	0.25 – 1	300 or 360
Hard	1000	10 – 25	1 – 10	3600

Table 12.2 Characteristics of disks

It should be noted that these figures only act as a guide. With advances in technology they are being constantly revised.

Short answer question 12.8

State three main differences between hard and floppy disks.

Answer to SAQ 12.8

Hard disks have:
i) much greater storage capacity
ii) shorter access times
iii) faster transfer rates

12.7 FLOPPY DISK CARE AND HANDLING

Most computer users know the basics of disk care. Disks can be damaged or destroyed easily by:

1. Touching the recording surface with your fingers or anything else.
2. Spilling liquid or other substances on the disk
3. Bending the disk
4. Writing on the disk label with a ballpoint pen or pencil
5. Exposing the disk to too much heat
6. Exposing the disk to stray magnetic fields.

When a floppy disk is not being used, put it in its storage box. This protects it from spillage, dust and smoke.

Avoid bringing disks near to magnetic fields as this can destroy the data on the disk. This is true for any electrical equipment containing components that generate magnetic fields, for example, laser printers, CD-ROM drives and some telephones. Avoid holding a floppy disk near the monitor, especially when you are switching it on and off, as the magnetic field radiated from the monitor may damage the disk. Avoid putting disks on top of the monitor or under the front edge of the screen.

Always label your floppy disks. Write on the label before sticking it on the disk. If you write on the label when it is on the disk, you may damage the disk: if this is unavoidable, use a felt-tip pen.

If you have important information stored on a floppy disk, make another copy for safety. Store copies of important information in a fireproof container, preferable in another site.

12.8 OTHER MAGNETIC STORAGE MEDIA

Audio cassette recording

In the early days of home computing this was a popular mass storage medium. Computers were designed to operate in conjunction with conventional domestic tape recorders. The main advantage was cheapness – it offered the lowest possible cost per bit. Data was recorded as audio frequency tones. The standard was known as Kansas City. In this system the bits were recorded as analogue audio tones: 8 cycles of 2400 Hz representing bit 1 and 4 cycles of 1200 Hz bit 0.

The storage capacity of a C30 tape was about 134k bytes. The data transfer rate was 300 bits per second with very poor access times (possibly many minutes). Generally it was unreliable and therefore prone to data corruption. Now obsolete.

12: Mass storage

 Short answer question 12.9

State how the bits 1 and 0 are represented in audio cassette recording.

 Answer to SAQ 12.9

8 cycles of 2400 Hz represents bit 1 and 4 cycles of 1200 Hz bit 0

Tape-Backup systems

A good reliable backup is important when you are using a large hard disk. Bear in mind that a small hard disk can store 20Mb and drives capable of storing several gigabytes (Gb) of data are now available. (1Gb = 1,000,000,000 bytes)

Because your data is probably worth more to you than the physical hardware on which it is stored, it is important to develop a good backup system.

A number of standards have now been developed:

1. DC-600 cartridge, invented by 3M. Available in capacities from 60 to 500/600 Mb
2. DC-2000 cartridge, also invented by 3M. Can store 80Mb or more
3. 4mm DAT (digital audiotape) catridges. DAT tapes can store over 1Gb
4. 8mm cartridges. These were developed by Sony for use in camcorders. Most units store over 2 Gb but even larger capacity units are available.

SUMMARY

- Mass storage is the term used to denote a large capacity backing store, such as floppy disk, hard disk and tape.
- The orientation of the magnetic dipoles within a ferromagnetic material is used to represent binary digits. One direction represents bit 0, while the opposite direction represents bit 1.
- Floppy disks are available in two sizes: $3\frac{1}{2}$ inch and $5\frac{1}{4}$ inch
- When a floppy disk is being written to or read from it rotates at a constant speed of 300 or 360 RPM
- Before a disk can be used it must be formatted by running the operating system disk FORMAT utility which organises the disk into tracks and sectors.
- The average access time for a floppy disk is about 100 to 200 mS
- To interface a floppy disk drive to a microcomputer a floppy disk controller (FDC) which has all of the necessary signals may be used.

12: Mass storage

- The Cyclic Redundancy Check (CRC) bytes on each sector of a disk are used for error checking.
- Most hard disks spin at 3600 RPM, about 10 times faster than a floppy disk.
- Hard disks have much greater storage capacity than floopy disks. Disks are now available which can store a number of gigabytes (Gb)
- The access time for a hard disk is about 10 to 25 mS: approximately 10 times faster than a floppy disk.
- Tape backup systems are now available which can store over 2 Gb of data.

END OF CHAPTER QUESTIONS

Section A: Multiple choice questions (Answers in Appendix A)

1. Which one of the following is an example of a backing storage device:
   a) ROM
   b) RAM
   c) MPU
   d) Hard disk

2. Most hard disks rotate at a speed of
   a) 300 RPM
   b) 360 RPM
   c) 3600 RPM
   d) 36000 RPM

3. The storage capacity of a $3\frac{1}{2}$ inch double-density (DD) disk is
   a) 360 kb
   b) 1.44 Mb
   c) 2.88 Mb
   d) 720 kb

4. A $3\frac{1}{2}$ inch disk should be write protected by
   a) taping over the write-protect hole
   b) positioning the slider to cover the hole
   c) positioning the slider away from the hole
   d) breaking off the slider

5. Which one of the following may be used to interface a floppy disk drive to a microcomputer?
   a) CRT controller
   b) decoder
   c) a serial to parallel interface
   d) FDC controller

6. Which one of the following signals is associated with floppy disk controllers?
   a) OE (output enable)
   b) strobe
   c) step
   d) busy

7. A Winchester drive refers to a
   a) floppy disk
   b) tape system
   c) hard disk
   d) combination of floppy and hard disk drives

8. The floppy disk controller signal 'DRIVE READY' is
   a) an output signal from the microcomputer to the FDC
   b) an input signal from the FDC to the microcomputer
   c) an output signal from the FDC to the floppy disk drive
   d) an input signal to the FDC from the floppy disk drive

9. The signal 'TRACK 00' associated with floppy disk controllers indicates that the read/write head is positioned over
   a) track 00
   b) track 79
   c) sector 00
   d) sector 79

10. The transfer rate in megabits per second, for a hard disk, lies between
    a) 0.25–1.00
    b) 100–200
    c) 10–25
    d) 1–10

SHORT ANSWER QUESTIONS

1. With the aid of a simple sketch explain how data is written to magnetic tape

2. With the aid of a block diagram explain the function of the following floppy disk controller signals
   i) DRQ
   ii) HLD
   iii) STEP
   iv) Select step direction
   v) Data from drive
   vi) Track 00
   vii) Track > 43
   viii) Write data
   ix) Write protect
   x) Drive ready

   Clearly indicate the directions of signals on your diagram.

3. In relation to disks define the following terms
   i) storage capacity
   ii) access time
   iii) transfer rate

4. LIST four dont's for handling floppy disks.

5. With the aid of a table compare the average access times and transfer rates for floppy disks and hard disks.

Chapter 13

Troubleshooting on Digital/Microprocessor Based Systems

First of all remember that a logical approach to testing and troubleshooting systems will always pay dividends. A prerequisite for troubleshooting on any equipment is a good knowledge of the system which you are attempting to test. The block/circuit diagrams, manual/s, and diagnostic software should also be available. Conventional test equipment, such as oscilloscopes and multimeters plays only a limited role in the testing and troubleshooting of bus structured microprocessor-based systems. Address, data and control information is transmitted along groups of parallel lines, called buses, from one part of the system to another. These parallel signals change state very rapidly. To overcome the problems of analysing bus-structured systems, specialised equipment such as logic analysers and signature analysers have been developed as well as a range of hand-held tools: logic probes, pulsers, comparators, clips and current tracers. The tools and equipment used for troubleshooting microprocessor-based products are introduced in this chapter.

13.1 LOGIC PROBE

A logic probe is capable of indicating the in-circuit activity of a single point in a digital system. Such probes will detect and indicate HIGH and LOW (1 or 0) logic levels, as well as 'bad' logic levels, including an open circuit, on a single line of a microcomputer circuit.

Separate LED indicators may be used to indicate the logic level of the point being monitored or an indicator lamp, near the tip of the probe, gives an indication of the logic level existing in the circuit under test. If three separate indicators are used they will be labelled high-low-pulse. When all three are on it indicates pulsed activity at the test node. If all three are off it indicates an open-circuit or high-impedance state.

If the probe uses a single indicator lamp then it can give any one of four indications: (1) off, (2) dim (about half brilliance), (3) bright (full brilliance), or (4) flashing on and off. Normally the probe is in the dim state, and must be driven to one of the other states by the voltage levels at the probe tip. The lamp is bright for a HIGH level and off for a LOW level. The lamp is dim for voltages between the 1 and 0 states and for open circuits or high impedance.

The probe may be powered from the system under test or a separate power supply. If a separate power supply is used, the power supply and microcomputer grounds must be connected together.

13: Troubleshooting on digital/microprocessor based systems

A logic probe is useful for verifying the operation of logic gates. Fig 13.1 shows the output of an AND gate being monitored by a logic probe. Both inputs to the gate are HIGH hence the probe indicates that the output is at a high level.

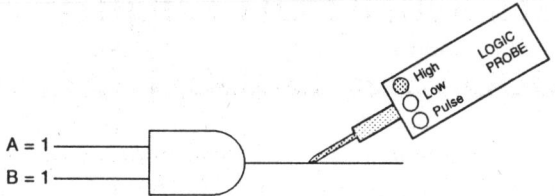

Fig 13.1 Using a logic probe

Although a logic probe is very useful for monitoring the logic state of a node in a system it is not as valuable when trying to locate faults in multiple-line circuits, such as address and data buses. For testing logic gates and other elements such as flip-flops the probe is often used in conjunction with a logic pulser.

 Short answer question 13.1

Assume that a logic probe, which has three LED indicators, is placed on the output of a functional microcomputer system clock. How would the probe respond?

 Answer to SAQ 13.1

Because the system clock is generating a continuous wavetrain of rectangular pulses the high and low leds would be ON and the pulse led would be flashing.

 Short answer question 13.2

How would a logic probe with a single indicator lamp show that a control bus signal is tri-stated (high impedance)?

 Answer to SAQ 13.2

The probe indicator would be dimly lit.

13.2 LOGIC PULSER

A logic pulser is a hand-held logic generator used for injecting controlled pulses into digital logic circuits such as microcomputers. Pulsers are available to provide either a single pulse or continuous pulses. A narrow pulse of short duration is generated whenever the push-button on the pulser is depressed. Alternatively, continuous low frequency pulses are generated if the button is held down. A flashing LED indicator on the probe indicates the output mode. The basic function of the pulser is to stimulate a node in a system.

Logic gate testing

A logic gate may be tested by pulsing the gate's input with a logic pulser, while monitoring the output with a logic probe. Fig 13.2 shows how to test a NOT gate.

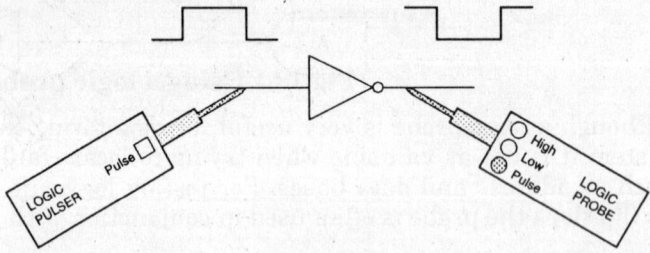

Fig 13.2 Checking a NOT gate using a logic probe and logic pulser.

The pulser is used to inject a single pulse into the gate, while the logic probe is placed at the output. If the gate is operating correctly the logic probe will respond to the pulse which was injected by the pulser. The pulse led on the probe should flash indicating a pulse at the output.

In Fig 13.3 the logic pulser generates a pulse opposite to the state of the top input to gate A, which results in its output briefly changing state, with the logic probe indicating the presence of a pulse. This assumes that the output of gate A is not shorted to a HIGH or a LOW level. Unless gate B is faulty or its output is held at a constant high or low (shorted to Vcc or ground) the probe at the output of gate B should also indicate a pulse.

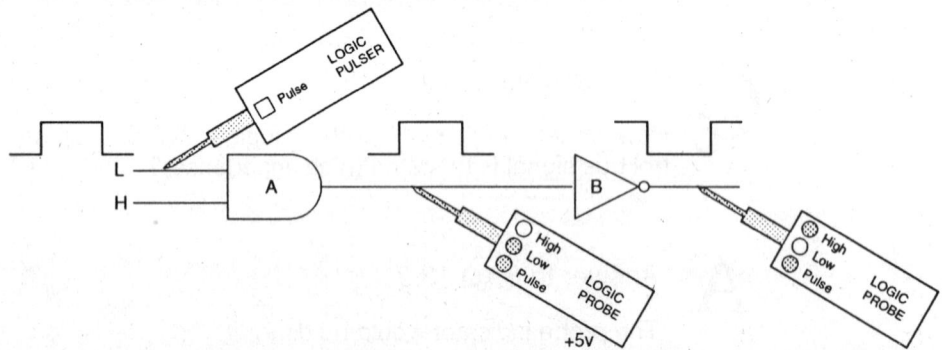

Fig 13.3 Logic circuitry testing with a pulser and probe.

If the probe placed between the two gates does not detect a pulse in response to the application of a signal at the input of gate A then the technique illustrated in Fig 13.4 may be used to establish if a short circuit to Vcc or ground exists. Assuming that there is continuity between gates A and B, if the pulser applies a pulse to the output of gate A then the logic probe should detect the presence of the pulse, if not, the line is either shorted to Vcc or Ground, so that the probe will indicate the presence of a constant HIGH or LOW.

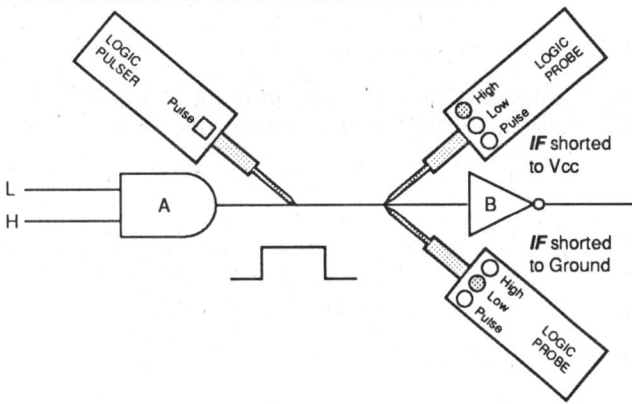

Fig 13.4 Checking a line shorted to Vcc or ground.

From the foregoing it is clear that the pulser probe combination may be used to detect shorts between a signal line and the power supply positive or ground. They can also be used to check for continuity in printed circuit board (PCB) tracks. This is shown in Fig 13.5, where the pulser is used to apply a pulse to the line. Because of the break in the PCB track the probe does not respond.

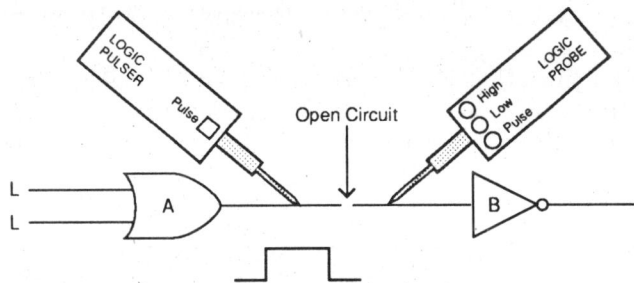

Fig 13.5 Using a pulser and probe to check for open circuits

Checking sequential logic elements

As well as checking combinational logic gates, sequential elements may also be checked using a logic pulser and probe. Fig 13.6 (a) illustrates an in-circuit J-K flip-flop which operates in the toggle mode. With no clock signal applied a logic probe may be used to verify that Q and $\overline{Q}$ are at opposite logic levels. In this case Q =0 and $\overline{Q}$ = 1. In (b) the logic pulser is used to inject a pulse into the clock input of the device. Assuming that it is not faulty, the output should toggle (change state). The Q output now goes high, while $\overline{Q}$ goes LOW. If the logic pulser is set to apply continuous pulses to the flip flop Fig 13.6 (c) shows that a probe placed at either Q or $\overline{Q}$ would indicate pulsed activity.

13: Troubleshooting on digital/microprocessor based systems

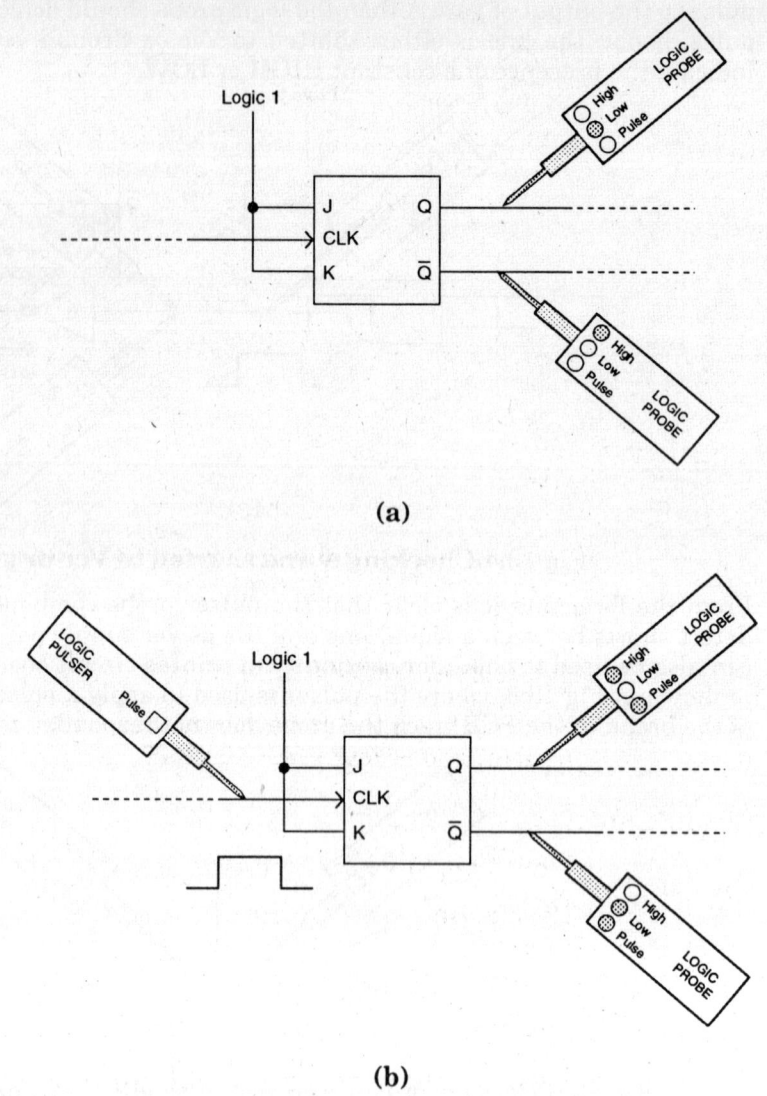

(a)

(b)

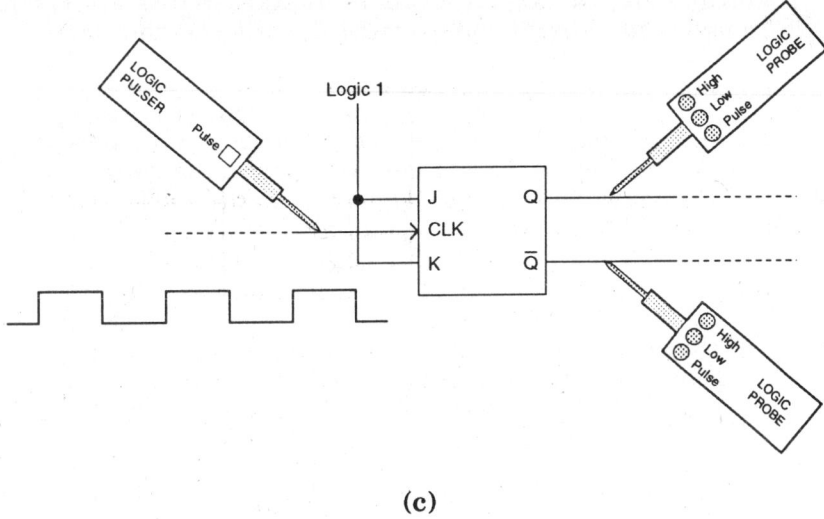

(c)

Fig 13.6 Checking sequential logic elements using a logic pulser and probe.

Q Short answer question 13.3

Which hand-held tool is often used with a logic probe to check for a suspected open-circuit in a PCB track?

A Answer to SAQ 13.3

A logic pulser

13.3 CURRENT TRACER

To measure electric current using a multimeter requires that the meter is inserted into the circuit. A current tracer is a troubleshooting tool that can detect a changing current in a wire or printed circuit board track without breaking the circuit. It is used when tests reveal a low impedance fault (drop in voltage and increase in current), such as a short circuit or a partial short.

It relies for its operation on the principle of electromagnetic induction which states that an electromotive force (emf) is induced in an inductive circuit when the current flowing in the circuit changes.

The current tracer has an insulated tip that contains a magnetic pickup coil. Whenever the current in a circuit changes the magnetic field associated with the current will also change and a voltage will be induced into the coil in the tip of the current tracer which causes a small led indicator to flash. The current tracer does not respond to static current levels, no matter how great the current may be.

Fortunately, the signal levels in digital circuits are changing continuously. Therefore the current and magnetic flux will also change.

Gate-to-Gate Faults

When a low impedance fault exists between two gates, the current tracer and logic pulser may be used to quickly pinpoint the defect. This is illustrated in Fig 13.7 (b) where the output of gate A has an internal short to ground. The procedure for tracing the current is as follows. Position the pulser between the two gates, and place the current tracer tip on the pulser pin as shown in Fig 13.7 (a). Pulse the line and using the control provided on the current tracer adjust its sensitivity so that the indicator just lights. First place the current tracer tip next to gate A, and then gate B, while continuing to pulse the line. The tracer will light only on the gate A side, since gate A, because of an internal short, is sinking most of the current. Had gate B been faulty then it would sink most of the current and the tracer would have lit at gate B but not gate A.

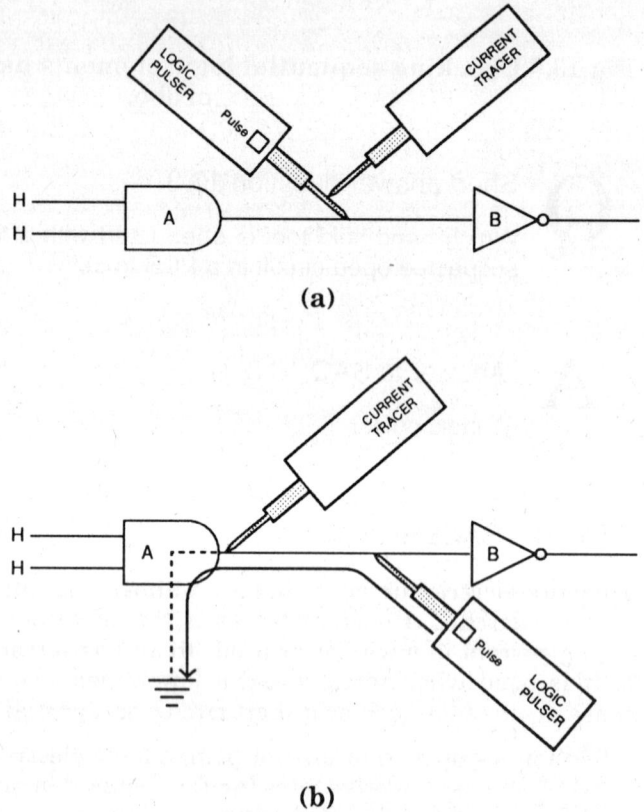

Fig 13.7 Using a current tracer: (a) setting up the current tracer (b) tracing the short

As well as gate-to-gate faults like that illustrated in the last example, the current tracer may also be used to check for shorts between printed circuit tracks. For instance, a solder splash between two tracks, as illustrated in Fig 13.8, would manifest itself as a low impedance fault.

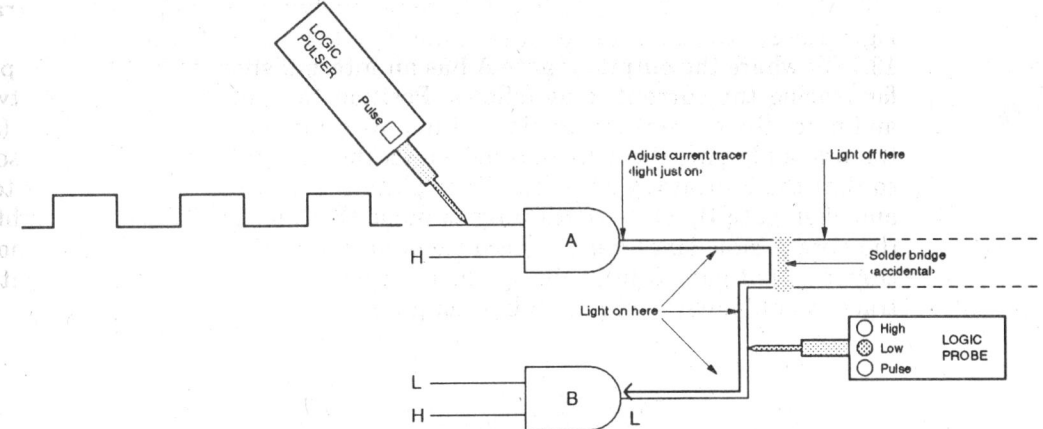

Fig 13.8 Locating solder bridges using a current tracer

When checking PCB tracks that may be shorted by solder bridges or other means, start the current tracer at the driver (in this case Gate A) and follow the trace. As the current tracer is moved from the output of gate A, the indicator light remains on until it passes the solder bridge. This is an indication that the current has found a low impedance path to ground. Backtract the tracer until the light comes on again and try to find the path of the current, which is indicated by the tracer light remaining on. In this case the light will remain on as the trace continues through the solder bridge to the output of gate B which is sinking the current. Visually inspect the area for solder splashes and the like. These principles also apply when testing for shorts in cable assemblies.

Because the current tracer operates on the principle that whatever is driving a low-impedance fault node or point in a circuit must be delivering the majority of the current, tracing the path of the current leads directly to the fault. The current tracer used in conjunction with a logic pulser (if necessary) may be used to locate the following types of faults:

(a) Shorted inputs on chips

(b) Solder bridges between tracks on PCBs

(c) Shorted conductors in cables

(d) Power supply shorts, such as Vcc to ground

(e) Shorts in a signal line to Vcc or ground

Multiple input gates

A standard TTL gate has a fan-out of 10, so its output can drive up to ten gate inputs in the same logic family. In Fig 13.9 the output of gate A provides a single input to four other gates. Assume that there is a short circuit in one of the gates B to E. In this case place the current tracer at the output pin of gate A and adjust the sensitivity control until the indicator light just comes on. Then check the input pins of gates B through E. If one of the input pins is shorted to ground, that pin will be the only one to light the indicator.

Should the tracer fail to light when placed on the output of gate A, it is likely that gate A is faulty. To check this, use the current tracer in the manner described for gate-to-gate faults.

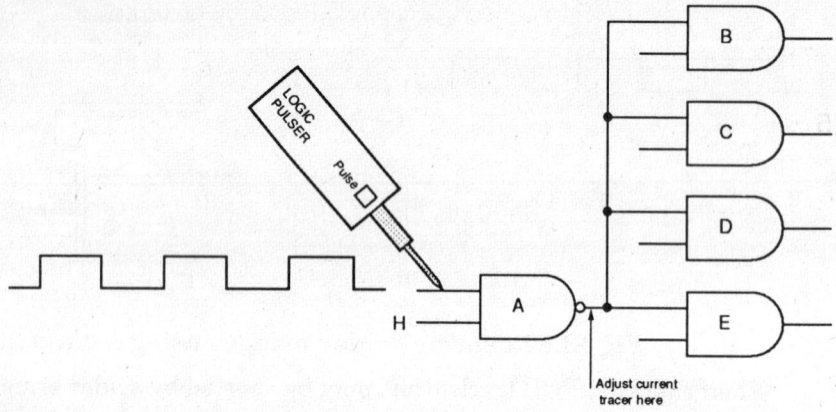

Fig 13.9 **Checking multiple input gates with a current tracer.**

Short answer question 13.4

Which two hand held tools are frequently used to find the faulty component in a digital system when a partial short circuit is suspected?

Answer to SAQ 13.4

The logic pulser and current tracer

13.4 LOGIC CLIP

The logic clip is a simple type of clip-on indicator which indicates the logic states of the pins on an IC by means of leds. No power supply connections need be made, since the clip powers itself from the IC under test by automatically locating the Vcc and ground pins. All pins on the clip are electrically buffered to minimise loading on any circuit being tested. Otherwise the clip might overload the IC and cause malfunction of the device under test. Logic clips may only be capable of checking a limited number of 14 and 16-pin chips within a logic family. Generally clips can test devices such as gates, flip-flops, counters, shift registers and the like.

13: Troubleshooting on digital/microprocessor based systems

 Short answer question 13.5

When using a logic clip to test a quad two-input logic gate isn't there a danger that the clip will overload the system and cause malfunction. Explain.

 Answer to SAQ 13.5

NO because the clip is adequately buffered

13.5 LOGIC COMPARATOR

This works on the principle of comparing a known good IC (the reference IC) with the IC under investigation. Fig 13.10 illustrates the principle of operation of the device. In use, the IC to be tested is first identified. A reference board with a good IC of the same type is then inserted in the comparator. The comparator is clipped onto the IC in question, and an immediate indication is given if the test IC operates differently from the reference IC. A lighted LED corresponds to a logic difference.

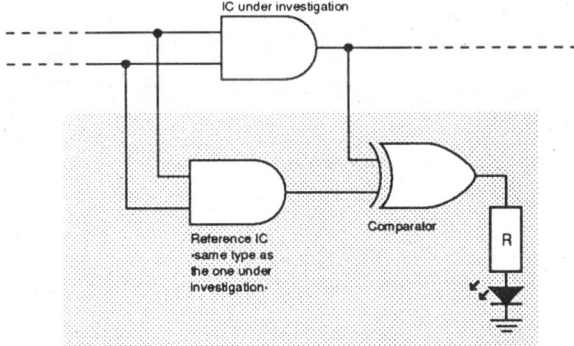

Fig 13.10 Principle of operation of a logic comparator

One of the disadvantages of logic comparators is that a separate reference card has to be stocked for each type of device that may have to be tested. The wide range of devices available within a logic family means that some devices are untestable by a logic comparator. As in the case of the logic clip, logic comparators are presently limited to 16-pin ICs, and are thus of little use in microcomputer work. However, 24-pin and 40-pin comparators may be developed in the future.

 Short answer question 13.6

State one disadvantage of using a logic comparator for testing digital ICs

13: Troubleshooting on digital/microprocessor based systems

> **A** **Answer to SAQ 13.6**
>
> A separate reference card (if available) has to be stocked for each type of device that may have to be tested. This makes it costly.

13.6 LOGIC ANALYSER

Microcomputers execute programs at high speed. This means that the information on the system buses changes very rapidly. Although hand-held tools play an important role when troubleshooting conventional logic networks they are, however, of limited use when applied to bus structured systems. For analysis and troubleshooting there is a need to be able to capture bus contents, while the program is running, and display the information on a screen. Oscilloscopes display one, two (or up to about eight) analogue signals on a CRT as a function of time, but most CROs are able to display only a periodic waveform. Since the bus signals are seldom repetitive the oscilloscope is of little use.

A logic analyser is a microprocessor-based instrument which is capable of capturing data from the system buses of a microcomputer while the program is running at full speed. The captured data may be displayed on a screen in different modes. It is used for the debugging of hardware and software.

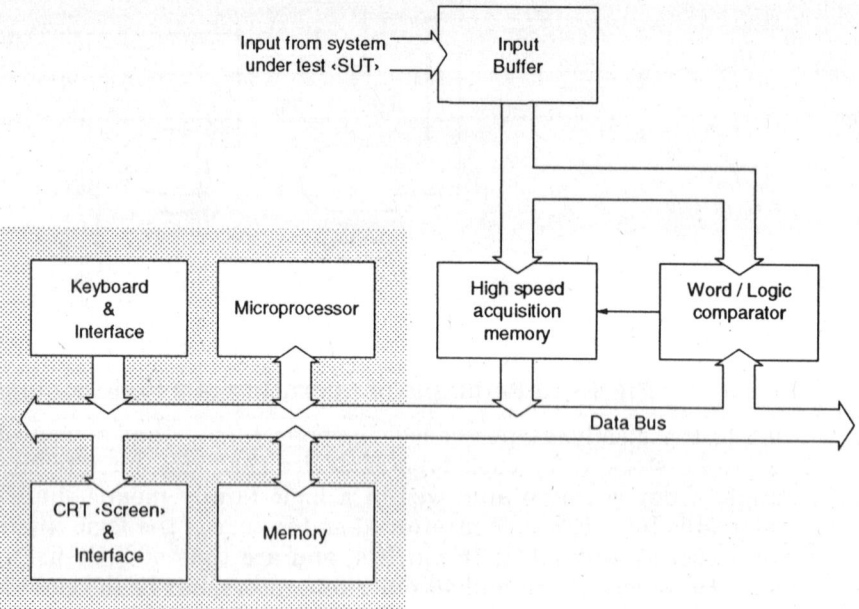

Fig 13.11 Block diagram of a logic analyser

As Fig 13.11 shows the logic analyser is a microprocessor-based product. As well as the usual components associated with a microprocessor (shown on the left of the diagram) the analyser has an input buffer, high speed acquisition memory, and a word or logic comparator.

In operation the logic analyser may be connected via a 40-pin clip to the microprocessor of the system under test. Typically 32 or more inputs (channels) can be used to follow the time behaviour of the signals found in a microcomputer system. The signals are fed into the analyser through an input buffer which minimises the loading of the instrument on the system being tested. When testing a computer, the technician or engineer is interested in capturing information pertaining to a certain part of a program and not just any information that happens to be captured by the analyser. To achieve this the analyser has some from of triggering which qualifies when the analyser should start capturing data. The high speed acquisition RAM acts as the recording medium, saving the logic levels at the inputs and allowing them to be replayed later for analysis. In a typical 32-channel device the memory would be organised as 32 bits wide by 1024 words deep, allowing the analyser to record for 1024 clock cycles. Note that bus information is captured at each clock pulse. Within the 32-bit word 16 address, 8 data and 8 status lines could be accommodated.

To illustrate how the analyser works suppose we wish to capture information after the address 2000H in a program.

The analyser would be configured to capture information from the system under test after the address 2000H appears on the address bus of the system. To achieve this the address 2000H is placed in the word/logic comparator. If we then execute the program the analyser will continually sample the input from the system and compare that input with the word in the logic comparator. When there is a match the logic comparator sends a signal to the acquisition memory which enables the captured data from 2000H onwards to be placed into the acquisition memory for a total of 1024 clock cycles. (assuming a memory of 1k bytes)

Because the instrument is based around a microcomputer the outputs from the acquisition memory may be formatted to provide one of the following user selectable displays:

(a) timing

(b) state

(c) Disassembly

In the timing mode it is possible to display captured data from a limited number of channels as a timing diagram.

In state mode the instrument can display the contents of its memory in binary, octal, decimal, or hexadecimal codes.

Many logic analysers have a disassembly feature which allows the captured data to be displayed as assembly language mnemonics.

As mentioned earlier the logic analyser may be used for software and hardware troubleshooting. It has the ability to capture information from the system buses while the program is running at full speed. Having captured the data from the buses we can sit down and analyse the activity of the buses and therefore determine whether or not the system is functioning correctly. From the observed data the cause of a fault can usually be localised. Many analysers are able to deal with asynchronous events such as interrupt requests from a peripheral.

13: Troubleshooting on digital/microprocessor based systems

 Short answer question 13.7

State one major advantage of a logic analyser compared with all other available test equipment for troubleshooting bus structured systems.

 Answer to SAQ 13.7

It has the ability to capture bus information from the system while the program is running at full speed. The captured data can then be recalled and displayed on the analyser and used to determine the likely cause of either hardware or software faults.

13.7 SIGNATURE ANALYSER

The traditional approach to testing and fault finding in an analogue system is to produce an annotated schematic which shows the voltage levels and waveforms at different points within the circuit. For instance, the amplifier, shown in Fig 13.12 could be tested by the application of a 1 kHz, 10mV peak signal at the input. Assuming an amplification factor of 200 the output signal would have a peak amplitude of 2 volts. A technician could test the amplifier by using a signal generator to apply the required test signal to the system. By using an oscilloscope the input and output waveforms could be checked. These could then be compared to the voltage levels and waveforms indicated on the circuit diagram.

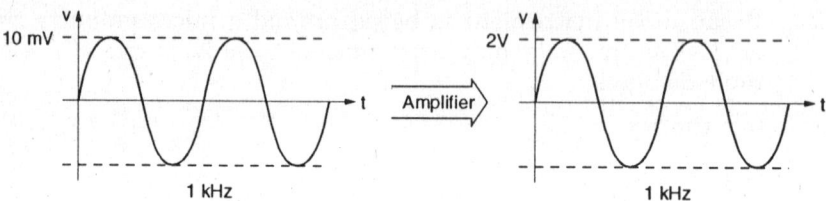

Fig 13.12 A conventional diagram showing voltage levels and expected waveforms

Adopting the same approach with microcomputers meets with several problems. For bus structured systems, where the data changes very rapidly, neither oscilloscopes nor multimeters yield meaningful information. Waveforms are long, complex and have a random appearance that makes all data streams look much alike. The signature analyser was developed as an instrument capable of recording these complex data streams yet presenting the information to a technician in an easy to understand manner. Like an oscilloscope it monitors the logic activity at a node in a system. The node must of course be stimulated by an appropriate test program. A signature analyser displays recorded information in the form of a 4-digit display and not as a picture like the oscilloscope. As shown in Fig 13.13 the basis of a signature analyser is a 16-bit shift register which has four feedback lines which are applied as inputs to a combination of EX-OR gates. The output from these gates is combined with the input signal from the node being tested in an EX-OR gate. The feedback paths ensure that all of the bits forming the data stream, and not just the last 16, contribute to the final signature. The signature which appears on the display uses the character set 0 to 9 and the letters ACFHPU.

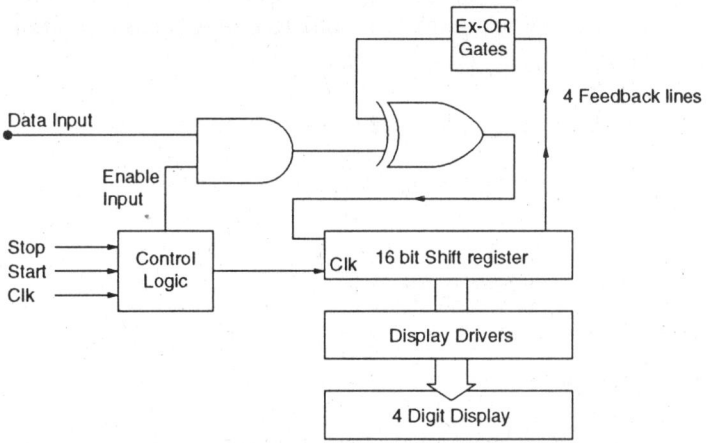

Fig 13.13 Principle of a signature analyser

Typical signatures, for a memory decoder chip are shown in Fig 13.14. To use the analyser signatures are obtained for a known good system using a test program. For troubleshooting the signatures obtained at various nodes in the system are compared with the reference signatures from the working system. Discrepancies indicate the faulty part of the system.

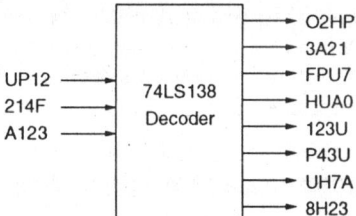

Fig 13.14 Typical signatures for a memory decode chip

It should be understood that the signature itself has no meaning and serves only as a token representing patterns of 1s and 0s in the data stream at the node being investigated.

Signature analysis is a simple test technique. Signatures are initially obtained by stimulating a known good system with a test program, and obtaining the signatures at various nodes in the system. These signatures are carefully documented. For troubleshooting, the same test program is applied to the same system, and a set of signatures obtained. The test signatures are then compared to the documented signatures. Differences point to the part of the system which is faulty. From that the individual faulty component may be located.

13: Troubleshooting on digital/microprocessor based systems

Short answer question 13.8

A set of signatures were obtained for a working microcomputer and carefully documented. The system was subsequently modified and some time later developed a fault. The signatures were not updated. Would it be advisable to use a signature analyser for test purposes?

Answer to SAQ 13.8

NO because the correct updated signatures are not available.

13.8 SELF-TEST PROGRAMS

The ROM inside a personal computer contains several routines, or modules, designed to operate the system. These include a Power-On Self Test (POST) module, consisting of a set of routines that test the:

motherboard
memory
disk controllers
video adapters
keyboard etc

This routine is useful when you troubleshoot system failures or problems. In addition to the POST test software in ROM, for IBM PCs and compatibles several types of diagnostic software are available to help you determine which PC component is defective. Usually you obtain the diagnostics disk and its accompanying problem-determination procedures, outlined in the guide-to-operations manual for the system. Armed with the diagnostics disks and the relevant manual/s troubleshooting is made much simpler.

The results of these tests are usually communicated to the operator using the computer's monitor to confirm satisfactory completion, or otherwise, of the tests.

Short answer question 13.9

Name TWO components which are usually tested by the POST program which resides in system firmware.

Answer to SAQ 13.9

The memory and the keyboard

13.9 MEMORY TESTING

The memory of a system consists of the ROMs (or EPROMS) which store the system firmware, and RAM. As mentioned previously the Power-On Self Test which is stored in the system ROM/S tests the memory (and other parts) when the system is first switched on.

ROM testing

The normal method of testing ROM involves forming a **checksum**. We will use the three byte imaginary RAM shown in Fig 13.15 to illustrate how it works. The three bytes 23H, 90H and 31H are added together to give a sum of E4H. The top location in the ROM is reserved for the checksum byte. The result of the addition is compared with the checksum figure. A difference, would of course, indicate a faulty ROM. If they do match the ROM is probably functional but there still remains a possibility that several errors have cancelled each other out, giving an apparent 'correct' checksum. In practice, the checksum technique can be applied to any size of device by adding together all its contents with the exception of the last location and ignoring any numeric overflow that occurs. A more exhaustive test involves CRC checking.

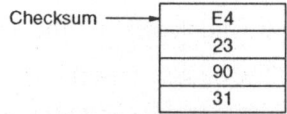

Fig 13.15 The ROM checksum test

A checksum ROM test program is usually implemented as part of the Power-On Self Test module, which is run during the power-up sequence of a microcomputer.

RAM testing

To test RAM devices involves writing a pattern into a memory location, reading it back and then checking that the byte which was written to memory has been read back successfully. The test bytes used for RAM checking are 55H and AAH (sometimes 00H and FFH). The test begins by filling the RAM under test with 55H = 0101 0101 in binary. Each location is then read and checked. The memory block is then filled with AAH = 1010 1010 in binary and again checked. Just like the ROM, RAM is also tested during the power-up sequence of the computer. The binary patterns written to and read from the RAM are known as the CHECKERBOARD pattern because they alternate between the two logic states, analogous to the alternation between black and white squares on a draughts board:

   55H = 0101 0101

   AAH = 1010 1010

The checkerboard method is a simple means of testing RAM. It would not necessarily detect certain kinds of faults that might occur in a RAM. For more exhaustive checking the WALKING ONES test is used. For this test, the following bit sequences will be sent to and read back from every RAM location in the memory. This test can be used to detect adjacent cell pickup which would manifest itself by

13: Troubleshooting on digital/microprocessor based systems

two adjacent bit positions being set to 1. This would be detected when the byte is read back for checking.

```
0000   0000
0000   0001
0000   0010
0000   0100
0000   1000
0001   0000
0010   0000
0100   0000
1000   0000
```

Short answer question 13.10

Name TWO tests which may be used for checking RAM and ROM. In each case state which test is more reliable.

Answer to SAQ 13.10

RAM: Checkerboard and Walking ones.

ROM: Checksum and Cyclic Redundancy Check (CRC)

Walking ones (for RAM) and CRC (for ROM)

SUMMARY

- Microcomputers are bus structured systems. When a program is running the information on the system buses changes rapidly. For troubleshooting this requires specialised test equipment.
- To aid testing and faultfinding a number of hand held tools are available:

    logic probes, logic pulsers, current tracers, logic clips, logic comparators

- A logic probe is capable of indicating the in-circuit activity of a node in a digital system. (high, low or pulsing)
- A logic pulser may be used to inject a single pulse or continuous pulses into a node in a digital system.
- The current tracer is suitable for tracking down low impedance faults such as short circuits or partial shorts in a system.
- A logic clip is a simple type of clip-on indicator which indicates the logic states of the pins on an in-circuit IC by means of leds.
- The logic comparator works on the principle of comparing a known good IC with a suspected faulty one.

- A logic analyser is capable of capturing information from the system buses while the program is running at full speed. Captured data may be examined to determine whether or not the system is working correctly.
- A logic analyser may be used for hardware and software debugging
- Signature analysis is a simple test technique. Documented signatures for a known good system are compared with signatures from the system under test.
- Personal computers run a Power-On Self Test (POST) program which checks various parts of the system at switch on time.
- The CHECKSUM test is frequently used for checking ROMs
- RAMs may be tested either by a CHECKERBOARD or WALKING ONES pattern

END OF CHAPTER QUESTIONS

Part A: Multiple choice questions (Answers in Appendix A)

1. Which one of the following is useful for tracking down low impedance faults?
    a) logic probe
    b) logic pulser
    c) current tracer
    d) logic clip

2. A logic probe with three leds is placed on a pin of an IC. The HIGH and LOW leds are on and the pulse led is flashing. This indicates that the node is:
    a) at logic 1
    b) at logic 0
    c) in a high impedance state
    d) receiving pulses

3. The pulse injected into the test node of a system by a logic pulser is
    a) a low frequency wide pulse
    b) a high frequency wide pulse
    c) wide
    d) narrow

4. When using a voltmeter to measure the supply voltage to the motherboard of a microcomputer you find the voltage level is very low. Assuming that the power supply itself is functional, which of the following would you use to determine the cause of the fault?
   a) a logic analyser
   b) a signature analyser
   c) logic clip
   d) current tracer

5. A logic analyser may be used
   a) only for hardware testing
   b) only for software testing
   c) for hardware and software debugging
   d) to obtain a signature of a node in a system

6. A signature analyser displays information on a
   a) 16-digit display
   b) SVGA monitor
   c) VGA monitor
   d) 4-digit display

7. A walking ones algorithm may be used to check
   a) the MPU
   b) ROM
   c) RAM
   d) the input/output port

8. A checksum algorithm may be used to check
   a) static RAM
   b) dynamic RAM
   c) ROM
   d) the microprocessor

9. Which of the following bytes are used for checking RAM?
   a) 01H and 10H
   b) 55H and AAH
   c) 5PH and PUH
   d) 1HH and HPH

10. A typical signature for a node in a digital system is
    a) 123E
    b) 456S
    c) 789U
    d) UBDD

SHORT ANSWER QUESTIONS

1. State ONE main difference between a logic probe and a logic pulser.
2. With the aid of a simple sketch explain the principle of a logic comparator
3. Using a simple sketch explain the principle of operation of a logic analyser

   State ONE advantage of a logic analyser compared with a signature analyser.
4. Explain the procedure for testing and faultfinding on a microprocessor based product using a signature analyser.
5. With the aid of a simple sketch explain how the checksum is calculated for an imaginary ROM which is storing the data 01H, 06H, FAH and 12H. The checksum is stored at the 5th (top) location in the ROM.
6. With the aid of a simple sketch explain how a RAM may be tested by the WALKING ONES method.
7. In relation to personal computers, what is the 'POST"?
8. Assume that you have to test a 4-bit asynchronous counter constructed from D-type flip-flops. Draw the circuit diagram and explain which hand-held tools you would select for the test. The DC voltage levels to each chip are normal.

Appendix A:
Answers to all multiple choice questions set at end of chapters

		Chapter number											
		1	2	3	4	5	6	7	8	9	10	11	12	13
Question number	1	B	C	D	C	D	B	D	B	A	C	C	D	C
	2	D	C	D	B	D	D	C	B	D	A	D	C	D
	3	C	A	A	C	C	C	A	D	C	D	C	D	D
	4	D	A	C	A	B	C	A	D	D	A	C	C	D
	5	A	D	D	A	D	A	B	D	B	D	D	D	C
	6	D	D	C	D	D	C	D	C	D	C	C	C	D
	7	D	B	C	C	A	A	D	D	A	D	B	C	C
	8	C	A	B	D	C	D	D	C	D	D	D	D	C
	9	A	C	C	C	C	D	C	C	A	D	D	A	B
	10	A	D	D	D	D	D	A	D	B	C	C	D	C

Appendix B:
A typical microcomputer clock circuit

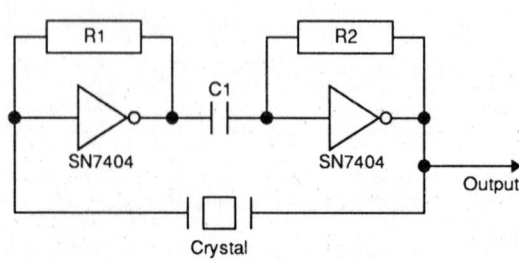

334

Appendix C: The CENTRONICS parallel interface using a 36-pin connector

Note: The direction of all signals is given with respect to the printer.

Signal pin no.	Return pin no.	Signal	Direction	Description
1	19	STROBE	in	Pulses on this line cause data to be read into the printer
2-9	20-27	DATA	in	Eight data lines. Each line has it's own signal ground return for use with twisted pair cables
10	28	ACKNLG	out	This indicates that the printer is ready to accept more data
11	29	BUSY	out	This signal is set HIGH to indicate that the printer cannot accept data.
12	30	PE	out	Signals that the printer is out of paper
13	-	SLCT	out	Signals that the printer is in the selected state
14	-	AUTO -FEED XT	in	If this is LOW, a line feed is added to each carriage return
15	-	Not conn.	-	Not used
16	-	0V	-	Signal ground level (logical common)
17	-	CHASSIS GROUND	-	Connected to printer chassis; not to signal ground (normally)
18	-	Not conn	-	Not used
19-30	-	GND	-	Signal ground for pins 1-12
31	-	INIT	in	A low pulse on this input causes the printer to be initialised and the print buffer is cleared
32	-	ERROR	out	This is LOW when: i. there is no paper ii. printer is off-line iii. or an error occurs
33	-	GND	-	Return signal ground
34	-	Not conn	-	Not used
35	-	-	-	Connected to +5V supply
36	-	SLCT IN	in	This signal is LOW for data entry

Appendix D: Pinout of the RS-232C 25-way connector

Pin	Description	Common name
1	Protective ground	
2	Transmitted data	TxD
3	Received data	RxD
4	Request to send	$\overline{\text{RTS}}$
5	Clear to send	$\overline{\text{CTS}}$
6	Data set ready	$\overline{\text{DSR}}$
7	Signal ground	
8	Data channel received line signal detector (Data carrier detect)	$\overline{\text{DCD}}$
9	Reserved for testing	
10	Reserved for testing	
11	Unassigned	
12	Secondary received line signal detector	
13	Secondary clear to send	
14	Secondary transmitted data	
15	Transmitted signal element timing	
16	Secondary received data	
17	Receiver signal element timing	
18	Unassigned	
19	Secondary request to send	
20	Data terminal ready	$\overline{\text{DTR}}$
21	Signal quality detector	
22	Ring detector	
23	Data signal rate select	
24	Transmit signal element timing	
25	Unassigned	

Notes:

i **Protective ground**: This pin is tied to the equipment frame and other external grounds as required.

ii Signal ground. Ground return for all RS-232 signals

iii The standard allows for two full duplex (data may be transmitted in both directions simultaneously) data channels.

Appendix E: Program Flowchart Symbols

Symbol	Comments
Terminal	This is the first or last symbol in a program or subprogram. Usually labelled start/stop or begin/end.
Process	Used to represent any kind of processing activity — details such as 'add number one to number two' are written inside the box
Decision	Used where a decision has to be made. The condition on which the decision is based is written inside the symbol
Pre-defined process	This is used to represent a process which has been detailed elsewhere (subroutine)
Input/output	The name of the variable is usually written inside the symbol
↓	Used to show the flow/path of a sequence of operations which are denoted by symbols

Appendix F: The Zilog Z80 microprocessor instruction set

When we speak of the microprocessor instruction set, we are talking about all the instructions that the microprocessor is able to understand and therefore carry out. The following tables list most of the instructions available with the Z80 microprocessor. The instructions are presented in their mnemonic form and the hexadecimal code of each instruction is also given. The following abbreviations are used.

A, B, C, D, E, H, L represent one of the internal MPU registers
'n' represents an 8-bit (one byte) value
'nn' represents a 16-bit value
(HL) represents the memory address currently held in register pair HL.
IX,IY are the index registers.

NZ = non-zero (Z=0)
Z = zero (Z=1)
NC = non-carry (C=0)
C = carry (C=1)
PO = parity odd
PE = parity even
P = sign positive (S=0)
M = sign negative (S=1)

Source code	Object code
ADC A,A	8F
ADC A,B	88
ADC A,C	89
ADC A,D	8A
ADC A,E	8B
ADC A,H	8C
ADC A,L	8D
ADC A,n	CE n
ADC A,(HL)	8E
ADC A,(IX + d)	DD 8E d
ADC A,(IY + D)	FD 8E d
ADC HL,BC	ED 4A
ADC HL, DE	ED 5A
ADC HL,HL	ED 6A
ADC HL, SP	ED 7A
ADD A,A	87
ADD A,B	80

Source code	Object code
ADD A,C	81
ADD A,D	82
ADD A,E	83
ADD A,H	84
ADD A,L	85
ADD A,n	C6 n
ADD A,(HL)	86
ADD A,(IX+d)	DD 86 d
ADD A,(IY+D)	FD 86 d
ADD HL,BC	09
ADD HL,DE	19
ADD HL,HL	29
ADD HL,SP	39
ADD IX,BC	DD 09
ADD IX,DE	DD 19
ADD IX,IX	DD 29
ADD IX,SP	DD 39

Appendix F

Source code	Object code
ADD IY,BC	FD 09
ADD IY,DE	FD 19
ADD IY,IY	FD 29
AND A	A7
AND B	A0
AND C	A1
AND D	A2
AND E	A3
AND H	A4
AND L	A5
AND n	E6 n
AND (HL)	A6
AND (IX+d)	DD A6 d
AND (IY+d)	FD A6 d
CALL nn	CD nn
CALL C,nn	DC nn
CALL M,nn	FC nn
CALL NC,nn	D4 nn
CALL NZ,nn	C4 nn
CALL P,nn	F4 nn
CALL PE,nn	EC nn
CALL PO,nn	E4 nn
CALL Z,nn	CC nn
CCF	3F
CP A	BF
CP B	B8
CP C	B9
CP D	BA
CP E	BB
CP H	BC
CP L	BD
CP n	FE n
CP (HL)	BE
CP (IX+d)	DD BE d
CP (IY+d)	FD BE d
CPD	ED A9

Source code	Object code
CPDR	ED B9
CPI	ED A1
CPIR	ED B1
CPL	2F
DAA	27
DEC A	3D
DEC B	05
DEC C	0D
DEC D	15
DEC E	1D
DEC H	25
DEC L	2D
DEC BC	0B
DEC DE	1B
DEC HL	2B
DEC IX	DD 2B
DEC IY	FD 2B
DEC SP	3B
DEC (HL)	35
DEC (IX+d)	DD 35 d
DEC (IY+d)	FD 35 d
DI	F3
DJNZ e	10 e
EI	FB
EX (SP),HL	E3
EX (SP),IX	DD E3
EX (SP),IY	FD E3
EX AF, AF'	08
EX DE,HL	EB
EXX	D9
HALT	76
IM 0	ED 46
IM 1	ED 56
IM 2	ED 5E
IN A,(n)	DB n
IN A,(C)	ED 78

Appendix F

Source code	Object code
IN B,(C)	ED 40
IN C,(C)	ED 48
IN D,(C)	ED 50
IN E,(C)	ED 58
IN H,(C)	ED 60
IN L,(C)	ED 68
INC A	3C
INC B	04
INC C	0C
INC D	14
INC E	1C
INC H	24
INC L	2C
INC BC	03
INC DE	13
INC HL	23
INC IX	DD 23
INC IY	FD 23
INC SP	33
INC (IX+d)	DD 34 d
INC (IY+d)	FD 34 d
INC (HL)	34
IND	ED AA
INDR	ED BA
INI	ED A2
INIR	ED B2
JP nn	C3 nn
JP (HL)	E9
JP (IX)	DD E9
JP (IY)	FD E9
JP C,nn	DA nn
JP M,nn	FA nn
JP NC,nn	D2 nn
JP NZ, nn	C2 nn
JP P,nn	F2 nn
JP PE,nn	EA nn

Source code	Object code
JP PO,nn	E2 nn
JP Z,nn	CA nn
JR C,e	38 e
JR NC,e	30 e
JR NZ,e	20 e
JR Z,e	28,e
JR e	18 e
LD A,A	7F
LD A,B	78
LD A,C	79
LD A,D	7A
LD A,E	7B
LD A,H	7C
LD A,I	ED 57
LD A,L	7D
LD A,n	3E n
LD A,R	ED 5F
LD A,(BC)	0A
LD A,(DE)	1A
LD A,(HL)	7E
LD A,(IX+d)	DD 7E d
LD A,(IY+d)	FD 7E d
LD A,(nn)	3A nn
LD B,A	47
LD B,B	40
LD B,C	41
LD B,D	42
LD B,E	43
LD B,H	44
LD B,L	45
LD B,n	06 n
LD B,(HL)	46
LD B,(IX+d)	DD 46 d
LD B,(IY+d)	FD 46 d
LD BC,nn	01 nn
LD BC,(nn)	ED 4B nn

Appendix F

Source code	Object code
LD C,A	4F
LD C,B	48
LD C,C	49
LD C,D	4A
LD C,E	4B
LD C,H	4C
LD C,L	4D
LD C,n	0E n
LD C,(HL)	4E
LD C,(IX+d)	DD 4E d
LD C,(IY+d)	FD 4E d
LD D,A	57
LD D,B	50
LD D,C	51
LD D,D	52
LD D,E	53
LD D,H	54
LD D,L	55
LD D,n	16 n
LD D,(HL)	56
LD D,(IX+d)	DD 56 d
LD D,(IY+d)	FD 56 d
LD DE, nn	11 nn
LD DE,(nn)	ED 5B nn
LD E,A	5F
LD E,B	58
LD E,C	59
LD E,D	5A
LD E,E	5B
LD E,H	5C
LD E,L	5D
LD E,n	1E n
LD E,(HL)	5E
LD E,(IX+d)	DD 5E d
LD E,(IY+d)	FD 5E d
LD H,A	67

Source code	Object code
LD H,B	60
LD H,C	61
LD H,D	62
LD H,E	63
LD H,H	64
LD H,L	65
LD H,n	26 n
LD H,(HL)	66
LD H,(IX+d)	DD 66 d
LD H,(IY+d)	FD 66 d
LD HL,nn	21 nn
LD HL,(nn)	2A nn
LD I,A	ED 47
LD IX,nn	DD 21 nn
LD IX,(nn)	DD 2A nn
LD IY,nn	FD 21 nn
LD IY,(nn)	FD 2A nn
LD L,A	6F
LD L,B	68
LD L,C	69
LD L,D	6A
LD L,E	6B
LD L,H	6C
LD L,L	6D
LD L,n	2E n
LD L,(HL)	6E
LD L,(IX+d)	DD 6E d
LD L,(IY+d)	FD 6E d
LD R,A	ED 4F
LD SP,HL	F9
LD SP,IX	DD F9
LD SP,IY	FD F9
LD SP,nn	31 nn
LD SP,(nn)	ED 7B nn
LD (BC),A	02
LD (DE),A	12

Appendix F

Source code	Object code
LD (HL),A	77
LD (HL),B	70
LD (HL),C	71
LD (HL),D	72
LD (HL),E	73
LD (HL),H	74
LD (HL),L	75
LD (HL),n	36 n
LD (IX+d),A	DD 77 d
LD (IX+d),B	DD 70 d
LD (IX+d),C	DD 71 d
LD (IX+d),D	DD 72 d
LD (IX+d),E	DD 73 d
LD (IX+d),H	DD 74 d
LD (IX+d),L	DD 75 d
LD (IX+d),n	DD 36 d n
LD (IY+d),A	FD 77 d
LD (IY+d),B	FD 70 d
LD (IY+d),C	FD 71 d
LD (IY+d),D	FD 72 d
LD (IY+d),E	FD 73 d
LD (IY+d),H	FD 74 d
LD (IY+d),L	FD 75 d
LD (IY+d),n	FD 36 d n
LD (nn),A	32 nn
LD (nn),BC	ED 43 nn
LD (nn),DE	ED 53 nn
LD (nn),HL	22 nn
LD (nn),IX	DD 22 nn
LD (nn),IY	FD 22 nn
LD (nn),SP	ED 73 nn
LDD	ED A8
LDDR	ED B8
LDI	ED A0
LDIR	ED B0
NEG	ED 44

Source code	Object code
NOP	00
OR A	B7
OR B	B0
OR C	B1
OR D	B2
OR E	B3
OR H	B4
OR L	B5
OR n	F6 n
OR (HL)	B6
OR (IX+d)	DD B6 d
OR (IY+d)	FD B6 d
OTDR	ED BB
OTIR	ED B3
OUT (C),A	ED 79
OUT (C),B	ED 41
OUT (C),C	ED 49
OUT (C),D	ED 51
OUT (C),E	ED 59
OUT (C),H	ED 61
OUT (C),L	ED 69
OUT (n),A	D3 n
OUTD	ED AB
OUTI	ED A3
POP AF	F1
POP BC	C1
POP DE	D1
POP HL	E1
POP IX	DD E1
POP IY	FD E1
PUSH AF	F5
PUSH BC	C5
PUSH DE	D5
PUSH HL	E5
PUSH IX	DD E5
PUSH IY	FD E5

Source code	Object code
RET	C9
RET C	D8
RET M	F8
RET NC	D0
RET NZ	C0
RET P	F0
RET PE	E8
RET PO	E0
RET Z	C8
RETI	ED 4D
RETN	ED 45
RL A	CB 17
RL B	CB 10
RL C	CB 11
RL D	CB 12
RL E	CB 13
RL H	CB 14
RL L	CB 15
RL (HL)	CB 16
RL (IX+d)	DD CB d nn
RL (IY+d)	FD CB d nn
RLA	17
RLC A	CB 07
RLC B	CB 00
RLC C	CB 01
RLC D	CB 02
RLC E	CB 03
RLC H	CB 04
RLC L	CB 05
RLC (HL)	CB 06
RLC (IX+d)	DD CB d 06
RLC (IY+d)	FD CB d 06
RLCA	07
RLD	ED 6F
RR A	CB 1F
RR B	CB 18

Source code	Object code
RR C	CB 19
RR D	CB 1A
RR E	CB 1B
RR H	CB 1C
RR L	CB 1D
RR (HL)	CB 1E
RR (IX+d)	DD CB d 1E
RR (IY+d)	FD CB d 1E
RRA	1F
RRC A	CB 0F
RRC B	CB 08
RRC C	CB 09
RRC D	CB 0A
RRC E	CB 0B
RRC H	CB 0C
RRC L	CB 0D
RRC (HL)	CB 0E
RRC (IX+d)	DD CB d 0E
RRC (IY+d)	FD CB d 0E
RRCA	0F
RRD	ED 67
RST 00H	C7
RST 08H	CF
RST 10H	D7
RST 18H	DF
RST 20H	E7
RST 28H	EF
RST 30H	F7
RST 38H	FF
SBC A,A	9F
SBC A,B	98
SBC A,C	99
SBC A,D	9A
SBC A,E	9B
SBC A,H	9C
SBC A,L	9D

Appendix F

Source code		Object code
SBC	A,n	DE n
SBC	A,(HL)	9E
SBC	A,(IX+d)	DD 9E d
SBC	A,(IY+d)	FD 9E d
SBC	HL,BC	ED 42
SBC	HL,DE	ED 52
SBC	HL,HL	ED 62
SBC	HL,SP	ED 72
SCF		37
SLA	A	CB 27
SLA	B	CB 20
SLA	C	CB 21
SLA	D	CB 22
SLA	E	CB 23
SLA	H	CB 24
SLA	L	CB 25
SLA	(HL)	CB 26
SLA	(IX+d)	DD CB d 26
SLA	(IY+d)	FD CB d 26
SRA	A	CB 2F
SRA	B	CB 28
SRA	C	CB 29
SRA	D	CB 2A
SRA	E	CB 2B
SRA	H	CB 2C
SRA	L	CB 2D
SRA	(HL)	CB 2E
SRA	(IX+d)	DD CB d 2E
SRA	(IY+d)	FD CB d 2E
SRL	A	CB 3F
SRL	B	CB 38

Source code		Object code
SRL	C	CB 39
SRL	D	CB 3A
SRL	E	CB 3B
SRL	H	CB 3C
SRL	L	CB 3D
SRL	(HL)	CB 3E
SRL	(IX+d)	DD CB d 3E
SRL	(IY+d)	FD CB d 3E
SUB	A	97
SUB	B	90
SUB	C	91
SUB	D	92
SUB	E	93
SUB	H	94
SUB	L	95
SUB	n	D6 n
SUB	(HL)	96
SUB	(IX+d)	DD 96 d
SUB	(IY+d)	FD 96 d
XOR	A	AF
XOR	B	A8
XOR	C	A9
XOR	D	AA
XOR	E	AB
XOR	H	AC
XOR	L	AD
XOR	n	EE n
XOR	(HL)	AE
XOR	(IX+d)	DD AE d
XOR	(IY+d)	FD AE d

Appendix G: The Z80 MPU Flag register

The Z80 flag register contains six bits of information which are set or reset by various MPU operations. Four of these are testable; that is, they are used as conditions for jump, call or return instructions. For instance, a jump (branch) in a program may be desired only if a specific bit in the flag register is set. The four testable bits are:

1   CARRY flag (C)
2   ZERO flag (Z)
3   SIGN flag (S)
4   Parity/Overflow (P/V).

The flag register can be accessed by the programmer and its format is as follows:

D7							D0
S	Z	X	H	X	P/V	N	C

Notes.
i   The two flags H and N are used for BCD arithmetic and cannot be tested
ii X means that the flag goes to an indeterminate state

Index

Access time *201, 207*
Accumulator *156, 165*
ACIA *234*
Acquisition memory *325*
Addition circuits *78-83, 157*
Address *12*
Address bus *12 154*
Address control logic *181*
Addressing modes *267-269*
Algorithms *258*
Alphanumeric codes *49*
Analogue-to-digital converter *243-244*
AND gate *57, 59*
Applications software *14, 17*
Architecture *146*
Arithmetic instructions *264*
Arithmetic and Logic Unit (ALU) *10, 152-153, 157*
ASCII code *48-50*
Assembler *17-18*
Assembly language *17*
Asynchronous *90*
Asynchronous 4-bit binary down counter *112*
Asynchronous 4-bit binary up-counter *107*
Asynchronous systems *107-113*
AT *5*
Audio cassette recording *309*
Average access time *308*

Backing storage *203 297*
Baud rate *235*
BCD *48-49*
BCD to 7-segment decoder *285*
BCD up-counter *109-110*
Bi-directional *12*
Binary addition *38*
Binary arithmetic *37*
Binary digit *2*
Binary division *40*
Binary fractions *35*
Binary multiplication *39*
Binary numbers *25*
Binary subtraction *38*
Bistable *90*
Bit *2*
Block diagram *9*
Boolean algebra *66-72*
Breakpoints *293*
Buffers *180, 182, 242*
Bugs *293*
Bus conflict *216*
Bus width *6*
Buses *11-12*
Byte *147*

CALL instruction *264-265*
Cassette recording *309*
Centronics *247*
CGA *249*
Checkerboard pattern *329*
Checking sequential logic elements *317*
Checksum *329*
Chip select *205*

Clear *93, 115, 116, 119*
Clock *151, Appendix B*
Clock waveforms *94*
Clocked S-R flip-flop *93*
Clones *5*
CMOS logic *129, 138, 140*
Combinational logic circuits *76*
Combinational logic gates *57-66*
Compiler *17*
Conditional jump instructions *264-265*
Control bus *12, 154*
Control circuits *152-153, 159*
Control structures *260*
Converting numbers from one base to another *30*
Counters *105*
CRC *303 329*
Criteria for selecting a logic family *129*
Current tracer *319-321*

D-type flip-flop *97*
DART *234*
Data bus *12 154*
Data bus control logic *180*
Data sheets *128, 208, 212*
Data transfer instructions *263*
Databases *15*
Debouncing *102*
Debugging *293*
Decimal numbers *23*
Decode cycle *183*
Decoder *214*
Decoding systems *216-219*
Delay routine *276-277, 284*
Digital computer *1*
Digital counters *105*
Digital to analogue converter *243*
DIL *4, 127*
Directly addressable memory *148*
Disk *300-302*
Disk drive *297, 303*
DISKCOPY *18*
DMA *182, 240*
Documentation *257*
Dot-matrix printer *248*
Down counter *112*
Dynamic RAMs *202*

EAPROM *204*
EBCDIC *51*
ECL *139*
Edge triggering *99*
EEPROM *204*
EGA *249*
Enable *205*
EPROM *204*
Error checking *235*
Even parity *51, 236*
Exclusive NOR *65*
Exclusive-OR gate *65*
Execute cycle *183, 185, 188, 191-193*
External data bus width *6*

346

Index

Fan-out *129, 131*
Faultfinding *314*
Fetch cycle *183, 184, 187, 190*
Fixed-point and floating-point numbers *46-47*
Flag register *166*
Flip-flops *90-104, 153*
Floppy disk care and handling *309*
Floppy disk controller *303*
Floppy disks *300-302*
Flowcharts *258*
FORMAT *18*
Frequency division *104*
Full-adder *85*

Gate *57*
Gate-to-Gate faults *320*
General purpose register *160*
Glitch *110*

Half-adder *79-83*
HALT *266*
Handling MOS devices *140*
Handshake lines *246*
Hard and floppy disks compared *308*
Hard disks *307*
Hardware *14, 17*
Hexadecimal *28*
High-level languages *16*
High-Speed TTL *136*

I/O mapped Input/output *239*
IC packages *127*
Index hole *301*
Inkjet printers *248*
Input devices *225*
Input output instructions *265*
Input/output ports *225-226*
Instruction decoder *153, 158*
Instruction register *156, 170-171*
Instruction set *262, Appendix F*
Integrated circuit *1, 127*
Integration injection logic *139*
Interfacing *241-246*
Interfacing examples *278-293*
Interpreter *18*
Interrupt I/O *240*
Inverter *61*
Iteration *260*

J-K flip-flop *100-102*
Jump & Branch (program flow control) instructions *264*

Keyboards *250*
Laser printers *249*
Latch *90*
Leading edge *94*
Least significant bit *148*
Level triggering *99*
Levels of integration *126*
Light emitting diodes *107, 280*
Logic analyser *314, 324*
Logic clip *322*
Logic comparator *323*
Logic families *126*
Logic gate testing *316*
Logic gates *56-65*
Logic probe *314*
Logic pulser *315*
Logical operations *264*

Low-Power Schottky TTL *136*
Low-power TTL *135*
LSI *127*

Machine code *16*
Magnetic media *298*
Magnetic tape *299, 310*
Main memory *297*
Maintenance and redesign *257*
Mass storage *297*
Master-slave (M-S) J-K flip-flop *100*
Mechanical switch debouncing *103*
Memories *199*
Memory addressing *148, 150*
Memory cell *199*
Memory decoding *214-219*
Memory locations *12, 148-149, 206*
Memory mapped I/O *239*
Memory maps *213, 239*
Memory testing *329*
Memory word *200*
Microcomputer *9*
Microcomputer programming *255*
Microprocessor *1, 3*
Microprocessor architecture *146, 155*
Microprocessor block diagram *154*
MIPS *151*
Mnemonic *262*
MOD numbers *109*
Modem *237*
Monitor *293*
MOS logic families *138-139*
Motherboard *7*
Mouse *251*
MPU *4*
MS-DOS *18*
MSI *126*

NAND gate *63*
Noise immunity *133*
Non-volatile *10*
NOP *266*
NOR gate *64*
NOT gate *61*
Number systems *23-37*

Object code *16*
Octal *27*
Odd parity *51, 236*
One's complement *42*
Operand *267*
Operating system *18*
Operation code *267*
Optical isolation *243*
OR gate *60*

Parallel I/O *225-233*
Parallel interfaces *247*
Parallel port *225*
Parity *51*
PC *5*
Periodic time *94*
Peripherals *248-251*
Personal computer *5*
PIA *225*
PIO *225, 227-229*
PIO programming modes *231*
POP *174*
Ports *11*

Index

Power dissipation 130
Preset 93
Printers 248-249
Problem specification 255
Processor speed 151
Program 14
Program coding 257
Program counter (PC) 156, 168-170
Program design 257
Program loops 274
Programmed I/O 240
Programmer's model of Z80 194
Programmer's model of the Z80 PIO 230
Programming examples 269-293
PROM 204
Propagation delay 129
Pseudo-code 261
PUSH 174-175

RAM signals and architecture 209-211
RAM testing 329
Random access memory 11, 168-169
Read access time 201
Read head 299
Read only memory 10
Read operation 201
Refreshing 202
Registers 115-119, 153
Reset 91, 305
ROM signals and architecture 205
ROM testing 329
RS232 247

S-R (Set-Reset) flip-flop 90-96
Schottky TTL 136
SCSI 247
Sector 300-302
Sector organisation 302
Selection 260
Self-test programs 328
Sequence 260
Sequential logic elements 90
Sequential logic systems 90
Serial communication 234-238
Serial data format 235
Serial input output 234
Serial interface 247
Shift registers 115-120
Signature analyser 326
SIMMS 219
Single stepping 294
SIO 234
SIPS 219
SMD 127
Software 14-17
Software development 255-257
Source code 17
Speed of operation of the microprocessor 151
Speed-power product 131
Spreadsheets 15
SRAMs 202
SSI 126
Stack 173
Stack pointer 172-175
Start bit 235
Status register 166

Stepper motor 291
Stop bits 235
Storage capacity 301, 308
Stored-program concept 2
Structured programming 259
Subprogram 172-173
Subroutine 172
SVGA 250
Synchronous 90
Synchronous and asynchronous systems 90
Synchronous binary up-counter 114-115
Systems software 15

Tape-backup systems 310
Testing gates 315-317
Testing RAM 329
Testing ROM 329
Time delays 276
Toggle 100
Top-down design 259
Trace table 293
Tracks 301
Traffic lights 289-291
Trailing edge 94
Transducer 244
Transfer rate 308
Transistor 1
Transistor transistor logic 134-137
Tri-state gates 84
Troubleshooting 314
Truth table 58
Two's complement 41-44

UART 234, 236-237
ULSI 127
Unconditional jump instructions 264-265
Unconnected (floating) TTL inputs 137
Universal logic 72
Unsigned binary 41
Unused CMOS inputs 138
Up-counter 107-112
USART 234
Utilities 18

VGA 249
Video displays 249
VLSI 127
Volatile 11
Voltage buffering 242

Walking ones 329
Winchester drive 307
Word 147, 200
Word lengths 147
Word processing 14
Write 201
Write enable 119
Write head 299
Write operation 201
Write protect notch 300

XT 5

Z80 PIO 227
Zilog Z80 194

Mathematics for Engineering
An Active-Learning Approach
D Clarke

ISBN: **1 85805 043 X** • Date: **Oct 1993** • Edition: **1st**
Extent: **300 pp (approx)** • Size: **275 x 215 mm**

> *Courses on which this book is expected to be used*
> This book provides a full course of study in mathematics for students following BTEC National Engineering and covers all the NII and NIII objectives.

The book is up-to-date and relates to current engineering practice. Mathematical techniques make full use of readily available information technology. It has been written specifically for engineering students by an engineer, and the activity-based approach gives a realistic context in which to follow the problem-solving routine of an engineer.

The book is divided into three main sections. Section 1 introduces the student to engineering mathematics through a project approach to the design of a motor car. Students acquire fundamental techniques through tackling the progressive tasks, with step-by-step support, and as confidence is built up, further mathematical topics are introduced. Throughout Section 1 cross references to the Section 2 Information Bank enable students to find easily all the necessary techniques and worked examples to solve the tasks in Section 1. Section 3 also has a project-based structure, and cross refers students to Section 2 for help, but it focuses on other engineering applications in order to reinforce and extend the techniques learned through Section 1.

Contents:

Section 1 – Project-based Application of Engineering Mathematics
Body Shape: Approach Area. Leading Angle. Capacity. *Fuel System:* Petrol. Electric. *Cooling System:* Heat Transfer. *Brakes:* Drums. Discs. *Gearbox:* Ratios. *Cylinder Design:* Engine Capacity. Cylinder Size. Piston Movement. *Electrics:* Alternator. Inition. Coil. *Suspension:* Springs. Dampers. *Transmission:* Drive. Clutch. *Testing:* Reliability. Petrol Consumption. Performance.

Section 2 – Information Bank
Primary Skills: Using Formulae. Using Calculators and Computers. Rearranging Formulae. Radians. Statistics. Trigonometry. Straight Line Graphs. Simultaneous Equations (including Matrices). Areas, Volumes and Surface Areas. Numerical Methods 1. Logarithms. Exponential Curves. Quadratic Equations. Differentiation 1. Integration 1.

Secondary Skills: Partial Fractions. Complex Numbers. Series. Binomial Theorem. Vectors (including Determinants). Differentiation 2. Integration 2. Numerical Methods 2. Maximum and Minimum. Differential Equations. Centroids. Second Moments of Area. Trigonometry 2.

Section 3 – Developing Skills
Further, short, projects in other engineering applications with tasks (with and without answers).

> ♠ **Free Lecturers' Supplement** ♠

Computer Studies

CS French

ISBN: **1 873981 18 X** • Date: **1993** • Edition: **4th**
Extent: **432 pp** • Size: **275 x 215 mm**

Courses on which this book is known to be used
GCSE; City & Guilds 726; BTEC; IDPM; BCS.
On reading lists of IDPM, BCS and ACP

This book aims to satisfy the GCSE and equivalent level Computer Studies text book requirement. It contains many illustrated examples to help students with coursework on word processing, spreadsheets and databases.

Notes on the Fourth Edition

The fourth edition reflects the continued shift of emphasis towards applications of computers, particularly applications packages and the features and usage of small desk-top and lap-top computers. Material is strengthened in the areas of applications development, Graphical User Interfaces (GUIs), and databases. The new edition has a new, larger format and revised layout.

Contents:

Introduction • Using Computers • **Applications of Computers** • Spreadsheets • Information Storage and Retrieval • Document Processing • Applications Areas • **Data and Programs** • Data Types and Data Representation • Number Bases • Designing Small Programs • Data Structures and Files • Simple Logic • **Hardware Features and Uses** • Hardware Overview • Interactive Devices • Input and Output Devices • Storage Devices • Choice of Hardware • Communication Systems • **How the Computer Works** • Arithmetic • Logic and Control • Elements of the Computer • The Computer's Own Language • Systems Architecture • **Software and Programming** • Software Types • Further Programming Methods • Low Level Languages • High Level Languages • Databases and 4GLs • Operating Systems • **Further Applications** • Batch Processing • Interactive Processing • Control and Manufacturing • Development of Applications • **Computers in Perspective** • Computers in the Organisation • Origins of Modern Computers • Social and Economic Aspects • **Appendices.**

Review Comments:

'A book to be recommended for its clarity and breadth of coverage.'
– **"Accountants Record"**

'A nice staccato style which is easy to read. – **"IDPM"**

♠ **Free Lecturers' Supplement** ♠

Also available as ELBS edition in member countries at local currency equivalent price of £2.50

Computer Science CS French

ISBN: **1 873981 19 8** • Date: **1992** • Edition: **4th**
Extent: **640 pp** • Size: **275 x 215 mm**

> *Courses on which this book is known to be used*
> A Level Computing; BTEC National and HNC/D Computer Studies; City & Guilds; BCS; AS Level Computer Science; BSc Applied Science.
> **On reading lists of ICM, IDPM, BCS and ACP**

This book provides a simplified approach to the understanding of Computer Science.

Notes on the Fourth Edition

This edition contains changes in content and layout which are aimed not just at covering the material on the latest syllabuses but at assisting the reader's study for the latest examinations. Parts targeted at contemporary computer applications and applications packages have been introduced. This reflects a significant shift in emphasis in examinations over recent years. Graphical User Interfaces (GUIs), development methodologies, desktop computers, applications packages and databases have been given more emphasis to reflect the examination requirements of developing and using computer systems. Obsolete material has been removed.

Contents:

Foundation Topics • Applications I: Document Processing • Storage • Input and Output • Applications II: GUIs and Multimedia • Computer Systems Organisation I • Programming I • File and File Processing • Applications III: Spreadsheets • Logic and Formal Notations • Computer Arithmetic • Computer Systems Organisation II • Software • Applications IV: Applications Areas • Programming II • Databases and 4GLs • Applications V: Information Storage and Retrieval • Systems Development • Applications VI: Business Industrial Computing • Computers in Contexts • Revision Test Questions.

Review Comments:

*'I think the presentation is superb and content perfect for my course work.' 'Good basic book – recommended by all academic staff in the department.' 'Still excellent value, and provides both good basis for teaching **and** private study.' 'Up-to-date information with clear graphical figures.'* – **Lecturers**

▲ **Free Lecturers' Supplement** ▲

Also available as ELBS edition in member countries at local currency equivalent price of £3.00

Computing
An Active-Learning Approach

PM Heathcote

ISBN: **1 870941 86 1** • Date: **1991** • Edition: **1st**
Extent: **352 pp** • Size: **275 x 215 mm**

Courses on which this book is known to be used
A Level Computing; BTEC Nat and Higher; ACCA Info Systems; BSc Software Eng; C & G 419 (DP); BTEC Cont Ed; BTEC First; Access to Computing; BTEC Nat Eng; AS; C & G 726; BA Business Studies.

Contents:
Introduction to Computers and Business Data Processing • Programming in Pascal • Data Structures • Databases • Systems Development • Programming Languages, Compilers and Interpreters • Internal Organisation of Computers • Operating Systems and Networks • Peripherals • Computer Applications and Social Implications.

The aim of this book is to provide the classroom support material needed on Advanced Level Computing and BTEC courses.

There are many excellent textbooks on computing at this level (including Computer Science by CS French) which give valuable support and wider reading/reference for the student outside classroom time.

This book, however, has been designed as an interactive teaching and learning aid, eliminating the need for hand outs or copious note taking. It incorporates the following features:

- concise explanation of principles
- questions at appropriate points within the text (with space allowed for student to fill in answers) to enable the student to test and broaden knowledge and understanding, develop ideas, supply discussion points and test application of principles.

Teachers can explain each part of a topic in whatever way they like and use the concise explanations as the 'skeleton' of the classroom work. Students take an active part in the learning process via the questions interspersed throughout the text.

Apart from its value during the course, this is also an ideal book around which each student can build his/her revision programme.

The lecturers' supplement is in the form of a PC-compatible disk. It provides tips on implementation of the course and outline answers to all in-text questions and chapter-end exercises and examination questions.

Review Comments:
'Excellent for encouraging student participation.' 'Can be used as a course companion for all Computing modules (BTEC).' 'Excellent presentation – in line with both our syllabus and teaching methods.' 'Brilliant! A very comprehensive text – really welcome [BTEC HNC Computer Studies].' 'Excellent for open learning students.' 'Brilliant book – excellent learning approach.' 'It is always a pleasure to come upon a book which is well presented and user friendly ... P Heathcote knows her stuff – and it shows!' – **Lecturers**

▲ **Free Lecturers' Supplement**   **Free Lecturers' Supplement** ▲

Introductory Pascal

BJ Holmes

ISBN: **1 85805 007 3** • Date: **1993** • Edition: **1st**
Extent: **224 pp** • Size: **245 x 190 mm**

> *Courses on which this book is expected to be used*
>
> A Level Computing, BTEC National and Higher National Computer Studies, GCSE Computer Studies, C & G 7261, IDPM Foundation, NCC.

The aim of this book is to introduce students to computer programming skills using Pascal. No prior knowledge of computing or computer concepts is assumed. Having covered the ground of this book students will be well placed to progress to *Pascal Programming* by the same author.

The approach of this book is to highlight the features of Pascal using carefully chosen examples with the development of the language statements and the programs being taken in manageable steps.

The author has used Turbo Pascal Version 5.0 from Borland International in the preparation and compilation of all the programs listed in this book.

Contents:

Facts and Figures: What is data? • Types of data • Size of data • Format of data • Computer memory • Pascal identifiers • Data declaration • **Processing Data:** Arithmetic • Input of data • Output of information • Formatted output • Program layout • Program development environment • Implementing a Pascal program • **Making Decisions:** If..then • If..then..else • Nested ifs • Boolean data type • Boolean expressions • Case • **Repeating Statements:** While..do • Repeat..until • Input of numbers • Input of characters • **Building Blocks:** What is a procedure? • Where are procedures written? • Procedure format • Calling a procedure • Parameters • Local declarations • Global declarations • Documentation • **Larger Programs:** Why design programs? • Pseudo-code • Test data and desk check • Documenting procedures • Coding procedures • Coding main program • Complete diagram • **Data Structures:** For..do • One-dimensional array • Input and output of data • Array of characters • Records • **Files of Information:** Text files • File processing activities • Input/output files • Report writing • Sorting • Searching • Direct access files • **Answers to end of chapter questions** • **Syntax diagrams** • **Index.**

♦ **Free Lecturers' Disk** ♦

Tackling Computer Projects

PM Heathcote

ISBN: **1 85805 002 2** • Date: **1992** • Edition: **1st**
Extent: **240 pp** • Size: **275 x 215 mm**

Courses on which this book is known to be used
A Level Computing, BTEC National and Higher National Computing

---

Contents:

Part 1: Choosing a Project. Analysis. Design. Using a Package. Pascal Techniques. Testing. The Report

Part 2: Specimen Project 1 – Gilbert and Sullivan Society Patrons List Analysis. Design. Testing. System Maintenance. User Manual. Appraisal.

Part 3: Specimen Project 2 – Short Course Database Analysis. Design. Testing. System Maintenance. Appraisal. User Manual. Appendices: Paradox Script. Test Runs.

Appendices: Turbo Pascal Editing Keys and Blank Forms

The aim of this book is to provide students with a comprehensive and practical guide on how to tackle a computing project for an Advanced Level or BTEC National computing course, using either a programming language or a software package. It will also be useful to students doing a project for a GCSE computing course or a Higher National computing course, since the principles remain the same at any level.

Students very often find it difficult to think of a suitable idea for a computer project, and having come up with an idea, find the analysis and design stages extremely difficult to get started on. This book gives them plenty of ideas for possible projects with advice on what constitutes a suitable project and a complete specimen project of each type (programming and package implementation) together with advice on how each stage (analysis, design, etc) is tackled.

The first project is implemented in Pascal and the accompanying listing is used to illustrate many useful techniques in Turbo Pascal such as pop-up windows and the use of function keys. The second example illustrates how to tackle a project using a software package instead of a suite of programs. Borland's Paradox database (Version 3.5) has been used, but the actual package is not of any significance here as the emphasis is on how to analyse, design, test and document the system.

Review Comments:

'It is ideal for our BTEC students to help them to tackle programming projects in a realistic and down-to-earth way, encouraging good practice – very readable too!' 'It tackles areas other texts ignore eg testing approaches and creation of a user manual, etc'. 'Well thought out and thorough advice for students on their project work for A Level – in fact for any level later too!' 'This is just the book required for students. It fills a gap in the market since other texts devote at most a single chapter to this 'grey area'. 'It is an excellent aid and should sell very well.'

– *Lecturers*

▲ **Free Lecturers' Supplement** ▲

You like this book? Perhaps we have another to help you with your studies:

	Title	Author	Price		Title	Author	Price
☐	Accounting & Finance for Business Students	Bendrey et al	£10.95	☐	Local Area Networks	Hodson	£6.95
☐	Advanced Level Accounting	Randall	£11.95	☐	Management Accounting	Lucey	£10.95
☐	Advanced Level Biology Practical	Hawkes/Eldridge	£8.95	☐	Management Information Systems	Lucey	£7.95
☐	Advanced Level Business Studies	Danks	£9.95	☐	Management, Theory & Practice	Cole	£10.95
☐	Advanced Level Maths	Solomon	£9.95	☐	Maths Attainment Tests Key Stage 1	Burndred	£3.75
☐	Advanced Level Maths Revision Course	Solomon	£4.95	☐	Maths Attainment Tests Key Stage 2	Burndred	£3.95
☐	Auditing	Millichamp	£9.95	☐	Maths Attainment Tests Key Stage 3	Burndred	£3.95
☐	BASIC Programming	Holmes	£7.95	☐	Maths for Engineering	Clarke	£7.95
☐	Business Accounting I Active Learning	Randall	£12.95	☐	Maths Key Stage 4 Vol. 1	Solomon	£6.50
☐	Business Maths & Statistics	Francis	£9.95	☐	Vol. 2	Solomon	£6.50
☐	Business Law	Abbott/Pendlebury	£10.95	☐	Vol. 3	Solomon	£6.50
☐	Company Law	Abbott	£9.95	☐	Modula-2 Programming	Holmes	£11.95
☐	Computer Science	French	£11.95	☐	MS Works	Weale	£5.95
☐	Computer Studies	French	£7.95	☐	Off to University?	Alger	£4.95
☐	Computing Active Learning	Heathcote	£9.95	☐	Operating Systems	Ritchie	£9.95
☐	Convert to C & C++	Holmes	£9.95	☐	Paradox 4.0 for Students Active Learning	Heathcote	£5.95
☐	Cost & Management Accounting Active Learning	Lucey	£9.95	☐	PASCAL CORE Active Learning	Boyle/Margetts	£9.95
☐	Costing	Lucey	£10.95	☐	PASCAL Programming	Holmes	£11.95
☐	Data Processing	French	£8.95	☐	Personnel Management	Cole	£10.95
☐	dBase for Business Students	Muir	£5.95	☐	Quantitative Methods for Computing Students	Catlow	£9.95
☐	Discovering Marketing Active Learning	Stokes	£9.95	☐	Quantitative Techniques	Lucey	£9.95
☐	Discovering the World of Business	Hillas	£8.95	☐	Quantitative Approaches to Decision Making	Oakshott	£9.95
☐	Easy Guide to Casio Scientific Calculator	Payne	£2.00	☐	Refresher in Basic Maths	Rowe	£4.95
☐	Economics for Professional & Business Students	Powell	£9.95	☐	Refresher in French	Francey	£7.95
☐	Elements of Marketing	Morden	£11.95	☐	Science Attainments Tests Key Stage 3	Burndred/Turnbull	£3.95
☐	English for Business	Chilver	£6.95	☐	Small Business Management Active Learning	Stokes	£9.95
☐	Excel for Bus Students	Muir	£5.95	☐	Spreadsheets for Accounting Students	West	£8.95
☐	Finance for Non-Financial Managers	Millichamp	£9.95	☐	Spreadsheets for Business Students	West	£5.95
☐	Financial Accounting Study Text	Jennings	£11.95	☐	Structured Programming In COBOL	Holmes	£11.95
☐	Financial Accounting Solutions Manual	Jennings	£8.95	☐	Students Guide to Accounting & Financial Reporting Standards	Black	£6.95
☐	Financial Management	Brockington	£9.95	☐	Systems Analysis & Design	Hughes	£9.95
☐	Financial Record Keeping	Lee/Jarvis	£8.95	☐	Tackling Computer Projects	Heathcote	£6.95
☐	First Course in Business Maths & Statistics	Rowe	£4.95	☐	Taxation	Rowes	£11.95
☐	First Course in Business Studies	Danks	£6.95	☐	Taxation Questions & Answers	Deane	£7.95
☐	First Course in Cost & Management Accounting	Lucey	£6.95	☐	Understanding Business & Finance	Hussey	£9.95
☐	First Course in Marketing	Jefkins	£6.95	☐	Understanding Business Statistics	Saunders/Cooper	£9.95
☐	First Course in Statistics	Booth	£5.95	☐	Understanding Computer Systems Architecture	Lacy	£10.95
☐	First Level Management Active Learning	Lang	£8.95				
☐	Foundation Accounting	Millichamp	£9.95				
☐	GCSE English	Tarbitt	£6.50				
☐	GCSE French	Kambuts/Wilson	£7.50				
☐	GCSE Mathematics	Solomon	£7.95				
☐	GCSE Maths Higher Level	Solomon	£7.95				
☐	GCSE Maths Practice Papers Higher	McCarthy	£3.95				
☐	GCSE Maths Practice Papers Intermediate	McCarthy	£3.95				
☐	GCSE Maths Revision Course Higher	McCarthy	£3.95				
☐	GCSE Maths Revision Course Intermediate	McCarthy	£3.95				
☐	GCSE Modern World History	Snellgrove	£6.50				
☐	GCSE Science Quizbook	Freemantle	£2.95				
☐	Information Technology Skills & Knowledge	Harris/Hogan	£7.95				
☐	Intermediate Accounting	Dyson	£7.95				
☐	Introductory Pascal	Holmes	£5.95				

DP Publications' books are available in most academic bookshops or, if you have difficulty finding what you want, UK customers can order direct from us at the following address:

DP Publications Ltd,
Aldine House, Aldine Place, London W12 8AW

Reference: C311

Add £2 postage and packing for one book, or £3 p&p for two or more books.

Please send me the titles indicated. I enclose a cheque for £_____.

Name _____

Address _____

_____

_____